Endorsements

Western liberal democracies appear to use imprisonment with 'good conscience', denying the violence which is the ever-present potential of the dehumanisation and demonisation of those incarcerated. Academic writing, while critical of the over-use of imprisonment, the ineffectiveness of imprisonment for reducing crime, and the over-imprisonment of particular social groups, too often uses the muted, rational-sounding language of risk-management, coupling rights with responsibilities, and bringing about change. This volume brings together rigorously researched examples of the violence of incarceration, showing that this is present in prisons, in immigration detention centres, and in children's institutions, and that it is present in different countries as well as across different forms of detention. The book challenges readers to look behind the penal language and see the violence and humiliation involved in imprisonment. It should be essential reading for academics, policy-makers, and practitioners concerned with detention in its many forms and many settings.

Professor Barbara Hudson
Centre for Criminology and Criminal Justice
Lancashire Law School
University of Central Lancashire, UK

Western governments boast about the 'rule of law' and the 'duty of care' governing the treatment of those men, women and children who are incarcerated. But the evidence of this carefully researched book is that from little known provincial asylums, to out of the way children's detention centres, to the notorious Abu Ghraib prison in Iraq, the experience of confinement still brutalises those who suffer it, and indeed, those we employ to manage it. The evidence presented here suggests that in many cases western governments are not in the least embarrassed that the current punitive drift, legitimated by the 'war on terror', is narrowing definitions of what would have once been thought of as the 'inhuman' or 'degrading' treatment of prisoners. The knock-on effect of this on routine institutional practices across the board is already discernible in America and among its allies. I can think of no better text for drawing attention to this punitive drift. It makes a compelling case against the escalating use of imprisonment, speaking on behalf of those who are trapped in an ever expanding network of brutal disciplinary institutions, the purpose of which is to reproduce (and reinforce)

the inequalities of power along gender, ethnic and class lines that continue to characterise modern societies.

Professor Mick Ryan
University of Greenwich
London, UK

An important collection based on detailed case studies across a number of jurisdictions by leading prison researchers. All, in various ways, trace the connections between the 'exceptional' forms of violence, terror, torture and abuse that have publicly surfaced in what Judith Butler calls the 'new war prison' and the routine and usually hidden practices of the 'normal' domestic prison or detention centre. Powerful stuff.

Professor David Brown
Law Faculty
University of New South Wales
Australia.

Incarceration is pointless, and so these voices tell us—voices much needed in the midst of global carceral insanity. Hear these voices please!

Professor Hal Pepinsky
Department of Criminal Justice
Indiana University
USA

The Violence of Incarceration pulls together many of the pressing and distressing issues that link criminal justice and 'the global war on terror'. From California to Ireland to the US airbase at Bagram, patterns of physical brutality and psychological cruelty repeat and reproduce like political fractals spinning off racism, misogyny and torture. With human rights and human dignity as its magnetic north, this powerful book helps map the often hidden and forgotten terrain of state repression.

Dr Christian Parenti
Author of *Lockdown America*, *The Soft Cage* and *The Freedom*.

This timely text addresses the exponential growth of imprisonment and carceral violence, across the globe. Written and edited by internationally noted critical scholars, these essays map the political utility of imprisonment, and the consequent disregard for human rights and the attendant violence of repressive prison regimes. The trends elucidated serve as a warning to us all.

Professor Robert Gaucher
Department of Criminology
University of Ottawa, Canada

The Violence of Incarceration

Routledge Advances in Criminology

The Violence of Incarceration

Edited by Phil Scraton
and Jude McCulloch

Routledge
Taylor & Francis Group
New York   London

First published 2009
by Routledge
711 Third Avenue, New York, NY 10017

Simultaneously published in the UK
by Routledge
2 Park Square, Milton Park, Abingdon, Oxfordshire OX14 4RN

Routledge is an imprint of the Taylor & Francis Group, an informa business

First issued in paperback 2012

Typeset in Sabon by IBT Global.

Library of Congress Cataloging in Publication Data

The violence of incarceration / edited by Phil Scraton and Jude McCulloch.
  p. cm. — (Routledge advances in criminology ; 5)
Includes bibliographical references and index.
ISBN-13: 978-0-415-96313-8 (hbk)
ISBN-10: 0-415-96313-3 (hbk)
ISBN-13: 978-0-203-89291-6 (ebk)
ISBN-10: 0-203-89291-7 (ebk)
 1. Prison violence. I. Scraton, Phil. II. McCulloch, Jude.
HV9025.V56 2008
365'.641—dc22
2008005150

ISBN13: 978-0-415-96313-8 (hbk)
ISBN13: 978-0-415-54246-3 (pbk)

Contents

vi *Contents*

Acknowledgments

The Violence of Incarceration was conceived in 2005 during Phil Scraton's visiting scholarship at Monash University, Melbourne. Following a public lecture at the Trades Hall, the home of struggle and resistance in the City, on the impunity of the powerful, we agreed on plans for two distinct but related projects. The first was to approach the international journal, *Social Justice*, with a proposal for a special issue on *Deaths in Custody and Detention*. The second was to contact a range of authors whose critical work on incarceration placed violence, interpersonal and institutionalised, at the centre of their analyses. The special issue was published in 2006 as *Social Justice* (Vol 33, No 4). Having received positive responses and abstracts from several colleagues, some of whom had contributed to the Special Issue, we approached Routledge with a proposal. We are grateful to Benjamin Holtzman for commissioning the text and for his patient support as the book came to fruition.

Negotiating an edited collection is always a tricky endeavour especially during the period between the proposal, the commission and the delivery of articles. We acknowledge the commitment and scholarship of our co-authors in writing for the volume and their acceptance that working together on a project from scratch at a distance is demanding and occasionally frustrating as individuals work at different paces and with diverse demands on their time. It is a tribute to the integrity of those involved that each of the collective who set out on this project, together with a few more we 'picked up along the way', delivered articles of immense significance, insight and experience that connect scholarship to activism while foregrounding the lives of the incarcerated.

We are indebted to the support and encouragement of those involved in the seminars and discussions at Monash, especially Criminology colleagues Bree Carlton, Sharon Pickering and Dean Wilson. Thanks also to Debbie Kilroy, Craig Minogue, Amanda George and Charandev Singh. In Belfast, we are grateful to our friends at Coiste na n-Iarchimí, especially Rosena Brown, Rosie McCorley, Laurence McKeown and Mike Ritchie. We acknowledge the broader support of our institutions and colleagues therein, the Institute of Criminology and Criminal Justice in the School of Law, Queen's University, and the School of Political and Social Inquiry, Monash University. Phil Scraton is particularly appreciative of the Monash scholarship that made collaboration possible.

We acknowledge the continuing and selfless support and solidarity of friends and families. Jude is grateful to all her friends including Annie Delaney, Ellen Kleimaker, Sue George and Sharon Jones, who have done the hard yards of political work over many decades. Thanks especially to her partner Mark Minchinton and her son Otis for all their encouragement and understanding. Phil thanks his long-time collaborator, Kathryn Chadwick, his co-worker on the women in prison research, Linda Moore, and Bree Carlton, Anna Eggert, Bill Rolston, Barry Goldson, Janet Johnstone, Karen Lee. Finally, his partner Deena Haydon and his sons Paul—partner Katrin Schoenig—and Sean, each of whom have contributed immensely to his research and writing.

Finally, we are deeply respectful of the energy, time and trust shown to us and to all who write in this text by prisoners, former prisoners and prisoners' families whose personal experiences are recounted throughout the following chapters. We believe that academic research has a fundamental responsibility to inquire, investigate and bear witness to that which happens behind the doors of closed institutions. While prisoners have shown immense strength and resilience in resisting the raw and the subtle manifestations of power in their daily lives, their voices are so readily silenced. When Annie Kelly took her own life in highly contested circumstances in the strip cell of a punishment block, Mourne House Women's Unit, she had written a last letter to her sister. In it she wrote, '*At the end of the day I know that if anything happens to me, there'll be an investigation . . . I know they'd all love me dead, but I'd make sure all is revealed first*'. The challenge for prison researchers is to respond to Annie's call to expose the extent of her suffering and to call to account those responsible. The 'challenge for every prisoner', states Nelson Mandela (1994: 340–341),

> . . . is how to survive prison intact, how to emerge from a prison undiminished, how to conserve and even replenish one's beliefs. The first task in accomplishing that is learning exactly what one must do to survive. To that end, one must know the enemy's purpose before adopting a strategy to undermine it. Prison is designed to break one's spirit and destroy one's resolve. To do this the authorities attempt to exploit every weakness, demolish every initiative, negate all signs of individuality—all with the idea of stamping out that spark that makes each of us human and each of us who we are.

Phil Scraton   Jude McCulloch
Belfast   Melbourne
November 2007

REFERENCES

Mandela, N. (1994) *Long Walk to Freedom: The Autobiography of Nelson Mandela*, New York: Little, Brown and Co.

1 The Violence of Incarceration
An Introduction

Jude McCulloch and Phil Scraton

She was born in the 1920s on Merseyside, England, imprisoned under order aged eleven. Classified 'feeble-minded,' her offending behaviour was unspecified 'persistent theft.' Incarceration lasted forty-five years, behind bars of harsh regimes. Judged aggressive and violent, she self-harmed. Jane Doe lives in recent history, an object of psychiatric and surgical experimentation. She is one of many women—and men—of great courage and determination whose private resistance to public degradation led eventually to release. Her twilight years have been lived out in day-to-day routines of a society which, for so long, denied her existence. No explanations, no apologies and no acknowledgment of the institutionalised brutalisation of a locked-in ward.

> For much of the 20th century Jane Doe and those similarly classified, including children born and brought up in 'mental hospitals,' endured enforced mutilation, electrically induced convulsions, drugging and ritual humiliation. Their bodies and minds constituted unrestricted test sites in medicine's obsession with the identification and eradication of individual pathology. They feared the perpetrators, the formalised physical abuse of the doctors accompanied by the routine, informal assaults of 'care' staff, and they feared the fate of absent friends; those who disappeared. A fear of death not by natural causes but by unlawful killing: experiments that failed, drug cocktails with fatal side-effects, restraint methods that suffocated and suicides of despair. These were the consequences of licensed assault and the institutionalisation of inhuman and degrading treatment. (Scraton 2002: 107–8)

The purpose of introducing a book on the violence of incarceration through glimpsing the experiences of one woman in 20th century England is to establish from the outset how people condemned by the State, committed to imprisonment by the rule of law and damaged by those in whose 'care' they are held, lose any effective means to influence their destinies. It is important to recall and reflect on her forty-five years of enforced incarceration. Once classified as a persistent offender whose 'mind' was 'feeble,' her pathological condition reinforced at five-yearly

intervals by psychiatrists' minimal reviews of her 'progress,' she was not
only locked away but became the property of the State and its professionals. Her body was utilized as they deemed appropriate. Within the
'virtually autonomous archipelago of incarceration in mental institutions
and special hospitals' (ibid), alongside the hidden penal archipelago, the
authority of those who turned the keys, who managed the regimes, who
delivered primary healthcare, who classified those behaviour disordered
and who pronounced on moral guidance was beyond independent scrutiny foregoing the public's interest. By their silence and acceptance all
involved in the processes and procedures of inhumane containment contributed to the timeless routine of institutional neglect and violence.

INDIFFERENT TO THE PAINS OF CONFINEMENT

Lack of public scrutiny and political accountability, alongside collective ambivalence and indifference, explains in part how psychiatric and
penal institutions sustained excessively punitive and often unlawful
practices. As Angela Davis (2003: 15) comments, 'people tend to take
prisons for granted,' reluctant 'to face the realities hidden within them.'
She continues:

> . . . the prison is present in our lives and, at the same time, it is absent
> from our lives. To think about this simultaneous presence and absence
> is to begin to acknowledge the part played by ideology in shaping the
> way we interact with our social surroundings. We take prisons for
> granted but are often afraid to face the realities they produce. (ibid.)

In a consistent vein, reflecting on the Holocaust, Nils Christie (1994:
163) notes the 'social production of moral indifference . . . created by
authorization, by routinization and by dehumanization of the victims
by ideological definitions and indoctrinations.' The Holocaust as 'process' was 'not directed by monsters' (ibid: 164) but was rational, 'run
with precision' and 'in harmony with the basic civilizing process . . . a
legitimate resident in the house of modernity' (ibid: 165). There are con-
sistencies, argues Christie, with the 'new penology' in its identification
and management of 'unruly groups,' its 'control of the dangerous classes'
(ibid: 167). A combination of mass media sensationalism and political
opportunism fuels the contemporary 'war on crime' in which there are
no limits to criminalisation and an ever-expanding commitment to the
management of crime prevention across all public sector institutions. It
is a universal 'war' in which any attempt to apply the brakes to penal
expansionism, to talk of alternatives to prison let alone raise the issue of
abolition, is portrayed as liberal and apologist. In this climate, prisons
are not only taken for granted, they are also demanded without concern

or conscience regarding the normalisation of 'legitimate' violence and violation within their walls.

Angela Davis (2005: 47) gives a powerful example of how women prisoners' experiences of strip and cavity searches, unequivocally 'sexual assault' in any other circumstances, are assumed to constitute a 'normal and routine aspect of women's imprisonment . . . self-justified by the mere fact of imprisonment.' For this is 'what happens to the citizen who is divested of her citizenship rights' making it right and appropriate 'that the prisoner be subjected to sexual coercion.' For Davis, such practices, administered in the collective name of the State's citizens, comprise 'powerful and profound' indicators that 'inform the kind of democracy we inhabit today.' A second, significant issue is the relationship between what comes to be normalised in the context of prisons and what is represented as aberrant. Redefined as sexual assault, the strip and/or cavity search constitutes one of several interlinked 'circuits of violence' connecting the 'ordinary' to the 'extraordinary' (ibid: 62). The 'ordinary' is characterized by routine violence permeating all prisons; the 'extraordinary' extends the continuum of violence to torture. Responding to the 'horrendous' brutalization of prisoners in Abu Ghraib and Guantánamo Bay, Angela Davis argues that the permissive, 'barbaric' practices adopted were a reflection and extension of the 'normalisation of torture within domestic prisons' (ibid:114). In 'highlight[ing] the links between the institution of the military prison and that of the domestic prison,' she notes:

> What is routinely accepted by prison guards can easily turn into the kind of torture that violates international standards, especially under the impact of racism. Fanon once made the point that violence is always there on the horizon of racism. Rather than rely on a taxonomy of those acts that are defined as torture and those that are not, it may be more revealing to examine how one set of institutionalised practices actually enables the other. (ibid: 63)

Drawing on cases within the United States, she establishes confirmation of 'the deep connections between sexual violence and the gendered processes of discipline and power embedded in systems of imprisonment' and their transfer between 'domestic imprisonment, military imprisonment, immigration detention' (ibid: 115). The torture, degradation and sexual coercion captured in the photographs and video footage from Abu Ghraib have foundations laid deep in the 'routine, quotidian violence that is justified as the everyday means of controlling prison populations in the United States' (ibid.). Such practices are not new, nor are they restricted in responsibility to the gratuitous acts of a small number of depraved men and women.

> Many . . . who know prison cruelty attribute it to the deliberate viciousness and sadism of wardens, keepers and guards. There are such brutal officials, but it is the institutional and routine aspects of prison

administration and life, rather than arbitrary personal sadism and de-
pravity, which accounts for most of the cruelty and personal demoral-
ization that goes on in our contemporary prisons. (Barnes and Teeters
1951: 419)

Writing on United States imprisonment in the late 1940s, Barnes and Teeters
argued that it 'supplies the method of carrying out the revengeful spirit of an
outraged society' bringing 'satisfaction for the wrongs, real or alleged, that
are brought upon it by the offender' resulting in the release of 'cruel impulses'
by guards seemingly inured to their 'sadistic' actions. Approval is granted,
respectability conferred, by the legitimacy of the institution. They conclude,
'it is probable that the most serious aspects of the prison as an institution'
are the consequences for the 'public mind' (ibid.). Fifty years later, Edward
Said (2000: 51) commented, 'Burning in the collective US unconscious is a
puritanical zeal decreeing the sternest possible attitude to anyone deemed
to be an unregenerate sinner.' Native Americans, demonised as 'wasteful
savages,' had been all but 'exterminated,' a 'tiny remnant' condemned 'to
reservations and concentration camps.' At the heart of United States policy,
an 'almost elemental anger' had consolidated with punishment 'conceived
in apocalyptic terms . . . sinners are condemned terminally, with the utmost
cruelty regardless of whether or not they suffer the cruellest agonies' (ibid.).

Felix Oviawe arrived at jail, hands tied, and was subjected to 'cruellest
agonies' from the moment he left the transport vehicle until he was thrown
in a cell with two others. He was told to strip and kneel. Forced to hold each
other by the ears, the three men knelt for hours while guards spat mucus on
their bodies. Left naked, the abused men used toilet paper to keep warm.
Their ritual humiliation and degradation by guards included plucking body
hairs with pliers, verbal abuse, kicking, punching, heads down toilet bowls,
enforced sexual acts on each other and unusual and degrading positions
while naked. Prisoners were made to chant 'America is number one!' Felix
Oviawe was not imprisoned in Abu Ghraib post-September 11 but in Union
County Jail in 1996 along with detainees from India, Finland, Albania,
Nigeria and Mauritania. He was an 'illegal,' a Nigerian state assemblyman
who fled Nigeria after the 1993 military coup seeking political asylum. He
was transferred from a detention centre to the jail in Elizabeth. His story is
one of many covered by Mark Dow (2004) in his painstaking, case-based
indictment of the use of violence, rape and abuse against detainees in United
States immigration prisons and ordinary jails. It demonstrates the casual yet
endemic violence that had consolidated within many United States places of
detention as the prison-industrial complex expanded beyond its investors'
wildest dreams.

Conceived in the immediate aftermath of the humiliations and killings
of prisoners in Afghanistan and Iraq, of the suicides and hunger strikes at
Guantánamo Bay, of the disappearances of detainees through extraordinary
rendition, this book explores the connections between these shameful events

and the inhumanity and degradation of domestic prisons within the 'allied' states. The central theme is that the revelations of extreme brutality perpetrated by allied soldiers represent the inevitable end product of domestic incarceration predicated on the use of violence up to and including lethal force. Before their deployment in Iraq, United States soldiers, many of them reservists and a significant number working as full-time corrections officers, were the recipients of a relentless diet of racist propaganda interweaving 'terrorism,' al-Qaida and Islam. Those taken prisoner, regardless of how or why they were detained, reckless as to guilt or innocence of any act, were captives beneath contempt.

> When the enemy is dehumanised, stripped of human identity, it is a small step to strip their clothes, to force them to simulate sexual acts and to coerce them into masturbating for the camera. The degradation inflicted on the body reflects denigration assumed in the mind. Photographs become a visible manifestation and record of subjugation. For all time, they represent the institutional power of personal abuse. In the photographs pleasure enjoyed by the captors increases in proportion to pain endured by their captives. Pornography is explicit in the representation; the overt expression of absolute power without responsibility and with assumed impunity. (Scraton 2007: 214)

Yet the 'torture, degradation and human rights violations at Abu Ghraib prison could not be dismissed as shameful acts of a small clique of cowboy soldiers' (ibid.). They were a manifestation of techniques that had become deeply institutionalised within the military and the CIA and criticised internally by the FBI. Further, they brought into sharp relief domestic prison conditions and violations within advanced democratic states self-styled as the 'coalition of the willing' in the 'war on terror.'

The following chapters include contributions from the United States, United Kingdom, Australia and the north of Ireland. Although these jurisdictions have distinct histories, cultures and political systems, each identifies as an advanced western liberal democracy professing a commitment to the rule of law and respect for human rights. The United States, self-appointed leader of the free world, identifies itself as a global exemplar of these principles and standards. In the recent period, the United Kingdom is the United States' most important ally and Australia almost certainly its most enthusiastic. Both states readily accept its assessment of its record on human rights. When pictures of prisoner abuse at Abu Ghraib surfaced in 2004, a major tenet of the reaction within the United States was to decry the damage done to its reputation as virtuous global citizen. Typical was the lament by one United States Senator:

> Worst of all, our nation, a nation that, to a degree unprecedented in human history, has sacrificed its blood and treasure to secure liberty and

> human rights around the world now must try to convince the world
> that the horrific images on their TV screens and front pages are not the
> real America, that what they see is not who we are. (Senator Susan M.
> Collins quoted in MacMaster 2004: 2)

This book has a number of aims. One is to expose as fiction the claim to the
political moral high ground made by the United States in particular and western liberal democracies more generally. Debunking the myth of pre-eminent
virtue is critical because such claims animate and legitimate global actions
such as the 'war on terror' that in turn are linked to violence and incarceration in the indefinite and punitive detention of tens of thousands of people
by the United States at places like Guantánamo Bay, Abu Ghraib in Iraq and
Bagram Air Base in Afghanistan. As William Pfaff (2007) cogently argues,
the claim to virtue underlies notions of Manifest Destiny as a claim to power.
In previous eras, the idea of Manifest Destiny involved spreading White
civilization; today such claims are likely to be made in terms of democracy
and human rights (Perera 2007: 128–129). Laying out a plan for unilateral
action and global conquest, the 2002 United States National Security Strategy
asserts that:

> America must stand firmly for the non-negotiable demands of human
> dignity: the rule of law; limits on the absolute power of the state; free
> speech; freedom of worship; equal justice; respect for women; religious
> and ethnic tolerance; and respect for private property. (Bush 2002: vi)

The myth of moral virtue works to hide, silence, minimize and deny the brutal, continuing history of violence and incarceration within western states
along with the violence and incarceration undertaken by or on behalf of western states beyond their national borders. The idea that torture and human
rights abuses are novel in the history of western nations requires an astonishing degree of historical amnesia (for example, see MacMaster 2004). It is not
intended to catalogue this history here but simply to note that the evidence
is plentiful for those who wish to know (see Eisenstein 2004; Jamieson and
McEvoy 2005). Beyond this, as contributors to this book argue, an understanding of the abuses at Abu Ghraib as exceptional aberrations requires a
denial of the everyday 'cruel but usual punishments' of contemporary incarceration in liberal democracies (Greene 2004). Each chapter in this book gives
testimony to the violence and gross violation of human rights that take place
daily in domestic prisons and detention centres in these states.

CHAPTERS AND THEMES

The first three chapters demonstrate how deeply violence has been embedded
in the daily exchanges between prisoners and between staff and prisoners

in liberal democracies. They concentrate on male prisons in the United Kingdom, Ireland, Australia and the United States. In subsequent chapters, historical contextualisation is given to the systemic violence and violations endured by women and child prisoners and detainees. Exploring recent histories not only establishes violence as 'currency' central to the operation of contemporary incarceration, but also acknowledges that jails and their regimes are contested. While unbridled institutionalised force has been, and remains, inherent in the culture of discipline and control, jails regularly have been sites of resistance and rebellion. Yet, demonstrable evidence of 'agency' among prisoners who individually or collectively engage in struggle from within does not negate the power of institutional force and coercion used regularly against individuals and organized protests. It is a force, as the chapters show, that extends to the use of lethal force, alongside death by neglect, with impunity.

Against the background of internment without trial, the removal of 'special category status' from those convicted of political offences and the ensuing 1981 Hunger Strike in which ten Republican prisoners died, Laurence McKeown (Chapter 2) analyses prisoner resistance and the 1983 mass escape from Long Kesh. It was, he argues, a 'crushing blow' to British government policy and to the Prison Service regime, its authority and legitimacy. Himself a hunger strike survivor, McKeown contextualises the planned breakout and the violent retaliation by prison guards that followed within the brutalisation of political prisoners throughout the history of protest and resistance within the prison (see also McKeown 2001).

In Chapter 3, Bree Carlton's account of the 1987 deaths of seven male prisoners in the Jika Jika High Security Unit at Victoria's Pentridge Prison, Australia, reveals the recent history of what she names the 'violent and abusive cultures' that prevailed in the hidden world of supermax incarceration. While two prisoners died in controversial circumstances within days of each other, five men perished in a fire following the failure to rescue them from barricaded cells. Revisiting the evidence presented at the inquests and inquiries and using prisoners' accounts, she constructs an alternative analysis of the events challenging the official version. What is uncovered is institutionalised physical and psychological violence deeply rooted within the organisational culture and operational history of the prison and its management. Such violence had become part of the routine exchanges that formed interpersonal relations between prisoners and between guards and prisoners (see Carlton 2007).

At the time that the seven prisoners died in Jika Jika, Scotland's 'high security' Victorian prison at Peterhead was embroiled in persistent prisoner protests and hostage-taking, which eventually spread to other jails. While conditions at Peterhead were dire and the regime harsh, the key issue for prisoners was the jail's history of routinised, endemic violence. The dominant perception within the jail, isolated on Scotland's far North-East coast, was that the 'hard men' of violence—the 'worst of the worst'—required the harsh restraints of coercive and punitive incarceration. Based on primary research carried out with prisoners in the jail and those released at the time (see Scraton, Sim and Skidmore 1991), Phil Scraton (Chapter 4) considers the Peterhead protests in the broader context of prisoner resistance in the United States. He contests the main premises of 'prison riot' theories and analyses the Peterhead protests through a combination of factors, not least the 'dominant and dominating culture of male violence and its associated levels of threat and fear.'

The chapters that follow focus on recent and current events. In Chapter 5, Barry Goldson considers the systemic violation of children's rights within a broader, global context raising issues of adult-centred power and its legitimacy. He emphasises the 'relative, or even absolute, impunity afforded to those who interpersonally and/or institutionally dispense violence to children.' He considers specifically the violence experienced by children in state institutions, detention and prisons within democratic societies and penal expansionism. Centred on the England and Wales jurisdiction, he uses primary research to illustrate how contemporary penal policies are 'tantamount to institutional and institutionalised child abuse' resulting in the 'deliberate, repeated and systematic imposition of harm' (see: Goldson 2002). With an increasing number of children dying in custody (Goldson and Coles 2005), he considers the impact of 'demonisation' and 'pathologisation' as social and political constructions of children in conflict with the law.

Reflecting on their established research and associated campaigns against the strip searching of women and girl prisoners, Jude McCulloch and Amanda George (Chapter 6) contest the proposition that the 'sexual humiliation' to which detainees at Abu Ghraib, Guantánamo Bay and other United States-supported sites of torture, inhuman and degrading treatment have been subjected is 'exceptional.' They argue that through routinisation and normalisation, women's experiences of strip searches as manifestations of 'sexual violence or coercion' are casually dismissed by the authorities that sanction their use. While focusing primarily on Australian prisons, they also draw on evidence from Canada and the north of Ireland to establish the debilitating impact of strip searches in the context of 'women's experiences of sexual assault and gendered violence.' In recounting the tragic circumstances of a woman's death in custody, they reveal the intense harm suffered by particularly vulnerable women through enforced strip searches.

Following on, Linda Moore and Phil Scraton (Chapter 7) draw on their primary research into the imprisonment of women and girls in the north of Ireland (see Scraton and Moore 2005; 2007). They contextualise the experiences of women and girl prisoners within gendered continua of 'violence' and of 'unsafety' derived in Liz Kelly's and Elizabeth Stanko's work, respectively. Accepting that these continua comprise the physical and sexual threats faced by all women, Moore and Scraton argue that women's prisons are an 'institutional manifestation of women's powerlessness and vulnerability.' Within the north of Ireland, however, the legacy of the Conflict and the brutalisation of women political prisoners lived on in the high security conditions, regime and punishments meted out to 'ordinary' women and girl prisoners by a predominantly male staff. The research reveals the persistence of harsh, uncompromising regimes in which low-security prisoners were subjected to high-security conditions, their basic physical and mental health needs neglected. Using case studies of the deaths of two women, they show that the most vulnerable women prisoners, often survivors of sexual violence, are warehoused rather than supported, their resistance perceived as non-cooperation requiring punishment rather than resilience to be encouraged.

While the previous chapters argue for gender-specific policies and regimes for women and girl prisoners, in Chapter 8 Cassandra Shaylor addresses the problems inherent in 'gender responsive justice' against a backdrop of the seemingly unstoppable expansion of women's incarceration in California. While not doubting the integrity of reformers in their attempts to provide penal policies, regimes and practices responsive to the distinctive and different 'needs and experiences of women in prison,' she argues persuasively that such initiatives and their associated campaigns risk 'perpetuating . . . outmoded notions of gender' while 'entrenching' and bolstering the prison-industrial complex. Consistent with the previous chapters, she establishes that prisons are a 'form of violence' inflicted on women, while the imprisonment of men 'offers no solution to interpersonal violence in our communities.' Prison abolitionism requires contextual and coherent vision involving self-determination within communities fully committed to affordable housing, equality of adequate healthcare and welfare, education and work opportunities.

Recording the unparalleled expansion of United States jails, Avery Gordon notes in Chapter 9 the significance of the 'growing reach of the United States military' globally supported by its 'corollary carceral complex.' Central to her position is that the 'routine treatment of conditions at Abu Ghraib and Guantánamo Bay as exceptional or isolated instances of abuses of state power has obscured the relationship between United States military prisons abroad and territorial United States civilian prisons.' She proposes that the isolation, dehumanisation and degradation extending to the use of torture have been central to the cruelties of subjugation inflicted on Native Americans and African Americans. As Cassandra Shaylor reveals the 'racialisation' of United States prisons, so Avery Gordon notes that in 'criminalising and capturing vanquished, threatening or unwanted populations' the United States reflects a long tradition of European enslavement, colonisation and Empire. The disproportionate level of incarceration of Black and Latino people, many caged in supermax jails, has consolidated military-style custody for civilian 'offenders.' In becoming the world leader in the use of imprisonment, the United States has condemned those held in captivity to a 'destiny' of 'permanent abandonment' overseen by ever-increasing technical apparatuses of physical restraint and coercion.

Dylan Rodríguez premises Chapter 10 on United States 'global state-craft and the technology of punishment' with the assertion that 'carceral violence' has been and remains central to United States 'national function and global dominance.' He considers that the United States prison represents a 'dynamic arrangement of intersecting trajectories of violence' that cannot be understood simply as the inevitable outcome of total institutions. Privilege is derived in structural inequalities and protected through the politics of law and order and regimes of imprisonment, the latter constituting a 'central presence in the social and racial formation of the United States.' Prisons thus reflect and reproduce the 'material relations of power' from which they arise and the legacy of slavery and genocide within the United States is evident in the 'normalisation' of 'racist bodily violence.'

In his analysis of the incarceration of Aboriginals in Australia, Chris Cunneen's Chapter 11 connects directly to Dylan Rodríguez's work. He broadly conceptualises violence to include direct physical assaults, cruel forms of ill-treatment and the neglect of prisoners. Acknowledging the 'over-representation of Indigenous people in criminal justice systems' internationally, he maintains that within police and prison custody violence is endemic and institutionalised. The State's 'monopoly of the use of violence' when directed towards Indigenous people can only be understood when 'symbiotically linked to the historical process of colonisation,' a process dependent on rule by terror. Consequently, the violence of incarceration is derived 'in dispossession from land and denial of sovereignty.' Cunneen shows how this legacy remains evident in contemporary incarceration, custody deaths and miscarriages of justice.

While pain and suffering were inflicted on Indigenous populations through techniques of punishment, the use of cruel forms of detention against refugees and asylum seekers demonstrates how the violence of incarceration extends beyond warehousing 'offenders.' In Chapter 12, Jude McCulloch and Sharon Pickering explore the imprisonment without trial of asylum seekers post-September 11. Focusing on the detention policies and practices of the Australian Government, they trace the 'politicised nature of border politics' and the 'sacrifice' of asylum seekers' human rights on the altar of political opportunism. Mandatory detention in locations and circumstances of severe dehumanization and debilitation are considered in terms of rights' violations and their deep impact on asylum seekers. As evident in other chapters in this book, McCulloch and Pickering analyse the State's techniques of denial, deflection and victim blaming as rationalizations for its use of severe forms of detention and internment. These processes, they argue, reflect a legacy of segregation, exiling and punishment of Indigenous people within Australia and the historic rejection by state institutions of human rights.

Chapter 13 considers the potential of independent monitoring in challenging the violence of incarceration and detention. Based primarily on work in England and Wales, Diana Medlicott explores the failure to prevent 'inhumane treatment and routine casual cruelty' within prisons despite a well-established system of external monitoring. Following discussion of the importance of national and international independent monitoring of prisons and other places of detention, she considers the recent moves to inhibit the role and functions of the Inspectorate in the England and Wales. Systemic failures in monitoring to prevent inhumane and degrading treatment, including issues of negligence, neglect, mental ill-health, staff abuse of prisoners with impunity and custody deaths, are explored through analysis of the treatment of women and children. She notes the broader context of unprecedented penal expansion, chronic overcrowding and weak strategies in which a 'culture of casual cruelty' has been allowed to 'flourish with impunity.' To an extent, that culture has become intractable and prisoners are viewed as 'inferior beings' in the 'psyche and belief systems' of prison guards. Finally, she discusses the potential of the Operational Protocol to the UN Convention Against Torture and Other Cruel, Inhuman or Degrading Treatment or Punishment in challenging institutionalised abuse and violence through the implementation of international standards.

In proposing the application of international rights standards as a means to end the violence of incarceration, this final chapter inadvertently opens a debate that, with a few exceptions, lies dormant yet present throughout the text. It concerns the extent to which, if at all, the emotional and physical abuse, cruelty and brutality that comprise the violence of incarceration can be eradicated through penal reform, stronger rights, increased transparency and greater accountability. For abolitionists, such reformism, however well-intentioned, facilitates a politics of incorporation in which places of detention become 'rights-compliant,' their managers and staff gain rights, management and protection diplomas and independent monitors annually report their visits and inspections. Taking England and Wales as an example, it is difficult not to be cynical about the introduction of a 'rights culture' to the operational policies, priorities and practices of prisons and detention centres. As Diana Medlicott shows, the not insignificant work of the Prisons Inspectorate has exposed repeatedly the institutional malaise within prisons, especially appalling regimes under which women and children are held. Yet Moore and Scraton's research in the north of Ireland demonstrates sharply how even the harshest external scrutiny can be deflected with disdain by prison management and the government departments to which they are responsible. The violence of incarceration is historically, socially and culturally imprinted on the foundations of the prison. It is moderated or hidden beneath the veneer of mission statements, glossy brochures and internet virtual tours.

As Thomas Mathiesen (1990) demonstrates, even on the terms of those who defend penal expansionism, prisons fail to deliver. He questions how what amounts to a 'prison fiasco' is denied and negated. The answer lies within three spheres:

> the widest public sphere, consisting above all of the whole range of modern mass media; in a narrower public sphere, consisting of institutions directly engaged in crime prevention such as the police, the courts, the prosecuting authorities and the prisons themselves; and in an even narrower sphere consisting of particular professional groups. (ibid: 139)

Yet these are the agencies and professionals whose processes and interventions should provide civic society with effective monitoring, reviews and accountability for the policies, practices and governance within the prison walls. As '*non-recognition* of the prison fiasco' has persisted, 'pretence takes over: the participants pretend the prison is a success' (ibid: 140).

Dealing with the consequences of the 'fiasco' in the short-term by arguing for penal reform and prisoners' rights without compromising the longer term objective of penal abolition is difficult. Angela Davis (2003: 103) notes that the 'anti-prison movement' works towards 'the abolition of the prison as the dominant mode of punishment' while simultaneously being committed fully to 'genuine solidarity with the millions of men, women and children who are behind bars.' Campaigning for 'more humane, habitable environments for people in prison without bolstering the permanence of the prison system' is a 'major challenge':

> How then do we accomplish this balancing act of passionately attending to the needs of prisoners—calling for less violent conditions, an end to sexual assault, improved physical and mental health care, greater access to drug programs, better education and work opportunities, unionization of prison labour, more connections with families and communities, shorter or alternative sentencing—and at the same time call for alternatives to sentencing altogether, no prison construction, and abolitionist strategies that question the place of prison in our future? (ibid: 103–4)

The alternative to incarceration, whatever the misrepresentation of abolitionism in the popular media, is not unidimensional but a 'constellation of alternative strategies and institutions' providing a 'continuum of alternatives.' This shift cannot be achieved without the 'demilitarization of schools, revitalization of education at all levels, a health system that provides free physical and mental health care to all, and a justice system based on reparation and reconciliation rather than retribution and vengeance' (ibid: 107). Only through eradicating the foundations of structural inequality can its institutional manifestations be eroded and the underlying roots of the violence of incarceration be tackled.

VIOLENCE, INCARCERATION AND NEOLIBERALISM

It is a remarkable testament to our inability to imagine the suffering of 'others,' and the power of dehumanizing discourses that surround those communities that suffer the weight of violence and incarceration, that illiberal and markedly uncivil practices of violence and incarceration within liberal democracies have had so little impact on understanding within these states of values of 'civilisation.' Even thoughtful critiques of punitive penal regimes assume that such practices do not impact on the *fundamental* nature of western societies as the home of civilized people. For example, James Austin and others reflecting on mass incarceration in the United States and the harshness of its penal regime comment that: '[a]s a civilized people we must not tolerate this' (Austin, Irwin and Kubrin 2003: 463). The idea that violence and incarceration may be uncivil but nevertheless undertaken by civilised people suggests that such practices, when carried out in putative liberal democracies, may be diminishing, troubling or confronting but not ultimately defining.

The failure to consider uncivil practices of violence and incarceration as defining is related to the long-held and firmly established notion of western democracies as the origin and natural home of ideas of freedom, equality and justice. The idea of western democracies as inherently civilised necessarily implies its 'example' to 'others' less civilised. The development of post-colonial studies and critical race scholarship has revealed liberal democracies' historical tendency towards violence and incarceration against identifiable groups socially, politically constructed and culturally represented as uncivilised. Democratic states have routinely denied access to rights and citizenship on the grounds of 'race,' at home and in 'their' colonies. The advent of rights and their denial on the presumption of racial inferiority supported by eugenicist assertions, masquerading as 'science,' form a basic liberal paradox (Goldberg 1993: 3–6). Exclusion from rights via renewed notions of dangerousness, related particularly to class and 'race,' was established at the inception of modern penal systems (Hudson 2003: 35–36). Ironically, the claims to moral virtue translated into Manifest Destiny laid the foundations for the violation of the rights and processes underpinning those claims. The brutality of slavery and colonisation were legitimised in terms of superior civilisation significantly derived on the idea of political virtue in which respect for individual rights and ideas of rule of law played a significant part (Eisenstein 2004; Saada 2003).

Currently, the United States, and its allies, the United Kingdom and Australia prominent among them, abandon human rights and rule of law because in the 'war on terror' they are battling a foe 'who hates freedom' and confronts liberal democracy's self-proclaimed respect for individual rights and the rule of law. Within this framework, the abuses of Abu Ghraib and Guantánamo Bay are not only committed by and with the support of 'civilised' states but are also rationalised through the 'defence of freedom' and the promotion of 'civilisation.' That such abuse is widely understood not to impinge on or undermine liberal democracy's claim to be 'civilised' is consistent with 'rule by terror' and the violence of incarceration central to the assertion of colonial power and authority. Historian L. P. Mathur, for example, writing about the British response to Indian nationalists in the early 19th century wrote: 'It is rather surprising and painful to note that civilised government like the British perpetrated barbaric punishments and showered unimaginable indignities on people who had sacrificed all for their motherland' (quoted in Anderson 2003: 48).

There are several reasons why the violence of incarceration should be understood as central rather than peripheral to western liberal democracies, particularly the states represented in this book. First is the extent of contemporary incarceration and its spiraling growth. At the forefront of penal expansionism is the United States where between 1975 and the turn of the millennium there was a five-fold increase in the numbers incarcerated and a doubling of prison admissions for African-Americans (Sparks 2003). The extent of mass incarceration in the United States is unprecedented in the history of liberal democracy, having no parallel in the western world. The systematic imprisonment of substantial proportions of communities over-represented as prisoners means that prison has become a regularised and normalised part of the life experience of some communities (Garland 2001).

It is also instructive that mass incarceration in the United States, not only in terms of numbers but also length of sentences, has failed to assuage public opinion that 'America is "soft" on crime' (Currie 1998: 38). While unequivocal and 'sobering evidence' exists that 'mass incarceration has had little impact on violent crime, we're told that "prison works"' (ibid.). Further, despite unprecedented costs of expansionism, 'we hear that "prison pays",' the irony being that 'we are told . . . not that we have overemphasized incarceration at the expense of other approaches to crime, but that we haven't incarcerated *enough*.' The myths, Elliott Currie argues, have become 'staples of the popular debate about crime and punishment,' the myths being: 'leniency' (soft on crime); 'efficacy' (the 'prison experiment' has been successful); 'costlessness' (prisons are value for money and, in the long term, *save* money).

While levels of mass incarceration in the United States are not matched in Britain, Australia and the north of Ireland, increases in imprisonment in these States are significant, particularly the massive rise in England and Wales since the mid-1990s. The upward spiral of incarceration combined with the over-representation of particular communities and groups of people as prisoners and detainees—including Indigenous people and asylum seekers in Australia, African Americans and Latinos in the United States, the mentally ill, sexually, physically and emotionally abused women and young people and the poor in all countries—means that incarceration is too frequently a defining experience for these individuals, groups and communities. The prisons and detention centres are also defining experiences for the increasing number of people who work inside these institutions, particularly where other employment opportunities and thus the ability to escape such employment have contracted (Gilmore-Wilson 2007).

A second reason why violence and incarceration might be considered defining of liberal democracies relates to the nature of incarcerated populations. In each of the states represented in this book, it is the poorest, most marginalised, least powerful and most vulnerable people who are imprisoned and detained in disproportionate numbers. The demographics of the prison and incarcerated populations tell a broader story about societies divided by 'race,' class, gender and age and prevalent or dominant collective values. Violence and incarceration work to maintain social hierarchies and hide the structural violence of global and domestic capitalism by 'disappearing' its victims. As Angela Davis (2003: 16) argues, prison:

> ... functions ideologically as an abstract site into which undesirables are deposited, relieving us of thinking about real issues afflicting those communities from which prisoners are drawn in such disproportionate numbers. . . . It relieves us of the responsibility of seriously engaging with the problems of our society, especially those produced by racism, and increasingly global capitalism. . . . The prison has become a black hole into which the detritus of contemporary capitalism is deposited.

The violence of incarceration is not reducible to the institutions that detain and imprison but is a significant and utilitarian element of the broader picture of structural violence that permeates liberal democracies.

The third reason, as the following chapters demonstrate, focuses on the conditions in which people are incarcerated. Not only does incarceration reflect broader social inequalities and structural violence, but it also plays a defining role in their amplification. Violence and incarceration are racialised, gendered and 'aged,' mirroring and extending the painful and burdensome legacies of slavery and colonisation, along with the myriad and intersecting oppressions of patriarchy and adultism including sexual coercion (Davis 2003; 2005). Further, this violence and incarceration produce structures of dominance that create new colonial relationships (see Cunneen 2001; Hogg 2001).

Finally, the violence of incarceration has remained unscathed by the 'advances' of liberal democratic states and their 'rights and opportunities' agendas. In fact, throughout the last three decades, neoliberalism has given birth to new punitive forms of violent incarceration. Neoliberalism and repressive social control are a 'package deal' through which the 'rhetoric of criminalisation and punishment legitimizes states that have reneged on their commitment to the social wage' (Mariani 2001). Neoliberalism has marked the ascendency of global corporations over nation-states and the rise of the strong or authoritarian state that rejects social support in favour of social control. As Joachim Hirsh (1997: 45–46) states:

> . . . we are dealing not with a 'hollowing-out' of the state as such, but rather of *liberal democracy*. . . . That is to say, the limitation on the interventionist capacities of the state reduces or even negates the ability of the political system to respond to the social demands that were traditionally expressed within the formal processes of democracy.

In a similar vein, Henry Giroux observes that what 'has emerged is not an impotent state, but a garrison state that increasingly protects corporate interests while stepping up the level of repression and militarization on the domestic front' (2002: 143). The language of criminal justice has become infused with military metaphors with wars on crime, drugs and most recently terror; signalling a shift from welfare to warfare or, as Andreas and Price (2001: 36) propose, to a 'crimefare' state. Increasingly, those who may have previously been identical as 'at risk' have come to be classified as 'the risk' to be monitored, controlled and incarcerated for the 'security' of law-abiding and patriotic citizens (Scraton 2004). The integration of national security into criminal justice necessarily involves identifying 'enemies within' through the continuous policing of an imagined border between the 'public' that is to be protected and the excluded and vilified dangerous 'other' (Zender 2000: 210). In considering these shifts in contemporary criminal justice and their impacts on violence and incarceration, it is important to keep in mind the historical antecedents of these developments. The blurring of the distinction between the rules of war and those of criminal justice that has consolidated over the past decades is resonant of the colonial past (Saada 2003). The geneology of violence and incarceration can be found in the violent repression of Indigenous people in Australia and the United States and the colonial conquests of England and the other European powers.

The point that violence and incarceration are distinctive and defining characteristics of western states is critical at a time when the foremost claimant to the virtues that supposedly characterise such states, the United States, is not only the vanguard of these uncivil practices domestically but has expanded its role to that of global jailer. A Presidential Military Order, declaring an extraordinary emergency for national defence purposes, passed by United States President George W. Bush in November 2001 allowed the arrest, detention and possible military trial of non-United States citizens by the United States' Defense Department, regardless of their location. It is estimated that 70,000 people have been detained in United States' extraterritorial penal camps around the world. There is now a real possibility that the mass incarceration and the brutality that accompanies it, an outstanding feature of the past decades in the United States, is central to its continuing global ambition.

Finally, a brief comment on 'agency' and resistance is necessary. In the debate concerning the appropriateness of capital punishment, the reformist argument, among other issues, often focuses on the moral 'right' of the State to extend its monopoly on the use of lethal force to the 'taking of life' as punishment. This construction is literal: 'taking life' meaning physical death. The reformist alternative is ever-lengthening deprivations of liberty up to and including 'life meaning life.' Yet custody, particularly in the harsh regimes of supermax security, but also extending to all forms of custody in which the majority of a sentence is served in isolation, allows the State to appropriate life. It might not be literal but, as so many prisoners have recorded, imprisonment is often a 'living death,' the death of the social, the familial, the spiritual. While much is made, quite rightly, of the use of harsh and degrading regimes to 'break' the will of political prisoners, it is often overlooked that this is an essential element of all prisons and other custodial settings in which the individual or the collective challenges the absolute authority of the institution. 'Agency,' a concept so popular with contemporary writers on imprisonment, undoubtedly exists by degree within prisoners' lived experiences and the minor skirmishes over time, regime, facilities and so on. When the exercise of agency poses a serious challenge to the authority of the guards, the managers and the medics, when verbal challenges tip over into active resistance, the limits of prisoners' agency are quickly contained and often fiercely policed.

REFERENCES

Anderson, C. (2003) 'The Politics of Convict Space: Indian Penal Settlements and the Andaman Islands' in C. Strange and A. Bashford (eds) *Isolation and Practices of Exclusion*, London: Routledge, pp 40–55.

Andreas, P. and Price, R. (2001) 'From War Fighting to Crime Fighting: Transforming the American National Security State,' *International Studies Review*, vol 3, no 3, pp.31–52

Austin, J., Irwin, J. and Kubrin, C. (2003) in T. Blomberg and S. Cohen (ed) *Punishment and Social Control*, New York: Aldine De Gruyter pp.433–470

Barnes, H. E. and Teeters, N. K. (1951) *New Horizons in Criminology*, New York: Prentice-Hall.

Bush, President G. W. (2002) *The National Security Strategy of the United States*, Washington, DC: The White House.

Carlton, B. (2007) *Imprisoning Resistance: Life and Death in an Australian Supermax*, Sydney: Institute of Criminology Press.

Christie, N. (1994) *Crime Control as Industry: Towards Gulags, Western Style*, London: Routledge, 2nd Edn.

Cunneen, C. (2001) *Conflict, Politics and Crime: Aboriginal Communities and the Police*, Sydney: Allen and Unwin.

Currie, E. (1998) *Crime and Punishment in America*, New York: Metropolitan Books.

Davis, A. (2003) *Are Prisons Obsolete?* New York: Seven Stories Press.

———. (2005) *Abolition Democracy: Beyond Empire, Prisons and Torture*, New York: Seven Stories Press.

Dow, M. (2004) *American Gulag: Inside U.S. Immigration Prisons*, Berkeley: University of California Press.

Eisenstein, Z. (2004) *Against Empire: Feminism, Racism and the West,* Melbourne: Spinifex Press.

Garland, D. (2001) 'The Meaning of Mass Imprisonment' in D. Garland (ed) *Mass Imprisonment: Social Causes and Consequences*, London: Sage pp.1–3

Gilmore-Wilson, R. (2007) *Golden Gulag: Prisons, Surplus, Crisis, and Opposition in Globalizing California*, Berkeley: University of California Press.

Giroux, H. (2002) 'Global Capitalism and the Return of the Garrison State,' *Arena Journal New Series*, no.19, pp.141–160.

Goldberg, D. (1993) *Racist Culture: Philosophy and Politics of Meaning*, Cambridge, MA: Blackwell.

Goldson, B. (2002) *Vulnerable Inside: Children in Secure and Penal Settings*, London: The Children's Society.

Goldson, B. and Coles, D. (2005) *In the Care of the State? Child Deaths in Penal Custody in England and Wales*, London: INQUEST.

Greene, J. (2004) 'From Abu Ghraib to America: Examining Our Harsh Prison Culture,' *Ideas for an Open Society: Occasional Papers from OSI-US Programs*, vol 4, October.

Hirsh, J. (1997) 'Globalization of Capital, Nation-States and Democracy,' *Studies in Political Economy*, no. 54, pp.39–58.

Hogg, R. (2001) 'Penality and Modes of Regulating Indigenous Peoples in Australia,' *Punishment and Society*, vol 3, no 3, pp.355–379.

Hudson, B. (2003) *Justice in the Risk Society: Challenging and Re-affirming Justice in Late Modernity*, London: Sage.

Jamieson, R. and McEvoy, K. (2005) 'State Crime by Proxy and Juridical Othering,' *British Journal of Criminology*, vol 45, no 4, pp.504–527.

MacMaster, N. (2004) 'Torture: From Algiers to Abu Ghraib,' *Race and Class*, pp.1–21.

Mathiesen, T. (1990) *Prison on Trial*, London, Sage.

McKeown, L. (2001) *Out of Time: Irish Republican Prisoners Long Kesh 1972–2000*, Belfast: Beyond the Pale.

Mariani, P. (2001) 'Overview: Law, Order, and Neoliberalism,' *Social Justice*, vol 28.

Perera, S, (2007) 'Our Patch: Domains of Whiteness, Geographies of Lack and Australia's Racial Horizon in the "War on Terror"' in S. Perera (ed) *Our Patch: Enacting Australian Sovereignty Post 2001* Perth: APINetwork pp.119–146.

Pfaff, W. (2007) 'Manifest Destiny: A New Direction for America,' *The New York Review of Books*, vol. LIV, no 2, pp.54–58.

Saada, E. (2003) 'The History Lessons: Power and Rule in Imperial Formations,' *Items and Issues,* Social Science Research Council, vol 4, no 4, Fall/Winter.

Said, E. (2000) 'Apocalypse Now,' *Index on Censorship*, vol 29, no 5: pp.49–53.

Scraton, P. (2002) 'Lost lives, hidden voices: "truth" and controversial deaths,' *Race and Class*, Vol 40, 1, pp. 107–118.

———. (2004) 'Streets of Terror: Marginalisation, Criminalisation and Moral Renewal,' *Social Justice*, vol 31, no 1–2, pp.130–158.

———. (2007) *Power, Conflict and Criminalisation*, London: Routledge.

Scraton, P. and Moore, L. (2005) *The Hurt Inside: The Imprisonment of Women and Girls in Northern Ireland*, Belfast: Northern Ireland Human Rights Commission.

———. (2007) *The Prison Within: The Imprisonment of Women at Hydebank Wood: 2004–2006*, Belfast: Northern Ireland Human Rights Commission.

Scraton, P., Sim, J. and Skidmore, P. (1991) *Prisons Under Protest*, Milton Keynes: The Open University Press.

Sparks, R. (2003) 'State Punishment in Advanced Capitalist Countries' in T. Blomberg and S. Cohen (eds) *Punishment and Social Control*, New York: Aldine De Gruyter, pp.19–44.

Zender, L. (2000) 'The Pursuit of Security' in T. Hope and R. Sparks (eds) *Crime, Risk and Insecurity*, London: Routledge, pp. 200–214.

2 An Afternoon in September 1983

Laurence McKeown

INTRODUCTION

The former Long Kesh/Maze prison camp is situated outside Lisburn, County Antrim, in the north of Ireland. Once home to several thousand political prisoners and those detained without trial (1971–1975) at the time of writing, in 2007 it is empty with many of the buildings under demolition. Its remaining prisoners were released in 2000 under the terms of the 1998 Good Friday Agreement, an internationally recognised agreement between the British and Irish governments involving all political parties in the north of Ireland.

Few other prisons in the world have had such a dramatic impact on the community. Previously an RAF camp during the Second World War, Long Kesh was reopened in 1972 to house those imprisoned without trial—trade unionists, students and Republican activists demanding civil rights. In 1975, when the policy of internment without trial became internationally notorious—in particular the revelations of ill treatment and brutality inflicted on those interned for which the British State was condemned at the European Court of Human Rights—the policy was dropped, the internees released and the name of the prison changed to HMP Maze.

By that time, Long Kesh did not only contain internees. Those convicted in the courts for political offences arising out of the conflict were also incarcerated there. They received political status, or 'special category status' as the British government preferred to name it. This was introduced in 1972 following a hunger strike by Republican prisoners in Belfast's Crumlin Road Prison at a time when talks between the British government and the Irish Republican Army (IRA) were taking place on the outside. The prisoners were housed according to their political affiliations, did not wear prison uniform or do prison work, organised their own educational and handicraft activities and established internal organisational structures, their appointed leaders liaising with the prison authorities.

In 1975, the situation changed when the Gardiner Commission recommended the release of the internees and the removal of political status from those convicted before the courts, introducing a new policy of 'criminalisation.' Anyone arrested and convicted post-1 March 1976 was to be treated as a 'common criminal,' regardless of offence or motivation. They would wear prison uniforms, undertake prison work, be integrated regardless of political affiliation and would not be permitted any internal command structures. To facilitate this change in policy, a new section of the prison was developed and special cellular units constructed. These were known as H-Blocks because of their distinctive shape. The H-Blocks of Long Kesh/Maze Prison became the site of the longest and harshest prison protest ever in Ireland, a protest culminating in the death of ten prisoners on hunger strike in 1981. One, Bobby Sands, was elected a Member of the British Parliament during his fast. Another, Kieran Doherty, was elected to the Irish Parliament. Together, this was a significant demonstration that their communities regarded them not as criminals but as political prisoners.[1]

More recently, the 1981 hunger strike is considered to have been a major influence not only on political developments within the Republican Movement but also on the course of Irish politics. An equally important and significant event, however, occurred less than two years after the end of the hunger strike. It was the 1983 escape from Long Kesh/Maze, effected by Republican prisoners. In H-Block 7 in the heart of what was deemed one of the most secure, if not the most secure, prisons in Europe, IRA prisoners seized control of the Block, held it for two hours without the knowledge of the prison authorities, hijacked the prison food lorry and drove to the front gates of the prison. Had it not been for a delay in the operation, all thirty-eight prisoners on board would have driven to freedom. In the event, half escaped. Nevertheless, the breakout was viewed as a major success, a massive morale boost to the prisoners and the Republican Movement, and an equally crushing blow to the British government, the prison authorities and security and intelligence agencies on the outside, none of whom had been aware of the planning and preparation of what was one of the IRA's most significant operations.

To fully comprehend the enormity of events on that day and the significance of the prisoners' actions, it is necessary to consider the physical, human and psychological barriers they confronted and overcame to make good the escape.

THE 'BLANKET PROTEST' AND HUNGER STRIKE, 1976 THROUGH 1981

In September 1976, the first Irish Republican prisoner sentenced under the newly introduced policy of 'criminalisation,' Kieran Nugent, refused to conform to the new prison regime and demanded to be treated as a political prisoner. He was stripped naked, placed in a cell and given only a blanket to cover himself. Thus began what became known as the 'blanket protest,' which lasted over five years, ending on 3 October 1981 following the death of the ten prisoners on hunger strike. At its height, there were more than 400 Republican prisoners on the protest. They lived their lives locked in cells twenty-four hours a day, had no radios, televisions, books, newspapers, magazines, writing papers, pens; no exercise; nothing but a piece of foam for a mattress, a piss pot and a container of water. From March 1978 to March 1981 they refused to wash, shave or have their hair cut. As a result they were often forcibly washed and shaved. In 1981, they began their hunger strike for five demands: the right to wear their own clothes, to not do prison work, to have free association and access to education facilities, to have a weekly visit and food parcel and to have their lost remission restored. The first of the prisoners to die on the fast, Bobby Sands, wrote:

> I believe I am but another of those wretched Irishmen born of a risen generation with a deeply rooted and unquenchable desire for freedom. I am dying not just to attempt to end the barbarity of H-Block, or to gain the rightful recognition of a political prisoner, but primarily because what is lost in here is lost for the Republic and those wretched oppressed whom I am deeply proud to know as the 'risen people'. (Sands 1981: 7–8)

POST-HUNGER STRIKE

When the hunger strike ended on the 3 October 1981, prisoners were granted only one of five demands: the right to wear their own clothes. This was a right extended to all prisoners in the north of Ireland, political or otherwise. Although it was only one of their demands, it was the most significant, symbolically of immense importance. The prisoners had always stated that they would 'wear no convict's uniform' and they adhered to that resolution. More importantly, on a practical level, having their own clothes allowed them to get out of their cells for the first time in five years, to eat meals in the canteen, to wash, to exercise, to associate together in the evenings and at weekends. Coming together in this manner, they were able to strategise on how they would achieve their outstanding demands.

It was clear to the prisoners that the physical, head-to-head type of confrontational approach to the prison authorities and prison policy was over. If they were to move forward to create the conditions and facilities they wanted, they would have to adopt a new approach to prison struggle. Prior to 1981, their actions could be defined as prison protest; post-1981 it became prison struggle. It became obvious that they could not sit apart from the prison system. To undermine it, they would have to enter into it and that would entail agreeing to do prison work. It was a rational decision but one that was not arrived at easily or without considerable emotions being expressed. Having refused to accept prison policy over a five-year period and enduring extreme conditions as a consequence, some prisoners felt that participation in the prison regime would betray those who had died on hunger strike. The counter-argument was that the only way to achieve the outstanding demands for which those on hunger strike had died was to destroy the prison system from within through engagement.

In October 1982, one year after the end of the hunger strike, Republican prisoners ceased their no-work protest and presented themselves for work. The prison authorities were jubilant and quickly allocated as many prisoners as possible to work duties, opening new workshops to facilitate the increased numbers. Republicans, it seemed, had finally succumbed to the prison system after years of protest. Their key leaders were now performing the duties of 'orderlies' in the wings and even in the administration centre of the H-Blocks, cleaning out the guards' mess and the governor's office, making tea and emptying rubbish bins. From the authorities' standpoint, it seemed that at long last the policy of criminalisation was beginning to work, if not entirely along the lines initially envisaged.

A FALSE SECURITY

Those who believed the official line, however, had become victims of their own propaganda and the failed policy of criminalisation. In their delight at witnessing 'conformity' to prison policy, they appeared to forget that prisoners were committed to the destruction of not only the prison system but also the British State in Ireland. Rather than being confined to their cells or Blocks (as befitting the containment of such subversives), the prisoners roamed the camp at will, going to and from workshops where they used machines and materials for their own purposes. Leo Green states:

> Our objective was to slow down the whole production process [in the workshops], change the climate of the place, and ultimately to burn or wreck the workshops. We were already being told to prepare for that.[2]

While planning the destruction of the workshops on a designated date, the prisoners also used the new situation for other purposes. Two activities remained key priorities for imprisoned Irish Republicans through the many decades, indeed centuries, of struggle. The first was escape to rejoin the struggle; the second was engagement in education and personal development while preparing for escape or release from prison. For Irish Republicans, escape has always been a political act and commitment.

Larry Marley was at the forefront of escape activity. Where others saw concrete walls, Larry saw obstacles to be climbed; where others saw metal gates, Larry saw locks to be opened. Most important, where others saw guards, Larry saw vulnerability and human weakness. Already, in 1975, he had made a successful escape from Newry Court House, remaining 'on the run' and active with the IRA until his recapture in 1976. Sent to the

Long Kesh Cages, where he was given political status, he soon attempted to escape again. It was on one such bid that he was caught with two others, Brendan McFarlane and Pat McGeown. All three lost political status, were sent to the H-Blocks and joined the protest for reinstatement. After the 1981 hunger strike and the new conditions that prevailed, Larry explored further possibilities for escape even though he was soon due for release.

NEW PRISONERS INTO THE H-BLOCKS

During the 1982 through 1983 period, other crucial elements came together, significantly influencing the course of future events in the prison. A number of high-profile IRA volunteers had been sentenced recently, including Martin Lynch (a former blanketman) and Bobby Storey from Belfast. Storey had been arrested several times throughout the 1970s, charged and placed on remand. Each time he was acquitted, despite being tried in Northern Ireland's Diplock court system where a single judge, sitting without a jury, decided on guilt or innocence. Storey did not rely on lawyers to fight his case; he played an active part, going over the detail in its minutiae.

Storey's judgement was trusted by the IRA leadership on the outside, as was that of Martin Lynch, who became Officer Commanding of the Republican prisoners shortly after his arrival in the H-Blocks. Storey was a member of the camp staff with responsibility for security and intelligence including all aspects of escape attempts. At this time, another prisoner arrived in the H-Blocks following a failed escape bid from the Long Kesh Cages, where prisoners convicted of offences before 1 March 1976 were still able to retain their 'special category status.' This was Gerry Kelly.[3] The new H-Blocks arrivals joined with Marley, McFarlane and others who had been on the protest for years and had established total collective trust and commitment. Plans were soon hatched to carry out what became one of the greatest escapes in the history of British penal institutions in Ireland or abroad.

AN ESCAPE COMMITTEE IS FORMED

Brendan McFarlane recalls:

> There was never a time when escape was away from my mind but obviously no one could even attempt it during the blanket protest because the environment wasn't conducive. But once you came out of those conditions the environment was more open and opportunities began to present themselves, either by going out to visits, the hospital, the gym, the workshops, all the different places you travelled about in the camp. Obviously acquiring apparatus to assist with escapes became much

easier too. You could also hide things easier. The camp staff set up an escape committee with Larry Marley to oversee it. Larry told me there was an idea of taking over the entire Block and effecting an escape on the prison food lorry. I said, 'Look, you couldn't do that without weapons.' I knew because I had looked at it on my travels around the Block. There were too many nerve centres. Larry said, 'Yes, I know, but the IRA's prepared to run with it. They're prepared to provide the weaponry.' I couldn't believe it. From looking at possible escapes on a small scale my confidence suddenly soared.

Gerry Kelly initially had doubts:

I was asked my opinion [of the plan] and I was very sceptical, not in the sense that I thought the plan wasn't good, it was very workable, very feasible, but I had worked on ideas like that in the past. Mass escapes weren't new in terms of concept. What we knew however was that they weren't going to work because of the need for weapons to be supplied from outside, which outside was always reluctant to provide. After speaking to Bobby Storey and learning what was available to us for the escape attempt I got more into it.[4] I got more enthused, more excited, more interested. I actually got much more confident also.

Bobby Storey, however, was able to provide reassurances to the IRA leadership:

The IRA certainly had concerns about weapons going into any prison especially the H Blocks so shortly after the hunger strikes and protests and knowing the level of hostility between the prisoners and the prison authorities but I was able to satisfy them on that account. The prisoners were disciplined IRA volunteers and as far as I was concerned the weapons would be used on the escape in the same manner as they would be in any other IRA operation on the outside. That is, in a totally limited, disciplined and specific capacity to carry out whatever was needed to be done.

CREATING THE CONDITIONS

The size of the planned escape, in terms of numbers of prisoners involved, was matched by the sheer audacity in believing that prisoners could take over an entire H-Block at the heart of a prison regarded as one of the most secure, if not the most secure, in Europe. To succeed, the plan required more than availability of weapons. A complete relaxation and breakdown in security precautions on the part of the guards was also necessary. To achieve that end, a major psychological conditioning of the guards had to be developed. And that required prisoners to adopt a radical break from previous attitudes and behaviour towards guards, in itself a major undertaking coming so soon after the blanket protest and hunger strikes when hostility between the two groups was at its height. Brendan McFarlane notes how they had to 'work on the screws, not just for escapes but in general to improve the quality of life in the Blocks.' He continues:

> We had to break down their domineering attitude and in a sense that was not too difficult to do because once we were out of our cells the screws were not going to be too aggressive. So we set out to create a relaxed environment. The only way any jail operates and functions is if there is a degree of co-operation between the administration and the prisoners in the way that daily life is structured. We needed to get onto first name terms with the screws. That would make it more difficult for them to enforce any restrictive policies. The big thing we had in our favour was that the NIO (Northern Ireland Office) wanted us out to work.[5]

> Because of my reputation from the time of the hunger strike and having attempted to escape in the past I was not allowed to work outside of the Blocks in the workshops. A screw actually came and told me that soon after we gave up the protest and then said to me, 'See the orderly's job in the stores, doing the yards? That's the one you want to go for. You're finished your work by eleven o'clock in the morning.' So I said, 'No problem, that'll do me.' That gave me the run of the Block any time of the day. Others took on other roles as orderlies in the circle, people like Tony McAllister and Gerry Kelly.

Bobby Storey recalls the priority of 'reduc[ing] tension in the Block':

> Any minor issue that came up we acted to divert or resolve it. While the other Blocks were going through all sorts of petty issues H7 was relatively calm. The screws relaxed. We were on first name terms with them all and as they relaxed and talked we were able to build up a psychological profile of them and assess how they would respond in certain situations. We were also able to move around the Block fairly freely even though this was against prison rules. As orderlies we could go from wing to wing and across the circle just by going to the grille and calling the screw over to unlock it. This meant that at any one time of the day we could have people positioned at all vantage points in the Block.

Gerry Kelly 'hadn't talked to screws in years':

> When we had political status it was our appointed leadership who had all the dealings with them but I knew I had to be in the circle to carry out my brief on the escape so had to deal with them. I remember talking

to 'Steve the Greek' who people had told me had been an animal during the blanket protest and when I asked him for something and called him, 'Steve,' the guy nearly did somersaults to get it for me.

Brendan McFarlane recalls the complete change of approach:

I saw me going over to the screw in the control room and asking did he want a cup of tea as I was making one for myself.[6] He would say, 'Aye,' so I would make it and pass it in the grille to him. Then I would ask if he wanted a bit of toast and go off and make it and bring it out on a plate. Well, you can't put a plate of toast through the grille so he would open the grille. See once he did it once, the grille to the control room opened every time you went over to it. I would say to the screw in the control room, 'Here, I'm brushing the circle I'll brush out the control room for you when I'm at it, no problem, away and get yourself a cup of coffee.' And he would walk out of the control room, leave the gate open and me in brushing it out. This was the nerve centre of the Block, supposed to be locked at all times. I could see all the controls and how they worked.

We had the situation for instance that a grille would be opened for me when the screw saw me approaching. I might be ten foot away but he would open it. Even the front gate of the Block—the screw would open it when he saw me coming. Similarly with Gerry Kelly, or Bobby Storey. When a screw saw them approach a grille he automatically opened it. They were conditioned to thinking, 'He's coming out here, he has a reason to be out here, I don't want him standing at the grilles waiting on me to open it.'

In less than a year, the Republican prisoners transformed the prison environment from one of confrontation on a daily basis to one where they had become a regular part of the daily maintenance of the prison. To the casual observer, the policy of criminalisation had worked. These prisoners had seemingly finished with protest, were no longer dangerous or subversive, had finally conformed to the system and just wanted to get on, complete their sentence, and get out.

THE ESCAPE

The illusion was shattered on the afternoon of Sunday 25 September 1983. From the circle of H-Block 7, Bobby Storey shouted the codeword, and in one swift, coordinated move, all prison guards in the circle and four wings were taken hostage. The operation was complex, given the layout of the Block, with prison guards stationed within easy access to alarm buttons.

Should individuals fail to carry out their allotted tasks, the escape would fail. Bobby Storey gives the following account:

> We took over the actual wings using a variety of weapons arresting up to 15 prison officers, one of whom received a flesh wound to his shoulder which was tended to by a POW [Prisoner of War] there and then. Others took over the circle area arresting 7 or 8 prison staff. The operation to take command of the Block went smoothly and according to plan except in the case of the warder in the control room who tried to raise the alarm. He had a gun pointed to his head and was told several times to move away from the alarm button. He made a move to push the alarm and was shot and injured. The escape leader immediately instructed two POWs to escort a prison medical officer attached to H7 that day to gather medical supplies from the treatment room and tend to the wounded guard. This lost us valuable minutes during what was a very tightly time-framed operation, but equally it was the natural and correct response. All the captured prison guards were taken to the classrooms, tied up and gagged. All other prisoners not going on the escape were locked in their cells.
>
> The prison officers arrested were hooded to avoid identification of POWs during the operation. Pillowcases where chosen as hoods so that they would not hinder breathing. The prison officers who complained of being too warm had their hoods lifted. Prison staff under arrest were told they were in no danger, so sit and do nothing to hinder the escape, which they did, and were treated as stated. A statement was read out to all prison officers under arrest. It accepted that prison officers would give accounts of what happened to them but urged them not to allow themselves to use the post-escape climate to tell lies or brutalise POWs—a plea ignored by the many prison staff later that day.
>
> The operation required that some prisoners be dressed in screws' uniforms, so we had to get a number of them [12] to remove their uniforms. We provided them with blankets to cover themselves. We also took whatever personal possessions they had in the pockets of the uniforms, put these into A4 envelopes, sealed them, put their name on them and placed the envelopes beside them where they sat. One of the guards, who was grossly overweight and had difficulty breathing with being tied, asked to be untied, and said that he would give his word not to interfere with the escape. He was untied.
>
> A statement was also read out to all POWs when we had taken control of the Block that all actions taken against Prison staff during the operation [to escape] must only be relative to ensuring the success of the operation, and for no other reason; also that any actions must be of

necessity and measured. Whilst such an instruction was not felt to be absolutely necessary it was important to the POWs that such an expression of professionalism and balance was stated.

Once the prisoners secured the inside of the Block, Brendan McFarlane, as he often did, walked to the outer front gate and produced a gun and ordered the guard off his position. When the food lorry arrived at H-Block 7, the driver was taken hostage, briefed about what was happening and told he was to drive the lorry out of the camp.[7] He was advised that a grenade was attached to the driver's seat of the lorry and that, should he attempt to jump from the lorry, the grenade would explode. One of the prisoners, Gerry Kelly, would travel alongside on the floor and would shoot the driver should he attempt to abandon the lorry. The driver was shown the gun and agreed to carry out the instructions. Thirty-seven prisoners climbed into the back of the lorry. Other prisoners, who acted as a backup to the operation, let the lorry out of the Block, locked the front gates and entrances and returned to their cells. The lorry passed through all internal gates without hindrance and arrived at the tally lodge, the main exit/entrance in the perimeter wall. A number of prisoners in prison guard uniforms overpowered the prison staff, taking control of the tally lodge. A delay in arriving at the front gate of the prison put the escape behind schedule. As Bobby Storey comments:

> The food lorry had been late getting to H7 and we also lost some time treating the injured guard so by the time we reached the tally lodge [front gate] a new work shift of screws was coming on and others going off. This meant a lot of screws had accumulated at the entrance.

Soon the prison guards massing at the tally lodge became aware of what was happening and they tried to prevent the escape. Hand-to-hand fighting broke out. Prison Officer James Ferris died of a heart attack after being stabbed with a screw driver. Bobby Storey realised the lorry would not make it out of the camp and he 'gave the order for the remaining prisoners to get out of the back of it and to make a run for it':

> With some of us dressed as screws and the screws coming on duty dressed as civilians the British soldiers guarding the perimeter wall of the camp were confused and did not open fire immediately. It was only later that they did, wounding several men. We just ran across fields. Some commandeered a number of cars and made their getaway. Several were caught immediately. Myself and two others made it some distance but once the alert was up the helicopters were sent up and we hid in a river, breathing through reeds when the chopper came into sight. We had hoped to stay there until nightfall but were discovered when a foot patrol of British soldiers and RUC men arrived.[8]

THE AFTERMATH OF THE ESCAPE

Once the alarm was raised at the tally lodge, the rest of the camp was locked down. Prisoners were returned to cells, unaware of what was happening. Shortly afterwards British Army helicopters appeared over the H-Blocks and British soldiers and the RUC entered the Blocks, beginning with H7. Seamus Finucane recalls:

> The Brits [British soldiers] and the RUC searched around the perimeter of the Block and then the exercise yards and catwalk outside the cells. They discovered a bag of rounds in the catwalk outside Bobby Storey's cell which was adjacent to our cell so they raided our cell. It was very aggressive; very frightening. They were very psyched up, shouting and screaming. They put rifles to our heads and shouted at us to get down. We tried to talk to them to calm the situation and regain control of what was happening. They roughed us up a bit on the ground and others searched the cell and then they left. They searched the rest of the wing and did a headcount of all prisoners then left the Block.

> It was then that the screws came into the Block. It was some time before they decided to move us across to H Block 8. 'A' wing was moved first. There were very senior prison governors present at that stage including assistant governor Bill McConnell and I think even the governor of the prison. I think 'A' wing was 'administratively moved' under the stewardship of the governor who could later say that there was no violence or brutality on the move but he then went off the scene and left the move to the assistant governors and more junior prison guards.[9] I think they handed over control to the POA [Prison Officers' Association] who wanted revenge because that's when the brutality started. The thing is, there had been no brutality of the screws in the Block at the time of the escape. All the hand to hand fighting and injuries occurred at the tally lodge at the perimeter wall.

> A screw who we knew as 'Big T' came down our wing while we were all locked up and shouted out that we were to strip down to the waist. I shouted out to him to ask what was going on. He came over to my cell, lifted the flap [of the door] and shouted in, 'Fuck up' but he left the flap up and we were able to see what was happening in the wing. We were in cell 25 and they started moving people from the cells across from us, starting with cell 3. People were taken out of their cells with their arms held up their backs. They were semi-naked and trying to carry things in their hands. Any radios or tobacco they had was taken from them and thrown up the wing. It was all very controlled; one prisoner out of the cell at a time. I could tell it was a very hostile situation and very heated.

When they came to my cell they took me up to the wash area of the wing to where they were stripping people. On the way up the wing I was banged into walls and grills and with my arms up my back it was very difficult to keep balance or try to stop myself from hitting against the walls. There were dogs in the wing. If you fell to the ground you were bitten by the dogs. Depending on your profile as a prisoner you were given various degrees of treatment during the strip search. I got roughed up quite a bit. I then had my arms handcuffed and I was run out to the circle. It was even more difficult to keep my balance with the cuffs on and again was knocked against walls and grilles. In the circle there were both white shirts [senior prison officers] and blue shirts [basic grade prison officers]. The number 1 Chief [prison officer] was also there. They tried to ascertain your identity—most of them would have known us all personally—so as to identify who had escaped. I got slapped around there also as I wouldn't cooperate with them. I was then taken out of the Block and ran across to H Block 8 through a gauntlet of screws and dogs. Your biggest fear was the dogs because if you fell the screws set them on you and they bit you. Several prisoners were bitten. We were all barefoot and naked from the waist up which made it all worse. All of this was witnessed by senior officers.

You were just glad to reach your cell in the other Block. It didn't matter that we were held there throughout the night without bedding or blankets. What took place was controlled and systematic. It was not the occasional 'rogue screw.' They had been humiliated by the escape and wanted to take that out on us.

Seán Murray soon realised the seriousness of what was happening:

The RUC left the Block and the POA took control and we had a very dangerous situation. They came in to the cells and told you to take your shoes and socks off. I refused because I knew rightly why they wanted them off. They pulled me out of the cell by the hair and I got beaten the whole way down the wing to the toilet area. I was stripped; physically stripped because we wouldn't strip for them. They turned you upside down, gave you your clothes back, you were handcuffed to a screw then run through the circle. You were being beaten and kicked. They had dogs. What saved me was that I was handcuffed to a young screw and I pulled him in the way of the dogs anytime they were close so he got bitten a few times. It depended on what screw you got. Some weren't really bothering. Others were out to get you.

Those in H-Block 7 who had not been part of the escape also experienced brutal retribution by the prison guards but the captured escapees feared for their very lives. Bobby Storey comments:

I was captured with 3 others; Joe Simpson, Sean McGlinchey and Peter Hamilton. We were immediately stripped naked and had our hands cuffed behind our backs. Our captors were a mixture of prison officers, RUC men and British army soldiers. We were beaten and interrogated about where other escapees may be hiding. We were then taken to a nearby Bridge and our ordeal continued until RUC jeeps arrived to transport us individually back to the H Blocks. Inside the Jeep I was assaulted continuously by the RUC who were in a state of near hysteria. When we arrived back at the jail a large crowd, by way of a mob, were waiting on us. All of them were prison officers. A section of them attempted to drag me away from the jail entrance. They ended up arguing about me with another section of the crowd who wrestled me away from the first group and dragged me into the jail. I was dragged still naked—although at this point my plastic cuffs had snapped allowing me some degree of covering up—and was kicked and punched at every step almost. I was eventually brought to a car park where there were scores of prison staff. They surrounded me and kicked, punched and batoned me. Their numbers almost assisted my plight as some got in the way and accidentally obstructed others. As the beating continued a senior prison officer shouted, 'No more batons; just kicks and punches.'

I was eventually dragged off to the prison reception building, between two prison officers. They invited every prison officer who walked towards us to assault me. Many did; a punch or a kick as they walked past me. I was then brought into the reception where I was placed in a cubicle. I was attacked there by a small group of prison officers on three occasions. One of them later told me that he joined in on the assault on me to divert others in the group from taking me out to a step and breaking my neck on it and making it to appear as though it were an accident, as they had talked of it.

I was then placed in a van with Peter Hamilton—both of us put on the floor of the vehicle. Prison staff had their feet on us, digging their heels into our naked backs and legs. When the van stopped I was dragged out by the ankles by two prison staff. I managed to twist around so that when I hit the ground it would be with my back. I was then dragged over rough ground which grated the skin off my back, shoulders and buttocks. I was dragged into a cell and received more assaults before I was locked in. I had several injuries, none of which were attended to that day.

In the days following the escape, the POA remained in control of the prison. Access to governors, doctors, solicitors and the Board of Visitors was denied for several days.[10] Seamus Finucane:

We were lucky to get fed. When we eventually got exercise many people were walking the yard without shoes or tops. It was 5 days after the escape before I got a visit with my brother Pat.[11] Until then we had been isolated without access to newspapers or radios or visits.

In the case of Brian Pettigrew, one of those assaulted by prison guards and bitten by dogs in the move from H7 to H8, it was ten days later before he was seen by a doctor. His injuries were still visible, however, and the doctor made a report detailing his injuries, confirming they were consistent with dog bites. Pat Finucane (solicitor) initiated a legal claim for damages on behalf of Brian, and in the case held in the High Court of Northern Ireland in 1988 former Lord Chief Justice Hutton ruled in his favour.

During the trial, damning evidence was revealed regarding the retributive behaviour of prison officers, not only on the evening of the 25 September, but in the days and weeks that followed. Prison officers and an Assistant Governor who denied allegations of assaults or dog attacks during the move from H7 to H8 were exposed as lying under oath. Minutes of a meeting between the Governor and POA representatives in the days following the escape, made available to the court, confirmed that the POA, against the advice of the Governor, took unilateral action concerning the running of the prison and the regime available to prisoners. The Deputy Governor, Duncan McLaughlin, who headed up an internal inquiry in the aftermath of the escape, reported to Sir James Hennessy (former Chief Inspector for Prisons appointed to carry out an inquiry into the escape on behalf of the British government) that he had met with a 'wall of silence.' Hennessy encountered similar difficulties throughout the course of his investigation.

The court awarded Brian Pettigrew £3,000 compensation for his injuries and, in his statement to the court, Lord Chief Justice Hutton commented, 'I consider that in the circumstances of this case the plaintiff should receive a sum for aggravated damages. I am also of the opinion . . . that the plaintiff is entitled to exemplary damages.' Explaining his decision to award exemplary damages, Judge Hutton referred to the case of Rookes v Barnard (1964) and to the comments of Lord Devlin who stated in that trial:

> Exemplary damages are essentially different from ordinary damages. The object of damages in the usual sense of the term is to compensate. The object of exemplary damages is to punish and deter.

Approximately eighty prisoners who were assaulted on the evening of the 25 September took similar legal cases. Each was settled out of court and compensation paid, £3,000 to those who suffered dog bites, £1,500 for other injuries.

An immediate consequence of the escape was closure of the prison workshops. Indirectly, Republicans achieved yet another one of their demands less than two years from the end of the 1981 hunger strike. Bill McConnell, the Assistant Governor present on the night of the movement of prisoners from H-Block 7 and who oversaw, but later denied in court, the brutality of prison guards, was executed by the IRA on the 8 March 1984. In its statement, the IRA said of his death, 'it should come as a salutary lesson to those in the administration presently advocating a return to a policy of beatings as a means of controlling political prisoners.'

Gerry Kelly, a successful escapee, was arrested in Amsterdam in 1986 close to a large stockpile of weapons believed to be destined for the IRA. Britain requested his extradition to which a Dutch court agreed but only on the grounds that the charge for which he had originally been imprisoned— the bombing of the Old Bailey courthouse in London—be dropped. The court accepted Kelly's defence that 'the bombing had been a legitimate act of war.' The British government agreed, granting Gerry Kelly a Royal Prerogative to assist the extradition process. No doubt the British government believed that back home in the north of Ireland Kelly would be sentenced to a lengthy jail term, or life imprisonment, for the central role he played in effecting the escape. In fact, he received seven years. Like all the other prisoners who appeared before the High Court in Belfast charged with escape or attempted escape, he benefited from conflicting evidence and the systemic deceit of prison guards' 'evidence.' Gerry Kelly was released from prison in 1989, just six years after the escape, and in 1992, along with Martin McGuiness, met with the British government in secret talks that heralded the beginning of the peace process in the north of Ireland. Currently he is an elected Member of the Legislative Assembly in the north of Ireland and a junior minister in the Office of the First and Deputy First Minister. A long road travelled from the Cages and H-Blocks of Long Kesh.

Besides Gerry Kelly, eighteen others successfully escaped; nineteen others were recaptured within twenty-four hours. Three who escaped died later on active service with the IRA: Séamus McElwaine, Poiric McKearney and Kieran Fleming. Others arrived in the United States, where lengthy extradition proceedings were initiated. Only one, however, was extradited back to Ireland and two others were extradited from the south of Ireland back to the north. Those who were never recaptured were finally granted freedom from prosecution as part of the ongoing peace process negotiations following the Good Friday Agreement.

In 2007, part of the former prison site at Long Kesh/Maze is planned to be preserved as a museum following a lengthy and successful campaign by Coiste na nIarchimí, the umbrella organisation for former Republican prisoners. Coiste's plans for the site include an iconic new building to house an International Centre for Conflict Resolution. The view of the former Republican prisoners is that the site should stand as a lesson to future generations, particularly those in government, that the way to deal with political issues is to engage with the political representatives of the communities, not to imprison them.

CONCLUSION

Walking through the remains of the prison in 2007, its gates lying open, trees growing through the tarmac and rust forming on the locks, it would be understandable—but wrong—to assume that in 1983 the prison was insecure. In fact, it was a highly secure prison. Two crucial elements, however, led to the breach of security on 25 September. Those involved in the planning, preparation and implementation of the escape were not 'mere prisoners' but highly intelligent, disciplined, committed, experienced and dedicated volunteers in the Irish Republican Army. While the focus of the prison authorities was confined within the prison walls, the focus of the Republican prisoners was on the overall struggle against Britain's presence in Ireland. For them the escape was viewed as another military operation against British forces and institutions, as had been the hunger strike and blanket protest. It continued the numerous other protests and actions Republican prisoners had taken over the years including the burning of the prison camp in 1974. Unlike the average social prisoner in a regime that has individualised him/her, Republican prisoners worked together for a common purpose regardless of personal cost, no better evidenced than in the death of their ten comrades on hunger strike in 1981.

By comparison, those guarding the prisoners were largely demotivated, apolitical, undisciplined, underskilled individuals who shared no common purpose or even camaraderie outside of the prison drinking club. This was the occupational culture displayed in the immediate aftermath of the escape when they indulged in gratuitous violence against the prisoners and throughout the subsequent days and nights when they denied prisoners their lawful access to solicitors, doctors and medical treatment. Despite the significantly contrasting characteristics of prisoners and guards, however, the prison might have remained secure had the two groups not been placed in close proximity—yet that was the essence of what the 'criminalisation' policy was designed to achieve. It was that gross disparity in ability, politics, competence, vision and collective application—the 'human element'—that proved to be the weakness in the prison security system, not the walls, the metal grilles or the locked cells: a weakness that the prisoners recognised and exploited not only on the day of the escape but also throughout the months of preparation and manipulation of the prison regime in H-Block 7, establishing the conditions necessary to effect the escape. On realising how they had been systematically 'duped' and made to look foolish, the guards exacted their revenge on Republican prisoners in general. This was not a 'the heat of the moment' response but a deliberate, calculated, organised and brutal retaliation.

A central tenet of the criminalisation policy was the language that went along with it: 'Godfathers,' 'mafia-style shoot-outs,' 'sectarian gangs' and 'men of violence.' The media, the churches and the academics (with a few notable and courageous exceptions) were passively complicit in adopting the new terminology even when it flew in the face of realities on the ground. In H-Block 7 in Long Kesh/Maze prison on the 25 September 1983 the supposed 'men of violence' had control of the entire Block for over two hours. Among the prison guards they took captive were at least three who were infamous for the brutal manner in which they had treated Republican prisoners during the blanket protest and hunger strike. They could easily have been singled out, put against a wall and summarily executed for 'war crimes.' No one would have known who carried out the executions except those who pulled the trigger. But the IRA and their volunteers do not act out of revenge. This would have been contrary to what volunteers had learnt when being inducted into the organisation. So the guards had nothing to fear from the prisoners unless they attempted to obstruct the operation, as one did and was given immediate medical treatment for his wound. When the behaviour of the volunteers/prisoners is compared with that of the guards later that evening, the classification of the former as 'men of violence' is deeply ironic. Particularly so, when the guards' violence was perpetrated in the belief that it carried the authority and backing, if not the direct permission, of the British state.

NOTES

1. For a full discussion of these issues see: Campbell et. al. 1994; McKeown 2001; O'Hearn 2006. See also: Sands 1983.
2. This statement and those from prisoners throughout this article are taken from interviews conducted by the author.
3. Gerry Kelly had been on a lengthy hunger strike in England in the early 1970s, along with Hugh Feeney and the Price sisters in their demand to be transferred to the north of Ireland. This was granted in 1973. He had made a number of attempts at escape whilst imprisoned in England and upon his transferral to Long Kesh.
4. At the time of the escape, seven hand guns were available to the prisoners, having been smuggled in from outside. On the day of the escape, the IRA provided substantial back-up on the outside, including the use of heavy calibre anti-aircraft weapons and landmines placed on roads, to be detonated after the escapees had passed, so as to prevent pursuit by the British Army and RUC.
5. The Northern Ireland Office was the seat of administration for the north of Ireland under Direct Rule from Westminster.
6. The control room in the Block was where all alarms points throughout the Block were monitored. The control room of each Block was in direct contact with the central control room in the central administration building.
7. Having built up the intelligence on the camp, Larry Marley knew that the food lorry was not searched at each gate, as it was supposed to be according to prison security regulations, but was casually waved on through by the guards.
8. Royal Ulster Constabulary was the police force of the north of Ireland at the time. The RUC was heavily criticised by nationalists as it was overwhelmingly made up of Protestants from the unionist community. As part of the

peace process, the Good Friday Agreement and the report of the Patten Commission, the RUC was reconstituted as the Police Service of Northern Ireland and a new policy of fifty/fifty per cent recruitment from the nationalist and unionist communities initiated.

9. In a subsequent court case taken by the prisoners for brutality and dog bites suffered on the evening of the 25th September, the court heard that Governor Whittington had been present at the start of the movement of prisoners from H7 to H8 but that, ' . . . he did not stay at H Block 7 for more than a few minutes and returned to the administration block where he had other duties to perform . . . ' (Judgment of Hutton LCJ, 17 November 1988 in the High Court in Northern Ireland in the case of Brian Pettigrew vs The Northern Ireland Office and the Governor of HMP Maze).

10. See Judgment of Hutton LCJ, 17 November 1988 in the High Court in Northern Ireland in the case of Brian Pettigrew vs the Northern Ireland Office and the Governor of HMP Maze.

11. Patrick Finucane, thirty-eight years, Antrim Road, north Belfast, shot dead in his home on 12 February 1989 by the Ulster Defence Association (UDA)/ Ulster Freedom Fighters (UFF). He was married with three children. Mr Finucane was a successful and respected Belfast solicitor who was assassinated after years of death threats from the RUC Special Branch. His clients passed many of the threats on to him after their interrogation at RUC holding centres. His death came several weeks after a British government Minister, Douglas Hogg, stated at Westminster that a number of solicitors in Northern Ireland were known to be sympathetic to one or other terrorist organisation. It has been revealed in the years since his death that British intelligence agent and UDA/UFF intelligence officer Brian Nelson had assisted the murder gang by supplying them with information on Mr Finucane's movements. It is also suspected that RUC Special Branch agents were directly involved. At an inquest into Mr Finucane's killing in September 1990 it was revealed one of the weapons used was reportedly stolen from a British Army barracks at Holywood, County Down. After the hearing, Mrs Finucane issued a statement directed at the British government and the RUC, stating that 'despite the ample evidence, allegations of collusion had never been investigated.'

REFERENCES

Campbell, B., McKeown, L. and O' Hagan, F. (1994) *Nor Meekly Serve My Time: The H Block Struggle 1976–1981*, Belfast: Beyond the Pale Publications (revd 2006).

McKeown, L. (2001) *Out of Time: Irish Republican Prisoners Long Kesh 1972–2000*, Belfast: Beyond the Pale Publications.

O'Hearn, D. (2006) *Bobby Sands: Nothing but an Unfinished Song*, London: Pluto Press.

Sands, B. (1981) *The Diary of Bobby Sands*, Dublin: Sinn Fein.

———. (1983) *Bobby Sands: One Day in My Life*, London: Pluto Press.

3 Entombing Resistance

Institutional Power and Polarisation in the Jika Jika High-Security Unit

Bree Carlton

In October 1987, prisoners held in the Australian State of Victoria's Pentridge Prison Jika Jika High-Security Unit built a barricade and lit a fire to draw attention to conditions. Five prisoners—James Loughnan, David McGauley, Arthur Gallagher, Robert Wright and Richard Morris—died when staff and the attending emergency crew failed to open the electronic doors in time. In late August, two months prior to the fatal fire, prisoners John Williams and Sean Downie died within two days of one another in unrelated, yet controversial circumstances. Prisoner accounts of life in Jika[1] prior to these deaths draw a disturbing picture of a violent and abusive institutional culture and a harsh high-security environment. Prisoner experiences represent an alternative version of events that contrast sharply with official representations. These competing accounts were publicly battled out in the Coroner's court more than twenty years ago.

Jika Jika was a hi-tech prison constructed to house the system's 'worst' male prisoners. Despite the emphasis on security, technology and efficiency, the supposedly modern and 'humane' complex was plagued with violent incidents and fraught with entrenched management problems. Between 1980 and 1987, there were multiple escapes, escape attempts, assaults, murders, prisoner campaigns, protest actions, barricades, fires, hunger strikes, acts of self-harm, attempted suicides and prisoner allegations of misconduct and brutality by prison staff (State Coroner's Office 1988–1989a; State Coroner's Office 1988–1989b; Prison Reform Group 1988). The impact of the harsh high-security environment on both staff and prisoners produced polarised relationships and an escalating atmosphere of tension. The pressure created through such conditions exacerbated an intense sense of fear and paranoia, while giving rise to a predatory culture of psychological and physical violence between prisoners and between officers and prisoners. During 1987, the seven deaths that occurred in Jika represented 38.8 per cent of the total number of deaths in the Victorian prison system during that year.[2] This is an astonishing figure for a division that on average represented only 1.4 per cent of the Victorian prison population (Office of Corrections Victoria 1987–1988).[3]

This chapter reconstructs the institutional circumstances, pressures and cultures of abusive violence that culminated in the fatal crisis. It unearths and centralises alternative accounts by prisoners who experienced Jika first-hand. In addition to providing a window into prisoner experiences of control, it argues that the troubling events and institutional conditions within the Jika complex are emblematic of high-security prisons designed to house the system's 'worst of the worst.' More broadly, this chapter contends high-security models are, through their prioritisation of security and control, harm and crisis producing. The highly controlled atmosphere, coercive disciplinary objectives and strategies, the operation of unaccountable power and institutional secrecy integral to such regimes enact a self-fulfilling prophecy and intensifying cycle of violence, resistance and security.

In Australia as elsewhere, the human costs of high-security are yet to be acknowledged. As human rights advocate Charandev Singh recently stated:

> The reproduction of what's called supermax units or high-security units or special handling units has always been linked in Australian colonised history to very high rates of deaths and killings and very severe human rights violations. . . . What the research has indicated is that it causes people to separate themselves from the capacity to be human, the capacity to empathise, the capacity to understand what is real and what is imagined; it constitutes a form of severe human suffering and control. . . . The lesson that's taught in these institutions is that violence, the use of unaccountable power and abuse is the norm. (Minc 2006, *Radio 2SER*)

There is an official unwillingness to acknowledge or account for such considerations and a string of high-security units proliferate post-Jika Jika. The Barwon Prison Acacia Unit in Victoria, Woodford Correctional Centre Maximum-Security Unit in Queensland (Fletcher 1999), and the Casuarina High-Security Unit in Western Australia (Carter 2001) comprise a continuum of high-security regimes associated with institutional disorder, abusive and violent cultures and deaths. A further prominent example, the Goulburn High-Risk Management Unit in NSW, has recently attracted much attention and criticism (Funnell 2006). Opened in 2001, Goulburn was designated by officials to house 'psychopaths, the career criminals, the violent standover men, the paranoid inmates and gang leaders' (*Australian* 16 July 2005). However, contrary to this official posturing, Goulburn has served to house a variety of prisoners, at the discretion of the New South Wales (NSW) corrective services Commissioner, including those on remand and the mentally ill (Funnell 2006). Within three years of its opening, Goulburn prisoners sent out an 'offer of hope,' stating: '[I]n this place where we are kept there is no sunlight, no fresh air, nothing but grey concrete, self mutilation, desperation, hunger strikes, sensory deprivation and psychological damage' (*Justice Action* 4 July 2003).

High-security units are repeatedly officially deployed to house 'new breeds' of 'high-risk' criminals and prisoners. Such threats are reinvented and repackaged each time a new facility is on the agenda. Presently, the focus rests with terrorism, and high-security units have been advanced domestically and internationally to house the 'worst' terrorists and terror suspects under the banner of the 'war on terror' (Davis 2005; Gordon 2006). Currently, in Victoria the development of a new multi-million dollar 'super prison' awaits construction in the already maximum-security section of the Barwon Prison. The twenty-seven-man block, according to officials, will house suspected and convicted terrorists and those engaged in organised crime (*Herald Sun* 31 May 2006). Officials justify the need for this new facility despite the fact a group of unconvicted men remanded for terrorist related offences are already isolated and shackled in high-security conditions in the Barwon Prison Acacia Unit.

This chapter focuses on accounts of Jika in order to draw attention to the ongoing reproduction of high-security units in spite of their associated harms. It begins by locating the experience of Jika Jika in the historical and political contexts of prevailing official objectives and coercive uses of modern hi-tech supermax models of confinement by western states. The case study is grounded in the growing body of research and literature documenting the various harms associated with the arbitrary and prolonged use of security driven systems of imprisonment (see: Haney 2003; Haney and Lynch 1997; Rhodes 2004).

PROLIFERATING COERCIVE CONTROL AND CRISIS IN HIGH-SECURITY

High-security prisons, also known as control units and later supermax, have been characterised by Cassandra Shaylor as the 'penultimate synthesis of technology and space in the service of social control and dehumanisation within the prison' (1988: 387). Once transferred to high-security, prisoners experience a repressive intensification of disciplinary control and coercion through the application of new technologies and psychologically geared management strategies (Davis 2003). These include prolonged periods of isolation, limited social interaction and periods spent outside cells and the use of restraints and shackles when prisoners are transported (Haney 2003). Physical separation of prisoners and guards, hi-tech monitoring equipment, constant surveillance, electronic controls, pastel colours, bullet-proof glass, a sealed interior environment, sensory deprivation and overload, limited prisoner 'privileges,' constant cell searches by specialist security squads and open-ended sentences are additional hallmarks. In high-security, technologies and psychological strategies are mutually reinforcing, giving new meaning to the expression 'total confinement.' Marion Federal Penitentiary, Illinois (Dunne 1992), Pelican Bay SHU (Haney and Lynch 1997) and the Lexington Control Unit Kentucky in the United States (O'Melveny 1992); the Wakefield Control Unit in the United Kingdom (Fitzgerald 1977); Kent Maximum-Security Unit, Canada (Jackson 1983); the Katingal Special Security Unit (Matthews 2006) and Jika Jika High-Security Unit in Australia are each pioneering examples of modern high-security regimes developed by western prison authorities.

The Jika Jika High-Security Unit in Victoria, Australia, was developed in line with international standards and trends in high-security design and management (State Coroner's Office, 1988–1989: 445). Most pertinent to overseas trends was the increasing use of segregation and classification systems operating on the principle of separating recalcitrant prisoners from the majority. In this respect, isolation has been used since the inception of the prison. However, in 1966 the landmark Mountbatten report into British prisons marked the beginning of a new era in prison security (Mountbatten 1966). Authorities commissioned the report following a series of sensational escapes by notorious high-security prisoners (Fitzgerald 1977: 49). Most significant was Mountbatten's recommendations that a centralised classification system determine the security risk of all prisoners from highest to lowest, and that all those classified high-security be centrally detained within single 'Alcatraz-type' segregation units (Fitzgerald 1977: 51–52). Mike Fitzgerald argues that the Mountbatten Report signified a repressive shift from 'treatment' and 'rehabilitation' within penal policy back to 'control' and 'security' (1977: 50). Indeed, the increasing implementation of segregation principles during this time has been criticised as fostering the widespread use of high-security units as 'prisons within prisons'. Zdenkowski and Brown recognise the political implications in Australia, arguing that above all segregation is used for the express purposes of 'eliminating prisoner rebellion and controlling prison activists before they are galvanised into concrete action' (1982: 148; see also: Churchill and Vanderwall 1992; Fitzgerald 1975; 1977).

The key to uncovering relationships between high-security and cycles of violence and harm lies primarily in the origins and official objectives informing the development of such institutions. Historically, threats of prisoner violence, dangerousness and non-compliance have been mobilised by officials to justify coercive practices, structures and technologies. As Dylan Rodríguez acknowledges 'state power enunciates domination over (and ownership of) human bodies as the measure of peace, security, and social order' (2003: 184). He argues further, 'here terror itself becomes the moral of the story—prisoners ought to live in fear, in return for the fear they have wrought (as retroactive threats to a presumably civilised order) and continue to extract (as caged, violent quasi-people always on the cusp of returning to freedom or overtaking the facility)' (2003: 186). In this way, discourses of dangerousness and dehumanisation underpin the very operation of power in high-security and serve to further justify official force and violence as legitimate and necessary to maintain control.

Modern high-security formed the basis for the application of pseudo-scientific principles and practices of 'behavioural modification' and 'adjustment.' These rose to prominence through an era of disturbing psychological experimentation and strategies designed for the purposes of counterinsurgency, interrogation and political imprisonment in the cold war period (Gordon 2006; Lucas 1976; McCoy 2006; Physicians for Human Rights 2005). During this time, research in the field of psychology, particularly cognitive science, revealed the powerful potential of manipulating human behaviour (McCoy 2006). In the 1950s and 1960s, studies uncovered the devastating impacts of sensory deprivation and prolonged isolation on the human psyche (McCoy 2006; Physicians for Human Rights 2005). Other research highlighted the impact of sleep deprivation, the administration of psychotropic drug and electroshock treatments, 'special' behavioural adjustment incentive programmes and social isolation (Fitzgerald 1975; McCoy 2006; Ryan 1992: 83–109). Much of this research and 'expertise,' gleaned from the imprisonment and interrogation of political dissidents in Northern Ireland, South Africa, Russia, East Germany and Korea, was applied in domestic prison systems in the 1960s and 1970s to deal with prisoner subversion and non-compliance (see; Fitzgerald 1977; Lucas 1976: 153–167; Ryan 1992). In 1970, United States psychologist Dr James McConnell stated in his paper titled 'Prisoners Can Be Brainwashed Now':

> It goes without saying that the only way you can gain complete control over a person's behaviour is to gain complete control over his environment. . . . I believe the day has come when we can combine sensory deprivation with drugs, hypnosis, and astute manipulation of reward and punishment to gain almost absolute control over an individual's behaviour. It should be possible then to achieve a very rapid and highly effective type of positive brainwashing that would allow us to make dramatic changes in a person's behaviour and personality. (cited in Ryan 1992: 95)

During this time, domestic prisons came to serve as a laboratory for the experimental application of a range of behavioural controls already described. A primary example is the controversial deployment of the Special Training and Rehabilitative Training (START) behavioural modification programmes in Marion Federal Penitentiary Illinois and the administration of painful drug aversion therapies in Vacaville, California (Ryan 1992: 83–109). The phrase 'behavioural modification' in this context fails to convey the full extent of institutional violence enacted through enforced isolation, sensory deprivation, use of shackles and the forced administration of drugs amongst a raft of other controversial 'treatments' (Ryan 1992).

These technologies are officially neutralised as painless spatial and psychological methods to achieve prisoner control. Such practices are bound up in and legitimated by neutralising professional terminology and discourses associated with security, punishment and incarceration (Rodríguez 2006: 148–149). However, as Lucas argues, whether the methods used are overtly physical or psychological, 'the intent is to apply stress to the individual in such a way that normal psychological functioning and defence mechanisms break down and the victim becomes amenable to behaviour manipulation' (1976: 156). In this sense, psychologically geared methods of control are devised to curb independent thinking, 'break' and 'remould' difficult or recalcitrant prisoners into a state of conformity and compliance (Rodríguez 2006; Ryan 1992). Such a project is synonymous with the exertion of official torture and violence, resulting in great physical and psychological pain and harm (Haney 2003).

Prisoner psychological and physical breakdown and despair in response to indefinite periods spent in isolation and sensory deprivation, extreme forms of prisoner resistance and corresponding official use of 'legitimate' yet abusive force, self-harm and suicide are some of the documented harms associated with supermax (Haney and Lynch 1997; Human Rights Watch 1997; Rhodes 2004). Aside from the violent and abusive cultures fostered by conditions, severe psychological and physical detrimental effects wrought by the damaging combination of sensory deprivation and isolation are well-documented in reports by prisoners, studies and clinical experience (Haney and Lynch 1997). These include depression, anxiety, hypersensitivity to external stimuli, hallucinations, perceptual distortions, temporal and spatial disorientation, deficiencies in task performance, impaired motor coordination, paranoia and problems with impulse control (Haney 2003: 130–132; Haney and Lynch 1997; Physicians for Human Rights 2005: 60–61). Such effects have been likened to those experienced by survivors of torture (Haney, 2003; Physicians for Human Rights, 2005: 62–63).

While perennially advocated by officials to house 'worst of the worst' or 'high risk' offenders, trends in western prison systems such as the United Kingdom, Australia and particularly the United States, where the supermax model predominates, suggest these prisons are becoming increasingly normalised (Davis 2005: 124–125; Funnell 2006: 70–74). In reality, the supermax is used to house a range of prisoners for various reasons including those considered disruptive, those concerned with their rights, women and the mentally ill (Human Rights Watch 2003). Reporting on supermax conditions in the State of Indiana, Human Rights Watch observed that once these institutions are opened, there is a tendency to fill them and 'standards for selecting prisoners for whom harsh conditions are warranted get diluted in practice' (Human Rights Watch 1997: 11). In addition, Human Rights Watch reports that once disruptive or difficult prisoners have been transferred to high-security, there is a tendency to keep them there for extensive periods in the interests of 'security,' thus threatening their physical and mental well-being and enhancing the likelihood of repeated criminal or disruptive behaviour and longer periods in high-security (Human Rights Watch 1997: 11). High-security conditions thus serve to magnify rather than prevent or subdue institutional disorder and violence.

Haney and Lynch (1997: 493) suggest there is a tendency by officials 'to account for violence within the prison walls through an exclusive focus on the characteristics of the prisoners who engage in it rather than the situation or context in which it occurs.' Scraton and Moore (2005: 68) also recognise that institutional violence, brutality and cruelty are the physical manifestation of 'ideologies fuelled by the representation of the captive as evil, as beneath contempt and beyond redemption.' The violent excesses and potentially lethal harms associated with high-security are rarely exposed, but on the rare occasions they are, such brutality is publicly countenanced and normalised through vengeful and justificatory discourses focused on the dangerousness, violence and criminality associated with the incarcerated. These powerful discourses relegate prisoners to a place beyond humanity, as though they are somehow expendable as human beings. Moreover, they further mask and justify the institutional violence and terror that underscore the operation of power in high-security.

The following account of life and death in Jika is constructed to highlight subjective prisoner-centred accounts of control in high-security. In addition, the experience of Jika Jika demonstrates the way that amplified levels of institutional secrecy and a lack of official transparency and accountability serve to shield and exacerbate institutional violence, disorder and crisis.

TROUBLED BEGINNINGS: SECURITY AS SELF-FULFILLING PROPHECY

Jika Jika opened in 1980. At the time of its conception the multi-million dollar complex was officially celebrated as an impressive technological first, an 'escape-proof,' 'anti-terrorist' yet humanely modern facility (Dixon and Austin 1978). Jika was geared towards total containment and security. From the outside, the complex resembled a spider-like futuristic space station (Lovell and Associates 1996). Groups of twelve prisoners were housed in detached 'units' and segregated into 'sides' in groups of six. The complex was completely sealed, providing no openings for fresh air. The units were connected via corridor spines that led to a central administration area and the entire facility was suspended on stilts. Prison officers and prisoners were physically divided by bullet-proof glass to enable supervision, and prisoners were subjected to constant video camera surveillance (Dixon and Austin 1978; Lovell and Associates 1996). Electronic consoles allowed prison officers to remotely control power, heating and prisoner access through the pneumatic steel doors within each Unit, thus limiting the need for physical contact with prisoners. Outside, prisoner recreation took place within the exercise yards enclosed by angular 'escape-proof' cages, and the perimeter of the complex was protected by advanced microwave technology and alarm systems (Austin and Dixon 1978).

At the time designers Payne and Yorke were honoured with awards, Jika Jika was already experiencing significant problems. Within two years, several prisoners attempted suicide and there were incidents of self-mutilation (Challinger 1982). There were prisoner assaults on other prisoners and despite the system of 'total surveillance,' prisoner Glen Davies was murdered by prisoner Edwin Eastwood in one of the passive recreation yards in April 1981 (State Coroner's Office 1982). The sliding doors often malfunctioned and prisoners were difficult to place in accommodation units due to various personality clashes and conflicting protection needs (Challinger 1982). The facility as a whole became too expensive to run and so staff were minimised, which meant that prisoners were confined to their cells for longer periods than initially anticipated. Due to these numerous problems, officials were confronted with the embarrassing task of defending an expensive and seemingly malfunctioning institution they had sold to the community as a forward thinking solution.

After Glen Davies died, officials commissioned an independent, internal investigation of Jika by criminologist Dennis Challinger (1982). This report revealed significant concerns about the adverse impacts of the sensory-deprived environment on prison officers and prisoners; a marked lack of officer training, experience and communication; a lack of clearly defined and supported prisoner programmes; and gross inadequacies in the grading and placement of prisoners (Challinger 1982). Challinger raised concerns that Jika was being used to hold a range of prisoners that did not fall within the officially defined categories of 'serious escapees' and 'potentially serious escapees,' protection prisoners and those deemed to pose a serious risk of physical violence to staff and other prisoners. Others included the psychiatrically ill, remand prisoners, those who posed conduct or management issues in other divisions and women prisoners (Challinger 1982).[4]

In Jika's early years institutional relationships began to show strain and antagonism developed between staff and prisoners. The electronic controls and physical separation created a situation where prisoner accommodation units became prison officer 'no-go' areas; prisoners existed on their side of the bullet proof glass, prison officers worked on the other side and seldom did the two sides associate (State Coroner's Office, 1988–1989: 455). Prisoners had little to occupy their time and, due to the inflexibility of the security-driven environment, limited work and educational programmes were offered. There was a sense of boredom and malcontent amongst officers prompted by the 'monotony' of unit work and the painstaking security procedures that slowed the process of moving around the complex. Low-ranking officers had to consult with senior staff over every issue, no matter how trivial, prior to making a decision; this also compounded frustration (Challinger 1982: 11).

Generally speaking, officials and staff responded to institutional problems produced by social and material conditions with control- and security-based solutions that intensified institutional instability and conflict. Serious security breaches in 1983 resulted in a security crackdown and managerial changes (State Coroner's Office, 1988–1989b: 440–450). The 'humane' aspects, initially celebrated as Jika's strengths, were eroded during this early period in the interests of tighter security. In 1983, the authorities decreed that the passive recreation yards should be concreted over due to the successful escape of four prisoners and corresponding allegation that prisoners had used the garden beds to conceal contraband (State Coroner's Office, 1988–1989b: 448). In 1984, Barry Quinn was murdered by a fellow prisoner who doused him with craft glue and set him alight in one of the day rooms (State Coroner's Office: 1985).

It was only a matter of weeks after Quinn's death that Minister for Community Welfare Services Pauline Toner announced that the Jika would be renamed 'K Division.' Toner publicly stated that the name change was prompted by complaints from the local Indigenous community who had campaigned against the appropriated use of the tribal name for a prison (*Age* 17 August 1984). While this may have been partly the case, this announcement also coincided with official attempts to counter the increasing public stigma associated with the name Jika Jika.

The early problems experienced in Jika are indicative of what is referred to here as the self-fulfilling prophecy of security. As Rodríguez argues, the state:

> Thrives from its own endemic insufficiency and structured institutional failure to evaporate or fully neutralise dissent, resistance, and incorrigibility among its captive subjects—in fact, the prison regime requires and produces such institutional crisis as a premise for its constant revision and reinvention of technologies of domination. (2006: 146)

The early years in Jika resulted in the erosion of basic freedoms, an escalation of security and punitive responses to what were essentially official insufficiencies and engrained institutional problems. Such responses failed to address matters in any meaningful or constructive way, serving instead to entrench problems while generating increased frustration and a polarising atmosphere.

EXPERIENCING POWER: PRISONER ACCOUNTS OF LIFE IN JIKA

Between 1985 and 1987, unmediated prisoner accounts of life in Jika began to publicly emerge, citing corrupt classification processes, unbearable conditions, prison officer mind games, abuse and misconduct and violent cultures as serious concerns (Prison Reform Group 1988). Prisoners reported experiences of isolation, frustration, paranoia, fear and aggression stemming from the high-security environment and conditions of sensory deprivation. Prisoners were sometimes confined for more than twenty-two hours a day within the highly controlled air-conditioned atmosphere with the same five to six prisoners and were thus isolated in restrictive yet overcrowded conditions. In such conditions, prisoners are subjected to 'sensory overload,' where they are unable to escape the intrusive noise or presence of others (Haney and Lynch 1997: 497). These conditions have been condemned by mental health experts and in United States court judgments (Haney and Lynch 1997: 497).

The impact of conditions and environment comprised an ongoing griev-ance for Jika prisoners. In 1984, prisoner James Bazley wrote a series of protest letters to the Victorian Attorney-General, characterising the regime and conditions in Jika as 'harsh, brutalising, institutional torture' (*Telegraph* 24 November 1984). He stated: ' . . . if I was to be asked the main difference between Jika and the infamous German concentration camps, I would say . . . there are no gas ovens in Jika' (*Telegraph* 24 November 1984). Another prisoner, John Dixon-Jenkins, concurred, stating:

> . . . if you were to see this place and look beyond the signs of very high-security that are everywhere, you would see a physical environment that looks better than any other part of Pentridge. This 'humane' look belies the total insanity of what takes place in here. (*Bendigo Advertiser* 8 September 1987)

One anonymous prisoner stated, 'the problem that we are forced to endure is the psychological pressure of day-to-day living in this artificial environ-ment. The psychological damage that is happening to prisoners in Jika is more intense than anywhere else in the prison system' (Prison Reform Group 1988: 6). In 1986, prisoner Robert Wright complained that:

> The units within Jika Jika are virtual echo chambers, as the minutest noise reverberates. . . . In the cells at night, one is able to hear the other prisoners using their toilets, flushing them, watching their television, even turning in their beds. . . . A degree of animosity will build up . . . violence can and does erupt. . . . People such as yourself would never realise or understand the stress this place gives after a period . . . you can find no way anywhere in the unit to escape all of this. (*Age* 29 July 1989)

Prisoners lamented that conditions were made worse by the lack of work and activities to occupy their time. Ongoing prisoner idleness, the tedium of the institutional routine and the harsh artificial surroundings produced a psychologically surreal and damaging experience. Prisoner Wayne King complained the daily monotony caused one day to blend into the next, 'you'd spend the day in the day room reading newspapers or playing one of the two games on the computer. The cells are all open and we're free to go in and out. We are let into the exercise yard for maybe half an hour a day (sometimes less)' (Prisoner Statement 3 November 1987; State Coroner's Office, 1988). Prisoner King characterised his time in Jika as 'a bad dream,' a 'mad experience.' Such sentiments were common amongst Jika prisoners and particularly ex-prisoners who reported long-term detrimental psychological effects. Ex-prisoner Maurie Dowdle reported during a press interview in 1987 after leaving Jika, he wished he 'could take off his head and rinse it under a tap . . . after two years in Jika I have lost reality. I don't care about anyone or anything' (*Age* 31 October 1987).

Prisoners' alleged conditions were compounded by an abusive managerial culture. Most prominent in prisoner accounts was the phenomenon of 'mind games,' a form of psychological power play exercised by prison officers over prisoners to antagonise and provoke. Prison officers were stationed in a fishbowl and controlled prisoner access about the units via security doors; they controlled lighting and power supply, hot water, heating and air conditioning via electronic consoles. Prisoners complained this power was abused, alleging officers refused to open doors for prisoners to access their cells or toilets (State Coroner's Office, 1988–1989a: 688–689). During the day, when prisoners were engaged in daily activities, the unit doors would slam shut unexpectedly, trapping prisoners in their cells or in the day room for long periods of time (State Coroner's Office, 1988–1989b: 2005). It was often the case that if an officer refused to open the door for a prisoner to go to the toilet, they would eventually have no choice but to relieve themselves by urinating on the floor of the day room in front of other prisoners (State Coroner's Office, 1988–1989b).

It was claimed that during the summer the heating would be turned up while in winter prisoners were constantly ill with colds due to the air-conditioning being turned on (State Coroner's Office, 1988–1989b). Prison officers also controlled the power supply and, it was reported, if a prisoner turned on the television, the officers would turn the power off; if a prisoner began to cook toast, the power would go off. Prisoners also complained that the hot water supply was often turned off for long periods, leaving prisoners with cold water to shower and wash with (Prisoner Statement, State Coroner's Office, 1988–1989a: 2198). Officers also allegedly used food, medical care, mail, visits and exercise as additional avenues to frustrate and provoke prisoners. Prisoners reported officers frequently dumped dirt and other foreign objects in their food (State Coroner's Office, 1988b: 2158; Interview, Reed, 15 May 2004); taunted prisoners by tampering with their mail (State Coroner's Office, 1988–1989b: 1132); took prisoners to the doors of the exercise yards only to return them to their cells without exercise (State Coroner's Office, 1988–1989b); interfered with visiting arrangements and maintained an obtrusive presence to the point where prisoners refused visits (State

Coroner's Office, 1988–1989a: 16–31). It was also commonly complained that prisoners who had settled into a unit well and were getting along with other prisoners would find themselves transferred unexpectedly to another unit where relations may not be so harmonious (State Coroner's Office, 1988–1989a). If relations were particularly bad in this respect, prisoners would be forced to go into self-imposed lockdown until a transfer could be arranged.

Prisoners alleged they were subject to the involuntary administration of drugs. Craig Minogue made these allegations public during the Jika fire inquest in 1988, stating his belief that prison officers drugged the food and milk of prisoners (*Herald* 5 December 1988). Minogue reported that the drugs had the effect of making prisoners sleepy and feeling like they had a hangover. He told the Coroner that because of the paranoia experienced by prisoners in Jika, they did regular checks and dissected milk cartons; it was not unusual to find penetration holes.

Staff and prison officials denied allegations that mind games took place. Jika Governor Herron stated he felt prisoners used the charge of mind games only when they were angered or upset at having been deprived of something they wanted (State Coroner's Office, 1988–1989b: 198). Supervisor of Classification Michael Ryan believed that the phenomenon of mind games constituted what prisoners 'imagined' as a type of psychological warfare (State Coroner's Office, 1988–1989b: 517). He maintained it was impossible for officers to control the air-conditioning as they would need to go beneath the floors of Jika to do so, and then they would be placing themselves in a position of discomfort. Nevertheless, ex-prison staff gave evidence during the Jika inquest to the effect that a group of younger officers recruited to Jika often indulged in mind games. Former officer Ian Wright commented that 'six young stirrers' let the power go to their heads and tormented prisoners by playing with the air-conditioning and refusing prisoner requests, among other things (*Advertiser* 21 March 1989).

The fact that certain officers acknowledged the occurrence of mind games within Jika and the implication that they had done little to circumvent or report such activities is indicative of the unspoken systemic nature of those practices. The mind games described by prisoners in Jika resembled the early experimental behavioural modification techniques discussed earlier. They specifically mirrored techniques deployed in North Korean POW camps in the 1950s including: systematic weakening and dislocation of close emotional ties; the segregation of 'natural leaders'; the punishment of prisoners who demonstrated uncooperative attitudes; the systematic withholding of all mail; preventing prisoners from writing home or to friends in the community regarding conditions of confinement; and, most important, 'placing individuals into new and ambiguous situations for which the standards are kept deliberately unclear and thus putting pressure on them to conform to what is desired in order to win favour and a reprieve from pressure' (Fitzgerald 1977: 64; see also Ryan 1992). The application of pressure on prisoners directly related to the issue of prisoner classification.

Prisoners complained that once classified and transferred to Jika, it was extremely difficult to get reclassified. Prisoners reported the classification procedures and bodies responsible for considering prisoner cases lacked accountability, fairness and consistency. Prisoners were refused access to their files and information about their cases and had their classification status altered immediately prior to appealing their case (Prison Reform Group 1988). It was believed that such processes were designed to keep prisoners considered to be 'controversial' or 'troublemakers' in Jika as long as possible.

Many Jika prisoners dealt with these pressures through individual and collective forms of resistance. Prisoners lobbied for their rights and wrote complaints, smuggled information out, refused orders, refused to comply with the regime, initiated hunger strikes and escapes. While much resistance was non-violent, many Jika prisoners also broke under pressure, reacting with violent outbursts. Under these circumstances, there were instances where some affected prisoners, internalising their pain, sought to deal with their situation by attempting suicide or through self-harm. The occurrence of violent incidents peaked in 1987 (*Herald* 30 January 1987). There were extensive instances of cell and property destruction, prisoner barricades, fires and the reporting of violent threats made by prisoners to officers. One anonymous prisoner stated, 'Most violence [in Jika] happens when a prisoner reaches the end of his tether and decides to take no more' (Prison Reform Group 1988: 5). Dixon-Jenkins echoed this observation, 'such are the never-ending mind games and overt suppression of my work . . . as terrible as it sounds, I sometimes have the urge to let go with just one potent blow' (*Bendigo Advertiser* 31 October 1987).

Complaints were made that prisoners known for their political involvement in prison campaigns were subjected to 'extra special' treatment. Prisoner reactive resistance therefore served to intensify polarisation, creating a context for prison officer reprisals and a culture of violence. Early official justifications for Jika focused on the objective of alleviating the alleged instances of brutality that marred the reputation of Jika's predecessor, the H Division maximum-security unit (State Coroner's Office, 1988–1989b: 445–450). The designers envisaged that through the physical separation of prison officers and prisoners, the safety of both parties could be ensured and the occurrence of violence prevented. Despite this, prisoner accounts suggested Jika had done very little to prevent the use of excessive and unacceptable force by prison officers or violence between prisoners (Prison Reform Group 1988).

Prisoners reported that certain officers engaged in standover tactics while subjecting prisoners to constant intimidation, verbal abuse, harassment and threats of violence (Prisoner Statement 7 August 1988; State Coroner's Office, 1988–1989b). It was alleged on occasions that officers rostered during the evenings drank on the job and, during routine security checks, disturbed prisoners who were trying to sleep by yelling insults and aggressively kicking cell doors (Exhibit 42, State Coroner's Office, 1988–1989b). In one instance, a prisoner complained it was not uncommon during the evenings for officers to come in drunk and play football up and down the corridor outside prisoner's cells to amuse themselves (Exhibit 32, State Coroner's Office, 1988–1989b). Such displays of aggression escalated existing feelings of terror and fear among prisoners. Prisoners charged that some prison officers pitted prisoner against prisoner for entertainment. In one circumstance, two prisoners reportedly assaulted two other prisoners with cricket bats (Prison Reform Group 1988). An anonymous prisoner also reported he was involved in a similar incident where an officer gave a Stanley knife to a fellow prisoner who in turn attacked him, slashing a fourteen-inch cut across his stomach (Prison Reform Group 1988).

Prisoners also alleged they had experienced and witnessed 'bashings' by prison officers (Prison Reform Group 1988). It was reported that these commonly occurred during unit transfers. Unit 2 was a smaller section of Jika used as a punishment or isolation section. Craig Minogue stated that when a prisoner was taken to Unit 2, a group of four to six officers would remove him, taking him into the central circle of Jika called Unit 7. Minogue claimed that during the transfer the prisoner would be stripped, roughed up, threatened and abused (State Coroner's Office, 1988–1989a: 683). Thereafter he would be placed in a cell with only a mattress.

Prisoner Olaf Dietrich alleged that in Jika he had been brutalised, placed in shackles and tortured with an electric cattle prod. He reported that six officers entered his cell and when he put up resistance they placed him in restraints. Dietrich alleged that he was left in this state for a number of days, until officers returned with a twenty-four-volt cattle prod, which they 'shoved' into his buttocks for 'lunchtime entertainment' (State Coroner's Office, 1988–1989b: 2270–2272). According to Dietrich, this form of abuse or torture was common in Jika. He recounted instances where officers used fire hoses to subdue prisoners and threw nooses into cells yelling, 'hang yourself':

> There's procedures down there, and methods that they use as a form of management. Some are warranted some are not. Some are used in vengeance . . . they actually ridicule you when you're curled up on the floor in pain and you're shackled after a beating. You're degraded. Sometimes you've got no clothes on for days lying on the concrete floor. It's just disgusting. Nobody will ever know the torture of that institution down there. (State Coroner's Office, 1988–1989b: 2271–2272)

The combination of Jika's oppressive environment, the psychological pressures created by security and management procedures and mind games, threats and brutality described by prisoners had a cumulative effect, pushing some to breaking point. Olaf Dietrich characterised his experience in Jika as 'oppressive' and 'soul-destroying' (Prisoner Statement 12 August

1988; State Coroner's Office, 1988–1989b). He stated, 'I consider myself to be a fairly tough person mentally, but after three months, the place started to get to me.' Reed stated of his experience:

> You were always being pushed . . . it was total control of everything. If you were in H Division you went to smash something you'd smash it. In Jika . . . what could you smash? The concrete? The bars? The bullet-proof glass? I mean, your bed was a concrete bed, the shelving there was stainless steel. (Interview, Reed 15 May 2004)

Some prisoners reported an overwhelming sense of fear for their safety and the omnipresent foreboding that something terrible would happen if officials refused to take action. Just months prior to the fire, John Dixon Jenkins reported, 'violence, not on my part, is growing closer and more obvious almost each day. It must be coming soon. . . . I may somehow die in here' (*Bendigo Advertiser* 31 October 1987).

CRISIS POINT: JIKA DEATHS, AUGUST THROUGH OCTOBER 1987

Matters escalated during 1987 and, in January of that year, emerging accounts of mismanagement and incidents of abuse and violence prompted a public statement by Attorney General Jim Kennan, who branded the complex a 'dehumanising electronic zoo' (*Herald* 30 October 1987). During this time, Prisoners Action Group spokesperson Jeff Lapidos publicly revealed he had obtained statistics through Freedom of Information documenting 2,500 incidents in Jika between 1985 and 1987 that were serious enough to report to the Attorney General (*Herald* 31 January 1987). However, it was not until the deaths of prisoners John Williams and Sean Downie in late August 1987 that the situation reached a fatal crisis point. Williams died on 22 August in Unit 5 and Downie died two days later in the punishment section of Unit 2. While the deaths occurred in what were essentially unrelated circumstances, allegations of official mismanagement and prison officer misconduct were raised at both inquest investigations (Hallenstein 1989; Dessau 1989). Evidence put forward by prison staff and the authorities was vehemently contested by prisoners who alleged that officer negligence, ill treatment and in the case of Sean Downie, criminal conduct and abuse, directly contributed to and caused the deaths.

The events and circumstances surrounding the death of Sean Downie were particularly controversial. Downie was a remand prisoner who was transferred to the punishment section of Unit 2 and left in his underwear with no personal property. Hours later an emergency response was launched when an alarm signalled there was smoke in Unit 2. The authorities reported that Downie cut up his mattress, lit a fire, causing considerable burns to his face

and upper body, and proceeded to hang himself with a sheet from a vent at the rear of his cell (Dessau 1989). Officials painted a picture of a disturbed, dangerous person who had failed to adjust to prison life and took his own life (Hallenstein 1989: 27–28). In contrast, prisoners alleged Downie had been brutalised during and immediately after his transfer. Unit 2 prisoner John Dixon Jenkins provided a police statement to this effect but was never called to give evidence at the inquest. Prisoners and the prison chaplain also gave evidence that the grilles in Jika were suicide proof and the holes too small to thread a sheet:

> In contrast to the old prison cells in other parts of Pentridge it was designed in such a way that it was difficult for people to damage themselves, including suicide or, for instance, particularly, in hanging. (State Coroner's Office, 1988–1989b: 89)

Duty prison officers initially reported they had not attended Downie's cell in the immediate period prior to his death. However, they later amended their statements, submitting they had in fact attended Downie's cell an hour prior to his death in response to a disturbance (Dessau 1989: 8–12). They told the inquest they had not previously informed the investigating police or Coroner of this visit because nothing worth reporting had occurred and they had forgotten about it. The Coroner found that Downie committed suicide (Dessau 1989). However, she found officials and staff contributed to Downie's death through neglect and mismanagement. She maintained her concerns about the unexplained cell visit by officers and recommended that such matters should be subject to further independent investigation.

Downie's death fueled further chaos in Jika. Prisoners escalated their campaigns of non-compliance, which in turn prompted retributive responses by prison staff and officials. Two months later prisoners initiated a fatal protest fire. The fire came about as a result of ongoing official unwillingness to address the institutional problems plaguing Jika, which by October 1987 reached crisis point. Robert Wright was Jika's longest serving prisoner, having been confined there for seven years. Immediately prior to the fire officials informed Wright that his application for reclassification was rejected. Wright had been advised he should therefore 'make a life for himself in Jika' (Hallenstein 1989: 3). While Wright's classification case was a trigger for the protest, on a fundamental level the fire was a collective action by despairing prisoners who intended to make their plight visible and prompt official action.

Prisoners smashed the contents of their cells and dayroom and built a barricade. Prisoners planned to use the toilets and plumbing as breathing devices; however, once the fire was lit, prisoners on Wright's side of the unit were unable to get sufficient fresh air and were quickly overcome by smoke (Hallenstein 1989). The rescue scene was chaotic and the emergency response largely inefficient. Prison officers were unable to open the electronic doors. The Governor of Jika directed officers to film the emergency response and guided them what to take pictures while a constant flow of officers flocking to the scene from other parts of Pentridge clogged the foyer of the unit forestalling the emergency efforts and using up breathing apparatus without purpose. The inquest investigation revealed gross shortcomings and culpability on the part of the prison authorities (Hallenstein 1989). Surviving prisoners gave evidence officers were well aware the protest fire was happening but failed to take action until after the fire was lit. It was also alleged that surviving prisoners were brutalised after the doors were finally opened. Prisoner Dietrich and other officers reported witnessing one of the deceased, Arthur Gallagher, brought out alive. However, while officers stood around arguing about who would administer mouth-to-mouth, he died (Murray 1990: 31).

The events and issues surrounding the fire and the deaths are too extensive to recount in this chapter. The inquests and inquiries that followed the fire were underscored by an official unwillingness to cooperate with the Coroner in his investigations. Rather, officials actively thwarted the investigation at every turn, refusing to provide information and attempting to silence and publicly discredit individual staff giving evidence that contradicted the official position (Inquest Exhibit 87 State Coroner's Office, 1988–1989). When all this failed to have the desired effect, officials attempted to forestall the inquest, questioning the Coroner's partiality (*Age* 30 May 1989). The Office of Corrections (OOC) also initiated a Supreme Court action arguing that the Coroner had exceeded his powers by admitting evidence outside his jurisdiction as set out in the Coroner's Act 1985 (Nathan 1989). All this comprised a campaign of avoidance in redressing the serious managerial and fatal operational failures and official culpability contributing to the fire and deaths.

After a lengthy inquest the Coroner found that, while the prisoners played a hand in their own deaths, the OOC had also contributed to the deaths through staff incompetence, lack of emergency training and mismanagement. The Coroner also made reference to prisoner allegations of prison officer mind games, abuse and misconduct during the fire, stating that while it was not his jurisdiction to comment on such matters, he believed the lack of sound administrative procedures, command control and discipline in Jika 'provided fertile ground for the spring of abuse' (Hallenstein 1989: 102). The obstructive conduct and behaviour of the OOC during the inquest constituted a large part of the findings, and are worth citing at length:

> The conduct of the OOC in this case raised deep and fundamental concern for our community's free institutions and its democratic style. Like any public institution, the OOC is accountable to the community it serves. Unlike many public institutions, the affairs of the OOC are behind closed walls and are not easily subject to public scrutiny. The

OOC has misinterpreted this position of advantage as a license for secrecy, rather than as requiring the maximum of openness and accountability. This OOC has used this position of advantage to try and manipulate the facts to try and prevent their proper investigation, and in a manner which could be described as corrupt. (Hallenstein 1989: 115)

Despite the criticisms and prisoner allegations made regarding the misconduct, violence and abuse that took place in Jika, there was neither restitution of justice for the families of the deceased nor any official validation of the personal costs and impacts on those who endured Jika. Subsequent public inquiries appointed to investigate allegations were neatly dismissed, thus exonerating and legitimising the OOC in the eyes of the public (Geschke 1990; Griffin 1989; Mulgrew 1989; Murray 1990). The fire ultimately led to Jika's temporary closure amid public controversy. Eventually, the electronic doors were taken out and the complex was reopened as a medium-security special unit for women.

CONCLUSION

In reconstructing the institutional atmosphere, events and allegations that culminated in crisis with the fatal 1987 protest fire, this chapter foregrounds alternative accounts of life and death in one of Australia's pioneering high-security prisons. The case study of Jika is situated in the growing international body of research and case studies documenting the harmful impacts of high-security. In Australia specifically, Jika is part of a continuum of similar institutions and practices associated with significant and ongoing human rights violations. The project of detailing and locating these violations, harms and controversial deaths in direct relation to such regimes presents a challenge to the overwhelming official discourses of denial geared to protect the ongoing development and use of high-security.

The excessive growth in the use of high-security and supermax prisons, most apparent in the United States, is of grave concern, particularly given conditions that fail to prompt a level of public attention or criticism commensurate with their impact. This is partly to do with the perennial justificatory discourses of dangerousness frequently recycled by officials. Yet, as Haney has suggested, when 'assessing the benefits and burdens of supermax confinement, it is important to keep in mind that correctional officials have not been given a mandate to engage in such extraordinary punitive and unprecedented measures' (2003: 129–130). As prisoner accounts of life in Jika attest, the infliction of physical and psychic terror and violence exist at the centre of high-security-related structures and practice. The pains that inevitably flow from such violence can only serve to entrench and exacerbate cultures of violence, disorder and in extreme cases, death. High-security prisons can thus be seen to reproduce and exacerbate many of the problems officials argue they are designed to address.

Clearly there is a need to consider alternative, rehabilitative rather than destructive solutions. The Barlinnie Special Unit represents a Scottish milestone in penal experimentation that emerged at a time when high-security was taken up by western prison authorities in the 1970s and 1980s. Barlinnie allowed freedom of movement; no uniforms; unlimited access to educational programmes, work and hobbies; and unlimited contact visits with family and friends. Prison officers and prisoners managed the unit collectively in a mutually supportive and respectful manner. Jimmy Boyle had been previously tagged one of the system's 'worst.' Initially written off by officials as beyond rehabilitation, Boyle was institutionalised since childhood and experienced the most brutalising aspects of prison life. However, once in Barlinnie, Boyle took on a prominent role in unit decision-making processes, engaged in education programmes, discovered his passion for sculpture and became a respected public spokesperson on prisoner rights and reform. Boyle stated of his time in Barlinnie, 'if you treat people like human beings they will act like human beings . . . everything has been tried from the downright brutal to the inhuman, but this is the only thing that has worked and even our critics must accept this' (1979: 263). According to Boyle, Barlinnie's achievements can be attributed to the emphasis on communication, 'seeing the individual as a person in his own right without relying on labelling or categorisation in order to identify. It is unique in the sense that two opposing factions have come together and worked towards building a community with a remarkable degree of success' (Boyle 1979: 263–264). In spite of its achievements, the Barlinnie Special Unit was closed in the early 1990s. In contrast, the proliferation of high-security continues.

Boyle's account of Barlinnie reminds us of the importance of revisiting past lessons lost. The year 2007 marked the 20th anniversary of the Jika protest fire and deaths. Pentridge Prison and Jika Jika were closed in December 1997. The site now comprises 'Pentridge Village,' a mixed residential and commercial development. Jika, now in ruins, awaits redevelopment. On the 29 October 2006, I returned with one of families of the deceased to mark the occasion of the fire and lay flowers. As we trawled through the crumbled asphalt, blocks of concrete and grassy mounds where the units once stood, the developer informed us that in time a five-star hotel is destined for the site. Jika survivor Craig Minogue wrote from prison in response to this, 'five star hotel—five men dead—five stars . . . it all fits well with the commodification of other people's suffering as entertainment.' The redevelopment of the site stands as a symbolic further levelling, burying of an unresolved and painful past.

In the post-9/11 context, it is imperative that a critical space is forged for rational debate about the conditions of those relegated to high-security.

Such a debate requires a focus on human rights, reason and humanity rather than retribution. Simplistic, populist law and order campaigns are effective in drumming up popular fears and prejudice through the use of imagery associated with racial otherness, social inadequacy and above all, 'dangerousness.' They work to benefit official impunity and hinder accountability in response to institutional violence and neglect. A further consequence and function of such official diversions is to forestall public identification with the imprisoned as victims of state violence. This results in the obviation of collective expressions of sympathy, support and solidarity, not only for those imprisoned but also for the families and friends suffering with the weighty burdens of loss and grief. Such expressions of support are essential to the process of healing and recovery. Critical scholars and researchers clearly have a role to play in these debates, to articulate and open up silences, confront official denial, uncover contested narratives and humanising accounts so the profound suffering that stems from state violence does not remain hidden, or worse, become normalised.

ACKNOWLEDGMENT

This chapter is adapted from the author's book, *Imprisoning Resistance: Life and Death in an Australian Supermax* (Sydney Institute of Criminology Series: Federation Press, 2007). Many thanks to Jude McCulloch, Phil Scraton, Mark Peel, Charandev Singh, Dean Wilson and Craig Minogue for their ongoing input and support.

NOTES

1. 'Jika' is a shortened name for the Jika Jika High-Security Unit. Despite the name change from Jika Jika to K Division in the mid-1980s, prisoners who experienced the regime have continued to remember the institution as 'Jika.' Therefore, in this chapter, I choose not to adhere to the official renaming to 'K Division' and use the names 'Jika Jika' and 'Jika' interchangeably.
2. From 1987 to 1988, there was a total of eighteen deaths in custody occurring within the Victorian prison system as a whole. Office of Corrections, *Annual Report*, 1987–1988.
3. The total daily average prison population in Victoria from 1987 to 1988 was 2017. The daily average for Jika Jika during this time was twenty-eight. It should be noted that from July to October in 1987, Jika averages fluctuated between thirty-nine and forty-two total prisoners. Office of Corrections, *Annual Report*, 1987–1988.
4. It is little acknowledged that women prisoners were held in Jika during the 1980s and 1990s (see Russell, 1998). A fire at Fairlea women's prison, and the decision by authorities to move recalcitrant women prisoners to Pentridge B Annex and Jika Jika, form but a small facet of a complex history of women, imprisonment, power and resistance in high security.

REFERENCES

Boyle, J. (1979) *A Sense of Freedom*, London: Macmillan Publishers.

Carter, K. (2000) 'The Casuarina Prison Riot: Official Discourse or Appreciative Inquiry,' *Current Issues in Criminal Justice*, vol 12, no 3, pp.363–375.

Challinger, D. (1982) 'Jika Jika: A Review of Victoria's Maximum-Security Prison,' Melbourne: Office of Corrections.

Churchill, W. and Vanderwall, J. J. (eds.) (1992) *Cages of Steel: The Politics of Imprisonment in the United States*, Washington: Maissoneuve Press.

Davis, A.Y. (2003) *Are Prisons Obsolete?*, New York: Seven Stories Press.

———. (2005) *Abolition Democracy: Beyond Empire, Prisons and Torture*, New York: Seven Stories Press.

Dessau, L. M. (1989) *Unpublished Finding of Inquisition upon the Body of Sean Fitzgerald Downie*, Melbourne: State Coroner's Office.

Dixon, B. and Austin, T. (1978) *Jika Jika Security Unit Commemoration Plaque*, Melbourne: Department of Social Welfare & Public Works Department.

Dunne, B. (1992) 'The US prison at Marion Illinois: An Instrument of Oppression,' in W. Churchill & J. J. Vanderwall (eds.), *Cages of Steel*, Washington: Maissoneuve Press pp.38–82.

Fitzgerald, M. (1975) 'Control Units and the Shape of Things to Come,' London: Radical Alternatives to Prison Publications.

———. (1977) *Prisoners in Revolt*, Harmondsworth: Penguin Books.

Fletcher, K. (1999) 'The Myth of the Supermax Solution,' *Alternative Law Journal*, vol 24, no 6, pp.274–278.

Funnell, N. (2006) 'Where the Norm Is not the Norm: Goulburn Correctional Centre and the Harm-U,' *Alternative Law Journal*, vol 31, no 2, pp.70—74.

Geschke, N. (1990) *Report on the Accountability of the Office of Corrections*, Melbourne: Office of the Victorian Ombudsman.

Griffin, J. (1989) *Inquiry into the Adequacy of Emergency Arrangements Adopted by the Office of Corrections since the Jika Jika Fire on 29 October 1987*, Melbourne: Office of Corrections.

Gordon, A. (2006) 'Abu Ghraib: Imprisonment and the War on Terror,' *Race and Class*, vol 48, no 1, pp.42–59.

Hallenstein, H. R. (1989) *Unpublished Finding of Inquisition upon the Bodies of James Richard Loughnan, David McGauley, Arthur Bernard Gallagher, Robert Lindsay Wright and Richard John Morris*, Melbourne: State Coroner's Office.

Haney, C. (2003) 'Mental Health Issues in Long-Term Solitary and 'Supermax' Confinement,' *Crime and Delinquency*, vol 49, no1, pp.124–156.

Haney, C. and Lynch, M. (1997) 'Regulating Prisons of the Future: A Psychological Analysis of Supermax and Solitary Confinement,' *New York University Review of Law and Social Change*, vol XXIII, no 4.

Human Rights Watch. (1997) *Cold Storage: Super Maximum-Security Confinement in Indiana*, New York: Human Rights Watch.

———. (2003) *Ill Equipped: US Prisons and Offenders With Mental Illness*, New York: Human Rights Watch.

Jackson, M. (1983) *Prisoners of Isolation: Solitary Confinement in Canada*, Toronto: University of Toronto Press.

Justice Action. (2003), 'Goulburn Prisoners Offer of Hope,' Sydney: Justice Action, July.

Lovell A. and Associates. (1996) *HM Pentridge and HM Metropolitan Prison (Coburg Prisons Complex) Conservation Management Plan*, Melbourne: Department of Treasury and Finance and the City of Moreland.

Lucas, W.E. (1976) 'Solitary Confinement: Isolation as Coercion to Conform,' *Australian and New Zealand Journal of Criminology*, vol 9, pp.153–167.

Matthews, B. (2006) *Intractable: Hell Has a Name: Katingal. Life Inside Australia's First Super-max Prison*, Sydney: Pan Macmillan.

McCoy, A. (2006) *A Question of Torture: CIA Interrogation From the Cold War to the War on Terror*, New York: Metropolitan Books.

Minc, A. (2006) 'Interview with Charander Singh' *Jailbreak*, Community Radio 2SER, Sydney, 9 May.

Mountbatten, Lord. (1966) *Report of the Inquiry into Prison Escapes and Security*, London: HMSO Home Office.

Mulgrew, T. (1989) Detective Chief Inspector, *Victoria Police Task Force Report on Allegations of Corruption Within the Office of Corrections*, Melbourne: Victorian Police Force.

Murray, B. L. (1990) *Report on the Behaviour of the Office of Corrections in relation to the Conduct of the Inquest by the State Coroner, Upon the bodies of James Richard Loughnan, David McGauley, Arthur Bernard Gallagher, Robert Lindsay Wright, Richard John Morris and in relation to the Inquest Conducted by the Deputy State Coroner, Ms. Linda Dessau, Upon the body of Sean Fitzgerald Downie*, Melbourne: State Parliament Victoria.

Nathan, J. (1989) 'Harmsworth v. The State Coroner,' Melbourne: Supreme Court of Victoria, 28 February, 9 March pp.989–999.

Office of Corrections Victoria (1987–1988) Annual Report, Melbourne: Government Printer.

O'Melveny, M. (1992) 'Portrait of a US Political Prison: The Lexington High-Security Unit for Women,' in W. Churchill & J.J. Vanderwall (eds.), *Cages of Steel*, Washington: Maissoneuve Press pp.112–127.

Physicians for Human Rights. (2005) *Break Them Down: Systematic Use of Torture by US Forces*, Washington: Physicians for Human Rights.

Prison Reform Group. (1988) *Jika Jika Revisited: A Collection of Prisoner Writings, The Doing Time Magazine,* Melbourne: Prison Reform Group.

Reed, P. (2004), Interview, Melbourne, 15 May.

Rhodes, L. (2004) *Total Confinement: Madness and Reason in the Maximum-Security Prison*, Berkeley: University of California Press.

Rodríguez, D. (2003) 'State Terror and the Reproduction of Imprisoned Dissent,' *Social Identities*, vol 9, no 2, pp.183–203.

———. (2006) *Forced Passages: Imprisoned Intellectuals and the US Prison Regime*, Minneapolis: University of Minnesota Press.

Russell, E. (1998) *Fairlea: The History of a Women's Prison in Australia 1956–1996*, Kew: The Public Correctional Enterprise CORE.

Ryan, M. (1992) 'Solitude as counter-insurgency: The US Isolation Model of Political Incarceration,' in W. Churchill & J. J. Vanderwall (eds) *Cages of Steel*, Washington: Maissoneuve Press pp.83–109.

Scraton, P.and Moore, L. (2005) 'Degradation, Harm and Survival in a Women's Prison,' *Social Policy and Society* vol 5, no 1, pp.67–78.

Shaylor, C. (Summer 1998) '"It's Like Living in a Black Hole" *New England Journal of Criminal and Civil Confinement*, vol 24, no 2, pp.385–416.

State Coroner's Office. (1982) Unpublished Transcript of Proceedings and Exhibits at Coroner's Investigation Into the Death of Glen Joseph Davies, Melbourne: State Coroner's Office.

———. (1985) Unpublished Transcript of Proceedings and Exhibits at Coroner's Investigation Into the Death of Barry Robert Quinn, Melbourne: State Coroner's Office.

———. (1988) Unpublished Transcript of Proceedings and Exhibits at Coroner's Investigation Into the Death of John Williams, Melbourne: State Coroner's Office.

———. (1988–1989a) Unpublished Transcript of Proceedings and Exhibits at Coroner's Investigation Into the Deaths of James Loughnan, David McGauley, Arthur Gallagher, Robert Wright and Richard Morris, Melbourne: State Coroner's Office.

———. (1988–1989b) Unpublished Transcript of Proceedings and Exhibits at Coroner's Investigation Into the Death of Sean Fitzgerald Downie, Melbourne: State Coroner's Office.

Zdenkowski, G., and Brown, D. (1982) *The Prison Struggle: Changing Australia's Penal System*, Ringwood: Penguin Books.

4 Protests and 'Riots' in the Violent Institution

Phil Scraton

According to interviews with many prisoners from diverse backgrounds, sentenced for different offences committed in contrasting circumstances, first arrival at prison, regardless of strength of body or resilience of mind, was always a moment of trepidation, fear and alienation. Trepidation regarding the unknown, fear of physical and emotional violence, alienation from institutionalised processes designed to sever the individual from personal and social context. In his autobiographical account of imprisonment, Trevor Hercules (1989: 24, 30) recalls the moment:

> I remember the van feeling cold as I hunched myself up against the window, one hand in my pocket while the other was in the middle of the seat cuffed to some white guy . . . I would have given anything to be outside in that cold, chilly night, that wonderful, fresh, chilly night . . . I was desperate to get out of this van. I even thought about escape, but that was not on. The door was secured by several locks with one screw sitting at the front of the van carrying the keys while several more sat at the back and the sides of the van. Besides, where was I going to go, me a black man with a white man attached to him, like some kind of monkey. . . . We had now arrived at the Scrubs. The driver bibbed his horn and the gates of hell swung open.

The experience of being cuffed, whether to a prison guard or in body chains, is the physical manifestation of the loss of freedom. It demonstrates that the authority of the prison, powerful and determining, is not consensual. It pays no regard to the politics of representation and accountability supposedly central to legitimacy within democratic societies. Much has been written about 'total institutions,' more recently challenging the assumption that it has the capacity to rob the individual of 'agency.' It is self-evident, given the long history of prisoner resistance—individual or collective—that the determining capacity of the prison is not absolute. Yet, political and professional autonomy given to managers and guards with immense discretionary operational powers declines the prisoner any semblance of civil rights.

The exchange of name for number is more than a symbolic indication of the prisoner's removal from civic society.

Within most advanced democratic states, regardless of claims made by their executives on state-of-the-art, virtual-tour-of-the-prison web-sites, prisons favour containment over rehabilitation, isolation over association and despair over hope. There was never a Golden Age that rescued the prisoner from Oscar Wilde's (undated: 46–47) 'bricks of shame' wherein 'vilest deeds like poison weeds, bloom well in prison-air.' A place where 'what is good in Man ... wastes and withers there.' Ron Phillips (in Fitzgerald 1997: 84) recalls his 'initial' moment, imposing 'a shattering change upon all the patterns simultaneously':

> The value of an hour changes, and all the apparatus built up over the years for dealing with the passage of time suddenly becomes obsolete. In normal life, few hours are entirely without incident or interest. In prison, many hours might pass, in which nothing happens. It becomes possible to look at a clock without receiving any information from it. It is not that time becomes irrelevant. In many senses, it becomes more important, for in the end that is what it's all about. No. It is merely that measured as the outside world measures it, time becomes intolerable. The prisoner has to learn to deal with time in a different way.

Further, the 'power of decision suddenly disappears, for anything which happens to the prisoner, including the most personal functions, happens because, or when someone else decides that it should.' What the loss of liberty means at this level is the 'illusion of control over personal destiny' and the imposition of personal 'impotence.' Speaking for so many others, Phillips considers the 'most terrible' realisation for the prisoner is the deprivation of 'value as a human being,' a change 'out of all recognition' ibid.) There is no mystery here. The stark and historically consistent reality of jail within democratic societies has been the purposeful defeat of the prisoner's personal and potentially collective will. While emphasising the state's authoritarian response to political prisoners, Nelson Mandela (1994: 340–1) notes the 'challenge for every prisoner ... is how to survive prison intact, how to emerge from a prison undiminished, how to conserve and even replenish one's beliefs':

> The first task in accomplishing that is learning exactly what one must do to survive. To that end, one must know the enemy's purpose before adopting a strategy to undermine it. Prison is designed to break one's spirit and destroy one's resolve. To do this the authorities attempt to exploit every weakness, demolish every initiative, negate all signs of individuality—all with the idea of stamping out that spark that makes each of us human and each of us who we are.

Survival against the odds is difficult for prisoners with little or no political cohesion or solidarity. Unremitting violence is often directed towards political prisoners yet their collective resistance and commitment to organising against the authority or legitimacy of the state provide mutual support and mobilisation against a common enemy (see: Campbell et al. 1994; McKeown 2001). For those not unified around political struggle, vulnerability is exacerbated by profoundly isolating, personal abuse and violence. Yet, as Brian Stratton (1973: 125) records in the following ultimatum issued to the authorities, the perpetration of violence by prison guards can spawn prisoner organisation and rebellion:

> We, the prisoners of Parkhurst convey to you that unless something is done very quickly to curb the brutality of a certain group of prison warders and an independent inquiry appointed to look into the conditions and complaints at Parkhurst, there will be a bloody riot, the like of which has never been seen in British Jails before.

FROM SAN QUENTIN TO ATTICA

Not long before he was shot dead by prison guards in California's notoriously violent San Quentin State Penitentiary, allegedly attempting to escape, George Jackson (1975: 94) reflected on his eleventh year inside. United States criminologists, he argued, crafted their 'neatly arranged . . . columns of figures' giving the 'impression of well-studied, detached, scientific analysis.' The African-American political activist revealed the stark reality behind the statistics. In the United States during the late 1960s, between thirty and forty per cent of the prison population was Black and the vast majority of prisoners were working class. In what was 'euphemistically called the "adjustment center" . . . far more accurately known as the hole,' most of the triple maximum security cells held 'black men—every one of them without exception from the working class.' Their incarceration was the inevitable consequence of a deeply authoritarian 'class- and race-sensitized society' whose 'ultimate expression of law is not order—it's prison' (ibid). Whatever their offences, whatever their personal culpability in their commission, most prisoners were 'victims of social injustice.' Prisons 'were not institutionalised on such a massive scale by the people' but were 'the creation of a closed society,' isolating those who 'disregard' or 'challenge' excesses of a class-ridden social order and its 'hypocritical establishment' (ibid). George Jackson's writings record United States race and class politics played out in the inherent hostility of state prisons. His experiences reflected a process of criminalisation within which the prison emerged as 'a symbol of state machinery which oppresses the poor and the powerless' (Thomas and Pooley 1980: 3).

Writing at the time, Tom Wicker (1975: 84–5) notes the 'violence and brutality,' particularly male rape, as routine, endemic and institutionalised.

While recognising 'not all the violence is employed by guards' against prisoners the 'most serious, if not the most prevalent, form of prison violence' was perpetrated by guards (ibid: 86). Prisoners had 'no real means of protecting themselves against official violence or gaining redress of grievances.' Prison management and guards 'take an entirely custodial view of their work, many fear and despise their charges.' Thus, 'force—instant and sometimes massive—is regarded as a necessary, even desirable, means of coping with their problems' (ibid). In this context, 'official violence' was 'an American prison commonplace' including well-documented evidence 'in numerous prisons' of '[b]eatings, tear gassings, Macings, "sweatbox" or "icebox" solitary confinement, gaggings, chainings, various kinds of floggings, and other numerous physical harassments' (ibid: 86–87). Alongside physical force, Wicker records the pervasiveness of 'psychological brutality,' ranging from forcibly keeping prisoners awake through the night to the 'prison's appalling lack of amenity—one shower and one pair of socks a week, one bar of soap and one roll of toilet paper a month,' inadequate food, 'skin searches' including 'rectal probe,' restricted visits, intercepted mail, 'arbitrary search and peremptory discipline' (ibid: 89).

In November 1970, at Folsom State Penitentiary, California, over 2,000 prisoners organised a strike, remaining in their cells for nineteen days 'in the face of constant hunger, discomfort, and continued psychological and physical intimidation' (Fitzgerald 1977: 202). Overtly political, the Folsom Prisoners' Manifesto of Demands and Anti-Oppression Platform called for an 'end to the injustice suffered by all prisoners, regardless of race, creed or color.' Referring to United States prisons as 'fascist concentration camps,' the text of the Manifesto stated that prison authorities institutionally denied prisoners respect regarding them as 'domesticated animals selected to do their bidding in slave labour and furnished as personal whipping dogs for their sadistic, psychopathic hate' (ibid: 203–4). The Manifesto included the unionisation of prisoners as a means to ending 'political persecution' and enabling 'peaceful dissent.' It referenced explicitly abuse of powers by prison managers and guards: tear-gassing dissenting prisoners locked in their cells; shooting prisoners; cruel and unusual punishment; physical brutality against prisoners held in San Quentin, Folsom and Soledad.

Within a year, on 9 September 1971 prisoners at Attica Correctional Facility, New York State, took control of the overcrowded prison. During the initial violence a prison guard and three prisoners were killed. New York State Police soon recovered most areas of the prison but over 1,200 prisoners occupied an exercise field, holding hostage thirty-nine prison guards and other employees. Guided by the Folsom Manifesto, the Attica activists issued a series of demands. Addressing the 'people of America,' the demands began with the context of the occupation: 'the unmitigated oppression wrought by the racist administration network of the prison.' 'We are MEN' the declaration proclaimed, 'not beasts and do not intend to be beaten or driven as such.' Representing the 'sound before the fury of those who are oppressed,' the occupation intended to 'change forever the ruthless brutalization and disregard for the prisoners here and throughout the United States.' It would 'bring closer to reality the demise of these prisons, institutions that serve no useful purpose to the People of America' (in Wicker 1975: 315).

Prisoners called for: 'amnesty, meaning freedom from any physical, mental and legal reprisals'; 'speedy and safe transportation out of confinement to a non-imperialistic country'; 'direct federal jurisdiction'; 'reconstruction of Attica Prison . . . by inmates and/or inmate supervision.' Finally, they sought negotiation with specified individuals, guaranteeing 'safe passage to and from this institution.' They invited *all the people* to come here and witness this degradation.' There followed fifteen 'practical proposals' dealing with prison conditions and regime, not least minimum wages, religious and political freedom, open communication, rehabilitation and education opportunities, guards' training, improved diet and healthcare, grievance procedures, less in-cell time, improved recreation facilities and an end to segregation and punishment.

Negotiations took place over four days, eventually in the presence of 'neutral' observers. At a delicate moment in the negotiations, Governor Nelson A. Rockefeller, who refused to visit the prison and identified the protest as a 'step in an ominous world trend' (in Parenti 1999: 166), ordered retaking the prison by force. Early on the 13 September, prisoners were given an ultimatum. They responded by threatening the lives of the hostages. The yard was tear-gassed and the state police opened fire into the fog. Twenty-nine prisoners and ten hostages were killed and eighty-nine injured. Official press releases stated that prisoners had summarily executed hostages. Eventually autopsies showed that all had been killed by police bullets. Inside Attica, reprisals against prisoners were sustained and prison guards alongside state police officers 'engaged in a day-long frenzy of verbal and physical brutality,' including prisoners being 'kicked in the head and the privates' and beaten and knocked to the ground' (Useem and Kimball 1989: 55). Prisoners were forced 'to run a gauntlet of guards and beaten the length of it' (ibid). Stripped naked, they were forced to crawl over broken glass. The putting down of the Attica rebellion, however, revealed a deep crisis of legitimacy within United States prisons and their management. Together with Californian prison protests, Attica 'indicated a nation-wide political consciousness among convicts' and its aftermath 'unveiled the state as brutal, desperate, and unprepared' (Parenti 1999: 166).

PETERHEAD, SCOTLAND'S GULAG

Opened in 1888, Peterhead Prison is located north of Aberdeen on Scotland's North-East coast. Designed to hold 208 male prisoners sentenced to penal servitude for a minimum of five years, by the early 20th century it held more than double its capacity. Access has always been difficult for most prisoners' families unable to make the long journey from the main Glasgow-Edinburgh population belt. By the 1980s, the prison no longer was overcrowded. It accommodated male prisoners, categorised A or B, serving sentences over eighteen months for whom allocation to a training prison was considered inappropriate. Peterhead's remote location also contributed to its isolation in terms of regime and staff. All prisons develop, even promote, an organisational culture in which the social lives of staff overlap with professional working relationships. In prison work, the closed institution coupled with prison officers' clubs on or close by the premises accentuates and sustains a distinctive occupational culture. Peterhead developed a reputation throughout the Scottish Prison Service (SPS) as a 'law unto itself.' It also was known as a hard, punitive jail.

While postwar statistics indicate that assaults by prisoners were considerably lower than in other Scottish prisons, 'Peterhead prisoners consistently received more punishments per head of population than did prisoners in other Scottish male prisons' (Scraton, Sim and Skidmore 1991: 11). Prison officers were armed as recently as 1959 and a whip known as 'the cat' was used as punishment until the 1950s. The 'impression of the Peterhead regime prior to the 1960s is that of arbitrary and excessive punishment . . . with loss of remission disproportionately inflicted' (ibid: 12). In 1966, changes in prisoner classification were introduced in Scotland. Prisoners under 35, identified as unwilling to participate in training, were sent to Peterhead. Those 'recalcitrant or subversive' or considered a 'bad influence on other prisoners' were transferred to the 'Special Segregation Unit' established at Inverness Prison, relatively close to Peterhead, where the regime was 'strict and privileges reduced to the minimum' (SHHD 1967: 7). This integrated an axis of punishment across the Peterhead and Inverness regimes.

In the enthusiasm to use classification as a means to control and discipline prisoners considered the least compliant, the most difficult to manage, the SPS relocated 'those who it was felt did not accept the legitimacy of the prison regimes into the solitary confinement unit at Peterhead and the segregation unit at Inverness' (ibid: 13). The intention was to resolve endemic problems concerning male long-term prisoners but it back-fired. By concentrating prisoners in a hostile and punitive Victorian prison, not fit for its purpose, located a very long distance from families, alienation and frustration led to persistent conflict: 'The increasing length of sentences, the repressive segregation techniques, the arbitrary classification system, the psychological and physical brutality each underpinned and provided sustenance to the violent behaviour of individuals' (ibid: 14). Peterhead was identified as 'the end of the road for many prisoners, it was Scotland's gulag, a prison of no hope.'

The endemic violence that dominated the operation of the Peterhead–Inverness axis is well illustrated in Jimmy Boyle's autobiographical account of life inside. Born and brought up in working class Glasgow, in 1967 he was imprisoned for murder following a childhood in reform schools and borstal. In prison, the 'pain' of his confinement 'was and still is tremendous,' his 'whole being was dead, my life was no longer . . . I was state-owned—forever' (Boyle, 1977: 155). Desperate and believing he 'would never experience freedom again' Boyle went before the Governor to gain an appellant visit. The Governor responded negatively and the prisoner 'could take no more.' He punched the Governor, was overpowered and put in solitary confinement. Later he heard heavy boots approaching the cell. Guards dressed in overalls, the 'heavy mob,' told him to strip. There would be no brutality. He took them at their word.

> No sooner had I stripped off than some of them moved in punching and kicking me . . . they beat me to the floor, leaving me in a pool of blood. There is something totally humiliating about being brutalised when naked. Nakedness leaves a feeling of helplessness. . . . There was this feeling of impotence. I lay on the floor in an absolute rage, hating myself for being such a bloody fool as to trust them. (Boyle 1977: 157)

Jimmy Boyle had been inducted into the all-pervasive culture of violence at the 'end of the road.' Despite his beating, he fought back, rousing a demonstration from his cell. The night guards put him in a strait-jacket. Left in a padded cell, he freed himself and throughout the night systematically destroyed the cell. He was 'covered in blood and filthy' but stood 'amid the wreckage . . . so proud.' His pain and suffering fed his violent response and he resolved that while the guards 'might beat me by sheer force of numbers . . . by fuck they would never beat my spirit into submission' (ibid: 158). On losing his appeal, he was taken to Inverness, the 'Siberia for prisoners in the Scottish penal system' (ibid: 167). Here he wrecked a Governor's office and was thrown in a 'silent cell.' Under heavy escort, handcuffed and naked, he went before the Governor. Back in the silent cell, he adopted a 'dirty protest.'

Eventually, he was transferred back to Peterhead. The 'atmosphere' was 'explosive . . . the slightest spark would blow the place sky high' (ibid: 172). Repeatedly pushed by a guard, he retaliated and a major confrontation between prisoners and guards occurred. There was a stand-off and he was put in solitary confinement in the punishment block: 'the door flew open and a mob of screws came in the door with batons in their hands . . . the "Batter Squad" out to extract their own pound of flesh' (ibid: 173).

> Eventually I passed out, waking to find myself alone. They sent for the doctor and when he came I stood in the corner like a wounded, frightened animal, refusing to trust anyone, but very dangerous. I refused to let him treat me telling him that he was one of them, part of them. The blood was splashed over the walls and running down my face and body. (ibid: 174)

There followed a long period in solitary where prisoners were beaten on arrival. He reflected that 'brutality . . . seemed to be getting worse in the long-term prisons.'

By late 1971, the cycle of violence cemented into his routine, Jimmy Boyle was in Peterhead when his mother died. Temporarily, he was transferred to Barlinnie in Glasgow to attend her funeral under heavy, armed escort: 'I was left to feel that by coming to the graveside I was desecrating it' (ibid: 200). Back in Peterhead, the prison was tense and following a disturbance in the recreation hall in which he was not involved, he was taken from his cell. He witnessed prisoners being beaten and thrown into cells. Without warning, a guard hit him from behind. As he retaliated, he 'heard them shouting for a straitjacket.'

> The blood was pouring down my face as the batons battered down on my head. . . . The jacket was being put onto me and tightened up "BASTARDS, BASTARDS, BASTARDS, BASTARDS" I screamed in utter frustration. During this fierce struggle we ended up near a sink full of dirty water. . . . I was well strapped into the straitjacket. . . . They lifted me and my head was pushed into the sink full of water to the sounds of someone calling out to drown the bastard. I was aware of a struggle between the screws, some of whom were frightened, trying to pull me out, while others were for drowning me. . . . I was coughing and swallowing water for what seemed to be an eternity . . . some, having lost control of themselves were still trying to push me under. I vividly remember mental flashes saying that it was all over, that I was dead. . . . I was being carried with my head near the ground and my legs up in the air, all the while being hit with sticks and boots. I could see the trail of blood I was leaving on the ground. My last memory of the affair was seeing a shiny boot bounce onto my face. . . . I lost consciousness. (ibid: 202)

A year earlier, in a classic understatement typical of those who observe prisons from a distance and whose perspective is carefully choreographed by governors, a Home Office researcher commented:

> There is a wide gulf between staff and prisoners and it is rare for staff to get close to prisoners. Violence is endemic. A wall of silence separates staff and inmates and punishments are accepted without argument. (McMillan 1971: 2)

By the early 1970s the Peterhead–Inverness axis had deteriorated to a level of extreme brutalisation. 'At one end of the continuum of institutionalised violence was the daily routine of bullying and intimidation; at the other was the inhumane, torturous punishment of the cages' (Scraton, Sim and Skidmore 1991: 15). Held in a confined 'cage' and stripped naked, the prisoner was subjected to full body searches three times daily despite having no interpersonal contact. Not only were the searches degrading but, given Jimmy Boyle's account, the treatment of prisoners was solely at the discretion of the guards. Following his most violent beating, he was transferred unconscious to Inverness, where he was examined and treated by a doctor. The injuries sustained by prisoners were known by other professionals, including medical staff, yet no one asked questions, sought explanations or made representations regarding the consequences of unbridled brutality. This provided guards with a licence to use extreme violence with impunity.

In 1974, Hugh Brown, Under-Secretary of State at the Scottish Office, recommended that, failing complete refurbishment, Peterhead should be closed. Hunger strikes and food refusal protests persisted alongside repeated allegations of staff brutality. In October 1978, a small group of prisoners set a fire and barricaded themselves inside a cell for 24 hours. While politicians, managers and staff repeatedly reassured the public that all was well, prisoners demonstrated they were not prepared to accept the hardening regime. In an interview with the Scottish Council for Civil Liberties (SCCL), a prisoner claimed the fire was a direct consequence of the unbearable conditions and regime, the last recourse to 'draw attention to the fact that they had been refused outside assistance with their complaints about conditions' (Robert Love Interview, SCCL, 4 April 1979). He also stated that prisoners in punishment cells were denied basic facilities and often held in isolation for a period longer than that imposed.

In their discussion of the causes and contexts of prison uprisings, Thomas and Pooley (1980: 8) note long-term prisoners 'will not tolerate unduly oppressive regimes' and will resist a 'tightening up' of a regime 'especially if such a procedure does not have any manifest security basis.' On 11 May 1979, the *Daily Record* published a letter smuggled out of Peterhead under the headline 'Zombie Cells Fury.' It claimed that the punishment block was a 'festering scandal,' where prisoners were held in solitary for 22 hours each day for as long as twelve months. Officials confirmed the block was worse than the Inverness cages and prisoners were held in solitary for up to a year. Within months, the anticipated protest erupted. The catalyst was the refusal of legal aid to prisoners preparing cases of inhuman and degrading treatment for the European Court. Ten prisoners broke out onto the roof and hoses were used as they barricaded themselves inside the roof.

Despite a commitment to refurbishing the jail, prisoners criticised the Secretary of State for his refusal to consult over conditions and staff brutality. An academic researcher, Russell Dobash, stated that he was 'shocked by the austere environment' (*Daily Record* 27 August 1979). Compared to all other Scottish prisons, Peterhead's conditions were 'exceptional in the negative sense.' He recommended its closure. The row over the previous protests continued with allegations that 42 prisoners were being held in solitary confinement in strip cells on 24-hour lock-up facing charges of

malicious damage, assault and fire raising. The spiral of violence continued. Protesters were dealt with harshly, receiving not only beatings from
guards but also long periods in solitary confinement, followed by exten-
sions to their sentences issued within the prison. By contrast, three guards
committed for trial accused of brutality against prisoners were acquitted.
The trial judge, however, considered that the prisoners' allegations 'carried
a certain ring of truth.'

Minor confrontations continued until May 1982, when a prisoner
reported a riot had occurred due to 'assaults and beatings meted out by
. . . warders' (letter from Alan Wardlow, *Newsline* 25 May 1982). His
allegations were verified by a prisoner's sister who stated that guards had
used violence to end a peaceful protest over conditions (letter from Sarah
Bryan, *The Scotsman* 22 May 1982). By November 1982, the official script
regarding Peterhead was set in stone. The Chief Inspector of Prisons for
Scotland recorded a well-adjusted and calm prison, the stability of which
was threatened by a group of violent men who engineered major conflict
from relatively minor disputes. Early the following year, a new ten-cell segregation block was announced for Peterhead, to accommodate the most
violent and disruptive prisoners within Scottish prisons. Prisoners inter-
preted this as a serious attempt to break the resolve of those who refused to
comply with the system. The regime would combine solitary confinement
and total surveillance.

In October 1983, a major disturbance broke out. Fifteen guards were
injured and three prisoners were locked in the 'cages.' The prison remained
tense, and in January 1984, twelve prisoners occupied the roof of the
prison. The eighteen-hour siege ended when the prison's riot squad stormed
the barricades. By March, the segregation unit was full to capacity and
prisoners embarked on a dirty protest. On 1 July, five prisoners on dirty
protest warned of 'trouble and tragedy.' They claimed that prisoners were
treated 'like animals,' deprived of newspapers, radios, tobacco, beds and
mattresses: 'rather than give us basic human needs the authorities would let
this protest go on for ten years, would rather have a disgruntled staff and
a permanent focal point of dissent within the prison system' (*The Scotsman* 19 July 1984). Prisoners were charged and found guilty of the January
'riot,' receiving a collective total of a further forty-five years in prison. One
prisoner, acquitted by the court, stated that prisoners felt 'the only way of
bringing the state of life in Peterhead to the public's attention is protest.'
The rooftop occupation was a 'warning of what could happen if the prisoners used the power they have shown that they possess to make their point
by violence' (*Glasgow Herald* 9 July 1984).

Throughout 1985, allegations of brutality by guards were rejected by the
Prison Service and the Scottish Office. Hostage takings continued, a guard
was charged with repeatedly assaulting a prisoner using handcuffs and a
prisoner was hospitalised having been beaten with batons, grabbed by his
testicles and kicked in the stomach. As 1986 progressed, tension within the

prison became 'unbearable' (*Glasgow Herald* 7 May 1986). Despite pleas from prisoners and their families and evidence from campaign groups, the official line continued to reflect denial allied to complacency. In October 1986, the Scottish Minister, Ian Lang, visited the prison and proclaimed conditions were 'very good'. He praised the 'professionalism' of the guards, was 'impressed with the atmosphere' and commented that staff were 'making every effort to ensure that the atmosphere is kept low key rather than highly charged' (*Glasgow Herald* 15 October 1986). Lang's statement was greeted with incredulity by prisoners' families, ex-prisoners, solicitors, campaigners and some politicians. It was the final blow to many prisoners who considered that their persistent complaints had been ignored. The die was cast. Within weeks, protests spread throughout Scotland's prisons.

A ninety-three-hour protest at Peterhead led to further charges of mobbing, rioting and hostage taking. Writing at the time of his trial, a prisoner, John Smith, made a plea in mitigation shared by other prisoners:

> Can anyone understand the full horrors of prison life even by visiting the prison? Of course not. No one can understand this without being part of it, feeling the anxieties, knowing the helplessness, living in desolation. . . . [Prison] is geared to use the men as labour, punish them if necessary and disregard their inner spirits as of no consequence. Physical and mental brutality does exist in Peterhead. . . . If the prison authorities insist on treating the prisoners like animals, then prisoners will naturally continue to act like animals. Prisoners, including myself, have been described as incurable psychopaths, subversive and hell-bent on destruction. This can only be described as an excuse rather than a truth. I ask you, have prisoners been given the chance to express themselves in any other way? (Submission to the High Court, Peterhead, 4 March 1987)

John Smith's plea cut no ice, and the protesters received additional ten-year sentences. Following a siege at Saughton Prison, Edinburgh, others received six- and seven-year sentences. A new official strategy emerged for dealing with protesters. Fibre-optic surveillance cameras and listening mechanisms already had been used by outside security specialists. The military's undercover Special Air Services (SAS) had also been deployed in ending the Peterhead siege, a new development in civil–military cooperation. Whatever these supposed 'advances' by the State, whatever the heavy sentences handed down by the courts, serious prison protests persisted throughout Scotland's jails involving roof-top occupations, barricaded cells, fires and hostage takings. There was no recognition that many prisoners, as John Smith had predicted, had become involved as a direct consequence of appalling conditions, physical and emotional suffering and a systemic denial of rights.

On 28 September, Peterhead's D Hall erupted. Within days, the protest reduced to three prisoners holding a guard hostage. He was regularly paraded by the prisoners on the prison roof. They indicated their intention to seriously injure him. On 3 October, the siege was ended and the guard released by the SAS using CS gas and stun grenades. Media coverage was widespread and public revulsion at the guard's humiliation brought universal condemnation. Despite this, and the use of military intervention, another hostage taking and siege occurred at Perth Prison. It ended when the authorities agreed to publish the prisoners' demands: the closure of Peterhead; improved parole opportunities; end to brutality.

The authorities denied that decrepit buildings, inhumane treatment, harsh regimes and mind-numbing segregation had nurtured rebellion. According to John Renton, Secretary of the Scottish Prison Officers' Association, control of the prisons had been 'lost' because 'we have been too soft' (*Glasgow Herald* 5 October 1987). He called for further isolation of those identified as an unmanageable hardcore. Andrew Coyle, then Chair of the Scottish Prison Governors' Committee, justified the clampdown on prisoners' work, association and recreation, considering 'identifying and controlling that small group of prisoners which abuse freedoms' as central to ensuring future stability (*The Independent* 7 October 1987). The Secretary of State for Scotland, Michael Rifkind, resolved to 'deal ruthlessly' with the 'small group of vicious animals' that infected an otherwise compliant and reasonable prison population (*BBC Radio 4*, 6 October 1987). In an outburst chillingly reminiscent of the red-necked response at Attica, the Leeds Prison Officers' Association Secretary, Graham Fenwick, proposed, 'the next time prisoners get on the roof they should be shot' (*Daily Record* 6 October 1987).

Supporting the prisoners' grievances while not condoning their violence, Dr Russell Dobash, a researcher into Scotland's prisons, stated:

> Frustration, angry feelings of hopelessness, a deep sense of deprivation and deep-rooted claims of injustice can trigger of unrest. The prisoners are not acting irrationally. For they are trying to highlight and make public their grievances. (*Daily Record* 6 October 1987)

John Carroll, a Glasgow solicitor with considerable experience of Peterhead, noted a refusal within the prison system to accept that some guards intimidated prisoners and this combined with a reluctance to initiate change and reform (*Sunday Mail* 4 October 1987). He argued that many prisoners were intelligent and rational, protesting to defend their rights, and they were aware that protests would lead to significantly longer sentences. The most insightful contribution to the debate, however, came from Ken Murray (1987), a Principal Officer who had initiated a ground-breaking programme for those classified as violent prisoners at Barlinnie Special Unit:

> Prisons are not natural habitats, they can't be. But they need not be unnatural places that they are in which fear and anger thrive. Prisons

are hostile places, prisoners are abused and debased in a variety of ways yet they are not deterred from re-offending . . . Prisoners most of the time are scared and they concentrate on the one major impera- tive in their life—survival . . . fear is the all-prevailing influence in the prison culture.

Murray had no doubt that the prison authorities and the politicians ulti- mately responsible had buried their heads in sand. His long experience of the legacy of Victorian prisons and the inheritance of violent regulation by guards 'above the law' highlighted key issues: inadequate accommodation; overcrowding in the local jails; 'slopping out'; mutual distrust between pris- oners and staff; staff brutality and cruelty; frustrations regarding parole and visits; poor complaints system.

Reflecting on their spectacular descent into chaos, Joe Sim (1994: 105) notes how violence within Scotland's prisons became institionalised, 'part of a normal routine . . . sustained and legitimated by a wider culture of masculinity.' He continues:

> First, they reinforce popular and professional discourses which equate male violence inside and outside with individual pathology. Second, they allow the state to maintain that something is being done about violence inside through the removal of these prisoners from normal circulation and into solitary confinement. Third, they normalise vio- lence in that the concentration of these prisoners allows other forms of prison violence to be seen as legitimate, a normal if regrettable part of prison life. (ibid: 105–6)

INSIDE THE REGIME

It was in this volatile climate that the Gateway Exchange set up an inde- pendent inquiry into the prisoners' protests at Peterhead. Primary access to interview prisoners was denied to the researchers. Early in February 1987, a questionnaire was delivered to prisoners. It was anticipated that some prisoners, fearing reprisals, would not participate. Forty-five responses were received and other information, written and oral, was drawn from former prisoners, prisoners' families and lawyers. The Independent Inquiry published a coherent, integrated report focusing on the history of Peterhead and the emergence and consolidation of its regime including hygiene and sanitation, privacy, work, food, recreation, education and staff relation- ships. The level of violence, staff brutality and the debilitating use of segre- gation were condemned universally by prisoners, often in graphic detail.[1]

> When I first came to Peterhead I spoke to staff with respect and civility. Now after 15 months of mental suffering and dehumanising treatment

I don't look on them as men. They do not care about the effect that this awful regime is having on me or other prisoners.

The majority of prison staff are indifferent to prisoners whom they think of as 'bodies.' I am a human being not a body.

I'd be willing to co-operate with staff if they treated me as a human being.

I don't trust them because they are always trying to find out my weak points so as to use them against me. If a screw treats me like a human being then I will treat him the same.

Older members of staff have the wrong attitude, they think we are all 'no hopers' and the 'scum of the earth.'

These five accounts reflect the dehumanisation reported by so many prisoners through which their status as citizens was removed and replaced by one less-than-human. There were constant references by guards to animal descriptions ('beast,' 'dog,' 'maggot') and to waste ('scum,' 'dross,' 'shit'). Prisoners also noted inconsistencies and provocations:

Nothing can be said to staff in confidence because at the end of the day it would be noted and relayed back no matter how significant.

Some staff may ignore petty rules, others may be zealous in applying them, if there is a personality clash between you and a member of staff then treatment can vary very wildly.

Some are O.K. but some are right bastards and treat you like shit.

You have a good squad and a dog squad who go out of their way to annoy you.

They do their utmost to antagonise me and get a reaction to justify locking me up.

How can you have a good relationship with a member of staff when you know that he will be right in there kicking the shit out of you if that's what the other staff were doing?

Prisoners viewed guards as turnkeys concerned only with locking prisoners in cells for as much of their shift as possible, drawing wages and making extra money through overtime payments. This contradicted the caring image portrayed by guards and their association in media comments. Prisoners stated:

They are not interested in the problems here unless it involves their wage packets. Warders are only here for the wages and are not interested in the job. Like most people in menial jobs they hate everything about their jobs.

Their attitude is terrible. If they could they would lock you up permanent. All their interests are centred around double shifts and money and this reflects the way I treat them. I treat contempt with contempt.

Staff in general have no time for prisoners and can't wait to lock them up . . . Most enjoy the silly games they play or watching you strip—humiliating you. They're all too quick to say 'I go home at night' or 'I get £500 a week' or 'You are my overtime this weekend.' . . . None of them would hesitate to put you on report, false or factual.

As prison walls are built not to keep prisoners in but prying eyes out, they can literally do as they wish—after all, who believes a prisoner, or wants to?

Prisoners experienced loss of identity, lack of respect and personal humiliation as defining elements in their relationships with guards. From the moment they arrived in prison, privacy lost and degradation assured, they experienced the diminution of the self. Personal mortification, what one prisoner referred to as the 'torturing' of the mind in which communication with staff was reduced to 'the language of violence, which is their language,' was the softer end of a continuum of violence deeply embedded in the culture of Peterhead. Further along the continuum, however:

If I don't communicate in that manner I am left to rot, until I react in the way they want me to. In all my time in Peterhead I have watched men who have resorted to violence. I can tell you that they have never had any choice because of the mental torture they are put through here. If you remain here you are not in the end capable of rational thought. You are no longer responsible.

Institutionally the experience of Peterhead was fear. Fear of losing dignity, rationality and sanity; fear of violence and its consequences. Solitary confinement, being sealed in the silent cell, represented the ultimate fear. While the average stretch in solitary was reported as three months for several it had been over twelve months. Its impact was devastating:

My head aches from morning until night. To put another human being into that silent cell you would have to be barbarous. The effects are severe! The thought of returning to Peterhead is very frightening. I've been locked up in the silent cell for 8 days. . . . When you step into the cell you see a box. That's the silent cell. Around this is all their strip lights and big heaters. The inside is about 3 square yards. There are two spy holes and two small air vents. It's a human furnace. I've had headaches all week. Sitting there in this cell is like having a band clasped around your throat.

Eighty-six per cent of prisoners felt unsafe inside and sixty-two per cent considered the fear of violence dominated their daily lives. Given the tensions, the culture of masculinity and 'hardmen' reputations prisoners feared other prisoners:

At any time a prisoner can snap and go crazy. The screws don't give a damn as long as it isn't their heads on the chopping block.

You can cross someone at any time not even realising you've done it, an incident could flare up and you could find yourself in the wrong place at the wrong time and end up involved unwittingly.

I have been assaulted four times by other prisoners two of which left me with large, visible scars for life. All of which made it necessary for me to be housed in the annexe at Peterhead.

The tense atmosphere fed off and into hostility between prisoners encouraging predators and 'feeding the paranoia that creeps up on you':

Peterhead is a dangerous place to be in for a great many reasons. It is not easy to avoid trouble when there is constant unrest on either side.

It is almost impossible to live at peace with each other due to our situation and tempers can flare up quite easily over the least little thing.

No one feels safe in prison. I for one don't. That's why I end up in so much trouble . . . I fear dying, loneliness, going insane, solitary confinement.

At Peterhead's core, like many other regimes at the time, was the unlawful use of force by guards. Commenting on the use of violence (understandably several declined) seventy-one per cent of prisoners reported assaults by guards and sixty-two per cent had witnessed assaults by guards on other prisoners. The latter was conservative given that most assaults on prisoners occur 'behind closed doors':

You hear it going on, the fighting and kicking, you hear your mates screaming but you're powerless. Either you protest and shout, knowing you're next or you put your pillow over your head and block it out.

Peterhead prisoners rejected the complaints system. They claimed it was stacked against them and represented a system that 'fabricated' and 'rewrote' evidence, denied legal representation, always took 'their [guards] word over ours' and placed prisoners in double jeopardy 'for making false allegations.' Procedures were not to be trusted and accountability existed only in name:

> Such is the atmosphere in Peterhead that you learn not to trust anyone. In my opinion, a situation created by staff. My motto: 'On guard.'

> I have experienced staff telling other prisoners that I have been grassing other prisoners for no apparent reason other than to put con against con and not con against screw. . . . When things are tense in here you can't help being afraid.

In a volatile climate of mistrust and fear, petty arguments and disagreements quickly escalated into fierce confrontation often provoked by guards:

> There's a total breakdown in communication between prisoners and staff. At any time trouble can flare. If you're singled out you are beaten or simply restrained even though you haven't struggled. Restraining technique is virtual strangulation.

> During any incident or argument staff are liable to lash out first, due to fear, and this is frightening as it usually involves anything up to 6 of them. Six lashing out with sticks can cause some damage to a person.

> You have to tread softly with staff as they can, and do, what they like with no comebacks. An assault here, or a report there. When there is the first sign of trouble they run out of the hall, lock you in and refuse to let you out. I was stabbed in the prison. Even after warning the authorities, they just don't care and they won't get involved.

Specific acts of brutality provided an account of routine violence endemic within the Peterhead regime:

> One evening, while going to my cell at lock up time, an officer started shouting at me for no apparent reason. Then he pushed me into a cell and started punching me about the head. As I wasn't in any fit state to defend myself, I put my hands through the windows to make him stop because it would attract attention. It resulted in another officer pulling the screw off me. I was then dragged down to the cells. The next day I was put in front of the Governor and charged with assault. The officer said I had assaulted him. . . . The Governor didn't believe

my side of the story. He said his staff don't go around beating up prisoners. I was sent to see the psychiatrist.

I have been quite lucky, one assault only. Punched, kicked, wrists bent, neck bent, ankles twisted, this was me being 'restrained' after an incident protesting the way another inmate had been treated.

They forced an internal search on me without a doctor and an officer jumped on my arm in the cell-block in Peterhead.

Christmas Day '86 they set about me with riot sticks for throwing a cup of tea out my door. They charged me with assaulting them with a knife and gun. I was found not guilty of these charges.

I have been very badly assaulted in the past by some staff. I have had my leg broken, my head bust open, and my face very badly marked.

I've had too many assaults to mention in various penal establishments. In PH only once—assault involved batons, feet, hands.

Several times, the most serious being in the yard leading to the silent cell. 4 staff beat me up which led to me being taken to an outside hospital for X-rays on my head plus bruising on my body and legs and face.

They kicked me unconscious for protesting and when they came back it was the same brutality all over again, beaten, stripped, handcuffed and thrown into an empty cell.

A prisoner had experienced three 'typical instances':

I refused to go to a 'separate cell-block' so I got punched, kicked, and dragged; Lit a fire in a cell in solitary confinement to keep warm so I got a black eye off the staff; Fingers fractured while being escorted to cell block after attempted escape; Nose broken after taking hot water for tea after being refused permission.

As already discussed, prison protests often result in systematic and sustained attacks by guards on prisoners. Following a series of protests in British jails, prisoners were prosecuted and given heavy sentences. Yet prisoners, including many not prosecuted, experience the use of calculated violence by 'riot squads' as a more than symbolic gesture in regaining control of the prison:

After the riot in '79 I was beaten unconscious for my assaults on staff, when my brother threatened the staff's families with revenge. I had my head split open with a baton in the silent cells.

The last time officers, clad in semi riot-gear, riot sticks like baseball bats, further officers outside my door: [date provided]. Struck by baton, used like bayonet, kidney, left leg gave way, jumped all over me, mainly booted, handcuffed arms up my back, squeezed testicles, etc (usual) internal life endangering injury, 10 inch scar, med. reports max. 24 hour life expectancy without emergency op. 16 hours left on floor, no doctor unless a deal that I fell.

How safe I feel depends on the situation at a given time, especially when the MUFTI squad are operating; then no one is safe.

1984; A Hall was destroyed; I was put into a windowless cell, with nothing apart from a mattress, 18 solid weeks. A 'pneumatic consolidated drill' with a jack hammer attachment pounded the floor of the above cell. One night I lit a fire in the hope that I would be taken from A Hall. The officers came in force dragged me from the cell, hit me with fists, sticks and kicked me all over the place, tried to break my arms and choke me.

Examples of 'routine' assaults by guards on others were provided by prisoners:

I saw my friend, T.P., being beat up in the exercise yard; my friend J.B. beat up on the corridor, another man in the hall.

Saw a member of the staff punch a guy then they grabbed him and forced an internal examination on him.

I saw an inmate assaulted on exercise at PH by 3 members of the staff. Witnessed this from my cell window.

I saw a prisoner punched in the face for refusing to drop his underpants without an M.O. present. I have heard prisoners getting beaten up but everyone is locked up before this takes place.

I have seen prisoners being put on report in the past for next to nothing and dragged to the cells and hit with sticks . . . I have seen it all.

Over many years, in many prisons, the instances I have personally witnessed of prisoners being assaulted by prison staff are too numerous to enumerate.

These comments reflect how staff assaults on prisoners formed part of Peterhead's established custom and practice. It was a regime within which a slap, a punch, a kick, a body search could occur any time as part of routine imposition of authority, the physical expression of discretionary power. Jimmy Boyle's beatings served as a warning to all who contested authority. Prisoners were less matter-of-fact regarding more serious or sustained attacks:

> The most recent was a man being kicked near to death and being left in a cell for 5½ hours before the Authorities would call a doctor. The man was badly injured and had to undergo an emergency operation to save his life. I was a witness.

> Of all the liberties I witnessed among them was an assault on a young cripple. This particular day his sticks were at surgery being adjusted. He intervened in a slanging match on behalf of another prisoner, the officer seized him by the throat and punched him 3 times or so in the face, officer later said that he had hit him with a stick. [The prisoner] got 14 days for assault.

> I saw him [a prison officer] whack a man over the head with several sets of steel handcuffs, bursting his head open which was later stitched up. I was only 4 yards away, as were 5 other prisoners. . . . At the time the warder hit the man on the head, five warders were holding on to the man; they all denied the warder hit the man with the cuffs.

> Once I saw a man almost beaten to death by about 15 screws. . . . Only extensive surgery saved this man's life. The screws used 'riot-sticks' as well as the 'black aspirin' [their boots].

> I heard an inmate being assaulted on Xmas night, battered with sticks. Heard the screams, he was taken to hospital. I saw him the next day with his arm all bandaged up and in a sling plus a bruise on cheek.

> [My] bruises were witnessed by a few prisoners one of which was placed on report and lost 14 days remission because he vented his anger at the state I was in. Only verbally I might add. The assault had taken place in the separate cells area.

Violence was not confined to assaults but also involved self-harm and what was perceived as the callous indifference of managers and officers. A prisoner had 'slashed his face twice in the past couple of weeks' but no one had 'lifted a finger to help him.' The prisoner giving this account asked, 'What state of mind is the poor guy in?' Prisoners also identified a spiral of violence sustained by a commitment to retaliation and retribution.

> My views on violence are simple enough: if they have a license to inflict brutal beatings—then you must do likewise at the earliest opportunity

as a defensive act to show them you're prepared to stand none of it. I don't believe in abusing or assaulting warders because they are locking me up. I treat them as they do me.

The only way I can communicate with these people is in a cell block. By tension, abuse, violence, hatred and excrement. They won't allow for a man to change, so fuck them. No way will they be able to talk to me because when I talked they didn't listen. Fuck them.

As discussed above, violence at Peterhead was part of its history. Its harsh regime was justified as the only means to keep Scotland's 'hard men' in check. Yet, it was also an expression of an institutionalised culture of masculinity emphasising and promoting physicality and aggression. Taunts such as 'Let's see how hard you are now' or 'You're with the big boys now' are familiar expressions of male group camaraderie idealising physical domination and breaking the 'enemy.' The treatment of Jimmy Boyle demonstrates the bigger the reputation, the greater the challenge. It was not a culture confined to staff–prisoner relations but one that was all-pervasive. It was evident in prisoner-on-prisoner bullying and intimidation. It surfaced in intra-staff relations when certain guards were perceived by colleagues as being 'too soft' on or 'too close' to prisoners.

THE REALITY AND CONSEQUENCES OF 'RELENTLESS FORCE'

Generous in complimenting our work as the 'most sophisticated version of the deprivation thesis,' Eamon Carrabine (2005: 900) quotes an earlier critique by Sparks et al. (1996: 61) in which the authors assert that the Peterhead research 'places its whole emphasis on the imposition of order by relentless force.' Consequently, they argue, the analysis neglects the 'many complexities of prison life' and 'significant variations in the social organisation of different prisons.' While not wanting to expend too much energy in rebuttal, central to the Peterhead research was overwhelming evidence of what happens to social and organisational relationships, to the 'complexities in prison life' when 'order' of dubious merit and legitimacy is imposed by unabated cruel and brutalising force. Potential for positive relations is not only limited or stunted, but it is also eliminated and replaced by deep-seated alienation and retaliation predicated on violence.

From the evidence presented in *Prisons Under Protest*, and revisited here, it is difficult to draw any other conclusion than dysfunctional relations and complicit management as inevitable consequences of a violent institution. Carrabine (2005: 900) is correct when he states, 'there are significant differences in how power is experienced by the confined.' Yet, there appears to be a fundamental misrepresentation of the Peterhead research.

There was no intention to confine the analysis to an explanation reducible exclusively to the dynamics of deprivation. As Useem and Kimble (1989: 219) note, prisoners do not riot or protest 'merely because they are deprived of amenities' to which they are accustomed on the outside.

Far from reducing the protests to a simplistic variant of deprivation theory, the Peterhead research emphasised the spectrum of contextual factors that, over an extended period of time, fed and nurtured tensions to breaking point. These included: the prison's history as a 'tough' and uncompromising jail; the seemingly unrestrained discretion of the guards and the implicit acceptance by managers of guards' abuses of power; the concentration of 'difficult' prisoners on one site; the appalling structural condition of prison buildings and cells; the excessive use of solitary confinement and segregation. Each factor plumbed into a dominant and dominating culture of male violence and its associated levels of threat and fear. It was not that under heavy duress, the administration collapsed. Nor was it that prisoners withdrew previous compliance to a functioning regime. The administration had never been any different, guards had always abused their powers and prisoners had never accepted the prison's *modus operandi*.

As Carrabine (2005: 910) states, prisons are 'in the final analysis, coercive institutions but force will usually remain in the background of interaction as an intimidating threat rather than in constant use, as various inducements, normative commitments and ritual compulsions form the routine sources of order.' At Peterhead, however, force was constantly in the foreground. 'Inducements,' 'commitments' and 'compulsions' had little constituency in a prison where disorder was a permanent feature of daily life and violence awaited at the turn of every corner, the sliding bolt of every door. As the research demonstrated, not all prisoners resisted forcefully or protested openly. Yet there was no legitimacy afforded to a regime in which violence against prisoners—meted out directly and physically in assaults and indirectly and psychologically through isolation—was institutionalised.

As discussed earlier, prison protests in United States jails, particularly the Attica rebellion, amounted to a collective resistance 'against a multitude of poor conditions, including rampant and widespread brutality of guards,' 'irrational limits' on basic amenities and restrictions on religious freedom (Midgley 2003: 283). A key issue was the 'lack of an impartial court forum to hear their [prisoners] grievances regarding inhumane treatment and illegal irregularities in their convictions' (Clarke 2003: 312). The Attica deprivations, as Clarke states, and the 'body count' that followed the ending of the protest disclosed an issue of 'national shame.' As John Midgley (2003: 283) concludes, 'Prison riots, like the urban riots of the same time, placed the otherwise obscure experience of prison under a national media spotlight' resulting in a 'public outcry over such graphic examples of overt abuse by both state actors and prison staff.' However loud and sustained the outcry, it took twenty-six years for former and current prisoners, who had suffered during the raid and the retribution that followed, to win a class action in the courts against prison and state officials. Further, since Attica the use of incarceration in the United States has reached unprecedented levels with half of all prisoners African-Americans and three-quarters people of colour (Rhodes 2004: 9). African-American women comprise forty-eight per cent of women in prison (Johnson: 2004: 34). Prison conditions are diverse but at the 'sharp end,' particularly those held in maximum security jails or control units, the situation is bleak and discriminatory. Writing on his return to Attica in 2001, David Gilbert (2005: 313–314) records:

> While Attica COs (correction officers) were always aggressive, it is now out of control. Even i [sic]—a veteran at navigating harassment shoals—have been screamed on far more times in this five months than in the preceding five years. And behind the shouts and insults is the threat—and all too frequently—of beatdowns. I don't have a way to accurately assess how often beatings happen or to compare that statistically to other years, but it is certainly a palpable reality.

In her primary research into the use of isolation in control units, Lorna Rhodes (2004: 60) shows how in responding to the 'worst of the worst,' prisoners classified the most dangerous and violent, guards 'believe that the inmates ultimately control their own fate.' Yet, as her research interviews and observations demonstrate, 'prisoners in these units can slip toward seeming nothing but bodies—beyond or unworthy of rehabilitation—to be managed by nothing more than a parsimonious economy of attention.' As a 'social' being, the prisoner 'withers on the other side of the bars,' stripped of dignity, respect and self-worth. The expectation to take responsibility and return, compliant, to the mainstream would require 'an almost superhuman ability to exercise his (or her) will.' For many prisoners control units, caged segregation, realises their worst fear—to be 'broken' by the punishing regime of isolation and loneliness.

Paula Johnson (2004: 274), in her excellent presentation of African-American women's accounts of their incarceration, notes the 'resolution' of issues of 'accountability and culpability . . . central to criminal adjudication and sentencing' is 'complex.' The administration of criminal justice 'is further complicated by frequently being fraught with conscious or unconscious race, gender and class biases.' Context is not confined to process. It extends to 'issues of structural inequality in society' alongside 'unequal treatment in criminal justice proceedings' thus 'render[ing] the ultimate determinations as suspect in many such circumstances.' The massive over-representation of people of colour in United States jails and the escalation in African-American women's imprisonment has to be placed within the structural determinants of 'race,' class and gender within United States communities.

Further, as Elliot Currie (1998: 30) argues, 'while we were busily jamming our prisons to the rafters with young, poor men, we were simultaneously generating the fastest rise in income inequality in recent history ... tolerating the descent of several million Americans into poverty. . . . ' He recounts the classic poverty trap in which the poor, disproportionately people of colour, 'became increasingly isolated, spatially and economically ... trapped in ever more impoverished and often chaotic neighborhoods' (ibid: 31). These are 'communities without stable jobs, without preventive health care, without school guidance counsellors or recreation facilities, with staggeringly inadequate mental health and child welfare services,' yet constantly 'bombarded by a particularly virulent ethic of consumption and instant gratification.' As Paula Johnson notes, imprisonment in jails in part is an inevitable outcome of imprisoned communities.

The politics of prison protest at Peterhead were not as visible, as apparent, as those at Attica. Yet the abusive dynamics within the prison (staff brutality, use of solitary, harsh regime, poor accommodation, lack of effective complaints system) coupled with guards' animosity towards prisoners as the 'lowest of the low,' the 'worst of the worst,' together comprised the circumstances in which prisoners rebelled. The seriousness of the Scottish protests was clear in the formulation of demands reminiscent of manifestoes proposed in the United States. In reasserting authority, prison guards at Peterhead, consistent with their history, administered both targeted and arbitrary physical beatings. Reducing prisoners to 'bodies,' to 'animals,' represented a deeply set process of dissociation and dehumanisation backed up by official denial. Most prison guards in Peterhead were from the same working class background, the same towns, schools, housing schemes and communities, as the prisoners. Their view of their neighbours was formed around 'rough-respectable,' 'criminal-honest,' 'violent-peaceful' binaries. To most guards prisoners were moral degenerates known by reputation for their predatory behaviour. They deserved little empathy and were unworthy of social interaction. Through their irresponsibility and pathology they had sacrificed any call on respect, on humanity. The downward spiral of mistreatment, abuse and violence created and sustained a mutuality of contempt. As with all forms of alienation, the guards and their managers were diminished by the inhumanity and degradation they perpetrated explicitly or condoned implicitly.

While the specific circumstances and distinct contexts of the protests covered here cannot be reduced to precise common denominators, to ignore the significance of violent, discriminatory and debilitating custom and practice fronted by the most confrontationary and conflictual elements of cultures of masculinity is naïve. Using theoretical models of 'disorganisation' and 'deprivation,' or a combination of both, to explain the dynamics of protests within violent places of detention neglects the significance of structural relations and inherent inequalities of class, 'race,' gender, sexuality and age and how they play out in the informal politics of prison. Ruth Wilson Gilmore (2007: 243) has no doubt that 'coming to grips with dehumanisation' is the lesson of the twentieth century, 'the age of genocide.' She states:

> Dehumanisation names the deliberate, as well as the mob-frenzied, ideological displacements central to any group's ability to annihilate another in the name of territory, wealth, ethnicity, religion. Dehumanisation is also a necessary factor in the acceptance that millions of people (sometimes including oneself) should spend part or all of their lives in cages.

It is also about how humanity is debased through institutionalised acceptance of the violence of incarceration.

ACKNOWLEDGEMENTS

Many thanks to my co-workers on the Peterhead project, Joe Sim and Paula Skidmore, and to Jimmy Boyle, whose book, *A Sense of Freedom*, continues to be an inspiration. Also to Kathryn Chadwick who worked with me on subsequent research in Scotland and to my partner, Deena Haydon, for her continual support and critical analysis. Special thanks to the prisoners who took significant risks in participating in the primary research.

NOTES

1. All direct quotes from prisoners in this section are from written statements to the independent inquiry into Peterhead research and published by Scraton, Sim and Skidmore (1991).

REFERENCES

Boyle, J. (1977) *A Sense of Freedom: An Autobiography*, Edinburgh: Canongate.
Campbell, B., McKeown, L. and O' Hagan, F. (1994) *Nor Meekly Serve My Time: The H Block Struggle 1976–1981*, Belfast: Beyond the Pale Publications (revd 2006).
Carrabine, E. (2005) 'Prison Riots, Social Order and the Problem of Legitimacy' *British Journal of Criminology*, 45 (6), pp. 896–913.
Clarke, M.T. (2003) 'Bringing the Federal Courthouses to Prisoners' in T. Herivel and P. Wright (eds) *Prison Nation: The Warehousing of America's Poor*, New York: Routledge, pp. 301–314.
Currie, E. (1998) *Crime and Punishment in America*, New York: Holt.
Fitzgerald, M. (1977) *Prisoners in Revolt*, Harmondsworth: Penguin.

Gilbert, D. (2005) 'Attica—Thirty Years Later' in J. James (ed) *The New Abolitionists: (Neo) Slave Narratives and Contemporary Prison Writings*, Albany: State University of New York, pp. 311–316.

Gilmore, R.W. (2007) *Golden Gulag: Prisons, Surplus, Crisis, and Opposition in Globalizing California*, Berkeley and Los Angeles: University of California Press.

Hercules, T. (1989) *Labelled a Black Villain*, London: Fourth Estate.

Jackson, G. (1975) *Blood in My Eye*, Harmondsworth: Penguin.

Johnson, P.C. (2004) *Inner Lives: Voices of African American Women in Prison*, New York: New York University Press.

Mandela, N. (1994) *Long Walk to Freedom: The Autobiography of Nelson Mandela*, Boston: Little, Brown and Co.

McKeown, L. (2001) *Out of Time: Irish Republican Prisoners Long Kesh 1972–2000*, Belfast: Beyond the Pale Publications.

McMillan, J. (1971) 'Some Notes and Observations on the Prison Subculture,' Unpublished Paper.

Midgley, J. (2003) 'Prison Litigation 1950–2000' in T. Herivel and P. Wright (eds) *Prison Nation: The Warehousing of America's Poor*, New York: Routledge, pp. 281–300.

Murray, K. (1987) 'Fear and Loathing in Our Prisons,' *The Scotsman*, 12 January.

Parenti, C. (1999) *Lockdown America: Police and Prisons in the Age of Crisis*, London: Verso.

Rhodes, L. A. (2004) *Total Confinement: Madness and Reason in the Maximum Security Prison*, Berkeley and Los Angeles: University of California Press.

Scraton, P., Sim, J. and Skidmore, P. (1991) *Prisons Under Protest*, Milton Keynes: Open University Press.

SHHD (1967) *Prisons in Scotland Report for 1967* Scottish Home and Health Department, Cmnd 3319, Edinburgh: HMSO.

Sim, J. (1994) 'Tougher than the Rest? Men in Prison' in T. Newburn and E. Stanko (eds) *Just Boys Doing Business?* London: Routledge, pp. 100–117.

Stratton, B. (1973) *Who Guards the Guards?* London: PROP.

Thomas, J.E. and Pooley, R. (1980) *The Exploding Prison*, London: Junction Books.

Useem, B. and Kimball, P. (1989) *States of Siege: U.S. Prison Riots 1971–1986*, New York: Oxford University Press.

Wicker, T. (1975) *A Time to Die. The Attica Prison Revolt*, London: The Bodley Head.

Wilde, O. (undated) *The Ballad of Reading Gaol*, London: Heron Books

5 Child Incarceration

Institutional Abuse, the Violent State and the Politics of Impunity

Barry Goldson

Violence against children cuts across boundaries. . . . Some children are particularly vulnerable. . . . And no country is immune, whether rich or poor. Violence against children is never justifiable. Nor is it inevitable. If its underlying causes are identified and addressed, violence against children is entirely preventable.

(Kofi Annan, United Nations Secretary-General, 2006: xi)

INTRODUCTION: THE RIGHTS-VIOLENCE OXYMORON

In 1990, the 'World Summit on Children' assembled in New York, constituting the largest gathering of state leaders in history. Together, the Heads of State declared that the 'well-being of children requires political action at the highest level,' and they pledged: 'we are determined to take that action. We ourselves make a solemn commitment to give high priority to the rights of children' (cited in Children's Rights Development Unit 1994: xi). The United Nations Convention on the Rights of the Child (UNCRC) is seen to embody such commitment, setting out the principles and detailed standards for: the rights of children; the care and protection of children; laws, policies and practices that impact on children; and both formal and informal relationships with children. With few exceptions—most notably the United States—governments around the world have adopted and ratified the UNCRC more quickly and more comprehensively than any other international convention.

Article 1 of the UNCRC provides that 'a child means every human being below the age of eighteen years unless, under the law applicable to the child, majority is attained earlier.' Furthermore, Article 19 states that governments: 'shall take *all* appropriate legislative, administrative, social and educational measures to protect the child from *all* forms of physical or mental violence, injury or abuse, neglect or negligent treatment, maltreatment or exploitation' (emphases added). The Convention deliberately defines 'violence' in broad terms and, in this sense, it is consistent with the definition since provided by the World Health Organisation (2002: 5):

· · · the intentional use of physical force or power, threatened or actual, against a child, by an individual or group, that either results in or has a high likelihood of resulting in actual or potential harm to the child's health, survival, development or dignity.

Despite the almost universal ratification of the UNCRC and concomitant 'State Party' duties to uphold the human rights of children and comprehensively safeguard them, however, widespread violence against children remains legal, state-authorised and socially approved. Across the world, children continue to endure the corrosive impositions of violence: sometimes random, sometimes organised, always insidiously pervasive.

In February 2003, Paulo Sergio Pinheiro was appointed, at Assistant Secretary-General level, to direct the 'United Nations Secretary-General's Study on Violence Against Children' (the Study). The principal objective of the Study was to investigate all forms of violence against the world's children and to analyse the impact of such phenomena. The Study was undertaken in collaboration with the Office of the High Commissioner for Human Rights, the United Nations Children's Fund and the World Health Organisation. Informed by comprehensive consultations with government departments, international human rights agencies, civil society organisations, research institutions and children and young people themselves, it comprises the most wide-ranging and detailed analysis of its type in history. The final report—published and presented to the United Nations General Assembly in November 2006 (Pinheiro 2006)—makes for depressing, even if salutary, reading.

Infanticide; cruelty; humiliation; degradation; neglect; abandonment; punishment; and emotional, psychological, physical and sexual abuse are all historically embedded expressions of violence against children that date back to ancient 'civilisations' (Ten Bensel et al. 1997). More recently, as the Study has revealed, some forms of violence, including the organised sexual exploitation and trafficking of children, the excesses of child labour and the impact of war on children, have, at least ostensibly, captured the global political imagination and are relatively high on international agendas. Despite such historical constancy and the contemporary international concerns focussing at the extremes, however, 'attention to violence against children in general continues to be fragmented and very limited—different forms of violence in the home, schools, institutions and the community are largely ignored in current debates in the international community' (Pinheiro 2006: xviii).

This chapter is ultimately located within a global context in which children's human rights are often severely compromised and their claims to dignity and integrity are systematically violated. Theoretical questions that centre on power, authority and legitimacy are core concerns—implicitly and/or explicitly. The differential and structurally mediated impositions of violence on children are also key, within which the primary relations of class, 'race' and gender are uppermost. The means by which violence against children is dispensed with relative, or even absolute, impunity is also crucially important. It is not practical in a single chapter to engage comprehensively with the depth and breadth of the wider context, however. Rather, the emphasis here rests with the abuse and violence endured by children in institutions and, more specifically still, with child prisoners in 'advanced' industrial democracies. At a time when new modes of punitiveness characterise many western criminal justice systems and rates of child incarceration spiral in several jurisdictions (Muncie 2005; Muncie and Goldson 2006; Pratt et al. 2005; Wacquant 1999), the analytical privileging of institutional abuse, state violence and the politics of impunity in relation to child prisoners is especially apt. More specifically still, this chapter critically examines the situation in England and Wales, not least because it comprises the jurisdiction where greater use of penal custody for children is made than most other industrialised democratic countries in the world (Goldson 2006a).

INSTITUTIONAL(ISED) ABUSE

From their earliest inception, and irrespective of their officially stated purpose and rationale (moral reclamation, care, education, rehabilitation, correction, punishment), institutions for children have essentially comprised repositories for managing the unwanted. In the Middle Ages, residential institutions for abandoned children were established by the Church in Italy before spreading across Europe (Carter 2005). In the nineteenth century, as industrialisation and urbanisation swept through much of Europe and North America, 'child-saving' and 'correctional' institutions for the 'deprived' and/or 'depraved' proliferated (Goldson 2004). Similarly, colonialism and imperialism impinged upon children further afield. In Australia and Canada, for example, entire generations of aboriginal children were forcibly removed from their families and communities and placed in institutions in which they were denied their Indigenous culture and exposed to violent 'resocialistion' (Pilger 1992; Pilkington 2002). In the post-World-War period large-scale institutions for children developed in many communist countries under the USSR sphere of influence, and only later did the violations perpetuated within such facilities—including the massive orphanages in Romania, for example—become widely known. In more recent times, the number of children placed in institutions has multiplied exponentially owing to 'natural disasters,' armed conflict, widespread population displacement and the HIV/AIDS pandemic that has afflicted huge areas of the majority world.

Related to this are migrant and refugee children, including those seeking asylum, who are placed in institutions while their cases are being decided. In England and Wales, for example, 'serious concerns' (Her Majesty's Chief

Inspector of Prisons 2007: 8) have been raised with regard to the 2,000 children per year held in 'immigration removal centres' and 'immigration short-term holding facilities.' Taken together, according to some accounts as many as eight million children live in institutions—state, Church, NGO and/or privately managed—ostensibly designed to 'care' for them (International Save the Children Alliance 2003). But, as the UN Study has revealed, many such children are routinely exposed to multiple forms of violence and abuse (Pinheiro 2006: 175–229). Such children are typically drawn from the poorest, most disadvantaged, structurally vulnerable and oppressed sections of their respective populations, and children from racial and ethnic minorities are routinely over-represented. The low level of social value accorded to such children ('unsuitable victims' with 'lesser status') renders them particularly prone, by omission or commission, to systematic maltreatment within socio-political contexts where those responsible operate with impunity. Whilst the institutional(ised) abuse of children is almost certainly unevenly distributed, over time and across space it commands a permanent presence.

Turning to the question of child prisoners, although it is difficult to retrieve and collate reliable comparative data, certain sources estimate that, at any given time, approximately one million children are incarcerated worldwide (Pinheiro 2006: 191). This is almost certainly an underestimate, however. For example, more than 600,000 children and young people are imprisoned annually in the United States alone (Annie E. Casey Foundation 2004: 9). Child imprisonment is particularly problematic, not least because children in penal detention are especially vulnerable to violation. Here too, the historical evidence is compelling. Taking England and Wales as a single example, the practices of child incarceration are well-established. Since the establishment of the first penal institution exclusively for children at Parkhurst Prison for boys in 1838, an array of carceral experiments have created and sustained a panoply of institutional forms: 'Reformatories'; 'Industrial Schools'; 'Borstals'; 'Approved Schools'; 'Remand Centres'; 'Detention Centres'; 'Community Homes with Education'; 'Youth Custody Centres'; 'Detention and Training Centres'; 'Young Offender Institutions'; 'Secure Children's Homes' and 'Secure Training Centres' (Goldson 2002a). The history of such institutions is characterised by a catalogue of failure, misery, scandal, human suffering, abuse and violence, repeatedly produced and reproduced through their regimes and standard operational practices. Moreover, such history is not confined to a single jurisdiction; it is replicated worldwide and its echoes continue to be heard within many contemporary juvenile/youth justice systems.

Indeed, throughout the course of the United Nations Study, a series of 'thematic consultations'—involving leading international experts—convened in order to provide subject-specific reports. In the 'Violence Against Children in Conflict with the Law' report, the Director of the Study observed that:

Children in conflict with the law . . . are one of the *most vulnerable* groups to the *worst forms of violence.* . . . Public opinion about the involvement of children in illegal activities and the search for immediate answers have led to the introduction of insane repressive methods . . . the *recurrent* and *banalised* use of *institutionalization* is surely problematic. (Pinheiro 2005: 17–18, emphases added)

Furthermore, the NGO Advisory Panel to the Study stated that: '"tough on crime" policies and negative media and public images of . . . socio-economically disadvantaged children'; 'the over-use of detention' and '*impunity* and *lack of accountability* by law enforcement agents, institutions and staff, [are] some of the key issues that facilitate violence against children in the justice system' (NGO Advisory Panel for the United Nations Secretary-General's Study on Violence Against Children 2005: 4, emphases added).

THE VIOLENT STATE

As stated, England and Wales comprises one of the most punitive sites of juvenile/youth justice in the modern industrialised democratic world. Within the specific jurisdiction, the phenomena that give rise to 'the worst forms of violence' against children in trouble abound. Officially sanctioned policies and practices—including the 'recurrent and banalised use of institutionalization'—are tantamount to institutional and institutionalised child abuse (Goldson 2006b), the deliberate, repeated and systematic imposition of harm. Yet those responsible continue to neutralise accountability, evade responsibility and, ultimately, operate with impunity. The remainder of this chapter subjects this paradox to critical scrutiny.

Power and Punishment

The state's power to punish and claim legitimacy for various applications of violence has become an increasingly conspicuous feature of the Anglo-American 'special relationship' in the modern era, both at home and abroad. Within the domestic sphere, this is particularly, although not exclusively, evident within the realm of criminal 'justice,' where recourse to incarceration has consolidated and expanded.

In the United States, therefore, 'mass imprisonment' (Garland 2001a: 5), 'carceral hyperinflation' (Miller 2001: 158) and 'hyper-incarceration' (Simon 2000: 285) are terms more-or-less routinely applied to analyses of contemporary criminal justice interventions. Over the course of a year, 13.5 million people pass through jails and prisons in the United States, the daily count of prisoners has surpassed 2.2 million yet continues to grow, and 60 billion dollars are spent each year on 'corrections' (Gibbons and Katzenbach 2006: 11). Paradoxically, modern America, the 'land of the free,' is a place where a 'society of captives' (Simon 2000: 285) occupy 'the new iron cage' (Garland 2001b: 197). The creation of a 'prison nation' (Herivel and Wright 2003), a phenomenon described as 'Lockdown' (Parenti 1999), bears little, if any, relation to the actual volume or severity of crime, however. Rather it is steeped in the cynical (re)politicisation of crime, in populist posturing, in crudely competitive electioneering exchanges and, ultimately, in essentialist 'zero tolerance' policy-making (Tonry 2004). As Garland (2001c: 191) has observed, mass incarceration:

> . . . is very much a *political* process. It is governed not by any criminological logic but instead by . . . political actors and the exigencies, political calculations and short-term interests that provide their motivations. In its detailed configuration, with all its incoherence and contradictions, [it] is thus a product of the decidedly aleatory history of political manoeuvres and calculations. (emphasis in original)

Similar processes are also evident in the United Kingdom—more particularly England and Wales.[1] Since 1997, for example, successive New Labour governments have legislated on more than fifty occasions in the criminal justice sphere and have created more than 3,000 new offences (Morris 2006). In a high-profile lecture—'Our Nation's Future'—the Prime Minister, Tony Blair (2006), boasted: 'prison sentences are longer . . . more people are in prison, prison places have expanded by 19,000 since 1997 and are due to expand still further.' Expressed as a rate per 100,000 of the national population, the prison population in England and Wales is the highest among countries of the European Union (Home Office 2003). Spending on prisons has increased by more than 35 per cent in real terms since 1997 (Home Office 2006: para. 3.42) and the pattern of penal expansion is scheduled to continue. A further 900 prison places will 'come on stream in autumn 2007'—taking total penal capacity to 80,400 in England and Wales—and the New Labour government plans to 'build an additional 8,000 places and keep under close review whether more are needed' (Home Office 2006: para 3.43). Meanwhile, statistical projections—based on the implications of current policy initiatives and assumptions about future sentencing trends—suggest that 'more' will indeed be 'needed.' By 2013, it is estimated that the total prison population in England and Wales will be as high as 106,550 (de Silva et al. 2006).

Statistical trends with regard to the imprisonment of children in the United States and in England and Wales follow similar upward trajectories. The number of child prisoners in the United States increased by forty-eight per cent between 1993 and 1999, for example (Annie E. Casey Foundation 2003). Since 1993 in England and Wales, the number of fifteen- through seventeen-year-old prisoners has increased by ninety per cent; there has been a 142 per cent increase in child remand prisoners, a 400 per cent increase in the numbers of girls in prison and an 800 per cent increase in the number of child prisoners aged fourteen and under (Goldson 2006b; Nacro 2005). Not unlike the general pattern of penal expansion, the incarceration of increasing numbers of children bears no direct relation to actual juvenile crime rates (Bateman 2006). Rather, the power to punish is exploited in order to serve broader political imperatives (Tonry 2004) and the abusive violation of children in conflict with the law is the inevitable consequence, the collateral damage, of such cynical machinations.

Neglect and Immiseration

Child poverty is entrenched, spatially uneven (Oppenheim 2007) and racialised (Palmer and Kenway 2007; Platt 2007) in the United Kingdom. When account is taken of key measures of 'well-being'—including material well-being, health and safety, education, peer and family relationships—children in the United Kingdom are more disadvantaged than their counterparts in any of the 21 Organisation for Economic Co-operations and Development (OECD) countries surveyed by Unicef (2007). It might be argued that widespread child poverty in an otherwise 'rich nation' itself comprises a material manifestation of violence. The overwhelmingly disproportionate presence of poor children within institutions in general, and penal institutions in particular, only serves to compound such violation.

Indeed, child prisoners are routinely drawn from some of the most structurally disadvantaged families, neighbourhoods and communities. Children for whom the fabric of life invariably stretches across poverty, family discord, state welfare, inadequate housing, circumscribed educational and employment opportunities, and the most pressing sense of personal distress are the very children to be found in penal institutions in England and Wales, as elsewhere (Challen and Walton 2004; Children's Rights Alliance for England 2002; Commission for Social Care Inspectorate et al. 2005; Goldson and Coles 2005; Worsley 2007). When the biographies of child prisoners are analysed, 'it is evident that on any count this is a significantly deprived, excluded, and abused population of children' (Association of Directors of Social Services et al. 2003: 6)

Class-specific, racialised and gendered processes of state neglect and immiseration (Goldson et al. 2002) and criminalisation and punishment (Gelsthorpe and Sharpe 2006; Webster 2006; White and Cunneen 2006) combine. Children in conflict with the law are, in short, routinely abused in the infrastructure of everyday life. It follows that child prisoners are both inherently and structurally vulnerable, a fact that is officially recognised and acknowledged by the Youth Justice Board (YJB)[2] and Government ministers. The YJB's 'Head of Placements,' for example, has noted that 'every day, up to 70 children and young people [entering penal institutions in England and Wales] are identified as vulnerable' (Minchin 2005: 2). Furthermore, in response to a question raised in Parliament, Gerry Sutcliffe, Under Secretary of State for Criminal Justice and Offender Management, has reported that in the month of February 2007 alone, 1,148 child prisoners were officially designated as 'vulnerable' in state penal institutions in England and Wales (Sutcliffe 2007).

Violence, Harm and Death

In England and Wales, children in conflict with the law can be incarcerated in any one of three types of institution: Young Offender Institutions (state and private prisons), Secure Training Centres (private jails owned and managed by global security corporations) and Secure Children's Homes (provided by Local Government Authorities and the private sector) (for a fuller discussion, see Goldson 2006c: 54–55). Approximately eighty-five per cent of child prisoners are detained in Young Offender Institutions. The institutionalisation of children with multiple needs and complex vulnerabilities in prisons is an intrinsically violent act. When account is taken of the basic facts, the inadequate nature of such institutions becomes absolutely transparent. The staff–child ratio in such institutions is typically four to sixty (Bennett 2005: para. 51). As a consequence of the 'substantial increase' of children being incarcerated in England and Wales, the YJB (2006a) is 'taking a number of steps including . . . compulsory cell sharing . . . in single cells that can be legitimately converted . . . and, working with the Prison Service, to bring back into service as quickly as possible cells that are currently out of commission.' Prison officers have no professional training to equip them to work with child prisoners and, at best, 'juvenile awareness' training for such staff lasts no longer than seven days and 'some establishments are finding it difficult to release staff even for this short period' (Her Majesty's Chief Inspector of Prisons 2006: 57).

As stated, the international evidence reveals that children in custodial institutions are particularly prone to violence and harm. The conditions and treatment typically endured by child prisoners in England and Wales confirm this. Her Majesty's Chief Inspector of Prisons (2006: 56) concedes that 'bullying remains a problem in most establishments.' Indeed, the world of the child prison (not unlike the adult prison) is sharply stratified, organised in accordance with informal pecking orders and hierarchies of power, control and intimidation. Child-on-child and staff-on-child bullying is systemic. Moreover, stratification is both complex and fluid, creating a permanent sense of insecurity and uncertainty. The most obvious expression of bullying is physical violence, much of which goes unreported—thus unrecorded—owing to the intense antipathy to the practice of 'grassing' within 'inmate' culture, and worse still the consequences of being labelled a 'grass.' Child prisoners are also exposed to many other forms of 'bullying,' however, including: sexual violence; verbal violence (name-calling, threats, racist, sexist and homophobic taunting); psychological violence; extortion and theft; and lending and trading cultures—particularly in relation to tobacco—involving exorbitant rates of interest that accumulate on a daily basis (Goldson 2002b; Medlicott 2001). Children's emotional, psychological and/or physical integrity is routinely violated in custodial institutions in England and Wales.

Moreover, institutionalised and officially sanctioned practices within child prisons in England and Wales, as elsewhere, frequently assume violent and harmful forms. Her Majesty's Chief Inspector of Prisons (2007: 41) has reported that: 'injuries sustained during restraint are often the highest single category of child protection referrals in an establishment; but few properly monitor the injuries that arise from the use of force.' Indeed, such approved 'control' techniques would almost certainly be described as child abuse in any other context. Thus, in 'setting the record straight,' a YJB 'Secure Development Manager' describes 'distraction techniques' as modes of intervention 'inflicting a short, sharp burst of pain or discomfort on a young person,' and 'nose distraction' as involving 'a member of staff passing his or her hand over the young person's head and, placing the index finger underneath the nose, applying smooth pressure upwards and backwards' (Reilly 2005: 6).

Prison Service statistics provided by the YJB to an inquiry chaired by Lord Carlile of Berriew, indicate that 5,133 'restraint' interventions were recorded in child prisons in England and Wales during the period January 2004 to September 2005 (Carlile 2006: para. 84). Furthermore, responses to Parliamentary Questions have revealed that 'restraint' was administered on 11,593 occasions in the four private child jails (Secure Training Centres) between January 1999 and June 2004 (ibid: paras. 100–101). In 2002, Beverley Hughes, Home Office Minister at the time, reported that between April 2000 and February 2002, 296 children sustained injuries resulting from 'restraint' in prisons, and in September 2004, Hilton Dawson MP, stated that there had been 200 injuries to child prisoners following 'restraint' in an eleven-month period (ibid: para. 118).

In addition to 'restraint,' the officially sanctioned practices of strip searching—'sometimes carried out by force' (Her Majesty's Chief Inspector of Prisons 2007: 41)—placing children in segregation (solitary confinement) and denying children sufficient access to exercise and fresh air are also deeply problematic. The 'Carlile Inquiry' was told that child prisoners were routinely required to submit to a full strip search during their 'reception' to prison: 'this meant that one of the very first experiences for a child going into a prison was to be asked to strip and reveal their body to an unknown adult' (Carlile 2006: para 154). Strip searching takes at least two forms: upper-body cavity searches whereby prison officers check the child's ears, nose and mouth, and lower-body cavity searches for which children are required to 'bend over or squat' (ibid: paras. 155–56). Her Majesty's Chief Inspector of Prisons has pondered:

> What is the rationale or the proportionality of routinely strip-searching children on arrival in prison, particularly for a population more

likely than average to have experienced abuse? And if the child resists, can you justify him or her being held down by adults, in painful wrist-locks, and forcibly undressed. (cited in Carlile 2006: para. 149)

Notwithstanding such concern, however, statistics from one Young Offender Institution alone, reveal that during the period January 2004 to June 2005, 3,379 strip searches were conducted on children immediately following their arrival at the prison (ibid, para. 158).

In the same way that euphemism is employed to describe processes of forceful physical intervention as 'distraction' and 'restraint,' most child prisons have 'renamed their segregation units, for example, as "care and separation" units' (Her Majesty's Chief Inspector of Prisons 2006: 56). The 'Carlile Inquiry' (2006: para. 188) also discovered that the terms 'Intensive Supervision Unit' and 'Reorientation Unit' were used to describe cells reserved for the segregation and solitary confinement of children, prisons within prisons where children can be held 'for days and even weeks at a time' (ibid: para. 207). Finally, at least for the purposes here, Her Majesty's Chief Inspector of Prisons (2007: 43) has observed that: 'access to exercise in the fresh air remains a major concern. In our survey, only around half the girls and a quarter of the boys said they were able to exercise every day, and in one establishment, none said they were able to do so.'

For all child prisoners, the combination of: their complex structural and inherent vulnerabilities; their daily experience of bullying; the officially approved practices of 'restraint,' strip searching and segregation and the abusive limits that are imposed upon exercise and access to fresh air perpetuate insecurity, fear and harm (Goldson 2002b). For some such prisoners, the cumulative violence is too much to bear. Self-harm is not uncommon and in a period of just eleven months there were 1,324 reported incidents by children in Young Offender Institutions in England and Wales (Her Majesty's Chief Inspector of Prisons 2006: 16). The pain of confinement is relieved only on release. For other child prisoners, 'release' takes a fatal form. Between July 1990 and September 2005, twenty-nine children died in penal custody in England and Wales, twenty-seven in state prisons and two in private jails (Goldson and Coles 2005).

THE POLITICS OF IMPUNITY

On one level, state agencies 'acknowledge' the abusive capacities of institutions, the high rate of child incarceration in England and Wales, widespread child impoverishment and structural disadvantage, the harmful and violent rhythm of penal regimes and, ultimately, the loss of twenty-nine children's lives. Numerous authoritative research reports, statutory inspections, academic articles and books, campaign initiatives, televised documentaries, radio broadcasts and journalistic pieces have profiled such phenomena

and, in this sense, it would be absurd to feign ignorance. But 'acknowledgement,' such as it is, is conditioned and filtered. The bald 'facts' of the
violations, abuses, harms and, ultimately, deaths, are registered, but the
wider contexts in which they are located, their true meanings and their
full implications are obfuscated. To paraphrase Cohen (2001: xii), they are
not fully 'digested,' they have 'sunk into consciousness without producing shifts in policy or public opinion,' without fundamentally destabilis-
ing the claimed legitimacy of child incarceration, without holding those
responsible to account. In a deeper sense, therefore, the violence is *denied*
(Goldson 2006c). Convenient rationalisations blur 'truth' and provide for
impunity, either consciously or unconsciously, via four intersecting and
mutually reinforcing processes, characterised here as: 'othering,' 'veiling,'
'euphemism' and 'circumscription.'

Othering

'Othering' processes underpin both *demonising* (the child as a dangerous
threat), and *pathologising* (the child as a pathetic victim) constructions of
children in conflict with the law. Paradoxically, each serves to excuse and/or
rationalise the violence of incarceration. Young (1999: 110) recalls that:

> Demonization is important in that it allows the problems of society to
> be blamed upon 'others.' . . . Here the customary inversion of causal
> reality occurs: instead of acknowledging that we have problems in
> society because of basic core contradictions in the social order, it is
> claimed that all the problems of society are because of the problems
> themselves. Get rid of the problems and society would be, *ipso facto*,
> problem free!

Essentialised 'othering' and demonisation thus provides for modes of symbolic reconstruction: from 'children *with* problems' to 'children *as* problems.' It invokes the classic 'deserving–undeserving' formulation. Child
prisoners may well be dredged from the deepest reservoirs of structural
neglect and institutionalised immiseration, but it is their 'offender' status
that is emphasised. Constructions of moral transgression effectively displace the significance of material context and the 'customary inversion of
causal reality occurs.' Children in conflict with the law are thus essentialised as the 'undeserving,' the 'threatening,' the 'bad.' Moreover, the very
terms 'child,' 'children' and 'childhood' are studiously avoided. 'Inmates,'
'prisoners,' 'trainees,' 'criminals,' 'lawbreakers,' 'offenders,' 'thugs' and
'yobs' are the preferred descriptors. In this way, 'othering' effectively neutralises sensitivity to the harm that penal custody imposes; it distorts and
undermines sensitivity to children's suffering and pain. If child prisoners
are routinely presented and conceptualised as a strata of the 'undeserving,'
if they are subjected to 'conceptual eviction' and 'removed from the category

of "child" altogether' (Jenks 1996: 128), then the treatment and conditions to which they are exposed are more readily conceived as legitimate modes of corrective intervention as distinct from state-sanctioned violence and institutionalised child abuse.

Alternatively, othering discourses are applied in forms that emphasise constructions of individual pathology: 'emotional fragility'; 'mental distress'; 'psychological instability'; 'failure to cope'; 'weakness' and 'inadequacy.' Such conceptualisations ultimately imply that incarcerated children are, at least in part, 'responsible' for their own suffering. Moreover, the same emphases serve not only to deflect attention from state responsibility and accountability (the excessive reliance on incarceration and the violent nature of penal regimes for children in England and Wales), but they also negate institutional culpability and obscure the physical, emotional and psychological violence intrinsic to child imprisonment. Critical analyses of policy and/or any consideration of the wider social, structural, material and institutional arrangements that define child prisoners' lived realities are peripheralised. This provides, in short, a deliberately limited 'way of seeing,' an insidious form of denial.

Veiling

The coexistence of the 'new punitiveness' (Goldson 2002a) and an obsession with the concept of 'safer custody' comprise an apparent contradiction within contemporary youth justice policy in England and Wales. The reform agenda grinds itself out through a seemingly infinite corpus of: intra- and inter-agency reconfigurations; strategy documents; aspirational statements; official circulars; performance targets; inspections; audits; and operational policies, procedures and practices. Recent illustrative 'highlights' include: a Ministerial 'Roundtable' on 'Suicide in Prisons'; the establishment of a Prison Service 'Safer Custody Group' to operationalise a 'Safer Custody Strategy'; revised versions of Prison Service Order 2700 ('Suicide and Self-Harm Prevention') and Prison Service Order 4950 ('Regimes for Under 18 Year Olds'); the development of 'violence reduction strategies' to counter inter-prisoner violence (particularly bullying); the appointment of 'Suicide Prevention Coordinators' in prisons; the creation of special projects to develop 'safer' prison design (including 'safer cells'); the introduction of practices and procedures to improve pre-reception, reception and induction processes in prisons (including health care and 'vulnerability' screening); the development of policies to facilitate more effective systems of intra-agency and inter-agency communication and information exchange; the establishment of refined allocation processes and 'placement' strategies located within a 'comprehensive performance monitoring framework'; and the implementation of more rigorous 'risk assessment' and 'child protection' policies, practices and procedures.[3]

Most recently, social workers have been deployed within prisons, 'safeguarding' arrangements have been applied linking child prisons with 'local safeguarding children boards' and provisions of the Children Act 2004 have imposed statutory responsibilities upon prison governors, to 'safeguard and promote the welfare' of child prisoners (Her Majesty's Chief Inspector of Prisons 2007: 40). More specifically, with regard to the question of deaths in penal custody, the Government has prepared an exceptionally detailed 'comprehensive update on the continuing work being undertaken to reduce the number of deaths in custody,' in which it claims 'substantial progress in a number of key areas' (House of Lords House of Commons Joint Committee on Human Rights 2007: 7).

The primary logic of 'safer custody' reform implies that corrosive penal regimes can be 'humanised'; the conditions that give rise to harm and even death can be 'designed out.' Ultimately, however, this serves to veil the underlying and historically constant violence of child incarceration and, in the final analysis, as Miller (1991: 18) has observed, there is no evidence to suggest that the innumerable policies, practices and procedures claiming to provide 'safe' institutional environments for child prisoners have ever succeeded or can ever succeed:

> Reformers come and reformers go. State institutions carry on. Nothing in their history suggests that they can sustain reform, no matter what money, staff, and programs are pumped into them. The same crises that have plagued them for 150 years intrude today. Though the casts may change, the players go on producing failure.

In reality, the concept of 'safer custody' or the 'caring prison' (Prisons and Probation Ombudsman 2004, Ev. 68) remains a contradiction in terms for child prisoners. At best, the reforming impulse amounts to the blind faith of good intention. At worst, it represents denial, a cynical means of veiling the violence of incarceration, a mechanism for imputing 'respectability' and sustaining a culture of impunity.

Euphemism

Christie (1981: 14) acknowledges that there are often 'kind thoughts behind kind words,' but he also problematises discourses that sanitise the practice of incarceration. He argues that euphemistic articulation—'innocent somnambulistic insulation'—renders prisons 'clean' and 'hygienic,' it denies human suffering, violence and harm. Following Christie, Cohen (1985: 276) explains how 'special vocabularies' are mobilised to 'soften and disguise the essential (and defining) feature of punishment systems—the planned infliction of pain.' With regard to contemporary practices of child incarceration in England and Wales, such euphemistic 'vocabularies' are mobilised in order to construct positive representations, both of the penal estate itself *and* the specific regimes and practices of custodial institutions.

In this way, Stern (1998: 157) notes that:

> ... prisons for children and young people are given a variety of names . . . the names are intended to show that these are not prisons, but places of good intent, where the previous bad influences of the young people's lives will be corrected by caring people.

Thus, the 'juvenile secure estate' is the preferred euphemism for describing the child prison system in England and Wales. Moreover, penal regimes and practices are presented as 'safe and effective' (Youth Justice Board 2006b: 33), and strategies for 'managing' the behaviour of prisoners are located within a 'child-centred culture' (Youth Justice Board 2006c: 1). Providing a 'calm, ordered and respectful living environment' (ibid: 7) is the claimed objective and, should it become necessary, disruptive child prisoners can be 'removed from normal location' and placed instead in 'intensive supervision units,' 'reorientation units' or 'care and separation units' (Carlile 2006: para 188; Her Majesty's Chief Inspector of Prisons 2006: 56).

Such euphemism is employed, to borrow the words of Orwell (1954: 245), 'not so much to express meanings as to destroy them.' It serves an anaesthetic function whereby practices that have resulted in 'allegations of abuse or rough handling' and have caused 'serious concern' for Her Majesty's Chief Inspector of Prisons (2006: 56) are packaged as 'caring' forms of 'restraint.' It masks and conceals inhumane practices whereby cells reserved for segregation and solitary confinement are described in terms of 'care' and 'supervision.' It denies truth in such a way that the ill-treatment of a child—stripped naked with the exception of a heavy canvas gown and locked in a concrete bunker under the fixed gaze of a surveillance camera—can be described as a benign placement in a 'safe cell' (Goldson and Coles 2005: 61–64).

Circumscription

Circumscription is particularly evident following a child's death in penal custody in England and Wales. In cases where the police are satisfied that there are no grounds for prosecution (including self-inflicted deaths), at least two separate but related processes are conventionally activated. First, an *investigation* into the specific circumstances surrounding the child's death in the penal institution will take place. Second, the Coroner's Court (covering the geographical area within which the child's body is finally located) will be notified, and the Coroner will preside over an *inquest*. Official representations of such processes imply that they facilitate detailed scrutiny. In reality, however, the statutory institutional framework within which post-death inquiry is located is seriously circumscribed. Paradoxically, investigations and inquests represent the 'political absence of an inquiring mind'

(Cohen 2001: 139); they provide the institutional apparatus through which impunity is guaranteed and perpetuated.

With regard to investigations, and despite recent reforms, the disclosure of information remains conditional and the Prisons and Probation Ombudsman's investigatory function is exercised on a non-statutory basis. The office has no power to compel the production of evidence. Inquests too have also been subject to recent reform, but they remain seriously limited in scope. The findings and recommendations reached by coroners and their juries following inquests into child deaths in penal custody are not published. As such, they cannot be systematically analysed, monitored or followed-up. In practice, investigations and inquests sustain a culture of defensiveness and institutional protection. They effectively comprise 'a board game with a limited number of fixed moves,' a legal process that 'depicts a wholly non-pictorial world' (Cohen 2001: 108).[4]

CONCLUSION: ACCOUNTABILITY AND ABOLITION

Informed global estimates suggest that 8 million children are held in institutions and, at any given time, 1 million children are incarcerated in penal custody across the world. Historical and contemporary international evidence reveals that children in institutions per se, and particularly those detained in penal facilities, are especially vulnerable to violence and abuse. This is not a phenomenon that 'belongs' exclusively to the 'majority poor world.' Indeed, it is present throughout 'advanced' industrialised democracies in the 'rich world.' By critically examining child incarceration in the United States and, more particularly still, England and Wales, this chapter has addressed institutional(ised) violence and the abuse of state power. There are good reasons to focus upon the Anglo-American context, not least because it comprises one of the world's most concentrated sites of incarceration. The tensions between international human rights obligations and the wanton violation of children are self-evident and are matters of official record.

Indeed, authoritative international human rights agencies have repeatedly expressed and recorded concerns about state policy and practice towards children in conflict with the law in England and Wales. For example, in January 1995, the United Nations Committee on the Rights of the Child reported serious violations of children's rights:

> Policy after policy 'has broken the terms of the UN Convention' . . . a report of the UN monitoring committee adds up to a devastating indictment of ministers' failure to meet the human rights of Britain's children . . . the report is not all bad . . . however, the 'positive aspects' cover only four paragraphs, and the remaining 39 are either critical or are recommendations for action [which include] . . . abandoning the plans for secure training centres for 12–14 year olds . . .

it also explicitly calls for 'serious consideration' to be given to raising the age of criminal responsibility. (*The Guardian*: 28 January 1995)

Such 'recommendations for action' were studiously ignored, however, and, when the UN Committee next formally reported the United Kingdom government's violation of international human rights standards, it drew specific attention to incarcerated children:

> ... [M]ore generally, the Committee is deeply concerned at the high increasing numbers of children in custody. . . . The Committee is also extremely concerned at the conditions that children experience in detention . . . and that children do not receive adequate protection or help . . . noting the very poor staff-child ratio, high levels of violence, bullying, self harm and suicide. (United Nations Committee on the Rights of the Child 2002: para. 57)

Equally, when the Council of Europe's Commissioner for Human Rights reviewed the circumstances of children in prison in England and Wales in 2005, he could only conclude that: 'the prison service is failing in its duty of care towards juvenile inmates' (Office for the Commissioner for Human Rights 2005: para 93). The United Kingdom government has not only failed to act on such international concern, but it has also compounded the problems further by intensifying and expanding child incarceration necessitating 'compulsory cell sharing . . . in single cells [and] bringing back into service as quickly as possible cells that are currently out of commission' (Youth Justice Board 2006a).

If the culture of impunity that surrounds the violation of children in penal institutions is to be disturbed, if—to recall Kofi Annan's words—the 'underlying causes [of abuse] are [to be] identified and addressed' in order to 'prevent' further 'violence against children,' then those responsible must be held to account. A starting point might involve the establishment of a comprehensive and fully independent commission of inquiry into child incarceration in England and Wales (Goldson and Coles 2005). To date, the United Kingdom Government has steadfastly opposed this proposition but, paradoxically, the United States might provide an unconventionally progressive example to its United Kingdom 'partner in crime.'

'The Commission on Safety and Abuse in America's Prisons' was formed, comprising 'respected civil leaders, experienced corrections administrators, scholars, advocates for the rights of prisoners, members of the religious community, and former prisoners' (Gibbons and Katzenbach 2006: 6). It commenced its inquiry in March 2005, a time when the prison population was well in excess of 2 million and 'there were accumulating doubts about the effectiveness and morality of [the prevailing] approach to confinement' (ibid: 8). The Commission's report was published in June 2006, and it exposes the violence of incarceration in stark forms. The report concludes:

'[T]his is the moment to confront confinement in the United States' (ibid: 17). A similar 'moment' has surely also dawned in England and Wales.

Politicians and state policymakers are not obliged to incarcerate record numbers of children in penal custody, exposing them to the violence discussed in this chapter and, indeed, throughout this book. They *choose* to do so. Moreover, they exercise this choice in the knowledge that child incarceration is irrational and spectacularly counter-productive when measured in terms of crime prevention and community safety and that it 'succeeds' only in imposing harm and, ultimately, death. Any truly independent commission of inquiry into child incarceration in England and Wales would, therefore, be obliged to seriously engage with the abolition of *all* prison service and private sector custodial institutions, and to consider retaining only the absolute minimum use of Secure Children's Homes for children whose behaviour places themselves and/or others at *demonstrable serious risk*. In the small number of cases where children might have their liberty restricted 'as a measure of last resort and for the shortest appropriate period of time' (UNCRC: Article 37b), the Commission would need to ensure that the full weight of all relevant international human rights standards, treaties, rules, conventions and safeguards apply as minimum and non-negotiable standards. Until such time, the state will continue to abuse its power to punish and violate children with impunity.

DEDICATION

This chapter is dedicated to the memory of Gurpreet Singh Mundy (Gilly), whose determination to confront and challenge state violence was inspirational and whose tireless pursuit of truth and justice was immense.

NOTES

1. The United Kingdom comprises three separate jurisdictions: England and Wales, Northern Ireland and Scotland. The complex origins and contested political histories of each of the jurisdictions are beyond the remit of this chapter. The emphasis is placed upon England and Wales where patterns of penal expansion are substantially greater than in the other two jurisdictions. This should not be taken to imply that penal politics, policy and practice and/or the conditions endured by child prisoners is unproblematic in either Northern Ireland (see for example, Davey et al., 2004; Kilkelly et al., 2002; Scraton and Moore, 2005) or in Scotland (see for example, McAra, 2006; Scraton and Chadwick, 1986; Whyte, 2003), however.
2. The YJB is the state agency vested with responsibility for 'placing' children in penal institutions once they have been remanded or sentenced to custody by the courts in England and Wales.
3. For a more detailed discussion and critical assessment of such reforms, see Goldson 2002b: 74–83 and Goldson and Coles 2005: 50–61.
4. A detailed critical analysis of investigations and inquests relating to child deaths in penal custody is provided in Goldson and Coles, 2005: 67–94. For

more general critique of the inquest process see: Liberty, 2003; Scraton, 1999; Scraton and Chadwick, 1987; Scraton et al., 1995; Thomas et al., 2002.

REFERENCES

Annan, K. (2006) 'Preface,' in P. S. Pinheiro *World Report on Violence Against Children*, Geneva: United Nations, pxi.

Annie E. Casey Foundation (2003) *Advocasey: Juvenile Justice at a Crossroads*, vol 5, no 1 Spring, Baltimore: Annie E Casey Foundation.

———. (2004) *Kids Count Data Book: Moving Youth From Risk to Opportunity*, Baltimore: Annie E Casey Foundation.

Association of Directors of Social Services, Local Government Association, Youth Justice Board for England and Wales (2003) *The Application of the Children Act (1989) to Children in Young Offender Institutions*, London: ADSS, LGA and YJB.

Bateman, T. (2006) 'Youth Crime and Justice: Statistical "Evidence," Recent Trends and Responses,' in B. Goldson and J. Muncie (eds.) *Youth Crime and Justice: Critical Issues*, London: Sage, pp. 65–77.

Bennett, The Honourable Mr Justice (2005) *Judgment Approved by the Court for Handing Down in R (on the application of Mrs Yvonne Scholes) v. The Secretary of State for the Home Department*, 30 November and 1 December, London: Royal Courts of Justice.

Blair, T. (2006) 'Our Nation's Future: Criminal Justice System,' Lecture presented at the University of Bristol, 23 June 2006. http://www.number10.gov.uk/output/Page9902.asp, visited on 13 August 2006.

Carlile, Lord. (2006) *The Lord Carlile of Berriew QC: An independent inquiry into the use of physical restraint, solitary confinement and forcible strip searching of children in prisons, secure training centres and local authority secure children's homes*, London: The Howard League for Penal Reform.

Carter, R. (2005) *Family Matters: A Study of Institutional Childcare in Central and Eastern Europe and the Former Soviet Union*, London: EveryChild.

Challen, M. and Walton, T. (2004) *Juveniles in Custody*, London: Her Majesty's Inspectorate of Prisons.

Children's Rights Alliance for England (2002) *Rethinking Child Iimprisonment: A Report on Young OffenderInstitutions*, London: Children's Rights Alliance for England.

Children's Rights Development Unit (1994) *The UK Agenda for Children*, London: Children's Rights Development Unit.

Christie, N. (1981) *Limits to Pain*, Oxford: Martin Robertson.

Cohen, S. (1985) *Visions of Social Control*, Cambridge: Polity.

———. (2001) *States of Denial: Knowing About Atrocities and Suffering*, Cambridge: Polity.

Commission for Social Care Inspectorate, The Healthcare Commission, Her Majesty's Inspectorate of Constabulary, Her Majesty's Inspectorate of Probation, Her Majesty's Inspectorate of Prisons, Her Majesty's Crown Prosecution Service Inspectorate, Her Majesty's Inspectorate of Courts Administration, The Office of Standards in Education (2005) *Safeguarding Children: The Second Joint Chief Inspectors' Report on Arrangements to Safeguard Children*, London: Department of Health Publications.

Davey, C., Dwyer, C., McAlister, S., Kilkelly, U., Kilpatrick, R., Lundy, L., Moore, L. and Scraton, P. (2004) *Children's Rights in Northern Ireland*. Belfast: Northern Ireland Commissioner for Children and Young People.

de Silva, N., Cowell, P., Chow, T. and Worthington, P. (2006) *Prison Population Projections 2006–2013*, England and Wales. London: Home Office.

Garland, D. (2001a) 'Introduction: The Meaning of Mass Imprisonment,' *Punishment and Society*, vol 3, no1, pp.5–7.

———. (2001b) 'Epilogue: The New Iron Cage,' *Punishment and Society*, vol 3, no 1, pp.197–199.

———. (2001c) *The Culture of Control: Crime and Social Order in Contemporary Society*, Oxford, Oxford University Press.

Gelsthorpe, L. and Sharpe, G. (2006) 'Gender, Youth Crime and Justice,' in B. Goldson and J. Muncie (eds.) *Youth Crime and Justice: Critical Issues*, London: Sage, pp. 47–61.

Gibbons, J. J. and Katzenbach, N. (2006) *Confronting Confinement: A Report of the Commission on Safety and Abuse in America's Prisons*, New York: Vera Institute of Justice.

Goldson, B. (2002a) 'New Punitiveness: The Politics of Child Incarceration,' in J. Muncie, G. Hughes and E. McLaughlin (eds) *Youth Justice: Critical Readings*, London: Sage, pp. 386–400.

———. (2002b) *Vulnerable Inside: Children in Secure and Penal Settings*, London: The Children's Society.

———. (2004) 'Victims or Threats? Children, Care and Control,' in J. Fink (ed) *Care: Personal Lives and Social Policy*. Bristol: The Policy Press in association with the Open University, pp. 77–109.

———. (2006a) 'Penal Custody: Intolerance, Irrationality and Indifference,' in B. Goldson and J. Muncie (eds) *Youth Crime and Justice: Critical Issues*, London: Sage, pp. 139–156.

———. (2006b) 'Damage, Harm and Death in Child Prisons in England and Wales: Questions of Abuse and Accountability,' *The Howard Journal of Criminal Justice*, vol 45, no 5, pp.449–467.

———. (2006c) 'Fatal Injustice: Rampant Punitiveness, Child Prisoner Deaths, and Institutionalised Denial—A Case for Comprehensive Independent Inquiry in England and Wales,' *Social Justice,* vol 33, no 4, pp.52–68.

Goldson, B. and Coles, D. (2005) *In the Care of the State? Child Deaths in Penal Custody*, London: Inquest.

Goldson, B., Lavalette, M. and McKechnie, J. (eds.) (2002) *Children, Welfare and the State*, London: Sage.

Her Majesty's Chief Inspector of Prisons (2006) *Annual Report of HM Chief Inspector of Prisons for England and Wales*, 2004–2005, London: The Stationery Office.

Her Majesty's Chief Inspector of Prisons (2007) *Annual Report 2005/06*, London: The Stationery Office.

Herivel, T. and Wright, P. (eds) (2003) *Prison Nation: The Warehousing of America's Poor.* New York: Routledge.

Home Office (2003) *World Prison Population List*, Findings 234. London: Home Office.

———. (2006) *Rebalancing the Criminal Justice System in Favour of the Law-Abiding Majority: Cutting Crime, Reducing Reoffending and Protecting the Public.* London: Home Office.

House of Lords House of Commons Joint Committee on Human Rights (2007) *Deaths in Custody: Further Developments*, Seventh Report of Session 2006–07, London: The Stationery Office.

International Save the Children Alliance (2003) *A Last Resort: The Growing Concern About Children in Residential Care*, London: Save the Children.

Jenks, C. (1996) *Childhood*, London: Routledge.

Kilkelly, U., Moore, L., and Convery, U. (2002) *In Our Care: Promoting the Rights of Children in Custody.* Belfast: Northern Ireland Human Rights Commission.

Liberty. (2003) *Deaths in Custody: Redress and Remedies*, London: The Civil Liberties Trust.

McAra, L. (2006) 'Welfare in Crisis? Key Developments in Scottish Youth Justice,' in J. Muncie and B. Goldson (eds) *Comparative Youth Justice: Critical Issues.* London: Sage, pp. 127–145.

Medlicott, D. (2001) *Surviving the Prison Place: Narratives of Suicidal Prisoners*, Aldershot: Ashgate.

Miller, J. (1991) *Last One Over the Wall: The Massachusetts Experiment in Closing Reform Schools*, Ohio: Ohio State University Press.

Miller, J. (2001) 'Bringing the Individual Back in: A Commentary on Wacquant and Anderson,' *Punishment and Society*, vol 3, no 1, pp.153–160.

Minchin, P. (2005) 'Placing Children and Young People,' in Youth Justice Board, *Secure Estate Bulletin*, October, London: Youth Justice Board for England and Wales, p. 2.

Morris, N. (2006) 'Blair's "Frenzied Law Making": A New Offence for Every Day Spent in Office,' *The Independent*, 16 August.

Muncie, J. (2005) 'The Globalization of Crime Control—The Case of Youth and Juvenile Justice: Neoliberalism, Policy Convergence and International Conventions,' *Theoretical Criminology*, vol 9, no 2, pp.35–64.

Muncie, J. and Goldson, B. (eds) (2006) *Comparative Youth Justice: Critical Issues.* London: Sage.

Nacro (2005) *A Better Alternative: Reducing Child Imprisonment*, London: Nacro.

NGO Advisory Panel for the United Nations Secretary-General's Study on Violence Against Children (2005) *Violence Against Children in Conflict with the Law: A Thematic Consultation*, Geneva: United Nations.

Office for the Commissioner for Human Rights (2005) *Report by Mr Alvaro Gil-Robles, Commissioner for Human Rights, on His Visit to the United Kingdom 4–12 November 2004*, Strasbourg: Council of Europe.

Oppenheim, C. (2007) 'Child poverty in London,' *Poverty: Journal of the Child Poverty Action Group*, vol 126, pp.15–17.

Orwell, G. (1954) *Nineteen Eighty Four*, London: Penguin.

Palmer, G. and Kenway, P. (2007) *Poverty Among Ethnic Groups: How and Why Does It Differ*, York: Joseph Rowntree Foundation.

Parenti, C. (1999) *Lockdown America: Police and Prisons in the Age of Crisis.* London and New York: Verso.

Pilger, J. (1992) *A Secret Country*, London: Vintage.

Pilkington, D. (2002) *Rabbit-proof Fence*, New York: Miramax Books.

Pinheiro, P. S. (2005) 'Opening Remarks from Paulo Sergio Pinheiro,' in NGO Advisory Panel for the United Nations Secretary-General's Study on Violence Against Children *Violence Against Children in Conflict with the Law: A Thematic Consultation*, Geneva: United Nations, pp. 18–19.

———. (2006) *World Report on Violence Against Children*, Geneva: United Nations.

Platt, L. (2007) *Poverty and Ethnicity in the UK*, Bristol: Policy Press.

Pratt, J., Brown, D., Brown, M., Hallsworth, S. and Morrison, W. (eds) (2005) *The New Punitiveness: Trends, Theories, Perspectives*, Cullompton: Willan.

Prisons and Probation Ombudsman for England and Wales (2004) 'Memorandum From Prisons and Probation Ombudsman for England and Wales,' House of Lords House of Commons Joint Committee on Human Rights, *Deaths in Custody Interim Report*, First Report of Session 2003–04, London: The Stationery Office.

Reilly, G. (2005) 'PCC: the facts,' in Youth Justice Board, *Secure Estate Bulletin*, November, London: Youth Justice Board for England and Wales.

Scraton, P. (1999) *Hillsborough: The Truth*, Edinburgh: Mainstream Publishing.

Scraton, P. and Chadwick, K. (1986) '"The Experiment that Went Wrong": The Crisis of Death in Youth Custody at the Glenochil Complex,' in B. Rolston, and M. Tomlinson (eds.) *The Expansion of European Prison Systems: Working Papers in European Criminology No. 7.* Belfast: European Group for the Study of Deviance and Social Control, pp. 145–161.

———. (1987) *In the Arms of the Law: Coroners' Inquests and Deaths in Custody*, London: Pluto.

Scraton, P., Jemphrey, A. and Coleman, S. (1995) *No Last Rights: The Denial of Justice and the Promotion of Myth in the Aftermath of the Hillsborough Disaster*, Liverpool: Liverpool City Council/Alden Press.

Scraton, P. and Moore, L. (2005) *The Hurt Inside: The Imprisonment of Women and Girls in Northern Ireland*. Belfast: Northern Ireland Human Rights Commission.

Simon, J. (2000) 'The "Society of Captives" in the Era of Hyper-incarceration,' *Theoretical Criminology*, vol 4, no 3, pp.285–308.

Stern, V. (1998) *A Sin Against the Future: Imprisonment in the World*, London: Penguin.

Sutcliffe, G. (2007) *Hansard, House of Commons, Column 1652W*, 28 March.

Ten Bensel, R., Rheinberger, M. and Radbill, S. (1997) 'Children in a world of violence: The roots of child maltreatment,' in R.E. Helfer, R. Kempe and D. Krugman (eds.) *The Battered Child*, Fifth Edition, Chicago: University of Chicago Press, pp. 3–28.

Thomas, L., Friedman, D. and Christian, L. (2002) *Inquests: A Practitioners Guide*, London: Legal Action Group.

Tonry, M. (2004) *Punishment and Politics: Evidence and Emulation in the Making of English Crime Control Policy*. Cullompton: Willan.

Unicef (2007) *Child Poverty in Perspective: An Overview of Child Well-Being in Rich Countries*, Florence: Unicef.

United Nations Committee on the Rights of the Child (2002) *Committee on the Rights of the Child Thirty First Session—Concluding Observations of the Committee on the Rights of the Child: United Kingdom of Great Britain and Northern Ireland*, Geneva: Office of the United Nations High Commissioner for Human Rights.

Wacquant, L. (1999) 'How Penal Commonsense Comes to Europeans: Notes on the Transatlantic Defusion of the Neo-liberal Doxa,' *European Societies*, vol 1, no 3.

Webster, C. (2006) '"Race," Youth Crime and Justice,' in B. Goldson and J. Muncie (eds.) *Youth Crime and Justice: Critical issues*, London: Sage, pp. 30–46.

White, R. and Cunneen, C. (2006) 'Social Class, Youth Crime and Justice,' in B. Goldson and J. Muncie (eds.) *Youth Crime and Justice: Critical issues*, London: Sage, pp. 17–29.

Whyte, B. (2003) 'Young and Persistent: Recent Developments in Youth Justice Policy and Practice in Scotland,' *Youth Justice*, vol 3, no 2, pp.74–85.

World Health Organisation (2002) *World Report on Violence and Health*, Geneva: WHO.

Worsley, R. (2007) *Young People in Custody 2004–2006*, London: HM Inspectorate of Prisons and the Youth Justice Board.

Young, J. (1999) *The Exclusive Society*, London: Sage

Youth Justice Board (2006a) 'The Secure Estate for Children and Young People is Nearing Operational Capacity,' http://www.youth-justice-board.gov.uk/YouthJusticeBoard, visited 8 August 2006.

———. (2006b) *Annual Report and Accounts*, London: The Stationery Office.

———. (2006c) *Managing the Behaviour of Children and Young People in the Secure Estate*, London: Youth Justice Board for England and Wales.

6 Naked Power
Strip Searching in Women's Prisons

Jude McCulloch and Amanda George

FBI agents who visited Abu Ghraib confirmed the use of isolation; they reported seeing detainees forced to strip naked and then placed in isolation with no clothes (Physicians for Human Rights 2005: 3).

I find in this day and age I can't understand how it is legal—women who are constantly slashing their arms, legs, throats and trying repeatedly to hang themselves are stripped naked, thrown in a suicide jacket.... 'Don't even give her a mattress, let her lie on the floor, let her lie in her own....' Women need help, counselling and therapy but to throw them in a strip cell, take away everything. I would hate to see a poor dog, bedding taken away treated like that (woman prisoner quoted in Scraton and Moore 2005a: 81).

INTRODUCTION

The publication of photographs depicting degradation and humiliation of prisoners at Abu Ghraib in 2004 focused world attention on the issue of torture and abuse. A report by Physicians for Human Rights on the use of psychological torture by United States forces in the 'war on terror' describes sexual humiliation, including forced nudity, at detention facilities in Iraq, Afghanistan and at Guantánamo Bay, Cuba (Physicians for Human Rights 2005: 25; 36–39; see also George Monbiot *The Guardian* 12 December 2006). While United States President George W. Bush dismissed the practices as not 'American,' critical scholars and prison activists quickly drew a link between the treatment of prisoners by United States forces in Iraq and of prisoners in United States domestic prisons. Judith Greene wrote: '[e]xperienced observers ... are quick to recognize that the Abu Ghraib photos reek of the cruel but usual methods of control used by many US prison personnel' (2004: 4). Avery Gordon makes the point that '[w]hile there is abundant cause for moral outrage and disgust, there is no warrant for being surprised or shocked that citizens of the US tortured, abused and ritually humiliated other human beings' (Gordon 2006: 44; see also Ratner and Ray 2004: 54). According to Gordon, the dehumanization exposed by the photographs 'is the *modus operandi* of the lawful, modern, state-of-the-art prison'. (ibid: 49)

Bree Carlton, similarly to Gordon and Davis, points to the continuities between the abuse at Abu Ghraib and the experience of domestic prisoners, using an Australian maximum security prison as a case study (Carlton 2006). In the aftermath of the publication of the Abu Ghraib photographs, an Australian politician referred to female prisoners in the state of Queensland being held in padded cells, often naked, in shackles, with their faces covered by masks. With a clear reference to the revelations of detainee abuse by coalition forces in the 'war on terror,' he said that '[t]his is not an overseas country or one in the Middle East; this is in Queensland' (B. Flegg, *Queensland Parliamentary Debates*, 2006: 675). The comment, consistent with much of the mainstream commentary, tends to suggest that the practices depicted in the photographs from Abu Ghraib are not the norm in prisons in western democratic countries.

Despite the tendency to see photographs of detainee abuse at Abu Ghraib as outside the accepted norm, 'forced nudity' and sexual humiliation in the form of routine strip searches have been aspects of women's imprisonment in western countries for at least twenty-five years. Prisoners and their supporters have always understood strip searching to constitute an official, deliberate and gendered strategy aimed at 'breaking down' prisoners, particularly women prisoners. Irish Republican prisoner Martina Anderson, argued that in implementing strip searches within women's prisons in Northern Ireland during the early 1980s:

> The British government is using women's nakedness to tyrannise them. We feel that our bodies are used like a weapon to penalize us, with the intention of making us collapse under the pressure. If we haven't collapsed now, I don't think that we will. (quoted in Stop the Strip Searches Campaign 1987: 2)

In spite of this long-documented history of strip searching within women's prisons, sexual humiliation of detainees in the 'war on terror' is frequently depicted as 'exceptional.' A report by Physicians for Human Rights, for example, states that '[t]he use of humiliation as a means of breaking down the resistance of detainees, including forced nudity . . . began when the "war on terror" began' (Physicians for Human Rights 2005: 5).

This historically inadequate understanding of the tactics used in the 'war on terror' and the widespread response of shock to the images of sexual humiliation and abuse at Abu Ghraib needs to be resituated in the context of routine strip searches of prisoners in western countries (Davis 2005: 46). The routine use of strip searches against prisoners, particularly female prisoners, means that '[s]exual abuse is surreptitiously incorporated into the most habitual aspects of women's imprisonment' (Davis 2003: 81). In addition to routine strip searches, it is common for women in distress, who are suicidal or engaging in self-harm, to be kept completely naked or almost completely naked in isolation cells (see, for example, Scraton and Moore 2005a: 81; 2005b: 69; 75). In this context, it is not possible to see the abuse, shown in the photographs from Abu Ghraib, as 'freakish irregularities' (Davis 2005: 50) outside the moral framework of western countries.

While strip searches are normalised within prison, prisoners, especially female prisoners, experience them as a form of sexual violence or coercion. Outside of the prisoner–prison officer relationship, the coerced removal of clothes would constitute sexual assault (George 1993). A Canadian prisoner testifying about her experience of strip searching said:

> How can they walk in there, rip my clothes and say 'Its [sic] okay, I was doing my job; it was professional.' Maybe if the tables were turned they wouldn't think so, but the tables aren't. I don't know how any man can do that to any woman and say it was their job. As far as I know, its [sic] a crime. A crime was committed there. And if something like that happened down the street, that's a crime. If you go in an apartment and rip girl's clothes off, that's a crime. That's sexual assault. (Arbour 1996: 75)

Although women prisoners experience strip searches as sexual assault, in keeping with dominant understandings of crime and violence, individual prisoners rather than the prison regime itself are popularly conceived as responsible for sexual assault within prisons. Male prisons in particular are understood to contain sexual offenders as well as being sites of sexual predation and victimization perpetrated and endured by prisoners. The spectre of male rape within prisons has widespread currency within the popular imagination (Korn 2004: 135–138). The failure to perceive routine practices of strip searches within prison as sexual coercion and institutionalised violence fits with a broader tendency to see crime and violence as residing almost exclusively within the realm of individuals as opposed to the state and its agents (Green and Ward 2004).

This chapter addresses this lacuna in focus and scholarship by examining the issue of routine strip searching within women's prisons. It concentrates in particular on the use of strip searches in Australian women's prisons, but also draws on the experiences of women prisoners in Northern Ireland and Canada. It considers the nature and extent of strip searches and the rationale or pretext for these type of searches. It describes and considers the impact of strip searches on women prisoners in the context of the experiences of sexual assault and gendered violence that women endure outside prison and the way that issues related to culture, religion and race compound the experience of strip search as violence and violation. The circumstances of a death in custody are used to highlight the way that strip searches in prison inflict harm and suffering on women by recalling and amplifying the sexual violence that female prisoners typically experience on the outside. Finally, it documents the range of actions taken to confront and intervene in the excessive and gratuitous use of strip searches in women's prisons and the shifts in practice that have occurred as a result.

NATURE AND EXTENT OF STRIP
SEARCHING IN WOMEN'S PRISONS

The first reports of the routine use of strip searches within prison come from Northern Ireland in the early 1980s (see Moore and Scraton, Chapter 7). A 1983 report describes the implementation of routine strip searches in that jurisdiction in 1982. A quote from a prison chaplain records that:

> Girls entering or leaving the women's prison for whatever reason, admission to prison, going to and on return from remand court or for trial, visiting hospital, parole, inter-jail visits, have to undergo a completely naked visual examination of all parts of their body front and back while the prisoner stands totally naked before prison female warders . . . I and my fellow priest consider this inhuman and degrading treatment. (Murray, quoted in Faul 1983: 1)

A booklet produced by the campaign to stop strip searching in Northern Ireland in 1987 maintained that over 4,000 searches had been carried out in the five years since their introduction in 1982 (Stop the Strip-Searches Campaign 1987). A 1993 article about the experience of women prisoners in the Australian state of Victoria titled 'Strip-searches: Sexual Assault by the State' documents the routine use of strip searches in that state's women's prison (George 1993:1). In a one-year period in 1995 in an Australian women's prison, 13,000 strip searches were conducted in a population averaging 100. In another Australian women's prison in a one-year period between 2001 and 2002, there were 18,889 strip searches in a prison population averaging 200. In its recent inquiry into Queensland women's prisons, the Queensland Anti-Discrimination Commission described what until late in 2005 was a routine day for a prisoner at the Crisis Support Unit (CSU), where women in distress or at risk of self-harm or suicide are incarcerated:

7.30am let out of cell, strip-searched, breakfast

11.00am strip-searched, locked down in cell

12.15pm strip-searched, lunch

4.00pm strip-searched, locked down in cell

5.10pm strip-searched, dinner

6.10pm strip-searched, locked down in cell

In addition, if the prisoner left or re-entered her cell after being in a shared area such as the exercise yard, she was strip searched on entry and exit, and any prisoner who left the unit for any reason would be strip searched on exit and re-entry. The women in the CSU who received the least number of strip searches were women detained in the padded cell, where they are 'generally held in a totally naked state and have no clothing on at all' (Anti-Discrimination Commission Queensland 2006: 71).

A strip search dictates that prisoners undress and stand completely naked in front of prison officers and perform certain actions ostensibly designed to reveal concealed contraband. In Australia, there are various permutations on the actions that must be performed including: lifting of breasts, opening the mouth and poking out the tongue, removal of dentures, turning around with legs parted whilst bending over and using the hands to separate the cheeks to permit visual inspection of the anus and outer vagina, squat and cough, squat facing the wall with hands up the wall and removal of tampon. Strip searches are also routinely carried out in combination with urine testing. Urine tests for illicit drugs are frequent in women's prisons. Sometimes strip searches are conducted in front of video surveillance cameras which are watched remotely by prison officers.

Strip searches are most frequently routine but can also be random or targeted, when a person is suspected of having contraband. Prison regulations typically establish routines whereby strip searches are required on entry to the prison, before and after visits with family, friends and professionals, before urine tests for drugs, before and after leaving the prison for court or day leaves, on being moved to a different part of the prison or at any other time when required. Outside prison police can generally only lawfully require a person to undergo a strip search when they have formed a suspicion on reasonable grounds that the person has drugs or a weapon. In prison, however, the very fact of being a prisoner satisfies the 'reasonableness' of this suspicion and no other justification is required. No prisoner is exempt from strip searching regardless of age, physical or mental health, convicted or remand, offence, religion or cultural background.

Physical force may be used to achieve the removal of clothing from prisoners who refuse to submit. Apart from physical coercion, the context of confinement and the life circumstances of women mean that strip searches are inherently coercive. Refusing a strip search is a prison offence that can lead to punishment. Physical resistance is likely to result in prison charges. Failure to submit will also lead to loss of contact visits with children, family or friends. Many women in prison are also mothers. In Australia, approximately three quarters of women are mothers (Corrections Victoria 2004b). As Corrections Victoria notes, 'given the importance of women maintaining contact with their families and especially their children most female prisoners would submit to strip searches to maintain contact' (Office of the Correctional Services Commissioner 2001). The frequency of strip searching combined with its sexually coercive nature has profoundly negative consequences for women, the majority of whom have suffered extensive histories of physical and sexual abuse outside prison.

IMPACT ON WOMEN

There are few systematic studies on the psychological impacts of strip searching. A 1989 report drawing on case studies from Northern Ireland and England described the feelings of humiliation and abuse experienced by those subject to the practice (United Campaign Against Strip-searching 1989). One aspect of strip searching that has been recognised as adding to feelings of humiliation is tampon removal (Office of the Correctional Services Commissioner 2001).

An Australian prisoner describes the process and her feelings:

> We are strip-searched after every visit. We are naked, told to bend over, touch our toes, spread our cheeks. If we've got our period, we have to take the tampon out in front of them. It's degrading and humiliating. (quoted in George 1993: 31)

The combination of strip searching with urine testing can also add to feelings of humiliation. Inspection personnel at one Australian prison recently reported that women, contrary to regulation, were 'instructed to hold their arms up away from their body' and required to supply urine samples while completely naked. They reported that, '[m]any women spoke of the lack of dignity and sense of violation they felt at being subject to these undignified procedures' (Office of the Inspector of Custodial Services 2006: 76).

The practice of routine strip searching can add to the isolation of women prisoners from people outside prison. As many women in prison are primary caregivers for children, this added isolation may be particularly painful for incarcerated women. The Anti-Discrimination Commission (2006: 73) in Queensland noted that:

> . . . a number of women . . . elected not to have contact visits at all because of their strong objections to being strip-searched. This is almost an impossible choice for women with children . . . in their attempts to maintain their relationships with their families they must have contact visits.

A Victorian review found that thirteen per cent of women denied themselves visits because of strip searches (Office of the Correctional Services Commissioner 2001: 32).

While the psychological impact of strip searches needs more systematic study, there is little doubt that strip searching produces feelings of humiliation in women. According to psychiatrists, victims/survivors of sexual humiliation often struggle with issues of shame and self-blame which undermine their sense of capability and autonomy. A review of strip searching by the anti-discrimination commissioner in Queensland maintains that female prisoners report:

> ... strip search diminished their self-esteem as human beings and greatly emphasized feelings of vulnerability and worthlessness. Strip-searches can greatly undermine the best attempts being made by prison authorities to rehabilitate women prisoners, through programs and counselling to rebuild self-esteem, cognitive and assertiveness skills. (Anti-Discrimination Commission Queensland 2006: 74)

The sexual coercion implicit in prison strip searches is experienced in the context of the violence and sexual coercion that women prisoners experience in the community. There is an extensive body of literature that supports the conclusion that the majority of female prisoners, up to eighty per cent, have been subject to sexual abuse outside prison (see, for example: Davies and Cook 1998: 17). Recent research across six Australian jurisdictions reported that women in prison had a rate of sexual abuse by a parent five times higher than women in the community and eighty-six per cent of these women sexually abused in childhood were later sexually victimized as adults. Overall, eighty-seven per cent of incarcerated women had experienced sexual, physical or emotional abuse in either childhood (sixty-three per cent) or adulthood (seventy-eight per cent) (Johnson 2004: xiv). A recent official review of strip searching in an Australian women's prison noted that:

> In initiating the review the Commission was mindful of the extensive body of research documentation confirming that the majority of female prisoners have themselves been victims of sexual abuse and violence in their childhood years and/or adult relationships. It was considered for such women the prison experience of strip-searching could prove particularly traumatic and be seen as an institutional perpetration of abuse. (Office of the Correctional Services Commissioner 2001: 3)

In R v Golden (2001: 83; 90), a case involving a male suspect and police in the Canadian Supreme Court, it was stated that:

> ... in our view it is unquestionable that they (strip searches) represent a significant invasion of privacy and are often a humiliating, degrading and traumatic experience for individuals subject to them ... strip searches are inherently humiliating and degrading for detainees regardless of the manner in which they are carried out and for this reason cannot be carried out simply as a matter of routine policy. . . . Women and minorities

in particular may have a real fear of strip searches and may experience such a search as equivalent to a sexual assault . . . the psychological effects of strip searches may also be particularly traumatic for individuals who have previously been subject to abuse.

An inquiry into the strip searching of women prisoners by a male emergency response team in a Canadian prison reported that:

> The process was intended to terrorize and therefore subdue. There is no doubt that it had the intended effect in this case. It also, unfortunately, had the effect of re-victimizing women who had had traumatic experiences in the past at the hands of men. Although this consequence was not intended, it should have been foreseen. (Arbour 1996: 88)

Beyond the gendered experience and violence of sexual assault, race, religion and culture may compound the psychologically damaging effects of strip searches. In the Abu Ghraib abuse scandal it has been suggested that the sexual modesty assumed to be associated with Muslim/Arab identity and religion were deliberately exploited to compound psychological harm. Physicians for Human Rights (2005: 11–12) reports that:

> There is evidence that US personnel directed sexual humiliation toward detainees because they knew that Arabs are particularly vulnerable to sexual humiliation and sought to exploit that vulnerability. Clinicians at the Centre for the Treatment of Torture Victims in Berlin, Germany [Berlin Centre], who treat a large population of Muslims, have found that Muslim victims of sexual torture forever carry a stigma. . . . With respect to forced nudity the Berlin Centre clinicians have found that merely being stripped naked implies the breaking of a strict taboo, which leaves victims feeling extremely exposed and humiliated.

Writing about the introduction of routine strip searches into the women's prison in Northern Ireland, prison chaplains maintained that:

> This new procedure has been a traumatic experience for young Catholic girls and older women, married and single, all of whom were reared and educated in Catholic houses and schools where the strictest standards of modesty were impressed upon them as a matter of conscience. (Faul 1983: 1)

Indigenous people, and Indigenous women in particular, are massively over-represented in Australian prisons (Department of Justice 2004). Rape and sexual violence were used as weapons of colonization, and Indigenous women continue to experience higher rates of sexual violence than non-Indigenous women. Indigenous women, discussing strip searches in prison, argue that 'to be forced to endure more sexual assault at the hands of the state is a total violation of our women's human rights. This humiliating, degrading and punitive practice is archaic and unnecessary' (Green 2005). Cultural difference may also impact on Indigenous women's experience of strip searches. One writer suggests the:

> Systemic humiliation of Murri [Indigenous people from the Australian state of Queensland] is best shown in the use of strip-searches . . . used as a tool of dominance and oppression. . . . In Murri culture adult women and men spend very little time together. Physical contact between the sexes is far more limited than in mainstream society. Even being in a room with males is uncomfortable for most Murri women, especially those from remote areas. To be strip-searched in the presence of men—particularly white men—is tantamount to torture. Many Murri women experience flashbacks to rape and sexual abuse during and after strip-searches. (Lucashenko and Kilroy 2005: 17)

Serious mental health issues are endemic in women's prisons, with an apparently strong correlation between experiences of childhood abuse, sexual assault, drug dependency and mental health issues. A substantial proportion of women prisoners have been diagnosed with psychiatric problems and many have attempted to take their own lives. Thirty-two per cent of Indigenous women in prison have attempted suicide and twenty-three per cent had self-harmed (Corrections Victoria 2004b:17). Of women from cultural and linguistically diverse backgrounds in prison twenty-two per cent have attempted suicide and twenty-eight per cent had self-harmed prior to prison (Corrections Victoria 2004b:14).

Women prisoners are 'amongst the most vulnerable, unwell and disadvantaged cohort in the community' (Federation of Community Legal Centres and Victorian Council of Social Services 2005: 6). Given the anecdotal evidence suggesting women experience strip search as a form of sexual abuse, it is worth considering the possibility that strip searches contribute to the poor mental health, suicide attempts and incidence of self-harm amongst female prisoners. Certainly the finding of those working with survivors of sexual humiliation and sexual torture in other contexts is suggestive. Physicians for Human Rights (2005: 12; 59–60) reports that:

> Staff members at CVT [Centre for Victims of Torture] say that sexual humiliation often leads to symptoms of PTSD [Post Traumatic Stress Disorder] and major depression, and that victims often relive the sessions of humiliation in the form of flashbacks and nightmares long after their detention. . . . Clinicians at the Berlin Centre similarly have found that victims of sexual torture often suffer form severe depression, anxiety, depersonalization, dissociative states, complex post-traumatic stress disorder, and multiple physical complaints such

as chronic headaches, eating disorders, and digestive problems. They also have found that suicides may occur unless a strong religious conviction forbids otherwise.

AN UNNECESSARY STRIP SEARCH AND A
TRAGIC DEATH: REMEMBERING RAPE?

Paula Richardson was a twenty-three-year-old Indigenous prisoner incarcerated at the Metropolitan Women's Correctional Centre (MWCC) in Melbourne, Victoria. On 11 September 1998 she hung herself with a shower curtain and died alone in a cell. Six weeks before she died, Paula had been subjected to a forced strip search. Just prior to being imprisoned Paula had been raped. While all strip searches share some characteristics with sexual assault, the most obvious being coercion and a diminished agency and control over one's own body, the circumstances of the forced strip search and the rape in this case shared a number of strikingly similar characteristics.

Paula was forcibly stripped by four prison officers, two male and two female, on the suspicion that she had concealed a soft-drink can. When she refused to hand over the can, three officers were called to assist. Paula was restrained, taken into an empty cell and held face down on the bed by three officers using arm locks. According to the officers, she was crying but passive. While she was held down, a male officer opened his 'cut down' knife (used to cut down hanging prisoners), held it behind her neck, and then cut down through the back of her overalls, her bra and her underpants. Her skin was also nicked. One officer then pulled out her overalls from under her so she was naked, to reveal the can. The refusal to allow the search and the possession of contraband (the soft-drink can) led to charges and loss of privileges. Three months previous to the strip search, shortly before being imprisoned, Paula was held face down in a lane and anally raped. This assault was reported to police.

Two days after the forced strip search Paula cut her wrists. One officer described her as 'acting childlike' and being in a foetal position in her cell and threatening to harm herself. Paula's mother described how Paula was allowed to telephone her after the search because her behaviour was incomprehensible to staff. During the phone call, Paula was inconsolable with distress and kept saying 'they've done it again, they've done it again.' Paula's mother knew about the rape prior to prison, but did not find out about the strip search until the coroner's inquest. The day after her phone call, Paula's mother contacted the prison extremely concerned about Paula's mental state and spoke to officers and health staff. Prison health records, the prison psychiatrist, prison officers and Paula's parents described how Paula's state of mind and behaviour rapidly deteriorated after the forced strip search. Six weeks later in another strip cell, where she was placed after another incident, Paula took her own life. The coroner who investigated her death described the forced strip search as 'unnecessary and invasive and an inappropriate way of dealing with the problem.' She also found that 'on the face of it, given in particular her recent history of rape, this episode may have been of great significance to Paula' (Heffey 2002: paras 18; 21).

The case study portrays in graphic detail the violence and coercion implicit in strip searches, and the way that this implicit force is backed up by raw power and overwhelming physical force when women resist. Paula's history as a survivor of rape is typical of women prisoners. The obvious similarities between the earlier rape and the prison strip search serve to highlight the continuities between the officially recognized crime of sexual assault and women's experience of strip searches as sexual assault. Paula's distress, mental deterioration and subsequent suicide make clear the high costs women prisoners and their families are forced to endure as a result of the routine use of strip searches. While the human costs of strip searching are high, the benefits of strip searching in terms of security and safety in prisons are far less clear.

PRISON SECURITY AND GOOD ORDER: RATIONALE OR PRETEXT?

When strip searching was first introduced in Armagh women's prison in Northern Ireland, the British government consistently claimed that is was necessary for two reasons, security and safe custody of prisoners (The Campaign to Stop Strip-searching 1987: 6). The official rationale remains the same today. Strip searches are part of the security matrix of a prison to ensure its 'good order and security' (Office of the Correctional Services Commission 2003: 1). Queensland Corrections maintains that 'the major objective of conducting searches is to prevent the entry of illicit drugs and other prohibited items, including equipment that could be used to escape from prison, or used for self or other types of harm' (Anti-Discrimination Commission Queensland 2006: 71). Strip searches are designed or justified on the basis of discovering and discouraging contraband and weapons.

Two thirds of women in Australian prisons, typical of women prisoners in most countries, were regular illicit drug users prior to prison, with young women having higher rates (Johnson 2004: xii; O'Connor 2004: 4). The major focus of strip searches in women's prisons is on detecting illicit drugs. The prison administration has a zero tolerance to illicit drug use in prison and combines strip-searching regimes with a programme of urine testing.

The rationale and justification for strip-searching regimes within women's prisons has been consistently critiqued and challenged. A report written five years after the introduction of strip searches at Armagh prison claimed that:

> Since 1982 and almost four thousand strip-searches later, nothing which would constitute a security risk has been found on the prisoners. The only items the authorities can claim to have found are: a £5 note, a bottle of perfume and two letters, all of which were found during ordinary rub-down body searches. How then can strip-searching be justified when these statistics unequestionably [sic] confirm that strip-searching is of no security value to the authorities whatsoever? (Stop the Strip-Searches Campaign 1987: 8)

As a result of the long-standing campaign against strip searching of women prisoners, there is increasing evidence about the failure of strip searches to contribute to 'good order and security' of prisons through detecting contraband. In Victoria, over the last fifteen years, community legal centres have made regular Freedom of Information (FOI) requests about the extent and success of strip searching within women's prisons. As Freedom of Information legislation has been gradually implemented in other states, this information has also being collected in other states.

Freedom of Information requests in 1995 revealed that over a one-year period in a Victoria maximum security prison there were 13,000 strip searches in a population of 100 prisoners. In two randomly selected months, no contraband was found in one month and two cigarettes were found in another. In Victoria's minimum security prison over this time, 523 strip searches took place with three separate findings of contraband which together comprised chewing gum packets, two cigarette lighters, three packets of meat and oregano. In another year at the same prison, the items found were foodstuffs, cigarettes, earrings, money and cassette tapes. During this time in Tasmania, senior prison staff reported that no contraband had been found in the previous five years on women prisoners (Diamond 1995: 99).

In 1996, the first private prison for women outside of the United States opened in Victoria. Over a two-year period, from 1998 to 2000, there were 11,891 strip searches and thirty-four items of contraband were found; however, the nature of the contraband was not revealed. When the State resumed control of the prison in 2001, there was a massive increase in strip searches so that in a one-year period from 2001 to 2002, 18,889 strip searches were carried out on a daily prison population averaging two hundred. Only one item of contraband was found. In Victoria's minimum security women's prison, some 736 strip searches over two years revealed one item of contraband. A Queensland Freedom of Information request in 2001 revealed that 8,400 strip searches of women prisoners succeeded in finding contraband consisting of 'two cigarettes, earrings, [and a] sanitary napkin (no blood)' (Kilroy 2002: 8).

The requirement to 'bend and part' the cheeks has been described in a review of strip searches as unnecessary 'because women wishing to conceal contraband would bank it vaginally rather than conceal it between the cheeks of their buttocks' (Office of the Correctional Services Commissioner

2001: 34). Requiring tampons to be removed and the 'squat and cough' are also pointless, because they are based on the false assumption that these actions, if performed while naked, will cause any secreted items to fall out. This reveals either a profound ignorance of women's anatomy or an indifference to the stated purpose of strip searches in favour of a deliberate strategy to humiliate and degrade women.

In 2002, after a long campaign by prison activists, Corrections Victoria instituted a three-year pilot to reduce the number of strip searches of women prisoners by changing a number of what were previously routine strip searches, into either random or targeted strip searches. This meant that for most women instead of having to strip search before and after family contact visits, they had them only after visits. The pilot reduced the number of strip searches from 21,000 a year to 14,000. There was also a change in the manner in which searches were done so that women took their tops and bottoms off separately so that they were not completely naked during the search (Corrections Victoria 2004a).

In order to ensure the efficacy of the pilot, Corrections Victoria developed a number of measures to determine whether the reduction in strip searches had any impact on the amount of 'unauthorized' drug activity in the prison and the amount and type of contraband seized. The measures used were the monitoring of urine tests, 'incidents' within the prison—assaults and self-harms and contraband seized in strip, cell and grounds searches. The study found that despite the massive reduction in strip searches and a significant increase in urine testing, there was a forty per cent *reduction* in urine positives and a reduction in the number of 'refusals' to urine tests. Moreover, although the number of strip searches had dramatically reduced, the same amount of contraband was seized. Only one item was seized during a routine strip search and four items were seized in targeted strip searches. The contraband seized comprised prescription medication and syringes.

This unchanged level of contraband seizure, Corrections Victoria surmised, was because other methods of searching were more successful in detection and that there had been an increase in 'dynamic' security, that is, prison officers using their faculties, watching, listening, etc. In addition, even though there was an increase in the women's prison population, there was a reduction in 'incidents' and overwhelmingly, women who were involved in 'incidents'—staff assaults, prisoner assault and self-harm incidents—had significant mental health issues.

The pilot provides convincing evidence that strip searches have dubious value in creating a 'safe' prison environment and that high levels of strip searching may well be counterproductive in combating illicit drug use by women. This is consistent with the point made by many women prisoners and supporters that strip searching, by increasing feelings of powerlessness, reducing self-esteem and amplifying and contributing to the experience of sexual abuse, deepens women's needs and desires to deal with feelings of pain through use of illicit drugs. According to former prisoner and prison rights activist Debbie Kilroy (2002: 15) 'it [the strip search] can only exacerbate depression, thoughts of suicide, incidents of self-harm, and ironically return women to the need for drugs to avoid the mental anguish inflicted by the abusive treatment.'

Prison activists have long believed that 'security and good order' is a pretext rather than a rationale for strip searches motivated by the will to dominate and control prisoners in a way that extends the punishment that loss of freedom itself entails. A 1963 CIA manual on interrogation states 'clothing allows detainees to retain a piece of his or her identity and thus increases capacity for resistance' (quoted in Physicians for Human Rights 2005: 56). The belief that strip searches are a form of institutionalised sexual abuse that exploits the apparent powerlessness of women prisoners has motivated prison activists in countries across the globe.

OPPOSING SEXUAL ASSAULT BY THE STATE

Campaigns against strip searching have been ongoing since they were first introduced in Northern Ireland (see, for example, Faul 1983). In Australia, a campaign against strip searches involving activists, serving and former prisoners, lawyers and academics has been in progress continuously since 1992. It aims to expose the nature of strip searches, their impact on women, their failure to meet their stated purpose, and most significantly to stop them. The campaign has developed international links with similar campaigns in the United States, Canada and Northern Ireland. The campaign has engaged in a range of strategies, including legal cases, advocacy, engagement with prison administration and politicians, Freedom of Information requests, complaints to anti-discrimination bodies, the publication of official reports and academic articles, community theatre and media. These strategies have had very limited success in changing prison policy and the practice of strip searching.

The campaign took a dramatic turn on a national level at an Australian Institute of Criminology Conference on Women Offenders in 2001. Prior to the conference, a group of women's prison activists from Australia and Canada, including one of the authors, Amanda George, held a two-day meeting to share information and to consider what the group wanted to achieve from the conference. A decision was made to focus on strip searches as a major issue. The majority of people attending the conference were not prison officers but higher level prison management and external bureaucracy: people who dictate the policies that mandate strip searches but who are unlikely to have witnessed them.

During a plenary session where the female heads of corrections from various jurisdictions were speaking, the activists asked if they could make a short public announcement. The pretext of a public announcement was used to stage a mock strip search. From the crowd, one woman's voice boomed that named 'prisoners' should get on stage. Onto the lighted stage, in the darkened room before an audience of several hundred, two women playing the role of prisoners were given instructions by another women, playing the role of guard, to perform a strip search. A pin dropping could have been heard in the room. The 'prisoners' stood naked and performed the actions that prisoners are typically 'requested' to comply with, lifting breasts and poking out tongues. During the search, other members of the group distributed leaflets containing statistical information about the number and futility of strip searches. The media had been alerted that something of interest would happen at the conference and as a result the issue received national news coverage (see: Davis 2003: 82).

After the conference, the Commissioner for Corrections in Victoria instigated the pilot referred to earlier. The Commissioner for Corrections from Canada was also on the stage during the strip search action. In 2004, there was a change in Canada's strip search policy. As a result of an Investigation by the Correctional Investigators Office, the Canadian Corrections Service formed the view that some of its routine strip searches were not supported by law, breached their human rights mandate and that in the future they could only be done on a 'reasonable grounds basis' (Correctional Service Canada 2004).

CONCLUSION

Strip searching is a long-standing and routine practice within prisons around the world, including prisons in states considered advanced democracies such as Northern Ireland, Canada, the United States, the United Kingdom and Australia. The revelation of serious abuse, including sexual humiliation at the United States detention facility Abu Ghraib in Iraq, was widely seen as evidence of a disgraceful breach of human rights deserving of condemnation. This response, however, must be located within the knowledge that sexual coercion and humiliation are regular and thoroughly normalised practices within western prisons. There is no reasonable basis on which to conclude, as some have, that sexual humiliation and coercion in detention are innovations of the 'war on terror.'

Routine strip searching of women prisoners has been institutionalised within women's prisons for twenty-five years. States attempt to deny that these acts constitute abuse by justifying them for a range of purposes relating to the security of the prison and the safety of those that reside and work there. However, strip searches do not effectively address their said purpose with mounting evidence that they deliver very little in terms of security and add significantly to the harm experienced by women prisoners. The pilot programme to reduce strip searches in Victoria suggests that strip searches are counter-productive in terms of security and safety in prison. Strip searches of women prisoners are experienced as a type of sexual coercion, which reinforces women's sense of powerlessness and undermines self-esteem and self-worth, adding to the distress and suffering of women. The circumstances surrounding the death of Paula Richardson, an Indigenous woman in an Australian prison, graphically demonstrate both the sexual violence that is integral to strip searching and the powerful resonances such practices have with the sexual violence experienced by women outside prison.

These negative psychological impacts of strip searches are intensified in a context where the majority of women prisoners have been physically, emotionally and sexually abused in the community prior to imprisonment. The coercive removal of prisoners' clothes amounts to a symbolic enactment of the stripping of rights that accompanies imprisonment. It is particularly resonant as an identity-stripping and negating act for women who so often have their identities and rights stripped through sexual assault outside prison. That the state through its practice of strip searching maintains and extends the experience of sexual abuse for women prisoners is a demonstration of Pat Carlen's (1988: 10) observation that prison incorporates and amplifies all the oppressions women, particularly poor women, Indigenous women and non-white women, face outside prison.

REFERENCES

Arbour, L. (1996) *Commission of Inquiry Into Certain Events at the Prison for Women in Kingston Public Works and Government Services*, Canada.
Anti-Discrimination Commission Queensland. (2006) *Women in Prison: A Report by the Anti-Discrimination Commission*, Queensland.
Carlen, P. (1988) *Sledgehammer: Women's Imprisonment at the Millenium*, London: Macmillan.
Carlton, B. (2006) 'From H Division to Abu Ghraib: Regimes of Justification and State-Inflicted Terror and Violence in Maximum Security' *Social Justice*, Vol 33, No. 4, pp. 15–36.
Correctional Service Canada. (2004) Memorandum to Wardens, 29 December 2004: obtained under Freedom of Information.
Corrections Victoria. (2004a) *Piloting a Way Forward: The Women's Prisons Region Strip-search Pilot*, obtained under under Freedom of Information.
Corrections Victoria. (2004b) *Better Pathways: An Integrated Response to Women's Offending and Re-offending*, Discussion Paper.
Davies, S. and Cook, S. (1998) 'Women, Imprisonment and Post Release Mortality,' *Just Policy*, vol 14, pp.15–21.
Davis, A. (2003) *Are Prisons Obsolete?* New York: Free Press.
Davis, A. (2005) *Abolition Democracy: Beyond Empire, Prisons and Torture*, New York: Free Press.
Department of Justice (2004) *Victorian Aboriginal Justice Agreement*, Victoria Government.
Faul, D. (1983) *The Stripping Naked of the Prisoner in Armagh Prison 1982–83*.
Diamond, R. (1995) *The Abuse of Power to Strip-search and Urine Test People in Custody in Australia*, Melbourne: Coalition Against Police Violence.

Federation of Community Legal Centres and Victorian Council of Social Services. (2005) *Request for a Systemic Review of Discrimination Against Women in Victorian Prisons.*

George, A. (1993) 'Strip-searches: Sexual Assault by the State' *Alternative Law Journal*, pp.31–33.

Gordon, A. (2006) Abu Ghraib Imprisoned and the war on terror; *Race and Class*, vol 48, no. 1, pp. 42–59.

Green, M. (2005) Untitled Keynote Address, *Is Prison Obsolete Conference*, Aboriginal Family Violence Prevention Legal Service, Melbourne: Sisters Inside.

Green, P. and Ward, T. (2004) *State Crime: Governments, Violence and Corruption* London: Pluto Press.

Greene, J. (2004) 'From Abu Ghraib to America: Examining Our Harsh Prison Culture' *Ideas for an Open Society*, Occasional Papers from OSI-US Programs, vol 4, October 2004.

Heffey, J (2002) Record of Investigation into Death Case No 2735/98 State Coroner Victoria.

Johnson, H. (2004) *Drugs and Crime: A Study of Incarcerated Female Offenders.* Canberra: Australian Institute of Criminology.

Kilroy, D. (2002) 'Stop the State Sexually Assaulting Women in Prison.' Expanding Our Horizons Conference, Understanding the Complexities of Violence Against Women.

Korn, N. (2004) *Life Behind Bars: Conversations with Australian Male Inmates*, Sydney: New Holland.

Lucashenko, M. and Kilroy, D. (2005) *A Black Woman and a Prison Cell*, Brisbane: Sisters Inside.

O'Connor, F. (2004) *Administration of Justice, Rule of Law and Democracy, Economic and Social Council*, Commission on Human Rights E/CN.4/ Sub.2/2004/9, 9 July.

Office of the Correctional Services Commission. (2003) *Project Management Plan: Piloting a way forward: Strip Searching Across the Women's Prisons Region.*

Office of the Correctional Services Commissioner. (2001) *Office of the Correctional Services Commissioner Services Commissioner's Review of Strip-searching Procedures at the Metropolitan Women's Correctional Centre and H M Prison Tarrengower.*

Office of Inspector of Custodial Services. (2006) *Report of an Announced Inspection of Bandyup Women's Prison.*

Physicians for Human Rights. (2005) *Break Them Down: Systematic Use of Psychological Torture by US Forces*, Washington: Physicians for Human Rights.

Queensland Parliamentary Debates. (2006) Legislative Assembly, 8 March.

Ratner, M. and Ray, E. (2004) *Guantánamo: What the World Should Know,* Melbourne: Scribe Publications.

R. v. Golden (2001) 3 S. C. R. 679.

Scraton, P. and Moore, L. (2005a) *The Hurt Inside: The Imprisonment of Women and Girls in Northern Ireland*, Belfast: Northern Ireland Human Rights Commission.

Scraton, P. and Moore, L. (2005b) 'Degradation, Harm and Survival in a Women's Prison,' *Social Policy and Society*, vol 5, no 1, pp.67–78.

Stop the Strip-Searches Campaign. (1987) *Stop Strip Searching*, Dublin.

United Campaign Against Strip-searching. (1989) *An Enquiry into the Psychological Effects of Strip-searching.*

7 The Imprisonment of Women and Girls in the North of Ireland

A 'Continuum of Violence'

Linda Moore and Phil Scraton

THE GENDERED PRISON

As stated in the first chapter, the enforced removal of a person's liberty, a citizen's status and the erosion of personal identity through the allocation of a number, a cell and a set of clothes are inherently violent processes. They are administered through procedures established ostensibly to prioritise security, order and safety underpinned by regimes of isolation, suspicion and fear. Prisons are essentially places of deprivation in which rights and needs are redefined as privileges to be earned through compliance and conformity. The slightest opposition to authority, questioning a prison instruction or a guard's order, can be met with severe punishment via broad discretion embedded in the institution's disciplinary code. The extent and commonality of the use of discretionary 'discipline' is evident across all jurisdictions within which certain prisons build and often celebrate their reputation as 'tough' jails boasting 'punitive' regimes. While the imagery of violence within prisons is that of prisoner-on-prisoner bullying, assault and wounding, the reality of violence, in scope and content, is not so specific. It extends to prisoner-on-staff and staff-on-prisoner violence. It includes acts of emotional, psychological and deeply personalised harm as well as physical or sexual assault. It extends from verbal abuse to beatings and death. It also encompasses self-harm and suicide as consequences of institutionalised negligence, neglect and intimidation. Recognition of the fatal consequences of punitive regimes is embodied in the principle of the state's 'duty of care' for those held in its jails and other forms of detention.

In recording, analysing and responding to the experiences of women in prison, it is essential not to restrict or overemphasise the significance of gender. As Angela Davis (2003: 61) states, 'women's prison practices are gendered, but so, too, are men's prison practices.' While prisons are isolated from the places in which they are located, 'the deeply gendered character of punishment both reflects and further entrenches the gendered structure of the larger society' (ibid). As Pat Carlen notes, women's imprisonment 'incorporates and amplifies all the antisocial modes of control that oppress women outside the prison' (1998: 10). What persists is the failure within the criminal justice system to accept that 'women's crimes are different to men's, committed in different circumstances.' Adjuncts to the mainstream male prison system, conditions and regimes for women regularly fall below minimum standards of decency and humanity. Carlen continues, 'so many women arrive in prison suffering from extreme health and social effects of poverty, addictions and physical and sexual abuse' yet no coherent or holistic policy is in place to manage their sentences (Carlen 2002: 15). As Jackie Lowthian (2000: 177) demonstrates, the institutional response further dehumanises through deterioration in healthcare, over-emphasis on security, increased risk of bullying, self-harm and suicide, curtailment of programmes and long periods of isolation.

The processes of dehumanisation within prisons mirrors gendered violence endured by women in essentially patriarchal social and societal relations. Reflecting on our primary research into the experiences of imprisoned women and girls, we note their vivid accounts demonstrated that while regimes and programmes within the prison 'were not gender specific in design or delivery, regulation, control and punishments were consistently gender specific' (Scraton and Moore 2005a: 76). Intimidation, degradation and humiliation varied in time, place, intensity and circumstance, yet were institutionally gendered. In analysing gender-oppressive regimes and the range and extent of subjugation within their operational practices, Liz Kelly's (1987, 1988) conceptualisation of a 'continuum of sexual violence' is apposite.

Liz Kelly found that in all women's lives, violence, its fear, its threat and its reality, was significant and ever-present, whether related to intimacy in the private sphere or danger in the public sphere. As Elizabeth Stanko (1985: 9) notes, within 'male-dominated society' women's 'experiences of sexual and physical violation take on an illusion of normality, ordinariness.' Taken together 'ordinariness' and 'continuum' cover a broad range of threatening and abusive behaviours including acts of emotional, physical and sexual violence. Analysis of the intimidation, fear and experience of violence should not be confined to interpersonal relations but should include collective and institutional manifestations. The continuum lifts the focus from the 'different forms of violence and abuse as discrete issues' to recognising 'commonalities between them in women's experience and theoretically as forms of violence underpinning patriarchal power and control' (Radford, Harne and Friedberg 2000: 2).

Stanko's concern centres on 'women's experiences of male violence' invariably 'filtered through an understanding of *men's* behaviour.' Viewed in this way, 'we easily draw lines between those aberrant (thus harmful) and those typical (thus unharmful) types of male behaviour' (Stanko 1985: 10). Absent from the 'commensensical separation between "aberrant" and "typical" is a woman-defined understanding of what is threatening, of what women consider to be potentially violent.' In describing their 'everyday encounters with men,' women's accounts reveal 'powerlessness' not only regarding actual physical attacks but in establishing and anticipating the threat or potential of violence at all levels (ibid: 11).

Vulnerability is directly connected to powerlessness, particularly the 'ever-present potential of sexual violation' (ibid: 12). Stanko notes the 'reality of physical and/or sexual vulnerability is part of women's experience of being in the world' (ibid: 12–13). Women, argues Stanko, 'learn to define their worlds and thus their experience as less than men's. In the social hierarchy of value, they are less.' Consequently, they 'internalise and silence many of their experiences of sexual/or physical intimidation and violation,' often feeling 'shame, humiliation and self-blame' for the unacceptable behaviour of men. Their experiences of all levels of 'intimidation' become 'welded to male dominance' that 'rests upon women's secondary position' (ibid: 17–18).

Writing on women's experience of prison as 'a kind of freedom' from domestic violence, Vetten and Bhana (2005: 265) note the profound 'similarities between imprisonment and abusive relationships.' Each is 'characterized by authoritarianism, a marked power imbalance, enforced restriction of movement and activities, lack of freedom of association, violence and enforcement of arbitrary and trivial demands.' Not only does this replication create problems for women regarding recovery, but it also requires the same strategies of survival used in resisting intimate abuse: 'compliance with others' demands, denial of one's own wishes and thoughts, defensive violence, suppression of feelings.'

The prison, then, becomes an institutional manifestation of women's powerlessness and vulnerability, and for girl and women prisoners the threat of violence and violation within the outside community remains significant in their experiences of prison. Also consistent are processes through which women are judged as 'good,' 'respectable' or 'moral.' There is a considerable literature on the dynamics underpinning the ascribed negative reputation of 'aberrant,' 'deviant' and 'criminal' women. Nonconformity and refusal to comply with gendered and sexual norms within patriarchies, however socially and culturally diverse, invariably results in discipline, banishment, punishment and even death. The imprisonment of women and girls cannot be removed from such frames of reference and determination. Once imprisoned, as Pat Carlen (1983: 155) memorably remarked, 'women are in no-woman's land.' Within the criminal justice system's public interrogation of their personal lives and their 'apposite history of maternal failures and dereliction of duty,' women offenders, as mothers or mothers-in-waiting, 'are seen as being outwith family, sociability, femininity and adulthood.'

As primary research into women in conflict with the law repeatedly demonstrates, their pathologisation operates on several apparently distinct yet, in application, inter-related levels. It incorporates prevalent assumptions in popular discourse supported by unsubstantiated premises within professional discourses that assume women's 'deviance' and 'crimes' to be exceptional, irrational, volatile and unpredictable: representing a denial of their passivity and servility. Consequently, as Heidensohn (1985: 74) notes, criminal women are categorised as 'abnormal' and pathological, the 'implicit assumption being' they are 'less reclaimable, more vile, more "unnatural" than male prisoners.'

Neither mentally ill nor treatable, the 'personality disordered' prisoner is portrayed as a 'residual deviant' beyond the scope of treatment. Once the classification is established, the status ascribed, the woman prisoner has 'little chance of having the label removed' (Carlen 1983: 209). Applied as a fixed, permanent category, there is 'little hope of change.' As Pat Carlen's primary research established, 'being seen as neither wholly mad nor wholly bad,' women prisoners are subjected 'to a disciplinary regime where they are actually infantilised at the same time as attempts are made to make them feel guilty about their double, triple, quadruple or even quintuple refusal of family, work, gender, health and reason' (ibid: 209).

In reviewing the contemporary history of medical intervention in the lives of women prisoners, Joe Sim (1990: 176) acknowledges the complexity and consistency associated with a 'disciplinary matrix' imposed exclusively in women's prisons. It combines 'individualization' and behaviour 'normalisation' within 'the perpetual surveillance of the women's physical and psychological response to imprisonment' and 'the advent of intensive technological control.' Despite resistance 'to medical and psychiatric categorization,' women prisoners experience 'continuing entrapment . . . within catch-all psychiatric categories such as behavioural and personality disorder' (ibid.). For the authorities, but also for the women, 'each return to prison' represents 'another failure,' their recidivism taken as proof that they had no intention or motivation to reform (Carlen 1983: 194). Consequently, the 'temporary classification "disorderly," gradually ossifies into the more permanent "disordered" . . . untreatable . . . beyond the remit of the treatment agencies, without hope and beyond recognition' (ibid.).

Strip searches are a powerful, painful element of women's subjugation in prison (see Jude McCulloch and Amanda George, Chapter 6). There has been considerable debate regarding the definition of 'strip search' particularly as it relates to women and girls. Prison authorities and managers often make the distinction between the removal of clothes for observation without touch and the physical inspection of the body. The latter they refer to as a strip search. That is not a distinction recognised by women prisoners (see: Scraton and Moore 2005b; 2007). They consider the removal of all clothes and the visual inspection of the body (prisoners instructed to open mouths, lift breasts, open legs) as a strip search. If a distinction is to be made, it is between removal of clothes—strip search, and the physical examination of the body—intimate cavity search. Angela Davis (2003: 81) considers sexual abuse 'is surreptitiously incorporated into one of the most habitual aspects of women's imprisonment, the strip search.' The State is 'directly implicated in this routinization of sexual abuse, both in permitting such conditions that render women vulnerable to explicit sexual coercion carried out by guards and other prison staff and by incorporating into routine policy such practices as the strip search and the body cavity search.'

In her work on Australian prisons, Amanda George (1995: 23) reveals the persistent 'sexual humiliation' of the strip search. Women and girls 'are naked, they bend over and spread their cheeks and if they are menstruating they must take out the tampon in front of the officer.' There was no requirement that the officers should be female. Tamara Walsh (2005: 20) states that in Queensland, where 'strip searches' are 'used excessively,' women and young women prisoners 'alleged that they had been raped by corrections officers.' Others reported 'they had been assaulted by corrections officers.' Men and women prisoners universally condemned strip searches as 'humiliating and degrading,' but for 'women who were survivors of domestic abuse' they resulted in additional 'significant trauma' (ibid).

The impact of strip searching is not confined to the physical experience of assault on the body. In discussing family visits, Pat Carlen (1983: 79) notes the inhibiting, emotional impact of strip searches, with women prisoners declining visits to avoid humiliation. At the moment of intense emotional strain in public, meeting and departing from their children, women were forced to endure a strip search before returning to the isolation of their cells. Women were 'torn between' the 'desire' to see their children and the 'desire to shield them from the pain of the experience' (ibid).

WOMEN'S IMPRISONMENT IN THE NORTH OF IRELAND: LEGACY OF CONFLICT

Until its closure in 1986, women prisoners in the north of Ireland were held in Armagh Jail, built between 1780 and 1819. Politically affiliated and 'ordinary' women prisoners were then transferred to the Mourne House Unit within a purpose-built, high-security prison, Maghaberry. Male prisoners arrived the following year and the male and female prisons were amalgamated in 1988. The recent history of women's imprisonment in the north of Ireland was dominated by the internment and incarceration of political prisoners and the British State's policy of 'criminalisation.' Regular strip searching was central to the punitive regimes endured by male and female prisoners. What is clear from the research is the 'profound impact' of strip searching on women's mental health. Sharon Pickering (2002: 179) reports associated trauma: 'Often making women's periods stop, anxiety attacks . . . designed to humiliate, to degrade.' In her detailed interviews with former women political prisoners, she records their resistance to being strip searched, 'usually result[ing] in them being forcibly held and clothes torn from their bodies' (ibid: 180). Physical assaults and consequent emotional trauma were exacerbated by being charged with breaches of prison rules and/or assaulting staff. Thus, use of discretionary force by officers was complemented by the use of formal punishment at an institutional level. At both levels, women prisoners, political or 'ordinary,' were left in no doubt that they were powerless to resist the authority and sanctions of the prison.

Powerlessness through violent humiliation is the overwhelming message of Karen Quinn's experience of a mass strip search of Republican women prisoners in March 1992. Locked alone in their cells women prisoners were subjected to forced strip searches by male and female guards in full riot gear. Listening to the 'screams of pain' coming from other women as they resisted the searches, she sat in her cell 'weeping' as male guards 'laughing all the time as they took it out on the women prisoners' (Calamati 2002: 87). Eventually it was her 'turn.' Confronted by women guards she refused to undress and attempted to resist, but 'there wasn't much I could do to hold off those four women in riot gear when they set on me and pinned me down . . . ' She was thrown to the floor and they began stripping her.

> I struggled as hard as I could. When they tried to pull my sweater off, it got stuck over my head and I couldn't breathe. Instinctively I raised my chin. Again they slammed my face onto the floor and one of the warders kept it pressed down with her knee. My arms were twisted so far back that I thought they'd break. I yelled that I was having my period but that didn't stop them. . . . They grabbed me by the hips and managed to get the trousers down below my waist and then they yanked them down over my ankles . . . I couldn't breathe for the pain . . . they managed to strip me naked. As I lay there on the ground they threw me a blanket and a sanitary napkin. The warder who held me down with her knee wasn't finished . . . as she was leaving, she landed me a violent kick in the ribs. (ibid: 87–88)

Karen was dragged from her cell to the association room and then returned to her cell. The doctor was 'shocked when he saw what they had done to me' and stated that 'maybe my jaw had been broken.'

> That night I was still in shock. I wasn't able to cry or even to feel anything. I felt devastated. I spent hours sitting on the end of my bed just staring into space. When the dawn came, I still couldn't believe what they had done to me . . . the following morning one of the warders who attacked me was on duty. I felt sick to my stomach at the sight of her; just a few hours before she had made me stand naked before her while my menstrual blood trickled down my legs. She was the one who should have been ashamed and embarrassed at what she had done to me. How could this woman, who had forcibly stripped twenty-one women, act as if nothing at all had happened when she came face to face with one of her victims? (ibid: 89)

It was a question also to be directed at prison management, its doctors and nurses, its clergy and board of visitors. In fact, Karen Quinn was charged with disobeying an order and she lost the right to any reduction in her sentence.

> I feel as if I had been raped . . . I was helpless to do anything to protect myself from the warders . . . they can attack me any time they feel like it. . . . Our bruises are fading, but the memory of what we were forced to endure will not fade so quickly. (ibid.)

Strip searching 'came to epitomise, for many, the resolve of the security services to have women submit to the process of criminalisation and surveillance by taking control of women's nakedness' (Pickering 2002: 181). The authorities were determined to 'break' women prisoners' resolve, thus ending their collective resistance to the regime. What was also particularly disturbing was the apparent enthusiasm displayed by male and female guards for unrestrained brutality against defenceless prisoners (see Fairweather et al. 1984).

The 'objectification' of women prisoners extended beyond breaking resistance and the attempted imposition of conformity. Having 'de-feminised' women through abuse, through the physical attacks on the women's bodies, it also sought to impose stereotypical constructions of femininity, of feminine appearance and motherhood (Pickering 2002: 176). Guards labelled women 'whores,' 'sluts,' 'bad mothers,' while imposing 'limitations and expectations based on their sex.' The authorities displayed 'firm assumptions about how women should behave' (ibid). A dual construction and application of women's sexuality—simultaneously emphasising femininity while negating femininity—reflected a concerted effort to 'render women impotent in an already debilitating powerless situation.' As a woman prisoner stated, 'They are always attacking your sexuality in order to degrade you, to humiliate you and in order to beat you' (ibid: 177).

MOURNE HOUSE WOMEN'S UNIT, MAGHABERRY

The 1998 Belfast (Good Friday) Agreement led to the 1998 Northern Ireland (Sentences Act) and the release of most politically affiliated prisoners. The prison population at Maghaberry remained diverse comprising: 'males and females; ordinary remand prisoners; sex offenders; asylum seekers; members of different Loyalist organisations, both on remand and on sentence; members of different Republican organisations on remand and on sentence; short-term sentenced ordinary prisoners, long-term sentenced ordinary prisoners, and so on' (House of Commons, Select Committee on Northern Ireland Affairs 2004: para 4). Mourne House retained relative autonomy. It had cells for fifty-nine prisoners, hospital, kitchens, workshops, education block and exercise yards. With its own gate, reception and walls, it was a prison within a prison. Despite the release of political prisoners, Mourne House, its regimes, its staffing levels and its atmosphere, operated as a maximum security unit. Yet, in its final operational year, a third of women admitted were fine defaulters and the majority of those sentenced were for less than three months. The daily population averaged thirty with 304 receptions through the year.

Following the September 2002 death of Annie Kelly in a punishment block strip cell and publication of a highly critical Inspectorate report, the Northern Ireland Human Rights Commission initiated an investigation into the human rights of women imprisoned in Northern Ireland, focusing on Articles 2 and 3 of the European Convention on Human Rights (the right to life and the right to be free from torture, inhuman and degrading treatment). Fieldwork was undertaken early in 2004 (see Scraton and Moore, 2005b). Women prisoners comprised life prisoners, remand prisoners, committals, short-termers, immigration detainees, Republican prisoners and 'young offenders.' From reception through to release, women were subject to constant reminders of their loss of autonomy and the power of the prison authorities. On arrival, women were subjected to full body searches or strip searches. Guards recorded distinguishing features and identifying marks before prisoners showered, dressed and were locked without any induction in the cells. All women prisoners interviewed found reception strip searches by guards 'degrading,' 'humiliating' and 'embarrassing.' Their comments ranged from abuse of privacy to physical violation. This extended to random strip searches after family visits or after court hearings.

The Inspectorate found that fifty per cent of women held in Mourne House 'did not feel safe on their first night,' reporting 'that they had not been given any written or spoken information about what was going to happen to them' (HMIP 2003: 166). Women commented:[1]

> It was scary. I didn't know what I was coming to. I didn't know anyone in prison or anything about a prison environment.

> I was absolutely petrified coming into prison. I came after long interrogation. I don't know how I coped. I came into reception. It was regimental: 'Get a shower.' 'Fill in this form.' No question: 'Are you alright?' It was all oppressive, no kind of reassurance. You were terrified.

Work experience was restricted to gardening or cleaning. Purpose-built workshops, praised by inspectors, were closed. An impressive range of education on offer was illusory as classes were cancelled frequently due to the guards' unavailability. The prison's high-security status prevented women's movement without a guard escort. Teachers were not permitted to collect prisoners and take them the short distance to the education block. The Head of Education was 'appalled' by the recent deterioration in regime and the guards' increasingly uncooperative attitude. He commented:

> Prison staff have a vision of education that is rigid. It is a group of girls in class, head down, working away with a teacher. Informal talking, chatting and coffee are seen as heinous crimes. We try to insist that there has to be give and take but it just gets tighter and tighter.

Long hours of lock up, never less than sixteen and often twenty-three, compounded women's isolation and feelings of powerlessness:

> The monotony is crucifying. Before I came in here I had such a busy lifestyle. I went from one end of the scale when I didn't have time to see the news at night to suddenly having hours and hours on my hands. That's what hit me when I first came in.

For mothers, limited telephone access contributed to their anxiety and frustration:

> My only priority in my day is contacting my children. There's nothing worse than a day goes by and you don't speak to them. There's nothing worse than going to bed that night knowing that you've not spoke to them.

Lack of child-centred visits created further stress for mothers and for children too young to comprehend the situation:

> If they were allowed to stay over, even twice a year in the place to see what the place is like. There was mine saying, 'Mummy, are you in a cage, is there bars around you?'

A few guards appeared to care, but the unsupportive and openly hostile attitude of the majority heightened women's sense of 'worthlessness':

> If you're a prisoner: 'Go to your cell and don't bother anyone else.' That's the attitude I get from them.

> The majority [of officers] simply don't care. They do their job as a means to an end. There's a minority who drive home the fact that you are prisoners, you're the scum of the earth, you're not deemed to fit with society.

A woman prisoner recalled an incident regarding officers' responses to two Romanian prisoners who were imprisoned with a baby:

> They [the Romanian women] found it hard enough with the language barrier because their English wasn't that great. The screws [officers] had a pretty nasty attitude to them, not the ones on during the day,

mainly at night. I was sitting in the cell one night last week or the week before and wee [baby] was very, very sick. I could hear her vomiting from my cell—she's directly across. They did tell her to fuck off and everything when she asked to see the doctor. That there shouldn't be allowed. OK fair enough, they've done what they've done, but they don't need to be treated like animals, because they're human beings.

Women observed prisoners with mental health problems being bullied by guards:

[T]his woman had twice that day tried to hang herself. One of the . . . officers said, 'could you leave the keys? I'm not content just looking through the flap, she could have a ligature round her neck.' 'No, don't be looking in at her. Don't even look at her. Fuck her.' That's the way it was going but it was top volume. 'Fuck the old bitch, let her go.' This was being boomed and everyone on our landing, even the hardened ones, thought it was outrageous. There wasn't an ounce of respect shown to her as a human being.

A former prisoner recalled an older woman held in a punishment block strip cell. She was desperate for a cigarette: 'She ate with her fingers. They'd [guards] taunt her by blowing smoke through the door. They would taunt her and laugh at her.' She continued:

She tried to hang herself and three of us saw her getting out of the ambulance. They walked her across the tarmac in February with a suicide blanket on. They had all the riot gear on. She was crying. They were bringing her back from hospital and she was put back in the punishment block. We just kept our heads down, just did our time.

Asked about intimidation by guards another prisoner focused on power:

The only form of power in their lives is when they don the uniform and come in here. They're the ones who are playing cards all day or in there [landing office] sleeping off a hangover. They just say 'no' to everything.

Further, eighty per cent of guards were male and regularly there were no women guards on night duty. A governor commented that the number of male guards was 'unhealthily high.' This had serious implications. A nurse stated: 'We got a call the other night that a female prisoner had stripped herself and was hanging and the prison officer couldn't go in until a female officer came across.'

Guards were not trained to recognise or respond to women's mental health problems: 'We're not trained to deal with psychiatric cases. All they do is tell you how to dress, wear your uniform, stick by the book manual.'

Guards and prisoners agreed that women with mental health problems regularly were inappropriately imprisoned. Limited contact between medical and discipline staff brought fragmentation: 'the doctor writes a care plan' but 'not in consultation with anybody.' The written care plan 'sits on the officers' desks and they don't even write on it.' Women prisoners considered lack of care contributed to the level of self-harm:

> I've never self-harmed myself but I know a lot of girls who have. They're just trying to find someone to talk to, to give them help. They need a counsellor. Young people cutting themselves. To me that's a cry for help. But instead of having someone to talk to they're just thrown in the punishment unit.

Women were transferred to the punishment block (named by the authorities as the 'special supervision unit') if they were considered disruptive, noncompliant or at risk of self-harm. 'Standard' cells had a steel-framed bed bolted to the floor, an open metal flush toilet and a hand basin bolted to the wall. A seventeen-year-old child and an older woman were interviewed in the punishment block. The child, in the block because she self-harmed, was dressed in a nondestructible short-sleeved gown. She had extensive, self-inflicted wounds to her legs and arms. The 'standard' regime consisted of a twenty-three hour lock-up with one hour's recreation alone. It was mid-winter; there was snow on the ground. She took no outside exercise because her clothing consisted of the gown and slippers. She had completed two days of a twenty-eight-day period of cellular confinement. Part of her 'care plan' was 'optimal contact' with other prisoners and staff. She had neither. She felt compelled to self-harm: 'It's how I cope.'

> I shouldn't be down here. There's nothing to do. It's worse in the night. I hear voices and see things. But no-one helps me . . . I should be in the hospital wing. This place needs a women's hospital or a special wing for nurses to control and deal with women with problems.

In a later interview, she had been downgraded to the 'basic' regime. 'Basic' cells in the punishment block comprised a raised plinth, a mattress (often removed), a padded nondestructible sleeping bag and a small plastic potty as a toilet. There was no running water. Forbidden underwear even during menstruation, it was 'hard' to hold the sanitary napkin in place. Denied privacy, her degradation and humiliation was palpable: 'Just look what they make me go to the toilet in. That's for night time. . . . It's a disgrace.'

The older woman was in poor physical and mental health, suffering from a serious bowel illness, an untreated skin condition, epilepsy and diabetes. Transferred to the block because allegedly she had thrown the contents of her colostomy bag at guards, her 'behaviour' was 'managed' by officers 'drip feeding' her cigarettes and refusing her tea unless she complied with instructions. Locked up twenty-three hours each day and allowed out of her cell to clean the corridors, she was in obvious need of physical health treatment and psychological care. A long-term prisoner stated:

> I find in this day and age I can't understand how it is legal. Women who are constantly slashing their arms, legs, throats and trying repeatedly to hang themselves are stripped naked, thrown in a suicide jacket. 'Don't even give her a mattress, let her lie on the floor, let her lie in her own. . . . ' Women need help, counselling and therapy but to throw them in a strip cell, take away everything. I would hate to see a poor dog, bedding taken away treated like that.

A young woman on the committals landing revealed her desperation and her experience of the institutional lack of care:

> I tried to hang myself. They wouldn't move me from the cell and it's just provoking. I just wanted to kill myself. There's no hope for me in here. I suffer from depression and phobia. I didn't get my medication for the first week. The doctor wasn't seeing me for a week. . . . I had no medical treatment for that week. They cut down my medication. I was put in a cell and locked down. Nothing given to us, just 'Away to your cell.'

Treatment by prison officers of those with mental health problems was a significant issue for all women prisoners interviewed. A remand prisoner commented:

> A lot of people hate being locked up, it drives them mental. I've seen it in here. I've seen people trying to drown themselves in the sink. Again that's a lot to do with the screws not being taught how to deal with those sort of prisoners properly. Even showing somebody a bit of compassion goes a long way.

A long-termer stated that most guards 'don't give a damn':

> They just want their day done and that's that. That's the attitude I get from them. If you're a prisoner, 'Go to your cell and don't bother anyone else.' I'm sure you know there's a lot of girls that cut themselves in here. There should be someone on site for those girls to talk to instead of nobody, really, other than the other girls and one or two staff.

With the women's healthcare centre closed, healthcare requiring an overnight stay took place in the male prison hospital. Because of the high-security, moving women prisoners to the main Maghaberry site was complicated and involved their accommodation in a holding cell until assessment. They were returned to the holding cell until their return to Mourne House. Women prisoners feared the male hospital:

> Going over to the male hospital is a nightmare. . . . It's a cell the men use. There's a toilet in it. There's no toilet roll, no privacy and it's just awful. You wouldn't even ask a man to use it.

> The hospital over the road is just for men. I was over there myself. It is very dirty and the men talk very dirty. It really upset me. There's men over there for rape and some of them men have raped young children. That really upset me. When I heard that I didn't feel safe around them.

A woman prisoner whose close friend had just taken her own life was transferred to the male prison hospital and 'locked up 23 hours a day.' She was held in strip conditions described without a hint of irony by a senior orderly as a 'basic suite.' Staff 'don't even talk to you and it's supposed to be a hospital . . . if you feel really down they don't care.' The isolation, particularly from other women, was the most difficult aspect of the twenty-three-hour lock up: 'I've never been in prison before. I hate getting locked up . . . it brings memories back to me.' She disclosed a history of sexual abuse, 'I'm lying trying to sleep, thinking about these things':

> In the hospital they [male prisoners] talk filthy and dirt with the other prisoners. A man exposed himself. Said, 'I'll give her one.' He thought 'I'll pull it out 'cos there's a woman there.' We were all outside together. One man is in for sexually abusing a child. We have to have association with them. They are crafty, some of them. I told them [staff] about what the man did but they never did anything about it. I did not feel safe around them.

A female nurse confirmed that:

> Women are very vulnerable in the main hospital. Vulnerable to verbal abuse although they are accompanied by staff . . . the male hospital is used as a place of safety but it's not appropriate.

DEATHS IN CUSTODY

From 1996 until its closure in June 2004, three women died in Mourne House. Janet Holmes, aged twenty from Derry, died in November 1996. A vulnerable young woman with a history of drug and alcohol problems, in prison Janet was distressed and had been transferred to the prison hospital where, the day before her death, she attempted to take her own life. Despite this attempt, Janet was returned from the hospital to an ordinary cell in Mourne House, offering multiple ligature points. A prison doctor assessed her fit to attend disciplinary hearings. Her punishment was removal of evening association, her radio and television and denial of access to the gymnasium. She took her own life by hanging during night time lock up. Following the inquest, the Belfast Coroner wrote to the Director General of the Prison Service recording his concern regarding the adjudication process in the prison, the training of guards, Janet Holmes' medical assessment prior to adjudication and the speed of access to her cell once the alarm had been raised.

In September 2002, nineteen-year-old Annie Kelly died by hanging in a punishment cell in Mourne House. Annie had been in conflict with the law since she was thirteen, following the tragic death of her brother. Considered to have behaviour problems too difficult to manage in a juvenile facility, at fifteen she was fast-tracked to a high-security prison. From 1997 to September 2002, she was committed to prison on twenty-eight occasions. Throughout her time in Mourne House, Annie was admitted to the male prison hospital on numerous occasions. She self-harmed, lacerating her arms, banging her head, inserting metal objects under her skin and strangling herself with ligatures, losing consciousness. Diagnosed 'personality disordered,' her medical assessments also record a bright and intelligent young woman suffering from low self-esteem.

Annie's violence towards guards was used as justification for segregation, unlocked only when three members of staff were present, protected by riot gear and a full-length shield. Annie's last letter home included a harrowing account of her transfer to the male hospital:

> Then they all held me out in the corridor. I only had the suicide dress on and I was told I could keep my pants cause I'd a s.t. [sanitary towel] on. But when the men were holding me they got a woman screw to pull my pants off. That shouldn't have happened. Then they covered me in a celatape to keep the dress closed and handcuffed me and dragged me off to the male hospital.

Annie told of her 'relief' at being returned to the punishment cell in Mourne House, having 'wrecked' the hospital cell. Despite being in an anti-suicide dress, she had 'hung myself a pile of times. I just rip the dress and make a noose. But I am only doing that cause of the way their treating me. The cell floor is covered in phiss [urine] cause they took the phiss pot out the other night.' Male guards were unable to search Annie enabling her to conceal lengthy ligatures. Annie wrote: 'At the end of the day I know that if any thing happens me there'll be an investigation.'

On the afternoon of 5 September 2002, a female guard looked through the cell spy-hole and saw Annie at the window, ligatures around her neck, her tongue out. Donning riot gear and assuming Annie was 'feigning,' the officers entered the cell where they realised that she was dead or dying. At the subsequent inquest, the jury found the 'main contributor' to Annie Kelly's death was 'lack of communication and training at all levels.' The jury criticised her 'very long periods of isolation' and the lack of appropriate 'female facilities.' Responding to evidence concerning the paucity of adolescent mental health care in Northern Ireland, the jury called for the provision of a 'therapeutic community.' The Greater Belfast Coroner wrote to the Secretary of State expressing his concerns. The Secretary of State responded that following the closure of Mourne House in June 2004 and the transfer of women to Hydebank Wood, young women were now accommodated in a 'low risk establishment with a relaxed and varied regime.'

On 3 March 2004, Roseanne Irvine, a thirty-four-year-old mother was found hanging in her cell in Mourne House during evening lock-up. Roseanne suffered mental health problems and alcohol dependency. From early 1994 until September 2001, she had numerous admissions to hospital, mental health and psychiatric units for anxiety, depression, alcohol intoxication, overdosing and self-harm. Previously imprisoned in Mourne House for setting fire to her home in an attempt to harm herself, she attempted to take her own life in prison. In the aftermath of this attempt, the Prison Officers Association corresponded with Prison Service management regarding serious deficiencies in female prisoners' healthcare. Roseanne spent two further periods in prison for breaching her bail and her probation order. On release, unable to cope with living unsupported, she was accommodated in various hostels. In 2004, following another suicide attempt, Roseanne was admitted to hospital, but subsequently discharged without medication. Allocated a place in a house occupied by men with multiple alcohol- and drugs-related problems, Roseanne was 'very frightened.' She set fire to her room at the hostel and within a week 'appeared in court in her pyjamas' charged with arson. She was remanded to Mourne House.

In prison, Roseanne told a guard she intended to hang herself. The guard opened an IMR21 [a 'prisoner at risk' document] and Roseanne was put in an anti-suicide gown, given an anti-suicide blanket, potty and a container of water and transferred to the punishment block. Scheduled to attend 'sick parade,' it was cancelled and the duty doctor was not informed of her condition. A guard recorded her distressed state. She had torn hair from her scalp. Yet that evening she was returned to an ordinary cell that offered multiple ligature points and access to a range of ligatures.

The following day, the doctor was delayed, dealing with male prisoners, and Roseanne was not examined. She told guards that she feared access to her daughter was under review. During a short evening unlock, Roseanne stated she had taken '5 Blues,' tablets given to her by another prisoner, in addition to her medication. A nurse assessed Roseanne and judged her fit to remain in her cell. The Governor, across in the male prison, was informed, and he ordered an immediate cell search. It did not happen and the women were locked in their cells for the night. At approximately 9:15 pm Roseanne was seen by a Night Guard sitting on her bed writing a note. She asked for the light to be switched off. Just over an hour later she was checked and found hanging by the neck from the ornate bars of the window.

The level of callous indifference of some prison guards towards the suffering of women prisoners is evident in the following account of the immediate aftermath of Roseanne's death:

> The next day I just sat and cried. I then had panic attacks. They didn't get the nurse over. I pushed the [emergency] button and they came to the door. I asked to see the nurse and they just said 'No.' They said, 'You're not allowed to push the button. It's for emergencies only.' I said I was having a panic attack. They said, 'Take deep breaths.' It was early evening. I sat up on the bed with a pillow and cried and cried.

Roseanne Irvine's death was foreseeable. A guard stated that she 'displayed the symptoms, the prior attempts' and the 'warning bells were there'. A professional worker commented that 'everyone realised that Roseanne had great needs,' yet provision 'fell short because no-one put their hand up for overall responsibility.' In February 2007, following a week-long inquest into Roseanne's death, an inquest jury endorsed these views, returning a damning narrative verdict. Roseanne had taken her own life while the 'balance of her mind was disturbed.' The jury noted the significance of 'the events leading up to her death' including her 'long history of mental health difficulties.' It stated: 'The prison system failed Roseanne.' There had been systemic 'defects' including 'severe lack of communication and inadequate recording,' a 'failure to act' on the IMR21 and a 'lack of healthcare and resources for women prisoners.' The jury concluded that prison was 'not a suitable environment for someone with a personality/ mental health disorder.' It recommended 'more ongoing training on suicide awareness for prison staff.' The Coroner announced that he would be writing to the Director of the Prison Service and to the Secretary of State for Northern Ireland.

THE GENDERED PRISON AND THE 'CONTINUUM OF UNSAFETY'

Elizabeth Stanko comments that 'Women's lives rest upon a continuum of unsafety.' Despite their diversity as women, 'they share a common awareness of their vulnerability' (1990: 85):

Women's heightened level of anxiety is born of an accurate reading of
their relationship to safety. It is not a misguided hysteria or paranoia.
Women's life experiences—as children, adolescents and adults—are set
in an everpresent sexual danger. Worry about personal safety is one
way women articulate what it means to be female and live, day-in,
day-out, in communities where women are targets of sexual violence.
(ibid: 86)

By the time the inquests into the Mourne House deaths of Annie Kelly
and Roseanne Irvine were held, women prisoners in the north of Ireland
had been transferred to a house in Hydebank Wood male Young Offender's Centre on the outskirts of Belfast. It was clear from discussions with
governors that their view of the Mourne House regime was one of stag-
nation and non-engagement by most guards. There was a poor industrial
relations context with senior guards presenting management as unable to
deal effectively with the powerful Prison Officers Association (the POA).
Matters were exacerbated by allegations reported in the media of relationships between male prison guards and women in Mourne House. Female
long-term prisoners were vilified in the local tabloids: 'Sex-starved Black
Widow snares warder; Jailhouse rocked by torrid allegations' (*Sunday Life*,
14 March 2004). Women were labelled 'the witches of East Wing,' the
'Fermanagh blonde' and the 'Ballymena bruiser.' Women prisoners consistently refuted the allegations, insisting that no sexual relations occurred.
The 'independent' investigation found serious managerial problems but no
evidence of sexual relationships. Subsequently, the Prison Service remained
silent as media attacks on the women persisted, leading to serious distress
for them and their children.

It was clear from the research that the rumour and innuendo, within
the prison and released to the media, was initiated and sustained by prison
guards. The women prisoners targeted would find newspapers left open
at pages in which salacious stories referred to them by name, with photographs taken at the time of their arrest or conviction constantly recycled:
'You come into the recreation room and it's there, right in your face. They
do it on purpose and they make sure all the others [prisoners] see it.' Following the transfer of women prisoners to Hydebank Wood, the rumours
connected the supposed 'sex scandal' to the closure of Mourne House. One
of the named women commented: 'We're getting blamed and it's causing
real problems for us with staff who don't want to work with us and with
prisoners coming in who know no better. Yet Headquarters [of the Prison
Service] won't issue a denial.' One life sentenced prisoner who was singled
out for this attention endured daily abuse in the prison, public vilification
and the anguish of knowing that her children were being bullied and tormented at school and in the community.

The victimisation of particular women through constructing and feeding
their negative reputations provides a clear example of how malicious prison

guards are able to use their position to intimidate and control the lives of prisoners. Prison managers' reluctance to intervene, to investigate and discipline guards or to challenge and correct stories suggested their acceptance and effectively institutionalised the deceit. Public portrayals of the 'bad woman,' especially when they combine grave crimes with sex scandals, are part of the stock-in-trade of tabloid journalism. Women so degraded have no come-back, no right of reply and no potential for redress. These events render targeted women vulnerable, fearful and unsafe. They exist on the continua of 'unsafety' and violence and they place their families and children at risk; harming mothers through hurting those close to them.

The research also revealed the direct harm done to women suffering from mental ill-health. As discussed earlier, this follows a well-established pattern of condemning women as untreatable through labelling them personality disordered. Again, this plays on popularly held assumptions that women prisoners, deviating from their gendered role, are either 'mad' or 'bad.' Not only does it have consequences for the labels applied but also for the treatment they receive. The lack of psychotherapeutic care in the community, their fast-track imprisonment and the lack of appropriate healthcare in prison not only leave them vulnerable and unsupported, but also create the conditions of self-fulfilment. Labelled 'disordered,' neglected and taunted, women who resist through anger and frustration, through self-harm or attempts on their own lives, are punished in the isolation of strip cells.

Many of the women interviewed for this research had direct experiences of sexual violence, in some cases from an early age. Far from being a safe and supportive environment, the prison was threatening—a profoundly unsafe place. Its 'continuum of unsafety' included strip searches, sexual abuse, solitary confinement, self-harm, institutional negligence, punishment block strip cells and violence directed towards those who resisted authority. In her definitive text on the operational practices of United States mental asylums for women, Phyllis Chesler (1972: 34–35) identified how the 'degradation and disenfranchisement of the self' was institutionally reinforced by the refusal of access to 'therapy, privacy and self-determination.' Women's boldness, assertiveness, questioning of those in authority and rejection of imposed expectations of femininity were met with 'punishment programs.' Those experiencing and seeking support for 'emotional distress' were 'punished for their conditioned and socially approved self-destructive behaviour' (ibid: 39). In this punitive context, attempts by women to take their own lives were 'like female tears, constitut[ing] an essential act of resignation and helplessness.' Those who succeeded 'tragically, outwitting or rejecting their [expected] feminine role, and at the only price possible: their death' (ibid: 49).

Women prisoners considered volatile or difficult to manage, particularly children and young women, experienced the full force of control and restraint, the 'legitimate use of force' at the discretion of the guards. There were numerous allegations of women being roughly treated or assaulted in circumstances where the forced removal of their bodies or their clothes escalated into violent confrontation. It is not difficult to draw parallels between the accounts of women political prisoners discussed earlier in this chapter and Annie Kelly's account of her treatment prior to her death. The verbal and physical abuse by particular prison guards, their callous disregard for troubled women and their apparent impunity against disciplinary proceedings reflected custom and practice in a Prison Service that had not recruited since the early 1990s and had not developed gender-specific or child-protection strategies, policies or training. Its reluctance to address the issue of strip searching, given the legacy of its use for inflicting pain and punishment on prisoners during the conflict, was a telling example of how deeply gendered responses were institutionalised.

Soon after the transfer of women from Mourne House, a life-sentence prisoner initiated a judicial review that included the use of strip searching at Hydebank Wood. The judge ruled that random strip searching did 'not recognise individual considerations of whether it [a search] is necessary.' It was for the Prison Service to demonstrate that searches were 'necessary and carried out in a proportionate way and as a proportionate reaction to the relevant mischief.' The Prison Service had 'failed to have proper and explicit regard to the relevant convention rights,' thus 'the current policy of strip searching at Hydebank cannot be demonstrated to be proportionate and necessary.' Subsequently, the Prison Service reviewed its policy and practice and reduced the use of strip searching to a random one in ten following visits. It retained the compulsory strip search on reception.

Following completion of the Mourne House research, the Human Rights Commission made numerous recommendations. It also called for an independent, public inquiry focusing on the deterioration in the regime and conditions in which women and girl children were held following the inspection of Mourne House in February 2002. An inquiry would seek disclosure of all available documentation regarding the administration and management of women's and girls' imprisonment calling oral evidence from senior managers to be tested under cross-examination. The terms of reference would include: the failure by the Director General and the Governor of Maghaberry to implement the Inspectorate's recommendations and its consequences for women and girl children prisoners held at Mourne House from 2002 to 2004; the circumstances surrounding the deaths in custody of Annie Kelly in September 2002 and of Roseanne Irvine in March 2004; the use of the punishment and segregation unit as a location for the cellular confinement of self-harming and suicidal women, including girl children; the circumstances in which prison officers were suspended and dismissed following allegations of inappropriate conduct. Following the inquest into the death of Roseanne Irvine, the Northern Ireland Affairs Committee established a generic investigation into healthcare in prisons in the north of Ireland and the Commission issued a further demand for an independent, public inquiry. The Commission's follow-up research was published in July 2007 (Scraton and Moore, 2007).

ACKNOWLEDGEMENTS

With acknowledgement to the Northern Ireland Human Rights Commission—this chapter does not necessarily reflect the views of the Commission. Many thanks to our families and friends for their personal and intellectual support. Warmest appreciation and thanks to the women interviewed for this study and the follow-up research and to the families of Annie Kelly and Roseanne Irvine.

NOTES

1. The following quotes and those throughout the article are taken from research interview transcripts with women prisoners and staff 2004–2006.

REFERENCES

Calamati, S. (2002) *Women's Stories From the North of Ireland*, Belfast: Beyond the Pale Publications.

Carlen, P. (1983) *Women's Imprisonment: A Study in Social Control*, London: Routledge and Kegan Paul.

———. (1998) *Sledgehammer: Women's Imprisonment at the Millenium*, London: Macmillan.

———. (2002) 'Introduction: Women and Punishment' in P. Carlen (ed) *Women and Punishment: The Struggle for Justice*, Cullompton: Willan Publishing, pp. 3–20.

Chesler, P. (1972) *Women and Madness*, New York: Avon 1972.

Davis, A.Y. (2003) *Are Prisons Obsolete?* New York: Seven Stories Press.

Fairweather, E., McDonough, R. and McFadyean, M. (1984) *Only the Rivers Run Free: Northern Ireland, The Women's War*, London: Pluto Press.

George, A. (1995) 'The Big Prison' in Hampton, B. (ed.) *Prisons and Women*, Kensington, NSW: UNSW Press, pp. 15–28.

Heidensohn, F. (1985) *Women and Crime*, London: Macmillan.

HMIP (2003) *HM Chief Inspector of Prisons, Report of a full announced Inspection of HM Prison Maghaberry, 13–17 May*, London: Home Office.

House of Commons Select Committee on Northern Ireland Affairs (2004) *Second Report*, London: The Stationary Office.

Kelly, L. (1987) 'The Continuum of Male Violence' in J. Hanmer and M. Maynard (eds.) *Women, Violence and Social Control*, London: Macmillan, pp. 46–60.

———. (1988) *Surviving Sexual Violence*, Cambridge: Polity.

Lowthian, J. (2002) 'Women's Prisons in England: Barriers to Reform' in P. Carlen [ed] *Women and Punishment: The Struggle for Justice*, Cullompton: Willan Publishing, pp. 155–181.

Pickering, S. (2002) *Women, Policing and Resistance in Northern Ireland*, Belfast: Beyond the Pale Publications.

Radford, J., Harne, L. and Friedberg, M. (2000) 'Introduction,' in J. Radford, M. Friedberg and L. Harne (eds) *Women, Violence and Strategies for Action: Feminist Research, Policy and Practice*, Buckingham: Open University Press, pp. 1–9.

Scraton, P. and Moore, L. (2005a) 'Degradation, Harm and Survival in a Woman's Prison,' *Social Policy & Society*, 5:1, 67–78.

———. (2005b) *The Hurt Inside: The Imprisonment of Women and Girls in Northern Ireland*, Belfast: Northern Ireland Human Rights Commission

———. (2007) *The Prison Within: The Imprisonment of Women at Hydebank Wood: 2004–2006*, Belfast: Northern Ireland Human Rights Commission

Sim, J. (1990) *Medical Power in Prisons*, Milton Keynes: Open University Press.

Stanko, E. A. (1985) *Intimate Intrusions: Women's Experience of Male Violence*, London: Routledge and Kegan Paul.

———. (1990) *Everyday Violence: How Women and Men Experience Sexual and Physical Danger*, London: Pandora Press.

Vetten, L. and Bhana, K. (2005) 'The Justice for Women Campaign: Incarcerated Domestic Violence Survivors in Post-Apartheid South Africa' in J. Sudbury (ed.) *Global Lockdown: Race, Gender, and the Prison-Industrial Complex*, London, Routledge, pp. 255–270.

Walsh, T. (2004) *Incorrections: Investigation Prison Release Practice and Policy in Queensland and Its Impact on Community Safety*, Queensland: QUT.

8 Neither Kind Nor Gentle
The Perils of 'Gender Responsive Justice'

Cassandra Shaylor

In the first decade of the 21st century, a remarkable and unprecedented event occurred at a hearing before the Senate Budget Subcommittee on Prisons in Sacramento, California. Over 2,500 women in prison showed up to protest AB 2066, a bill that would expand the California prison system for women by 4,500 beds. Of course, these women were not allowed to appear in person at a hearing ostensibly held to consider their fate. As gasps broke out around the committee room, advocates released a twenty-five-foot-long scroll stretching from one end of the room to the other, page after page of a petition circulated and signed by people in women's prisons to protest a plan allegedly introduced in their names.[1]

The story of the bill against which 3,300 people in California's women's prisons organised (Huang Interview, 30 March 2007)[2] forms a backdrop against which the complicated and contested understandings of gender within the prison industrial complex (PIC) can be examined. This article asks: How are outmoded understandings of gender and their connection to race and sexuality relied on and perpetuated by the penal system? What impact do these normative conceptualisations have within and beyond the prison on those who identify as women? On men? On transgender people? What are the ways in which well-meaning reformers (often self-identified feminists and politically progressive people) are interpolated by the seemingly positive rhetoric and strategies presented by an institution that continues to put people in cages? In particular, what is the role of 'Gender Responsive Justice,' a concept promoted as one which identifies and meets the different needs and experiences of women in prison—in perpetuating not only outmoded notions of gender but further entrenching the PIC itself? Finally, how can an abolitionist approach to the problem of the PIC transform such notions and effects?

Before considering these questions directly, I offer a series of reflections problematising the categories that help to constitute hidden ideologies of punishment. As an abolitionist and the co-director of *Justice Now*, one of only two explicitly abolitionist organisations in the United States, I believe that part of what makes radical ideas become common sense is the practiced intention to change language to reflect values.[3] The mission of *Justice*

Now is to work with people in women's prisons and local communities towards building a world without prisons. We believe that prisons and policing do not make communities safe and whole but, in fact, the current system severely damages those it imprisons and the communities most affected by systems of imprisonment. As abolitionists, we see prisons as a form of violence against women—and all others locked inside. We maintain that imprisoning men offers no solution to interpersonal violence in our communities. We are committed not only to challenging what we see happening in prisons and the PIC more broadly, but in building a different world where all have affordable housing, food, healthcare, economic opportunity and freedom from individual and state violence. This vision includes creating new ways to respond when people hurt each other, ways no longer reliant on violence and control (Justice Now 2005). Such a vision also requires that we model the ways of being we attempt to create. This entails granting people the right to self-determination and respecting their personal assertions of their needs.

For many years, advocates have used the terms 'women prisoners' or 'men prisoners.' Increasingly, however, a growing understanding of the ways in which these phrases reduce individuals solely to their status as prisoners is giving way to referencing *where people are located at a given point in their lives* rather than using the descriptor 'prisoner' in order to describe *who they are*. Because people in prison have multiple identities (including, but not limited to, artist, parent, legal advocate, sibling, organiser, partner, business-person and teacher) and are members of communities outside the prison system and eventually leave prison, we call for a move away from such narrowly conceived notions of identity.

Further, in this chapter, I employ the terms 'people in women's prisons' or 'people in men's prisons.' This acknowledges that it is the state that determines the specific institutions in which to imprison particular people based on a rigid gender binary not necessarily reflecting people's self-identity. For example, the California Department of Corrections segregates people into women's and men's institutions through assessment derived in biologically based criteria—namely genital inspection—regardless of how the person consigned to prison self-identifies. According to Alex Lee, former Director of the Transgender/Gender Variant People in Prison Project, this policy is consistent throughout prisons and jails in the United States. Using sweeping categories like 'women in prison' or 'men in prison' erases trans-identified people, continuing to allow the state to act as final arbiter of gender identity.[4] That said, there may be moments when I use 'women' or 'men' as blanket categories or refer to women's prisons and men's prisons in part to make analysis more clear and because the majority of people in prison choose to be referenced as women or men. When appropriate, I will refer to people as transgendered, gender variant, or gender nonconforming specifically to work against a binary logic of gender undergirding the larger social systems that abolitionists, among other radical activists, challenge.

In February 2005, the California Department of Corrections and Rehabilitation (CDCR) established the Gender Responsive Strategies Commission (GRSC), comprised primarily of CDCR officials, criminologists and representatives from various government departments, to 'assess and make recommendations on proposed strategies, policies and plans specific to women offenders' (CDCR 2006). In January 2006, the GRSC identified 4,500 people suitable for release from women's prisons based on ascribed statuses of 'nonviolent' and 'low-risk' (CURB 2007: 5). The recommendation put forward by the GRSC and later introduced as Assembly Bill AB 2066 by Assembly Member Sally Lieber (D-Mountain View) proposed that rather than releasing those 4,500 people back to their communities, instead they should be placed in as-of-yet nonexistent 'Female Rehabilitative Community Correctional Centers' (FRCCCs) (CURB 2007: 5).

The FRCCCs were presented by the GRSC as 'community-based alternatives to incarceration' (ibid). Despite being presented as a 'kinder, gentler' approach to women's imprisonment, the FRCCCs replicated existing structures of punishment while expanding the penal system. Rather than releasing the 4,500 people identified as unnecessarily imprisoned, new institutions were recommended. In deference to what often functions as the most influential political lobby in the state, namely the powerful California Correctional Prison Officers' Association (CCPOA), the proposed FRCCCs were to be operated by private contractors while people imprisoned in them would be guarded by CDCR correctional officers—unionised prison guards. Even though the CDCR states that these new 'residential' facilities would be run by 'community organisations,' the structure of the programmes—significantly the employment of members of the CCPOA—failed to recognise that no truly community-based organisation would bid to obtain one of these contracts.

The recommendation for the FRCCCs was incorporated into Governor Arnold Schwarzenegger's August 2006 Special Session on Prisons, at which he proposed a number of other prison expansion projects. As evidence of the intention to deploy the GRSC's recommendation as a means for expanding the penal system, in June 2006 the Governor's office explicitly stated that moving approximately 40 per cent of the women's prison population to these new facilities would make room for 'an entire prison worth of space that could be used for male prisoners' (Braz 2006: 87). Clearly, the proposal would not release anyone and, in contrast, would expand the capacity of the women's prison system by 40 per cent in two years (CDCR 2006: 5). I present this example of a disturbing and alarmingly proliferating trend of 'gender responsive justice' to highlight how gender is used to facilitate the work of the PIC.

Conventional understandings of gender that rely on a belief in 'difference' reinforce binary understandings of gender within the PIC. Such limited approaches do significant work for the PIC, including: prevention of gender self-determination; promotion of stereotypes of prisoners used to justify the continued existence of the prison; employment of the rhetoric of reform to distract from the underlying goals of building the system; disregard for imprisoned people's personal assertions of what reform, rehabilitation, and safety might mean by infantilising those identified as women, demonising those identified as men, and erasing those who self-identify as transgendered.

Feminist reformers initially introduced the language and attendant strategies of what they termed 'gender responsive justice' as a way to highlight what they understood to be different needs of women not addressed adequately by a prison system designed for men. The interventions these (mainly) academics have made during the last two decades have focused on attempts to change the system itself by promoting policies, training and restructuring plans to departments of correction (including jails, state prisons and federal penitentiaries) across the United States. As the pendulum has swung back from a focus purely on repression and punishment towards the use of language of 'rehabilitation' and 'reform' (a pendulum swinging consistently since the birth of the penitentiary), departments of correction have taken up the language of reformers, using it to their own ends. Most often, this manifests in professed commitments by prison administrators to change the structure, climate, and purpose of the prison towards rehabilitating people in prison and reintegrating them into communities from which they were removed. Typically, such assertions fail to result in any substantial shifts in how prisons or the systems that funnel people into them operate. In fact the co-opted approaches of reformers are used often as a screen behind which to grow and strengthen the PIC. The story of an expansionist project presented as a way to 'help' women in prison related earlier is one example of the dangers of a belief in and commitment to reforming a system that can be re-formed only to the extent that it becomes further entrenched.

Criminologists Barbara Bloom and Barbara Owen, along with psychologist Stephanie Covington, produced a massive report in 1993 for the National Institute of Corrections entitled *Gender-Responsive Strategies: Research, Practice, and Guiding Principles for Women Offenders* in an effort to present arguments about gender difference that 'have implications for *managing women* in the criminal justice system' (Bloom et al. 1993: 11, emphasis added). The larger discourse of 'gender responsiveness,' defined by Bloom and Covington (2000: v) as 'creating an environment . . . that reflects an understanding of the realities of women's lives and addresses the issues of the women' rests on a liberal feminist foundation. Liberal feminist underpinnings of gender responsive strategies rely on the specious notion that the prison system can at any point meet the complex and changing needs of *women* and, further, that an understanding of *woman* that remains encased in a stronghold of gender fixity certainly will not make it so. By capitulating to the notion that an acceptable role for the state is to 'manage' those it deems women, self-identified feminists end up doing the work of the state to control women, albeit with a plan for 'nicer' cells and 'better' programmes.

What is known in criminology as gender responsive justice depends on a belief in rehabilitation—a concept introduced by the penal system itself at its origin to replace corporal punishment—and resting on the idea that there is something fundamentally wrong with people in prison that needs to be fixed and that imprisonment can serve that function. An uncritical use of rehabilitation rhetoric fails to allow for an analysis of the ideological underpinnings of what is constituted as 'crime' and how that plays out in who is targeted for imprisonment (Davis 2003). In reality, people end up in prison for many complex reasons. Not insignificantly, institutional racism, and a larger social hatred of impoverished people, predetermines who becomes locked away even as a system of global capital benefits from the PIC. To promote rehabilitation as a laudable goal cedes to the state the construction of people in prison as flawed individuals who can be improved by the prison system.

Notably, gender responsive justice forms part of a larger shift happening in the prison system within the United States and abroad, a move away from a focus on punishment and back towards reform. In the United States, there have been more than a few indicators of a shift. A renewed focus on rehabilitation is reflected in the discursive practice of correctional systems, including changing the names of systems. In July 2005, the California Department of Corrections added the word 'rehabilitation' to the name of the department, ostensibly to signal a new era in a system that had been roundly criticised by the courts, the media and the public for abuse, mismanagement and excessive spending. At the same time that Governor Schwarzenegger announced the new 'R' and his commitment to rehabilitation, he cut vocational and educational programming in the system. A number of states closed or have considered closing prisons, albeit in most instances for economic reasons, but closures have required a change in language. The federal courts have taken strong stances on the unconstitutionality of confinement conditions, including a federal takeover of the healthcare delivery system in California. Moreover, as mentioned earlier, departments of correction increasingly employ consultants such as Bloom and Owen to implement 'gender responsive' programmes. There are plans for the introduction of gender responsiveness in Hawaii, Missouri and Minnesota.

The discourse of gender responsiveness is employed at local and state level by United States departments of correction, often to deleterious effect. In Massachusetts, for example, after ten years of mixed-sex imprisonment in Hampden County, the state is building a separate women's jail rather than decarcerating or developing alternatives for the growing population of women in the jail system. The jail will imprison over 350 women from Hampden and surrounding counties, at a cost over twenty-six million dollars (Walsh 2006). The Department of Women's Justice Services in Cook County, Illinois (which runs the Chicago jail) now implements gender responsive programmes for women (NCJRS 2007) and the Ohio Department of Rehabilitation and Correction (DRC) is implementing gender responsive 'best practice' (Ohio DRC 2006).

The potential dangerous impacts of gender responsiveness extend beyond the growth of prison systems themselves. It now contributes to the expansion of markets for imprisonment-related services. According to the Ohio DRC, 'the Orbis Partners, Inc. [guided by Bloom and Covington] developed a case management model to serve as a guide in the delivery of gender responsive case management services for women who are incarcerated or under probation/parole,' and the National Institute of Corrections is seeking applications from jurisdictions to implement and evaluate the case management plan (DRC 2006).

Further, the promotion of the approach abroad is beginning. In England, a recent report commissioned by the Home Office on 'women with particular vulnerabilities in the criminal justice system' made recommendations for what Baroness Jean Corston, who conducted the review, called 'a radical new approach, treating women both holistically and individually—a woman-centred approach' (Corston 2007: 2). In an uncanny parallel to the California expansion plan, she proposes, among other recommendations, that 'the government should announce within six months a clear strategy to replace existing women's prisons with suitable, geographically dispersed, small, multifunctional custodial centres within 10 years' (2007: 5). This movement and its effects are not new. Gender responsive justice recapitulates historical systems of imprisonment introduced as improvements designed to organise against increased repression or curb an unmanageable, unsustainable system (Morris and Rothman 1995). Unfortunately, an approach that relies on the belief that the system can be transformed toward a greater good if only X could be changed results in the further entrenchment of the idea that imprisonment is inevitable, appropriate and necessary.

Prison historians have found the negative effects of reform especially obvious in the evolution of prisons for women (Freedman 1981). The modern women's prison evolved from well-meaning efforts to challenge the repressive masculinist prison system to which (White) women initially were confined (Davis 2003). The original 'reformatories' for women were introduced to imprison poor and working-class White women who were trained to be domestic workers on their release. Black women were still enslaved during this period, and consequently endured a different form of punishment until slavery was abolished. Given the legacy of anti-Black racism, it is no surprise that laws quickly were passed after the Civil War to target and imprison Black people, and the racial make-up of the prison population shifted dramatically, as did the form of punishment, to a more repressive regime. Black and Native American women often were segregated within reformatories or, in the case of Black women, were subjected to the convict lease system instead of the 'feminizing' approaches of reformatories. Although born of good intentions, reformatories for women pointed to the contradictions within the imprisonment system as a whole. It can be reformed only to the extent that such reforms support its continued existence.

Discourses of rehabilitation too often keep gender responsive justice advocates from speaking directly to the people for whom they purport to advocate. Proponents of gender responsive justice too often speak for, rather than listen to, the political positions and expressed needs of people in prison. In California, supporters of gender responsiveness fail to work with women inside or their advocates on the outside, neglect to find out what strategies people in women's prisons support and routinely ignore, belittle and reject these perspectives when they are presented. For example, Executive Director of the California Commission on the Status of Women, Mary Wiberg, told a *Justice Now* advocate that garnering 2,500 signatures to protest AB 2066 was meaningless. Wiberg added that if she had 'all the time in the world,' she too could go into any prison in the state and persuade 2,500 people to sign anything she proposed (Tong Interview, 22 February 2007). Wiberg assumes that anti-prison organisers have no (real) work to do and 'all the time in the world' to waste. More significantly, she dismisses the political organising, independent thinking and free will of over 160,000 people imprisoned in California.

An insidious effect of gender responsive justice, its purported benevolent focus on women's special needs, often obscures other sexist and racist proposals and practices buried under the cover of gender responsiveness. In a particularly disturbing example, on 18 July 2006, the Healthcare Subcommittee of the GRSC proposed a policy to offer sterilisation to women in prison during labour or immediately after delivery, a practice that can be traced historically to the eugenics and racial purity movements born of the post-industrial West (GRSC 18 July 2006). The minutes of the meeting of the California Department of Corrections and Rehabilitation Gender Responsive Strategies Commission (dated 18 July 2006) read:

> The Health Care Subcommittee discussed and made the following recommendations: Birth Control and Sterilization: The committee discussed the cost effectiveness of elective sterilization, either post-partum or coinciding with Cesarean section. There would be no cost increase in terms of transportation and admission if they were at the hospital having a Cesarean section performed. The current contract language reads as, 'Doing what is medically necessary.' This is derived from the Title 15, which states that sterilization is an elective surgery and the CDCR does not provide elective surgeries. To prevent amending Title 15, this language could be incorporated into the Inmate Medical Services Policies and Procedures (IMSP&P), Volume 4, Chapter 24. This could then be integrated into the contract in order to cover the IMSP&P.

Amending Title 15, the portion of the Penal Code governing the administration of prisons, would require legislative approval. What is proposed is an end run around the legislature by amending internal policies and incorporating it into contracts with hospitals.

The proposal was put forward by Subcommittee Chair, Dawn Martin, Health Care Manager at Valley State Prison for Women (VSPW), where all pregnant women in California's state prison system are held. Though anti-prison advocate members of the GRSC have argued vociferously against this coercive proposal (Shain Interview, 26 March 2007) and representatives of the CDCR have denied pursuing what is, in effect, a policy of eugenics, *Justice Now* has documented several instances of women of colour, disproportionately Black women, being sterilised without their knowledge or consent (Levi Interview, 15 March 2007).

Further, during the summer after the GRSC presented the sterilisation proposal, *Justice Now* Human Rights Director, Robin Levi, documented the case of a woman in her mid-twenties, pregnant with her first child, who was pressured near the end of her pregnancy *and near the end of her prison sentence* by medical staff at VSPW to consent to sterilisation. She refused consent and expressed anger that she had been placed in such a situation. Moreover, she also indicated that other women had the same experience with VSPW medical staff (Levi Interview, 15 March 2007). Human Rights Documenters inside prison and *Justice Now* staff are working to uncover how widespread this practice is and whether any women have been sterilised as a result, following assurances by the CDCR that they did not adopt the GRSC Healthcare Committee's proposal.

Justice Now's Human Rights Documentation Program is a collaborative effort between people in women's prisons and *Justice Now* staff and interns. Using a 'participatory documentation approach,' people in prison are trained in human rights standards and documentation techniques, are supported in documenting their own and other people's experiences of human rights violations and collaborate with staff to produce and publicise human rights reports on abusive prison conditions. Based on the issues identified by people in prison as primary concerns, *Justice Now* focuses on issues related to the Right to Family, including inadequate reproductive health care and the denial of appropriate pre- and postnatal care, and forced and coerced sterilisation. Though a handful of organisations in the United States use participatory documentation approaches, this is unique work with people in prison. Our concern when launching the programme was that due to the reality of retaliation against people in prison for organising inside, very few women would be interested in becoming documenters. In fact, the response has been overwhelming and in addition to almost twenty documenters trained, there is a waiting list.

Gender responsive justice relies on outmoded, essentialist notions of femininity and female-ness to normalise ideas of women as the kinder, gentler sex, most valued for their roles as care givers and their place in a 'cult of domesticity' (Cott 1997). It also assumes that women are more deserving than men in relocation to (ostensibly) less punitive environments. The dangerous corollary to this approach is its reinforcement of male stereotypes of violence and dangerousness and, in the specific context of incarceration, specifically in need of harsh conditions and lengthy sentences as well as undeserving of and uninterested in contact with children and family. Such an approach relies on understandings of sex and gender that delimit the ways in which people are allowed to be and to be understood in the world, exclude people who do not conform to normative notions of male and female, and support the work of the state in promoting heteronormativity. Abolitionism demands more complex understandings of gender than those produced and promoted by the state, whose hegemonic renderings of gender exclude trans-identified and gender nonconforming people.

In the last quarter century, activists and scholars working in philosophy, history, cultural studies and identity-based movements have theorised complications of traditionally conceived genders.[5] Of course, reformers and abolitionists need to deal with the consequences of specific differences. Most women can bear children, and some women are prone to cancers that do not affect men. In addition, women have higher rates of HIV, Hepatitis C, and other diseases—mainly because of the legacy of sexism that has informed healthcare for women in and out of prison. Women also provide primary care for children to a greater degree than men. However, these differences constitute cultural constructs and should not be used to justify shifts in modes of punishment that assume that men are not or cannot be caregivers and, therefore, do not require changes in the oppressive regimes under which they live in prison. Further, self-identified reformers' refusal to look beyond 'the differing realities of the two genders' (Bloom, Owen et al. 1993) inculcates stereotypical notions of sex and gender by ignoring other gender formations.

Such binary conceptualisations of human biology fail to address issues of particular concern to transgendered people in prison, including, but not limited to, health issues, the construction and celebration of complex kinship structures, and a vulnerability to violence, often in response to their gender identity. Arguably in the context of incarceration, the refusal of the right to gender self-determination produces the greatest harm to gender nonconforming people, most if not all of whom face discrimination, harassment, and violence on a constant basis. Transgender prisoners are targeted for sexual assault and rape because of their gender variance. They are denied hormone treatments causing serious medical and psychological complications. They often are subjected repeatedly to strip searches, sometimes classified 'gender checks,' through which guards force trans people to expose their genitals merely to satisfy their curiosity and/or sadistic desires (Lee Interview, 6 November 2006).

Although the penitentiary was founded on a masculinist approach to punishment, this model does not benefit men in prison any more than women or transgender people. The current punishment regime assumes a harmful and violent masculinity even though such constructions of masculinity, not unlike those that equate femaleness with caregiving, are not inevitably linked to biological and/or essential maleness. Therefore, a masculinist approach to dealing with harms should be eliminated for all people, regardless of sex or gender identity.

This dominant understanding of masculinity is necessarily racialised. Popular representations and cultural stereotypes of prisoners as large, menacing Black men or as muscular, tattooed Latinos feed conceptualisations of aggressive masculinity that must be contained within prison walls. Such stereotypical representations undermine the efforts of advocates who work on behalf of people in women's prisons by operating at the expense of people in men's prisons. The failure to recognise the prison as a system that creates and promotes violence in the service of constructing an already violent and uncontrollable group of men (mainly of colour) allows the perpetuation of a particularly destructive form of institutional racism. Further, as long as institutionalised racism, sexism, and heteronormativity circulate unchallenged, White men, women of all races and transgendered people will be swept into cages as well. The prison system benefits from the production and reproduction of this particular form of (violent) masculinity because it justifies the continued existence of the institution. Ultimately the prison is self perpetuating, even during periods of reform, in part because it is designed to contain that which it produces. Because the system is predicated on a masculinist formulation, inextricably bound up with racism, abolition offers the only solution to interrupt that cycle of violence.

Moreover, a gender responsive approach has an equally damaging effect on how 'women' are constructed and understood both within and outside prison. Increasingly the discourse of gender responsiveness, and its promotion of ideas of essential difference, is being taken up by reformers who would self-identify as radical, as much as by those who work in direct collaboration with the system. Anti-prison advocates employ gender responsive justice language to argue, for example, that 'women are not men' and therefore should be treated differently. They base this conclusion not on disparate healthcare needs, but on conventional ideas of normative femininity. Writes one such male anti-prison organiser in an article entitled 'Women are Not Men; Tell the CdoC [sic]':

> Women have special needs that are different than men's, and CdoC ignores these needs to the detriment of the health and rehabilitative efforts of the women. It is a *tragedy* that women in California prisons are forced to live in T-shirts, jeans and sneakers. No feminine clothes are allowed: no dresses, skirts, slacks, blouses or sweaters can be worn. They wear the same clothes as the men. Self-respect and a positive self-image are critical for successful rehabilitation, yet *women are demeaned daily by having to dress as men*. There are restrictions on

hairstyles and limited choices in cosmetics and jewelry too. (Weinstein
2005: 11; emphases added)

Taking this statement on its own terms, the refusal to allow any persons to
choose what they want to wear diminishes self-expression and individuality
irrespective of their gender. In contrast to Weinstein's position, I have spoken with many people in women's prisons who express dismay at the idea
of gender-specific grooming standards that require women to wear clothing specifically marked W for women rather than unmarked, unisex clothing or clothing marked M for men. Specifically, many people whose larger
bodies do not fit into standard-issue clothes designated for women and
some masculine or not-female-identified people in women's prisons object
to the CDCR's dress code. A limited understanding of sartorial preferences
that operates within normative notions of sex and gender ignores those
who identify as trans men in women's prisons. This erasure compounds the
invisibility of those whom the state would erase and/or exterminate.

Self-presentation is not part of the larger problem, but reliance on stereotypical femininity fails to identify the ways through which the penal
system relies on a culture of humiliation and control that destroys the ability of *all* people to determine for themselves who and how they want to
be in the world. Further, Weinstein perpetuates sexist assumptions about
women by naturalising the jump from concerns about 'health and rehabilitative efforts' to a focus on appearance, emphasising the loss of ability to
wear a dress as 'tragic.' This reinforces stereotypes of women as vain, self-
centred and superficial and lacking commitment to and engagement with
political struggles. More urgently, such rhetorical appeals to vacuous senti-
mentality ultimately drain energy from the difficult work that needs to be
undertaken. It is work that includes focusing on the fact that many people
in prison die in drawn-out, gruesome ways, commonly without pain management, away from their families. Often they lose all contact with their
children for the rest of their lives through fast-track adoptions. Routinely
their mental health deteriorates as they are locked in cages twenty-four
hours a day. Each of these horrific realities does more disservice to people
in women's prisons than does being made to wear t-shirts and jeans.

In fact, the main concerns of the hundreds of Californians in wom-
en's prisons have very little to do with superficial stereotypical mark-
ers of traditional feminine gender expression. To the contrary, women in
prison typically express deep concern about: decarcerating the population through parole and sentencing reforms, returning to their communities with their physical and mental health intact, maintaining their rights
to and connections with their children, finding meaningful employment
and housing upon release, identifying egregious human rights abuses and
exposing them to a public largely ignorant about what happens behind
prison walls, organising for significant legislative and social change,
engaging in policy work to shift the current investment away from prisons

and toward community health. Further, those who do choose to focus on reform of the system need to recognise that the problems with which they are concerned are not unique to women. The need for adequate medical and mental healthcare, the importance of educational and vocational training programmes, the development of meaningful, translatable job skills, the need for harm reduction and voluntary, non-punitive drug treatment, expanded family visitation rights apply to men and transgendered persons in prison as well.

As scholar-activist Angela Davis has argued, studying prison history inevitably points to the deep connections between reform efforts across history and the expansion and fortification of the PIC. When penal history is considered, it becomes clear that the system is capable of reform insofar as it consistently has been reformed into a more expansive, often more brutal institution. Throughout the history of reform movements that have attempted to distinguish women's needs from men's, even the best intentions persistently result in negative outcomes.

In her work on White middle-class women reformers of the nineteenth and early twentieth centuries, historian Estelle Freedman discusses those who have fought for separate institutions for women based on their difference from men. Freedman's account of history resonates eerily with the present day movement for gender responsive justice:

> Women's prison reform has a complicated relationship to the history of American feminism. Prison reformers had important feminist insights: that is, they recognized sexual inequalities and at times spoke out against them. In contrast to women in the temperance and abolitionist movements, however, they only rarely became women's rights activists. Rather, prison reformers in the nineteenth century adopted a 'separate but equal' political strategy that derived, in part, from the nature of their work. Abolitionists wanted to emancipate individuals from an oppressive institution, slavery: women who applied this principle to their own sex often demanded freedom from legal restraint. Prison reformers, however, did not reject the institution that controlled criminals. Instead, they wanted to improve penal treatment of women, and to do so they eventually became keepers in their own prison. Arguments about individual liberty were unlikely to develop, in this setting, while arguments about sexual differences flourished in support of their cause. (Freedman 1981: 13)

The introduction of women's prisons to protect women in men's institutions, and to train White working-class women to be domestic workers, led to the spread of new institutions for women across the United States. Rather than diminishing the number of women in prison overall, such efforts led to the rise in the number of prisons being taken for granted and, in the foggy climate of national security, being actively encouraged.

Typically, reform efforts seek to improve the system by pouring in more resources. Consequently, in the current moment a focus on gender responsiveness interrupts and actively detracts from abolitionist efforts that prioritise decarceration, stop prison construction and meet the needs of prison-decimated communities. Rather than building newer, nicer cages that increase the capacity of the CDCR, true gender justice requires arguments for the release of the 4,500 women whose present and futures are at stake in the consolidation of the FRCCCs. True gender justice would allow those newly free people to live with their families and reallocate resources dedicated to building new facilities to supporting those individuals. The people released could be provided with six months of housing within their communities at a fraction of the cost of housing them in an FRCCC. Abolitionists call for support for programmes and endeavours outside the purview of the CDRC, namely organisations developing alternatives to imprisonment, alternative responses to violence and community-run re-entry programmes. Often cited as a model of community-based alternatives to imprisonment, *A New Way of Life* in the Watts neighbourhood of Los Angeles is a sober-living re-entry programme run by Susan Burton, herself a formerly imprisoned person.

A New Way of Life states as its goals: to provide a clean, safe, sober-living home environment where women and their children can feel welcomed and supported in their transition to becoming independent members of the community; to offer education, job training and skill-building opportunities for women to prepare themselves for self-sufficiency; to provide leadership as a community advocate for the rights of women prisoners, the formerly incarcerated, and their families. The organisation has outlined its values which include the following assertions:

> We believe all people, including former prisoners, are valuable and should be treated with dignity and respect. We believe that prisons and punishment are not effective tools for positive change and that treatment better serves the individual and society. We believe everyone who is given a chance, regardless of the past, can excel with support and community intervention. We believe in the power of mentoring to help people achieve their dreams. By motivating, supporting, and creating opportunities for others to excel, mentors are valuable role models that build confidence and self-esteem. We believe in the ability to empower people by educating them about systems of societal dysfunction, thereby transforming their beliefs.

Periods of reform do not bode well for abolitionists and their allies precisely because reform allows the state to appear benevolent while co-opting the strategies and support of well-meaning people in order to bolster the existing system. Nevertheless, the swing of the pendulum back toward reform also signals that people in prison and those working in solidarity with them on the outside are gaining momentum and building power. Further, radical organisers pushing for abolition of the system as well as those who engage in non-reformist reform are having an impact. At least in California, it no longer is possible for the state to build prisons with the expectation of tax-payer support. Polls conducted over many years have consistently shown that Californians do not want more resources poured into prisons.[6]

On the last night of the 2005 through 2006 California legislative session, the proposal for the 4,500-bed expansion stalled on the floor of the Assembly, an outcome that would not have occurred but for the work of abolitionists and our allies. Unfortunately, in his proposal to spend $10.9 billion to expand California's prison and jail systems, Governor Schwarzenegger proposed 4,350 new beds in FRCCCs. Assembly member Sally Lieber reintroduced a bill (now AB 76) for 2,900 new beds in FRCCCs in the 2007 to 2008 session. Nevertheless, fewer politicians in Sacramento support the plan. While the initial bill had three legislators listed as authors, eleven as co-authors, and no opposition, the new version has only one author. A growing number of opponents and thousands of people in women's prisons are actively organising against it. Over 150 feminist scholars, activists, and policy makers from across the United States signed an open letter opposing the prison expansion plan (Justice Now 2006).

Though the tendency of legislators has been to support prison expansion in California, mainly due to the financial influence of the CCPOA, a few are beginning to resist the trend toward so-called kinder, gentler imprisonment. In fact, in August 2006, after a tremendous effort by abolitionist organisers, a principal co-author of the original bill, Assembly member Jackie Goldberg (D-Los Angeles), removed her name from AB 2066 before it was reintroduced as AB 76. In an Opinion Editorial, Goldberg noted:

> It is with much deliberation that I have reached the conclusion that AB 2066 is a fraud, a realisation that has caused me to change my mind about legislation that once had my name on it. The recent contract bid proposal put out by CDCR for AB 2066 is filled with problems that would almost certainly result in a reduction of services, less family visitation, and countless other custodial issues. AB 2066 will also have the effect of expanding our already mammoth prison system by creating more beds to incarcerate men and women, and further exacerbate the already shocking medical and human rights abuses by decentralising control of California's prison system. . . . I urge the Legislature to not be pressured into enacting short-sighted legislation as a temporary fix to one problem among many in a prison system that is crying for true reform.[7]

Though this statement has been circulated widely by advocates, no mainstream print media covered the news that a politician had removed her name from the legislation and termed it a fraud. No newspaper in California ran Goldberg's opinion editorial. Such bold action by a policy maker demonstrates that people in prison and those working with them in solidarity can have an impact. Goldberg's reversal offers hope to abolitionists and models thoughtful and progressive political action for other legislators.

GENDER JUSTICE PLATFORM

As a radical alternative to gender responsive justice, *Justice Now* has developed a Platform for Gender Justice, including specific policy recommendations for California that could be replicated in other locations and proposals for ways of understanding true gender justice more broadly. *Justice Now* is an active member of Californians United for a Responsible Budget Coalition (CURB), a statewide coalition of over forty organisations working to curb prison spending by reducing the number of people in prison and the number of prisons in California. Its staff contributed to the creation of a position paper entitled '50 Ways to Reduce the Number of People in Prison in California.' Some of the suggestions included in the Gender Justice Platform are drawn from that document, which enumerates an even greater number of strategies for reducing the prison population than can be addressed in this venue (CURB 2007).

A Gender Justice Platform demands decarceration, both the closure of prisons and parole reform. Regarding closure, in California one state women's prison should be closed within two years by releasing the 4,500 women identified by the CDCR as posing no risk to the public. Such legislation should include a stipulation that the institution would not be reassigned as a prison, jail or detention facility for people of any gender as well as a stipulation that the re-purposing of the prison site be informed by an evaluation of the needs of the community where the prison currently is located. The only way to guarantee a population reduction is to reduce the number of beds in the system. Regarding parole reform, given that in California sixty per cent of people in prison are held for technical parole violations (e.g. missing an appointment with a parole officer, failing a drug test) and not for committing an offence, legislation preventing the return of people to jail or prison on technical parole violations would significantly reduce the population. Resources currently slated to run the Parole Department could be reallocated for housing, healthcare and job training and placement.

The Platform also demands moratoria on prison construction and spending. Throughout the history of the prison system, overcrowding and abusive conditions have never been ameliorated through a rise in prison construction. Instead, building new facilities always has resulted in increased numbers of imprisoned people. The recent trend of constructing 'specialty prisons,' including women's gender responsive facilities, geriatric prisons, prison hospices and nurseries, belies the reality that such institutions immediately become overcrowded. Further, they are often sites of more egregious human rights abuses than traditional prisons. As such, *Justice Now* recommends the legislation of a cap on the prison population, prison building and prison staffing (including non-custodial staffing). As flagrant violations of human rights, domestic law, and ethical medical practice occur regularly with impunity in the prison system, there is no indication that added staff or construction of specialty prisons will promote exposure of and accountability for such abuses in prisons of a smaller or more narrowly conceived nature.

The Gender Justice Platform also prioritises facilitating reunification with families and communities on re-entry. Bans created through the 1996 Federal Welfare Reform Act deny basic entitlements such as food stamps, public housing and medical benefits to people with drug convictions and/or outstanding warrants. Abolitionists demand that such bans be repealed. Moreover, we condemn and call for an end to the practice of denying people employment because of a history of contact with the prison system. Currently in the United States, a person (invariably a woman) who has a child under the age of three and has more than eighteen months of prison time permanently loses all parental rights should her child be placed in foster care during her imprisonment. Laws allowing fast-track adoption by streamlining children of people in prison from foster care to adoption must be repealed. At a minimum, funds must be allocated to provide support to families that they may maintain ties during a period of imprisonment in order to insure that children are able to reunite with their parents upon their decarceration.

Further, governments should be required to provide non-correctionally controlled social programmes as alternatives to imprisonment. Local, state and national governments must use the public funds saved through decarceration to reward counties that reduce the number of imprisoned residents with funds earmarked to provide non-locked, non-correctionally controlled social programmes administered through agencies not affiliated with law enforcement. Such programmes would include vocational training, education, healthcare and housing.

It is essential that the complex and changing understandings of gender are respected. More broadly throughout public culture but specifically in the context of the penal system, the Platform calls for a refusal of essentialist notions of sex and gender and the roles and expectations assigned accordingly. The existence of transgender, gender variant and gender nonconforming people requires validation within the PIC. More significantly, historical precedents that punish gender non-conformity with marginalisation, discrimination and violence must be curtailed. Abolitionists recognise that violence and discrimination are rampant across the system because that is the nature of the prison. Alongside women, men and gender non-conforming people should be guaranteed freedom from violence. Everyone's right to gender self-determination, both inside prisons and in the world at large, should be honoured as the struggle towards transformation from systems of imprisonment progresses.

The approaches to gender employed by reformers using a gender responsive framework and by the system itself facilitate the work of the PIC functioning primarily to maintain current power structures within and beyond the United States and benefiting those persons and industries who profit from it, at the expense of profound human suffering and premature death. Advocates and organisers argue that the strategy of gender responsiveness is being deployed in this political moment for myriad reasons. The practical, material effects of this approach result in the expansion of the system and the diminution of particular people within. This includes the literal eradication of Black and Brown peoples in the case of documented eugenicist practices. The penal system's co-option of the rhetoric of rehabilitation and reform obscures the further entrenchment of imprisonment through new construction, population growth and financial investments. It obfuscates the continued (re)allocation of public resources to the prison/security industries rather than to those communities from which imprisoned people are taken. This move toward reform forces the question of what it means to pursue radical anti-prison work, particularly when those who make radical critiques of the existing system see their work being taken up to justify its continued existence. The current resurgence of a climate of reform has been facilitated, in part, through organisers who expose the harmful economic, social and material effects of the system. Consequently, this historical moment also demands that anti-prison organisers carefully maintain a position that does not allow our work to be used against us, whether we identify as abolitionists or not.

NOTES

1. The language of the current petition reads: 'We, the undersigned petitioners, respectfully voice our adamant opposition to prison expansion. We oppose proposals to expand California's prison system, including the expansion of the women's and/or men's prison systems by building a whole new system of mini prisons—Female Rehabilitative Community Correctional Centers (FRCCCs)—across the state. Proponents of this mini prison expansion proposal reference our 'needs' to justify this expansion. But they have not stopped to ask us what we need or want. In 2006, over 1,000 of us jointly submitted a twenty-five-foot long petition to the Governor and Legislature to defeat this proposal. This year, Governor Arnold Schwarzenegger, in his 21 December 2006 proposal to spend $10.9 billion to expand California's prison and jail systems, included a proposal for 4,350 new beds in FRCCCs, and in the Legislature; Assembly member Sally Lieber has introduced AB 76 for 2,900 new beds in FRCCCs. We remain firmly opposed to this mini prison and all prison expansion proposals, for the following reasons: 1) We believe real change can only occur before a number is attached to an individual's name. Continuing to use state funds for prison expansion will only drain more resources from the services we truly need and that address the root causes leading to people's imprisonment. 2) Building mini prisons for women does not respond to our needs or the needs of our children, families or communities. The proposed mini prisons are being sold as a way to bring us closer to home, but in actuality, the California Department of Corrections and Rehabilitation (CDCR) contract bid proposal would further limit family visitation. 3) Expanding the prison system will exacerbate the already egregious human rights abuses and gross medical neglect we face in prison. Decentralisation will make much-needed oversight even more difficult than

it already is. 4) Prisons are destructive, abusive and inhumane. No place staffed by correctional officers will ever be 'community-based' or an 'alternative to incarceration' because the same negative environment causing so many of the problems we currently face will continue to exist. As people currently imprisoned at Central California Women's Facility, Valley State Prison for Women and California Institution for Women, we are particularly vulnerable to the negative consequences of these prison expansion proposals. Regretfully, our imprisonment precludes us from personally presenting this petition.'

2. The interviews referenced in text were conducted by the author in the course of her primary research.
3. Critical Resistance (CR) is the only other avowedly abolitionist organisation in the United States. The mission of CR is 'to build an international movement to end the Prison Industrial Complex by challenging the belief that caging and controlling people makes us safe.'
4. For discussion of the formation of alternative gender identities and the 'othering' of people who do not fit into one of two categories see: Fausto-Sterling (2000); Feinberg (1999); Kessler (1998); Nestle (2002).
5. For discussions of the complicated nature of gender identity see: Butler (1996) and (2004); Wittig (1992).
6. Beginning in the mid-1980s, prison boosters in California successfully achieved expansion by relying on methods that do not require taxpayer approval, namely using 'lease revenue bonds' which are not required to be put on the ballot for voter authorization. For a discussion of the political economy of prison expansion in California, see Gilmore (2007).
7. Unpublished OpEd, on file at *Californians United for a Responsible Budget* (CURB).

REFERENCES

Bloom, B. and Covington, S. (2000) *Gendered Justice: Programming for Women in Correctional Settings*, San Francisco, CA: American Society of Criminology.
Bloom, B., Owen, B., et al. (1993) *Gender-Responsive Strategies: Research, Practice, and Guiding Principles for Women Offenders*, Washington, DC: National Institute of Corrections, U.S. Department of Justice.
Braz, R. (2006) 'Kinder, Gentler, Gender Responsive Cages: Prison Expansion is Not Prison Reform', *Women, Girls & Criminal Justice*, October–November, 87–91.
Butler, J. (1996) *Gender Trouble: Feminism and the Subversion of Identity*, New York: Routledge.
———. (2004) *Undoing Gender*, New York: Routledge.
CDCR (2006) *Gender Responsive Program Accomplishments for Female Offenders*, California Department of Corrections and Rehabilitation. 20 February <http://www.cdcr.ca.gov/communications/docs/GRP_Accomplishments.pdf>
Corston, J. (2007) *The Corston Report: A Review of Women With Particular Vulnerabilities in the Criminal Justice System*. Home Office, March 15. <http://www.homeoffice.gov.uk/documents/corston-report>
Cott, N. (1997) *The Bonds of Womanhood: 'Woman's Sphere' in New England, 1780–1835*, New Haven: Yale University Press.
CURB (2007) *How 'Gender Responsive Prisons' harm Women, Children and Families: Special Report on Reducing the Number of People in California's Women's Prisons*. California United for a Responsible Budget.

Davis, A. Y. (2003) *Are Prisons Obsolete?* New York: Seven Stories Press.

DRC. (2006) *Ohio Department of Rehabilitation and Corrections Best Practices Tool Kit: Gender Responsive Strategies*, Accessed 2 April 2007.

Fausto-Sterling, A. (2000) *Sexing the Body: Gender Politics and the Construction of Sexuality*, New York: Basic Books.

Feinberg, L. (1999) *Trans Liberation: Beyond Pink or Blue*, Boston: Beacon Press.

Freedman, E. (1981) *Their Sisters' Keepers: Women's Prison Reform in America, 1830–1930*. Ann Arbor: University of Michigan Press.

Gilmore, R. W. (2007) *Golden Gulag*, Berkeley and Los Angeles: University of California Press.

GRSC (2006) *Minutes of Gender Responsive Strategies Commission Meeting.* 18 July.

Justice Now. (2005) 'Mission Statement' Oakland, California: Justice Now.

Kessler, S. (1998) *Lessons from the Intersexed*, Rutgers: Rutgers University Press.

Morris, N. and Rothman, D.J. (eds.) (1995) *The Oxford History of the Prison*, New York: Oxford University Press.

NCJRS. (2007) 'Women & Girls in the Criminal Justice System: Programs.' 2 April. <http://www.ncjrs.gov/spotlight/wgcjs/programs.html>

Nestle, J. (2002) *GenderQueer: Voices From Beyond the Sexual Binary*, Los Angeles: Alyson Books.

Ohio DRC. (2006) *Ohio Department of Rehabilitation and Corrections Best Practices Tool Kit: Gender Responsive Strategies*, Ohio: DRC 2 April.

Walsh, E. (2006) 'More Funds Sought for New Jail', *Springfield Republican*, 21 April.

Weinstein, C. (2005) 'Women Are Not Men—Tell the CDoC.' *Prison Focus* vol 22, 10–13.

Wittig, M. (1992) *The Straight Mind and Other Essays*. Boston: Beacon Press.

9 The United States Military Prison
The Normalcy of Exceptional Brutality[1]

Avery F. Gordon

IN THE SHADOW OF THE 'WAR ON TERROR'

> *If you're African or Native American how central torture is to the American way of life is hardly a new idea.*
>
> Mumia Abu-Jamal (2006)

> *The tradition of the oppressed teaches us that the state of emergency in which we live is not the exception but the rule.*
>
> Walter Benjamin (1969: 257)

In May 2006, when the Bush Administration appeared before the United Nations Committee Against Torture to answer queries about the secret detention, treatment and illegal rendition of prisoners in the 'war on terror,' hundreds of United States non-governmental organisations and grassroots groups filed over twenty shadow reports to the UN Committee (Amnesty International 2006), including one 456 pages long, coauthored by the American Friends Service Committee (2006) and entitled *In the Shadows of the War on Terror: Persistent Police Brutality and Abuse in the United States*. At the same time, the Vera Institute of Justice's (2006) Commission on Safety and Abuse in America's Prisons had quietly finished holding national hearings into violence, sexual abuse, degradation and 'other serious safety failures' in United States prisons and jails. A year earlier in March 2005, when the *Washington Post* first exposed the CIA's rendition programme and the existence of secret CIA-run prisons in Europe, Channel 4 aired Deborah Davies's graphic documentary on brutality in stateside prisons, *Torture: America's Brutal Prisons*, a film all but unknown in the United States (*Channel 4*, 2 March 2005). Virtually simultaneously with the now infamous photographs of the torture of Iraqi prisoners at Abu Ghraib, Mark Dow (2004) published his detailed exposé of the secret, indefinite and repressive imprisonment of immigrants, *American Gulag: Inside U.S. Immigration Prisons*.

The ongoing news of torture, abuse and legal disablement of prisoners of war and so-called enemy combatants in Afghanistan, Iraq, Cuba and elsewhere has given the United States military prison unprecedented public attention. Rarely do any prisons, much less the especially secretive military prison, emerge from the edge of geo-social consciousness where they reside, and thus our ability today to name some of their locations—Abu Ghraib, Guantánamo Bay, Diego Garcia, Bagram, Sherbarghan—is significant. The growing reach of the United States military into countries not its own, often with coerced or blackmailed permission, and the expansion of its corollary carceral complex is an extremely important and dangerous phenomenon. Secretive and closed, with expulsion and discredit the penalty for whistle-blowing, we know little about this vast military machine. The ongoing attention to prisoners of the 'war on terror' and to the normally hidden United States military prison is thus significant and laudable. However, the routine treatment of the conditions at Abu-Ghraib and Guantánamo Bay as exceptional or isolated instances of the abuse of state power has obscured the relationship between United States military prisons abroad and territorial United States civilian prisons. In this chapter, I briefly address this relationship, which I believe must be understood to ensure immediate redress and release for prisoners of war, to avoid the future isolation and dehumanisation of all prisoners held by the United States, and to grapple with the larger socio-political issues at stake. I begin with two presumptions or starting points.

First, while there is abundant cause for moral outrage and disgust, there is no warrant for being surprised or shocked that citizens of the United States tortured, abused and ritually humiliated other human beings and that the State's political and military leaders covered up their authorisation of it. There is no cause whatsoever for either angry or startled or presidential assertions that abuse and torture are not 'American,' not things that American citizens do or condone. In fact, while President Bush claimed that the Abu Ghraib photographs 'do not represent America' (see Danner 2004b: 74), neither Schlesinger nor Fay could sustain the 'bad apples' theory in their reports. Again and again, they provide the very evidence of its inadequacy (see Danner 2004a; Puar 2004: 522–34). American exceptionalism—the assertion that the United States is an inherently more democratic, egalitarian and just society than all others—has always been a lie. The current George W. Bush government has indeed formulated a policy of exceptionalism, claiming as a sovereign God-given Christian nation its right to exempt itself from the same laws that govern the conduct of other nations, but this policy is closer to the government's own definition of a rogue state than it is to a model democracy.

You do not need to believe in 'the evidence of things not seen,' as I do, to acknowledge the truth of this lie (Baldwin 1985; Gordon 1997). Certainly, since the invention of photography, the visual evidence is usually available. Often, it is an artifact or a souvenir of the presumed normalcy and legitimacy of the actions it shows. In this, the amateur photographs of Abu-Ghraib most closely resemble the photographs of lynchings in the United States between the 1880s and the 1930s, resemble them not only in their images of White women and men smiling and grinning at the mutilated bodies of Black women and men hanging from trees and posts, but also in the extent to which they were openly distributed and sold as keepsakes of an afternoon well-spent (see Allen et al. 2000; Solomon-Godeau unpublished). I note, as an important aside, that though they have been demanded, there has been no state acknowledgement or press interest in the *official* videotapes and photographs, those from the CCTV surveillance cameras ubiquitous in all prisons. As Shafiq Rasul and Asif Iqbal, two former Guantánamo Bay prisoners stated:

> We should point out that there were—and no doubt still are—cameras everywhere in the interrogation areas. We are aware that evidence that could contradict what is being said officially is in existence. We know that CCTV cameras, videotapes, and photographs exist since we were regularly filmed and photographed during interrogations and at other times, as well. (Rasul and Iqbal 2005: 28)[2]

Second presumption: Torture and cruelty towards prisoners, which is a general effect of the larger pattern, historically ancient, of criminalising and capturing vanquished, threatening or unwanted populations, is by no means an American or national phenomenon. The United States is certainly a global leader in both the use of punitive and extra-legal long-term imprisonment for achieving a variety of social and economic control objectives and a leader in developing and exporting specific techniques and portable technologies for securing unpopular terms of order. But it is not unique, and as Eduardo Galeano (1978: 305) said many years ago of the authoritarian regimes which dominated Latin America in the post-World War II period: 'it would be unjust not to credit [their] ruling classes with a certain creative capacity in this field.' In this case, credit belongs especially to France who pioneered and taught the United States, Israel, and many Latin American countries current standard operating procedures for urban warfare/ counterinsurgency wars of occupation.

Not surprisingly, France's former Foreign Legion and paratroopers, veterans of the Congo, Madagascar, Ivory Coast and other postcolonial wars, provide an experienced cadre of mercenaries and private security guards to the estimated 400 private security companies, almost exclusively Anglo-American, operating in Iraq today (see Claude 2005; Macmaster 2004). It is fitting to credit also the occupying British Army in Northern Ireland for, among other things, modelling advanced techniques for criminalising political opposition and the security uses to which the name terrorist could be put. In fact, it is the memory of Bobby Sands and the Irish Republican prisoners, who refused the mantle of prisoner of war, that has been most consistently evoked by the Guantánamo Bay hunger strikers today.[3]

PERSONNEL

The connection between the United States military prison and the United States civilian prison can be seen at four overlapping levels: personnel, punishment regime, law and geopolitics. At the most basic level, the connection begins with the literal sharing of personnel and occurs through two conduits, the assignment of Army Reserves and National Guard members and the appointment of United States prison managers and directors.

The modern military prison system began in 1875, in collaboration with the forerunner to the American Correctional Association (the American Prison Association) when the United States Military Prison—known now as the maximum security United States Disciplinary Barracks—at Fort Leavenworth, Kansas was established. The military correctional system, as it is known currently, is primarily oriented to confining soldiers and historically has done so mostly for desertion, mutiny, and treason. Each branch of the military service—Air Force, Navy, Marine Corps and Army—operates prisons, but only the Army and Marine Corps, responsible for operating prisoner of war camps and detention facilities for captives in the 'war on terror,' permit a career military occupation as prison guard (see Haasenritter 2003).

The United States Army maintains an active duty force of about 500,000 soldiers, but only approximately 1,000 to 2,000 of these are certified for prison guard duty after completing a four-week course at the mock prison at Fort Leonard Wood in Missouri. These military police (MP) are, according to Col. George Millan, director for training at the United States Military Police School, mainly stationed in United States territorial military prisons, creating a demand for military prison guards overseas. As the 'war on terror' expands and the number of United States military bases increases, the Army and the Marine Corps have gained custodial responsibility not only for a small but growing number of soldiers who refuse to fight or who desert but also for a large number of prisoners of war, enemy combatants and civilian security threats (see Laufer 2006).

It is difficult to acquire an exact and accurate number of United States military prisons and the number of prisoners held in them. Though clearly most have been released, the BBC estimated that 60,000 individuals have been taken prisoner in the United States-led wars, starting in 2001 in Afghanistan and in 2003 in Iraq (*BBC News*, 2005). At last count in 2005, the United States officially reported a total of 2,322 prisoners in fifty-eight military prisons in the United States and eleven detention centres in Europe and Asia (U.S. Department of Justice 2006). These figures are obvious undercounts. They do not include prisons in the 'war on terror' theaters, secret CIA or intelligence prisons or 'ghost detainees,' prisoners secretly held without record, information the United States military will not release.[4] And as Paglen and Thompson (2006: 147) learned:

> Questions specifically about CIA black sites . . . were attempting to make distinctions where none seemed in order . . . [B]lack sites were indistinguishable from military prisons, which were in turn indistinguishable from informal prisons run by the United States' warlord allies, which were in turn indistinguishable from the American occupation itself.

To the best of our knowledge, the 'one' prison on the vast military base in Guantánamo Bay, Cuba, consists of six facilities or 'camps,' now holding approximately 460 to 480 out of an original 800 or so prisoners. In Iraq, approximately 13,000 people are imprisoned in United States-run detention centres, the number of which varies from four to ten and, like at Guantánamo, one prison may itself consist of several distinct facilities (see Human Rights Watch 2005). Recent reports indicate that since June 2004, almost 18,700 Iraqi prisoners have been released, suggesting very high rates of imprisonment. The working estimate of the number of prisoners held by the United States military in Afghanistan is 500; it has been estimated that as many as 3,000 prisoners have been held in the north, at Sherbarghan (see Golden and Schmitt 2006; Smith 2004). What is notable is the presumption of continued growth. In Iraq, the sheer number of prisoners continually expands as occupation and civil war intensify. In August 2006, a new $60 million super-maximum facility was opened at Camp Cropper, near Baghdad's airport (see Graham 2005: A15; *CBS News*, 17 September 2006).

At Guantánamo Bay, despite consistent calls to close it, a new $38 million super-maximum prison opened in October 2006 to permanently house the 114 'most dangerous' and to confine what's expected to be an influx of prisoners in newly opened theaters in the 'war on terror' (Iran, North Korea, parts of Africa). The large complex at Bagram in Afghanistan, once a processing facility for captives transferred elsewhere, has become an expanding permanent facility, replacing or supplementing the estimated two dozen military and unknown number of secret CIA prisons (such as the 'Salt Pit' near Kabul or the 'Dark Prison') in the country. If Chalmers Johnson is correct that an 'honest count' (including Royal Air Force bases in Britain which he claims are more properly United States military and espionage installations) of 'our military empire would probably top 1,000 different bases in other people's countries,' and if we make the reasonable assumption that every military base has at least one prison or detention facility, in popular parlance, a brig, then the scope of military imprisonment is potentially staggering.[5]

This demand has been largely filled by the Army Reserve and by civilian prison guards in the Reserve (Moniz and Eisler 2004). In general, the 1.2 million members of the United States Reserve Forces and National Guard are crucial to the ability of the United States Defense Department to wage multiple front wars with a 'volunteer' army, and the increasingly conscripted nature of their service has emerged as a major source of dis-satisfaction and disobedience. A survey conducted by the American Cor-rectional Association indicated that since April 2003, over 5,000 civilian prison guards have been called up to active military duty and the potential exists for that number to rise by as much as 9,000. The United States Army publishes no information on the specific jobs to which these civilian prison guards are assigned. However, according to Lt. Col. Mark S. Inch, Corrections and Internment Branch Chief in the Office of the Provost Marshal General,

> . . . the military personnel who are more likely to perform enemy pris-oner of war and detention operations during war reside almost *exclu-sively* in the Army Reserve and Army National Guard. Therefore, the synergy between the reservist's civilian employment in the corrections field and his or her duty to confine enemy combatants in Afghanistan . . . Guantánamo Bay, Cuba, and Iraq . . . could not be more evident and essential to mission success. (Inch 2003, emphasis added)

This 'synergy,' or as Maj. Gen. Ryder (2003) calls it, 'professional bond,' is quite extensive. For example, the 300th Military Police Brigade, the majority of whom are Michigan prison guards, designed Camp Delta at Guantánamo Bay. The senior non-commissioned officer of the Brigade, Command Sgt. Major John Vannatta, is the superintendent of the Miami Correctional Facility in Indiana and now 'replicate[s] many of his familiar civilian responsibilities as . . . Camp Delta's "superintendent."' Sixty other 'professional correctional officers' are in 'key administrative and leadership positions' in Cuba. In Afghanistan, members of the 327th Military Police Battalion, many of whom are Chicago area prison guards and police, cur-rently run detention operations there. Capt. Michael Mcintyre and Master Sgt Don Bowen, 'designers of the emerging Iraqi prison system,' both work at the United States Penitentiary at Terre Haute, Indiana. The best-known Army Reserve and National Guard unit, the 800th Military Police Brigade, was put in charge of 're-establishing Iraq's jail and prison system' as well as staffing and managing the Army's prisons for enemy combatants and prisoners of war. This unit produced the two most famous reserve sol-diers—Army Reserve Staff Sergeant Ivan L. 'Chip' Frederick II and Corpo-real Charles A. Graner Jr.

Frederick, convicted and sentenced in October 2004, was a prison guard in Virginia. He confessed, as part of a plea deal, 'to beating and humiliat-ing Iraqi prisoners while taking souvenir pictures of the deeds.' . . . Freder-ick said he wrapped loose wires around a prisoner's finger and threatened to electrocute him if he fell off a narrow box. He confessed also to punching a prisoner and ordering him to masturbate in front of others 'just to humiliate him' (Morin 2004: A4). His defence was that the environment was 'stressful' and 'chaotic' and that he was poorly trained, notwithstanding that he was identified in the Psychological Assessment of the Taguba Report (Annex 1) as a 'ringleader' by virtue of his expertise in what is known euphemistically as the 'field of corrections.'

Until the moment in January 2005 when he was sentenced to ten years in federal prison, Graner, Lynndie England's boyfriend and the soldier famously shown smiling behind a pyramid of naked Iraqi prisoners, had been employed by State Correctional Institute at Greene (SCI-Greene). Graner was familiar to prison activists, particularly the Pennsylvania Abolitionists, since he had been implicated repeatedly in violence against prisoners at the super maximum security prison in western Pennsylvania, best known to those outside the state as the prison on whose death row Mumia Abu-Jamal sits. Prison activists and the Pennsylvania Department of Corrections documented many instances of prisoner abuse at SCI-Greene, starting in 1988, and reaching a peak in 1998. This was two years after Graner arrived, with 'good riddance' according to his former warden, from a six-year stint as a prison guard at Feyette County prison. At that time, guards were accused of routinely beating and humiliating prisoners, including 'through a sadistic game of Simon Says in which guards struck prisoners who failed to comply with barked instructions.' According to Army reports, Graner, like many others, was called up for active duty in May 2003 and given supervisory positions at Abu Ghraib precisely because of his experience as a prison guard (see: Pennsylvania Abolitionists 2004; Pierce 2004).

Graner was not the only individual given command responsibilities despite a known history of abuse accusations. Much attention has been rightly paid to the role General Geoffrey Miller's transfer from Guantánamo Bay to Abu Ghraib played in establishing norms and standards at the prison. His recommendation to 'GTMO-ise' Iraqi prisons was in part what prompted General Taguba to hold Miller responsible for the abuse of prisoners (see Center for Constitutional Rights 2006). But as Leah Caldwell points out, this should not obscure the important role a group of lesser non-military officials played. As she details, in May 2003, before Miller's arrival, Attorney General Ashcroft appointed a group of American prison managers to oversee the preparation and transformation of Iraqi prisons for United States military use. These officials worked through the International Criminal Investigative Training Program (ICITAP), which trains, consults and assists in the development of other countries' police forces and prison systems.

ICITAP is 'a successor to the police training program run by the Agency for International Development' that was terminated 'in the mid-70s . . . when it became public knowledge that U.S. AID officials were training police and prison officials around the world in techniques of . . . torture' and counterinsurgency tactics against leftists and popular movements (Caldwell 2004; see also Call 1998). The new ICITAP—begun in 1986 to oversee elections in El Salvador—is supposed to have put its past behind it, but was subject to a major Congressional investigation in 2000 for criminal misconduct and serious mismanagement. Through ICITAP, Ashcroft appointed a team of four executives, each of whom had, on their watch, a documented record of human rights violations, prisoner deaths or severe injury, and a record of transferring prisoners to other state prisons, a type of internal rendition programme. Of the four, all were taken to court and two were forced to resign.

John J. Armstrong, in 2004 the assistant director of operations of American prisons in Iraq, was the head of Connecticut's Commission of Corrections from 1995–2003. He opened Connecticut's first super-maximum prison, was the featured subject of a 2001 Amnesty International report on abuse of women in prisons and was forced to resign after settling lawsuits brought by the families of two of the 200 Connecticut prisoners who died after being transferred to Wallens Ridge, a super-maximum security prison in Virginia. Gary DeLand, former director of the Utah Department of Corrections in the 1980s, was the subject of many complaints, legal and otherwise, by prisoners of inadequate medical care and cruel and unusual punishment, according to attorney Brian Barnard. Terry Stewart, a consultant for a private prison company, Advanced Correctional Management, formerly directed the Arizona Department of Corrections from 1995 to 2002 where he 'accumulated many accusations of human rights violations' (Caldwell 2004; see also Butterfield 2004; Butterfield and Lichtblau 2004). Although he was found not guilty in court, under his command, among other things, 600 prisoners who had revolted over unacceptable prison conditions were left outside for four days in the heat, without food, water or toilets. Finally, Lane McCotter, former director of three prison systems (Texas 1985–1987), New Mexico (1987–1991) and Utah (1992–1997), is now an executive with a private prison company, Management and Training Corporation, that operates sixteen prisons. McCotter was forced to resign as director of the Utah Department of Corrections when a prisoner, shackled naked to a chair for sixteen hours, died. Abu Ghraib was apparently his choice as 'best site for America's main prison' and he worked closely with DeLand to refurbish the prison for use by the United States military. In the month before the Justice Department sent him to Iraq, it issued a report, following the death of a prisoner, criticising the lack of medical and mental health care at one of Management and Training Corporation's jails.

PUNISHMENT REGIME

No one working in the United States-run military or civilian prisons in Iraq, Cuba, Afghanistan or elsewhere has been charged with torture, inflicting cruel and unusual punishment or war crimes. Soldiers of the lowest rank have been charged with lesser offences, such as dereliction of duty, indecency, assault. Since 2002, at least 111 prisoners have died in custody in Iraq and Afghanistan. According to Human Rights First (Shamsi and Pearlstein 2006), only twelve prisoner deaths have resulted in punishment of any kind for any United States official, and the steepest sentence for anyone involved in a 'torture-related death' is five months in jail.

One reason is that 'torture and other abuses against detainees in US custody in Iraq were authorized' by commanding MPs and officers even after the conditions and activities at Abu Ghraib prison were made public, as the remarkable report, *No Blood, No Foul: Soldiers' Accounts of Detainee Abuse in Iraq*, demonstrates (Human Rights Watch 2006). This report provides a particularly chilling window into the nature of military imprisonment, and its first-hand accounts highlight how ordinary violence had become in the military prisons in Iraq.

Indeed, civilian and military prison guards and officials take for granted that in United States prisons abuse of power and torture are common, despite the sanctioned ignorance that pretends otherwise (Elsner 2004). Torture, humiliation, degradation, sexual assault, assault with weapons and dogs, extortion, blood sport consistently have been part of United States prison culture and behaviour. Angola, Attica, Marion, Florence, Corcoran—the names of these prisons carry their histories in tow in part because they broke through the invisibility barrier, bringing the images and stories of intolerable violence and deprivation into public view. Prisoners, prisoner rights advocates, human rights organisations such as Amnesty International and Human Rights Watch, civil rights organisations, such as the ACLU and the National Lawyer's Guild, scholars in a number of fields, not to mention various Departments of Corrections and state and federal Departments of Justice have all corroborated that 'racialized sadism,' to use William Pinar's term, is routine and has a history exactly co-extensive with the history of imprisonment in the United States, which is itself co-extensive with the history of the United States (see Christianson 1998; Conroy 2001; Davis 2004; Franklin 1989; Pinar, unpublished manuscript; Williams, K. 2006).

The normalcy of exceptional brutality—a shared punishment regime— is the second point of connection between the military and civilian prison. The presumed normalcy explains why there was, according to the Taguba report, an 'easy ... collaboration' between the Reservists and the professional Military Police. The comfortable collaboration went approved and unremarked on until photographs of its activities became public and became a 'scandal,' as much for becoming public as for its occurrence. The presumed normalcy also explains why, when asked by the FBI, no-one interviewed reported observing any 'misconduct' or 'mistreatment' of those detained at Abu Ghraib. The guards described what they saw and often what they did: prisoners handcuffed to the wall with nylon bags over their heads being deprived of sleep; prisoners spread-eagled on the floor yelling and flailing; men ordered to strip, placed in isolation and then subjected to deafening music and/or extreme temperatures; the punitive use of electric shock and stun guns; ritual humiliation and sexual assault; police guards repetitively kicking prisoners in the stomach; intimidation and threats to harm or kill family members; burning and branding. None of it 'rose to the level of mistreatment' in the minds of their observers because they were, to quote the respondents in the report, *'no different from . . . procedures we observed used by guards in US jails.'*[6]

The FBI interviewed most of those involved in policing at Abu Ghraib. Nobody initially claimed they saw any behaviour that could be construed as mistreatment, much less torture as defined in international law. What they witnessed they considered to be acceptable prison guard behaviour. And they were right. The Abu Ghraib photographs did not expose a few 'bad apples,' or an exceptional instance of brutality or perversity. The Abu Ghraib photographs exposed the dehumanisation that is the *modus operandi* of the lawful, modern, state-of-the-art prison.[7]

Nowhere is this more clear than in the growth, over the past two-and-a-half decades, of super-maximum imprisonment, the cutting edge in carceral technology, and arguably the prototype for the retooling of the military prison for the 'war on terror.' For example, the model federal super-maximum penitentiary in Florence, Colorado, where Zacarias Moussaoui was sent as his death sentence, to 'rot' in high-tech solitary confinement, along with Ramzi Ahmed, Theodore Kaczynski, Terry Nichols, Richard Reid and Eric Rudoph, is already effectively a 'war on terror' prison (Serrano 2006: A1). The most recently built prison in Baghdad is a supermax facility. In Afghanistan, under the auspices of a $10 million prison construction and training programme (for Afghan prison guards), 'American financed contractors' are renovating—to supermax standards—a former Soviet jail near Kabul (Golden and Schmitt 2006). In October 2006, a new supermax prison, Camp 6, was installed at Guantánamo Bay by Halliburton subsidiary Kellog, Brown & Root, at a cost of $38 million. Because 'there is no such thing as a medium security terrorist,' according to Rear Admiral Harry Harris commander of the prison network, and because there have been continual uprisings at the prison, Camp 6's 24-hour lockdown regime will replace the other units (Williams, C. 2006).

It is a cruel irony that the 'first step in the development of the modern supermax prison' was the conversion, in 1933, of the former military prison at Alcatraz Island, California, into a fortified 'custody prison,' designed to 'concentrate,' 'isolate,' 'segregate' and control 'the most serious disciplinary problems' in a context dedicated, FBI Director Hoover emphasised, to severe and unremitting punishment (Ward and Werlich 2003: 53–75). The history of the development of the supermax prison is beyond the scope of this chapter, but it is important to reflect on two relevant aspects. First, in many ways, Alcatraz was a public-relations-directed invention masterminded by Hoover to demonstrate publicly that the era's great gangsters, like Al Capone, ever popular as outlaws, were defeated by legitimate forces of law and order. The supermax prison today pretends to the same delivery of order and public safety in the face of gangsters running underground economies and societies. Second, the modern supermax prison was designed specifically to create a confinement regime that would end resistance to authority. As early as 1973, as Ward and Werlich show, political prisoners were being sent to Marion. The conversion of the federal prison at Marion into the contemporary supermax regime and into what came to be known as the Marion model was the direct result of prisoner strikes against brutal conditions at the prison and the spectre of another Attica. Here, too we find an important precedent for the criminalisation of dissent, a core function of mass imprisonment.

In the United States, there are seven million people, disproportionately Black and Latino, in prison or jail or on probation/ parole, well over half of whom have been convicted of non-violent drug-related and petty economic crimes (U.S. Department of Justice 2006). And yet, two per cent of the prison population is in what is called administrative segregation, without even the restricted due process ordinary prisoners possess. There are fifty-seven designated supermax prisons in forty states, fortified security units, prisons within a prison. As I suggest later, administrative segregation has become a condition and an identity and thus the count of designated facilities is a poor measure of scale (see Mears and Watson 2006 and the website Supermaxed.com). Under conditions of supermax imprisonment, men and women are electronically monitored and locked down twenty-three or twenty-four hours a day in small windowless cells, sealed with solid steel doors, only permitted to leave their cells shackled and handcuffed and supervised by at least two guards, perhaps a few times a week for showers and solitary exercise in a human-size cage. Administratively segregated prisoners are almost always caged.

In general, United States prisons are highly militarised, with vertical command structures, obedience norms and paranoid us/them cultures virtually indistinguishable from soldiering. The increasingly unfettered permission to use lethal force and the presence *inside* the prison of technologically sophisticated weaponry and surveillance equipment (metal detectors, x-ray machines, leg irons, waist chains, handcuffs, 'black boxes,' holding cages, 'violent prisoner restraint chairs,' psychiatric screens, chain-link fences, tasers, stun guns, pepper spray, tear gas canisters, gas grenades . . . mini-14- and 9- millimetre rifles, 12-gauge shotguns) has intensified the militaristic aspects of policing (Haney 2006). As Craig Haney points out, prisoners today are always, as if in war, under 'gun cover,' even while sleeping. Particularly in security housing units, where prisoners are in solitary confinement, 'excessive' force is not only permitted, it is routine: forced cell extractions, discharge of electronic stun devices, chemical sprays, shotguns with rubber and real bullets, the use of psychotropic drugs for pacification, sensory deprivation and sensory overload are the *normal punishment regime*. The convergence is striking: waging war looks more and more like a high security prison; prison looks more and more like waging a security war.

THE LAW

These practices violate the International Covenant on Civil and Political Rights and the United Nations Standard Minimum Rules for the Treatment of Prisoners, but the United States does not recognise the latter and its reservations to the former are sufficiently extensive to constitute effective non-recognition. In fact, the United States has established different standards, the third point of connection between the military and civilian prison: the laws governing them. I can only briefly touch on the complex and developing legal questions, and my point is this limited one. While the recently enacted Military Commissions Act makes sweeping changes in a number of areas, including to federal *habeas corpus* law and to the laws governing military trials, there is ample precedent in United States civil rights and constitutional case law for its treatment of prisoners of the 'war on terror.'

Over the past ten years, through a variety of means and given impetus by the 1996 Prisoners' Litigation Reform Act, the United States has severely disabled prisoners' political and civil rights, not only as voters, but as subjects with standing to access the law itself (see Mauer and Chesney-Lind 2002). The prisoner—with restricted access to independent legal counsel, held incommunicado in secretive locations inaccessible to the public, charged with violating internal bureaucratic rules, promised trials adjudicated by the very authorities who hold him/her, legally limited in his right to stand before the law independent of his/her captors—this prisoner is as readily found in United States maximum and super-maximum prisons as he or she is found in Iraq, Cuba or Afghanistan. Civil death, especially when accompanied by total isolation in extreme conditions of dehumanisation, has become pre-emptive, an intimidating and effective means for preventing the exercise of political and social will by destroying at its source, the socially and legally recognised person, and replacing that person with war's familiar figure: the enemy.

Indeed, in addition to intensifying prisoners' civil disabilities, the courts have eroded, if not effectively ended, the Eighth Amendment protection against cruel and unusual punishment in a series of cases centred on establishing the legality of super-maximum regimes of confinement, the combination of isolation and force described earlier. The courts have consistently authorised super-maximum imprisonment *sui generis* and they have done so by treating it not as punishment, but as a set of *administrative* procedures for managing high-security populations (Dayan 2003: 99). These procedures, formerly understood as punishments, are now treated as *security* measures whose need, nature and scope is the prison authority's, not the court's, right to determine. As security measures, these procedures and practices are not subject to the Eighth Amendment prohibition against cruel and unusual punishment because they are not considered punishments. Rather, procedures that were once treated as violations of the Eighth Amendment, as cruel and unusual punishments,

are now sanctioned as 'ordinary' or acceptable practices required for the maintenance of security.

Legal permission to treat what was once considered cruel and unusual punishment as 'ordinary incidents' of prison life entered the prison environment with its embedded classification logics, profound distrust of educated and politicised resistance, and powerful will to institutionally reproduce, stretching what constitutes a special disciplinary problem or an urgent threat to the physical safety of persons to the distinctive point, utterly characteristic of the criminal justice *mentalité* and prison culture, where the arbitrary and the paranoid meet. Consequently, administrative segregation is neither a temporary nor an exceptional response to situational security or disciplinary needs. Rather, it is a portable regime applicable anywhere, and once it is applied to you, in effect, it becomes you. The supermax prison is thus not merely a place. It is a condition and an identity, increasingly a type of prisoner who belongs *permanently*, because it is in his or her enemy nature to permanently pose a threat to 'our' security and who is classified as such in corrupt and demeaning administrative hearings where senior police officers act as legal counsel for the prisoner.

As Joan Dayan has brilliantly shown, the Supreme Court's Eighth Amendment cases are precisely the legal and linguistic basis for the 'detainee interrogation' memos prepared for the 'war on terror' (Dayan 2004). The recently declassified Pentagon *Working Group Report on Detainee Interrogations* (2003) asserts that 'illegal alien enemy combatants' possess neither the international rights conveyed to war captives by the Geneva Convention nor United States constitutional rights, which was, of course, the purpose of inventing the category in the first place. The report's treatment of complex questions of legal applicability and notably the applicability of international law is particularly obfuscating. Most relevant here is the claim that 'detainees' are not 'convicts' and thus since the proscription against cruel and unusual punishment was 'designed to protect those convicted of crimes,' even if a 'detainee could establish standing to challenge his treatment, the claim would not lie under the 8th Amendment' (Pentagon 2003: 36). The question of when conviction is necessary for imprisonment is particularly serious since in the United States slavery remains constitutionally enabled under one circumstance—conviction of a felony. The Bush government seeks imprisonment without trial and legal conviction, via administrative fiat, when conviction by United States judicial authority confers criminality and disables international law. To affirm that the prisoner is not a convict, however, is precisely to affirm his or her status under international law. The prisoner of war is emphatically not a convicted criminal.

To deal with the legalistic contortions, the working group argued that if enemy combatants were, in the end, 'mistakenly' found to hold constitutional rights for being held by the United States, only the Eighth Amendment, the prohibition against cruel and unusual punishment, not the right to due process, would apply (Pentagon 2003: 40). However, as their survey of Eighth Amendment cases shows, legal proof of constitutional violation has become all but impossible today. As the Report notes, the 'maintenance of order in the prison'—and 'it follows . . . obtaining intelligence vital to the protection of untold thousands of American citizens'—provides a legitimate state interest in 'various deprivations' that might otherwise be considered cruel and unusual. Moreover, to be considered cruel and unusual, such deprivations must be more than 'restrictive' or 'harsh'; they must exceed the normal conditions that are 'simply part of the penalty' itself. Yet deprivations cannot be 'assessed under a totality of the circumstances approach.'

Whether in terms of conditions of confinement or intensity of violence, Eighth Amendment violation requires demonstration of *intentional*, explicitly motivated, and *unusual cruelty*, meted out as *punishment*. Each qualification must be present together: explicit intent, unusual cruelty, punishment. However, recall that 'the necessities of prison security and discipline' are grounds for superceding all legally recognised rights of prisoners and grounds for redefining the very definition of penalty, punishment itself. Thus, the *administration* of individuals or groups who threaten *security* and who refuse to *comply* with orders by any means the prison deems necessary becomes the penalty for being the enemy by no longer being rendered as a punishment to which limit standards can be applied.

The intent of the Working Group Report was to legally justify a major change in the status and treatment of a new category of prisoner of war. Yet, its narrow apportioning of what constitutes *torture* and what is only *abuse*, or what is *prolonged harm* versus *lasting* or *permanent damage* and its insistence that Eighth Amendment violation requires demonstration of *specific, deliberate intent to inflict cruelty or excessive punishment* (not outcome) under conditions in which 'evolving standards of decency' are determined by ('with great deference given to') prison authorities are echoes of a social reality already settled, in law and in practice, in the civilian prison where the state's power to civilly disable and to maintain compliance and order is absolute.

GEOPOLITICAL TERMS OF ORDER

Long-term exposure to super-maximum imprisonment leads to madness and death. Yet, military and civilian prisoners spend more and more time in it, while the number of people in prison for life also escalates dramatically, up eighty-three per cent from 1992 to 2003 (see Haney 2003; Haney and Lynch 1997; Mauer et al. 2004; Rhodes 2004). Ward and Werlich (2003: 53–75) estimate that between 1984 and 2000 the average term in supermax control units increased from thirty-six to sixty months. Their estimate is based on prisoner stay in Florence, Arizona, the most notorious security housing unit in the United States, but the general pattern is confirmed in

California and elsewhere. It is difficult to convey what happens to someone confined indefinitely in conditions designed to break down all resistance to authority, self or another's, in twenty-four to forty-eight hours. Those who beat it have a worn and dignified strength that nevertheless shows the cost of the battle. The others become shadows, mournful spectres. Under such deficient and deadly conditions, the prisoner is no longer (and the extent to which they were before is questionable) conceived as human in any meaningful sense at all. Today, more than ever, the original impulse behind the specific wording of the United States Constitution's Thirteenth Amendment, that which abolished chattel slavery, is clear: *[N]either slavery nor involuntary servitude, except as a punishment for crime whereof the party shall have been duly convicted, shall exist within the United States, or any place subject to their jurisdiction.*

The increasing erosion of the distinction enshrined in the Eighth Amendment between cruelty and decency and between the humane and the barbaric is tied to the production of a permanent prison population. Permanent not only in the sense of always available but permanent also in the sense of perpetuity, of assigning to certain groups of people—in the United States, Blacks, Indians and Latinos—the caste and stigmata of the perpetual prisoner. The modern transatlantic slave system, which captured millions of Africans, inventively introduced permanent or hereditary enslavement, thereby making being a slave no longer a temporary social status, however despised or dishonoured, but rather a constitutive condition of one's social and juridical being. The significance of slavery to the historical development of the United States prison system and to who became and still today most frequently becomes a prisoner is well-known (see, for example, Davis 2003; Davis and James 1998; Lichtenstein 1996; Mancini 1996; Oshinsky 1996; Rodríguez 2006). But racism, by which I mean 'group vulnerability to premature death' (Gilmore 2002), explains not just who becomes a prisoner but also *what the prisoner becomes.* In the United States, where slavery was most elaborated and remained essential to national development, the fundamental racial ontology of permanent slavery was transferred, after the formal abolition of slavery, to the prisoner who became, with the scientific legitimacy of criminal anthropology, and bearing always the double burden of racialist ontology, an inferior race in and of themselves. 'The captive,' Orlando Patterson (1982: 38) has written, 'always appears . . . as marked by an original indelible defect which weighs endlessly upon his destiny.'

And what is the destiny of the captive today? In two words, permanent abandonment. As Ruth Wilson Gilmore has argued, abandonment is the 'rigorously coordinated and organised setting aside of people and resources' (Gilmore, unpublished; see also Gilmore 2006; Leyshon and Thrift 1995: 312–41). Abandonment by the state to the state is a core feature of the expansion of a parasitic security/ war economy rooted in mass imprisonment. A means of socio-economic and political dispossession, mass imprisonment warehouses surplus labour, that is people, the majority of whom are Black, for whom no room will be made in the legal capitalist economy. It removes from civil society, potentially active, angry and demanding political subjects, to a remote and closed place where they are civilly disabled and socially dead. Penal management of social and economic inequality effectively abandons individuals and communities to a vast system of repressive and deadly social control whose reach extends well beyond its seemingly targeted population while leaving the so-called free society also abandoned, bereft of these individuals' and communities' company and contributions.

From the vantage point of the United States, where mass imprisonment and its constituent role in what passes for economic development has advanced to unprecedented and alarmingly taken-for-granted levels, and, where African-American communities in particular are staggering under the historical weight of what Gilmore aptly describes as 'rounds and rounds' of regimes of abandonment, the tendency towards permanent captivity is perhaps more evident than elsewhere.[8] As suggested earlier, the expansion of supermax imprisonment is one important indicator and means. Another is the extension of civil disability. The collateral consequences of felony conviction in the United States include loss of civil rights and citizenship rights while imprisoned (or while paroled or on probation) and now increasingly upon final release, that is to say, indefinitely: loss of access to the law, to the right to vote, to serve on a jury, to hold public office, to live in certain neighbourhoods, to live in public housing, to associate with certain individuals, to hold certain jobs.

Perpetual civil disability requires, in effect, treating the prisoner and the former prisoner as socially dead, as having lost the right to belong, a condition of liminal social existence (a living dead person) lacking public worth, social standing and honour. Upon application, social death is always permanent, a condition or a taint which appears to belong to the captive (or slave), his or her essential mark so to speak. And in this it is a powerful legitimising and racialising tool for justifying indefinitely imprisoning people who might otherwise be your neighbours or fellow citizens/residents or friendly or even utterly strange strangers. Orlando Patterson rightly called social death an 'idiom of power.' And, he strikingly described how a society's outsiders (foreigners, infidels, prisoners of war) and a society's insiders (criminals, the destitute) could be conceived as people who did not and could never belong: 'The one fell because he was the enemy, the other became the enemy because he had fallen' (Patterson 1982: 44).

Being or becoming the enemy returns us to the complicated imbrication of imprisonment and war. An increasingly permanent captive population in the United States has been created out of the spoils of Indian wars, Civil wars, anti-communist cold wars, 'wars on crime,' 'wars on drugs,' and now a 'war on terror.' While war has always been the handmaiden of captivity and imprisonment, what is distinctive in the post-World War II period is the invention of perpetual wars, general wars without end, making false promises of security, waged against ever-shifting spectral enemies, driven by ideologies of order and counter-insurgency and by policies to contain and quarantine the effects of global poverty (see Davis 2006; Wilkin 2002).[9] Endless war, endless captivity. Permanent war, perpetual prisoners of war.

In the early history of warfare, there was no recognition of a status of prisoner of war. The defeated enemy, considered the property of the victor, was either killed or enslaved. Despite the Geneva Conventions and international laws governing the conduct of warfare, the United States has retained, as befits its imperial power, the ancient right of the strong and the conqueror to enslave their fallen enemies. Thus, in the 'war on terror,' there are no longer prisoners of war in the modern, post-Westphalian sense, only 'enemy combatants,' fallen captives. Here, in the new permanent security war, the 'foreign' enemy captured, tortured, ritually humiliated, detained indefinitely, often secretly, tragically finds his/her complement in the 'internal' enemy. They are both raw material of an organised abandonment in the service of a parasitical war economy; both subjects of a corrupt, malleable law that indicts without substantive representation; both subject to a crushing punishment renamed administration; both of whose social death and dishonour is presented as the necessary price for 'our' safety and security. Sometimes, of course, the external and the internal enemy are one and the same.

These are the terms of the 'war on terror' the United States is waging and soliciting in every part of the world. It does not act alone, however: Europe's xeno-racist carceral complex for refugees, asylum seekers and the economically precarious (see Fekete 2004; 2005); Israel's genocidal occupation and enclosure of the Palestinians in a concentration camp state; South Africa's adoption of a United States-style war on crime and its consequent imprisonment of ever larger numbers of Black youth, sadly the Soweto generation and their children (Samara 2005); soaring rates of imprisonment—the second highest in the world—in Russia and its previously or presently occupied territories (Turkmenistan, Ukraine, Kazakhstan, Latvia, Lithuania, Estonia, Kyrgyzstan, Moldova and Chechnya); the transformation of the Caribbean Basin into an off-shore-banking-tourist-prison archipelago and so on.[10] Increasingly, long-term captive populations worldwide are created by a 'global state security apparatus' (Wilkin 2002: 634) with many participating nation states, facilitating the fastest growing business sector in the world.

Bloated militarism in a crushing world economy dependent on the 'productive' destruction of places, communities, social wealth, shared intelligence, and the systematic abandonment of entire peoples is the road to ruin upon which the United States and its allies travel. This way of life is not sustainable, despite the imperial announcements of victory and invincibility. In the meantime, it is necessary to raise the call and the movements for the abolition of permanent war and the captivity and negation that accompany it. Worldwide, most individuals do not favour and many actively oppose the occupation war in Iraq. Even in the United States, where majorities have supported it, these have significantly declined. This presents an opportunity to transform strong sentiment against one war in Iraq and its estimated $700 billion price tag into a stronger movement for what Seymour Melman (1961; 1970; 1984; 1988; 2001), after a lifetime fighting for it, calls conversion: the transition from a militaristic or war social-economy to a peace social-economy. This will involve, as a first step, understanding the broader patterns underlying the behaviour of soldiers and police in Iraq and the larger context in which the military prison operates and bringing these understandings as necessities into the political mobilisations against the war in Iraq and the ongoing 'war on terror.'

Mass imprisonment and organised abandonment play a central role today in the perpetuation and expansion of a 'secure' or security-centred world economy and in its extreme and untenable social costs, one of which is our young people and their right to a future, to a destiny determined by them. One of the ugliest and most suppressed facts about the expansion of imprisonment in the world today, whether in the United States or France or the United Kingdom or South Africa or Brazil or Turkey or Nigeria, is that the vast majority of the world's prisoners are young, as are its soldiers. Thus, our young men and women, our most vulnerable young, those in need of the greatest care and protection, are increasingly faced with the choice—rendered starkly in the photographs taken at Abu Ghraib and in United States insistence that Iraqi independence be contingent on its possessing a United States-approved militarised police force—of being prisoner or police/soldier. The Mothers of the Plaza de Mayo would call this state of affairs military civil authoritarianism. It is a contraction of possibility for living—a captive destiny—that is a cruel patrimony and a shameful inheritance. Peace is never just the absence of a war. It is, as Melman described it, the 'moving peacefully' towards the elimination of institutions and decision-making powers that plan, make, support and love war. It is necessary today, and it is inconceivable without the abolition of its handmaiden—mass imprisonment.

NOTES

1. This essay draws on ideas and research presented in Gordon, A. (2006a) 'Abu Ghraib: Imprisonment and the War on Terror,' *Race & Class*, 48, 1: 42–59 and Gordon, A. (2006b) 'D'où viennent les tortionnaires d'Abou Ghraib?,' *Le Monde Diplomatique*, November 2006.
2. No doubt, these were one source for Secretary Rumsfeld's original warning that should all the unreleased photographs be made public, 'it's going to make matters worse' and for the Defense Department's refusal to release 'secret' photographs and videotapes following a federal judge's order; see 'Rumsfeld: Unreleased Images 'Cruel and Inhuman',' www.cnn.com (8 May 2004); and Zernike (2005).
3. 'I do not plan to stop until either I die or we are respected. People will definitely die. Bobby Sands petitioned the British government to stop the

illegitimate internment of Irishmen without trial. He had the courage of his convictions and he starved himself to death. Nobody should believe for one moment that my brothers here have less courage,' said Binyan Mohammed, quoted in Gillan (2005). On the Guantánamo hunger strikers, see Gordon (2006b).

4. On CIA-run secret prisons in the Middle East and Europe, see the break-out story by the *Washington Post's* Dana Priest, 2 November 2005: A01, and subsequent reports; Grey (2006); Paglen and Thompson (2006). Human Rights Watch also issued a number of independent studies on rendition and secret prisons. On the Pentagon's failure to investigate 'ghost detainees,' see Benjamin and Scherer (2006).

5. Johnson (2004a and b) argues that the Defense Department official figures for 2003 of 702 overseas military bases in about 130 countries and 6,000 bases in the United States and its territories significantly undercounts the actual number of bases the United States occupies globally because bases in Kosovo, Afghanistan, Iraq, Israel, Kuwait, Kyrgyzstan, Qatar and Uzbekistan are omitted. Official figures list only one Marine base at Okinawa Japan, failing to capture the size and scope of the American military colony there; see also Singer (2003).

6. The ACLU successfully sued for documents related to overseas detention facilities under the Freedom of Information Act and the extensive archive, heavily redacted, is online at: www.aclu.org.

7. The photographs certainly did not expose the relative merits of using torture to secure needed information, as some have suggested. As Elaine Scarry (1985: 28–9) pointed out some time ago, 'The idea that the need for information is the motive for the physical cruelty arises from the tone and form of the questioning rather than from its content: the questions, no matter how contemptuously irrelevant their content, are announced, delivered, *as though* they motivated the cruelty, *as if* the answers to them were crucial.' United States military officials have admitted that eighty-five to ninety per cent of the detainees at Abu Ghraib (and at Guantánamo Bay) were of no intelligence value (see Danner 2004a).

8. It is certainly what is at stake in the 2005 and 2007 revolts by French *banlieu* and inner-city youth against then Interior Minister and now President Nicholas Sarkozy's law and order policies. Though charged with lacking political awareness, the youth seem to understand the link between the government's promotion of neo-liberal market policies, the erosion of the social state, and the building of a security policing complex in which they are the raw material for precisely the kind of development abandonment involves.

9. In Immanuel Kant's famous 1795 essay, 'Perpetual Peace: A Philosophical Sketch,' he makes a rather convincing case that perpetual war is the norm, in fact has been characteristically what states do. Given that the presence or absence of monarchical rule has made little difference in the ongoing history of omnipresent warfare, we may be mistaken in claiming that permanent war is a post-World War II invention.

10. Hélène Châtelain, the director, with René Lefort of the celebrated documentary on the 1971 prisoner revolts in France *Les Prisons aussi*, has made a recent film, *Goulag* (2005), about the extensive Soviet prison system that forms the infrastructure for its current system. The International Centre for Prison Studies, King's College, University of London has an online data base of world prison rates at www.kcl.ac.uk/depsta/rel/icps/worldbrief. The United States and Russia have the largest prison population rates in the world. St. Kitts and Nevis are third (559), Bermuda is fourth (532), Virgin Islands is

sixth (521), Cuba is eighth (487), Belize and Suriname, the Cayman Islands, Bahamas, and Dominica are eleventh through fifteenth. Puerto Rico, Barbados, Netherland Antilles, Panama, St. Vincent, Aruba, Trinidad and Tobago, French Guyane, St. Lucia, Antigua—are all in the top thirty-five.

REFERENCES

Abu-Jamal, M. (2006) *The United States of Torture*, viewed 21 November 2007, http://www.prisonradio.org/2006Mumia.htm

Allen, J., Als, H., Lewis, J. and Litwack, L. (2000) *Without Sanctuary: Lynching Photography in America*, Santa Fe: Twin Palms Publishers.

American Friends Service Committee. (2006) *In the Shadows of the War on Terror: Persistent Police Brutality and Abuse in the United States*, viewed 21 November 2007, www.afsc.org/news/2006/human-rights-report.htm

Amnesty International. (2006) *Supplementary Briefing to the UN Committee Against Torture*, viewed 21 November 2007, http://www.web.amnesty.org/library/index/engamr510612006

Baldwin, J. (1985) *The Evidence of Things Not Seen,* New York: Holt, Rinehart & Winston.

BBC News (2005) 'US detainee death toll "hits 108",' 16 March. http://news.bbc.co.uk/2/hi/america/4355779.stm.

Benjamin, M. and Scherer, M. (2006) *The Pentagon's Ghost Investigation*, 17 May, viewed 21 November 2007, www.salon.com

Benjamin, W. (1969) 'Theses of the Philosophy of History' in H. Arendt (ed.) *Illumination*, New York: Schocken.

Butterfield, F. (2004) 'Mistreatment of Prisoners is Called Routine in U.S.,' *The New York Times,* 8 May.

Butterfield, F. and Lichtblau, E. (2004) 'Screening of Prison Officials is Faulted by Lawmakers,' *The New York Times*, 21 May.

Caldwell, L. (2004) 'The Masterminds of Torture, Humiliation and Abuse,' *Prison Legal News*, vol 15, no 9, September.

Call, C. (1998) 'Institutional Learning within ICITAP,' in R. Oakley, M. Dziedzic and E. Goldberg (eds) *Policing the New World Disorder,* viewed 21 November 2007, www.ndu.edu/inss/books/Books%20-%201998/Policing%20the%20New%20World%20Disorder%20-%20May%2098/chapter9.html, pp. 315–363.

Center for Constitutional Rights. (2006) *Report on Torture and Cruel, Inhuman, and Degrading Treatment of Prisoners at Guantàanamo Bay, Cuba*, New York: Center for Constitutional Rights.

Christianson, S. (1998) *With Liberty for Some: 500 Years of Imprisonment in America,* Boston: Northeastern University Press.

Claude, P. (2005) 'Profession: mercenaire francais en Iraq,' *Le Monde*, 26 November: 3.

Conroy, J. (2001) *Unspeakable Acts, Ordinary People: The Dynamics of Torture*, Berkeley: University of California Press.

Danner, M. (2004a) 'The Logic of Torture,' *New York Review of Books*, vol 51, p.11.

———. (2004b) *Torture and Truth: America, Abu Ghraib, and the War on Terror*, New York: New York Review Books.

Davis, A. (2003) *Are Prisons Obsolete?* New York: Seven Stories Press.

———. (2004) *Abolition Democracy: Beyond Prisons, Torture and Empire*, New York: Seven Stories Press.

Davis, A. and James, J. (1998) *The Angela Y. Davis Reader*, London: Blackwell Publishers.

Davis, M. (2006) *Planet of Slums*, London: Verso Books.

Dayan, J. (2003) 'Servile Law,' in E. Cadava and A. Levy (eds) *Cities Without Citizens*, Philadelphia: Slought Foundation, pp. 87–117.

——. (2004) 'Cruel and Unusual: The End of the Eighth Amendment,' *Boston Review*, October/November.

Dow, M. (2004) *American Gulag: Inside U.S. Immigration Prisons*, California: University of California Press.

Elsner, A. (2004) 'Abuse Common in US Prisons, Activists Say,' *Reuters Wire*, 6 May.

Fekete, L. (2004) 'Anti-Muslim Racism and the European Security State,' *Race & Class* vol 46, p.1.

——. (2005) 'The Deportation Machine,' *European Race Bulletin*, vol 51.

Franklin, H. B. (1998) *Prison Literature in America: The Victim as Criminal and Artist*, New York: Oxford University Press.

Galeano, E. (1978) *Open Veins of Latin America: Five Centuries of the Pillage of a Continent*, New York: Monthly Review Press.

Gillan, A. (2005) 'Hunger Strikers Pledge to Die in Guantánamo,' *The Guardian*, 9 September.

Gilmore, R. W. (2002) 'Race and Globalization' in R. Johnson, P. Taylor and M. Watts (eds) *Geographies of Global Change: Remapping the World*, London: Blackwell, pp. 261–274.

——. (2006) *Golden Gulag: Prisons, Surplus, Crisis, and Opposition in Globalizing California*, Berkeley: University of California Press.

——. (unpublished) 'Tossed Overboard: Katrina, Imprisonment, and the Politics of Abandonment.'

Golden, T. and Schmitt, E. (2006) 'A Growing Afghan Prison Rivals Bleak Guantánamo,' *The New York Times*, 26 February.

Gordon, A. (1997) *Ghostly Matters: Haunting and the Sociological Imagination*, Minneapolis: University of Minnesota Press.

——. (2006a) 'Abu Ghraib: Imprisonment and the War on Terror,' *Race & Class*, vol 48, no1, pp.42–59.

——. (2006b) 'D'où viennent les tortionnaires d'Abou Ghraib?,' *Le Monde Diplomatique*, November 2006.

Graham, B. (2005) 'U.S. to Expand Prison Facilities in Iraq,' *Washington Post*, 10 May.

Grey, S. (2006) *Ghost Plane: The True Story of The CIA Torture Program*, New York: St. Martin's Press.

Haasenritter, D. (2003) 'The Military Correctional System: An Overview,' *Corrections Today*, December.

Haney, C. (2003) 'Mental Health Issues in Long-Term Solitary and 'Supermax' Confinement,' *Crime & Delinquency*, vol 49, p.124.

——. (2006) 'Prison Overcrowding: Harmful Consequences and Dysfunctional Reactions,' Testimony to Commission on Safety and Abuse in America's Prisons, www.prisoncommission.org/public_hearing_2.asp

Haney, C. & Lynch, M. (1997) 'Regulating Prisons of the Future: A Psychological Analysis of Supermax and Solitary Confinement,' *New York University Review of Law & Social Change*, XXIII, 4.

Human Rights Watch. (2005) *U.S. Detention Facilities in Iraq*, viewed 21 November 2007, http://hrw.org/english/docs/2004/05/07/iraq8560.htm

————. (2006) ''No Blood, No Foul': Soldiers' Accounts of Detainee Abuse in Iraq,' *Human Rights Watch*, vol 18, no 3(G), July.

Inch, M. (2003) 'Twice the Citizens,' *Corrections Today*, December.

Johnson, C. (2004a) *America's Empire of Bases*, viewed 15 January 2004, www.TomDispatch.com

————. (2004b) *Sorrows of Empire: Militarism, Secrecy, and the End of the Republic*, New York: Metropolitan Books.

Laufer, P. (2006) *Mission Rejected: U.S. Soldiers Who Say No To Iraq*, Vermont: Chelsea Green Publishing Company.

Leyshon, A. and Thrift, N. (1995) 'Geographies of Financial Exclusion: Financial Abandonment in Britain and the United States,' *Transactions of the Institute of British Geographers*, vol 20, pp.312–41.

Lichtenstein, A. (1996) *Twice the Work of Free Labour: The Political Economy of Convict Labour in the New South*, London: Verso.

Macmaster, N. (2004) 'Torture: from Algeria to Abu Ghraib,' *Race & Class*, vol 42, no 2, pp. 1–21.

Mancini, M. (1996) *One Dies. Get Another: Convict Leasing in the American South. 1866–1928*, Columbia: South Carolina Press.

Mauer, M. and Chesney-Lind, M. (2002) *Invisible Punishment: The Collateral Consequences of Mass Imprisonment*, New York: The New Press.

Mauer, M., King, R. and Young, M. (2004) *The Meaning of 'Life': Long Prison Sentences in Context*, Washington, DC: The Sentencing Project.

Mears, D. and Watson, J. (2006) 'Towards a Fair and Balanced Assessment of Supermax Prisons,' *Justice Quarterly*, vol 23, no 2.

Melman, S. (1961) *The Peace Race*, New York: Ballantine Books.

————. (1970) *Pentagon Capitalism*, New York: McGraw-Hill.

————. (1984) *The Permanent War Economy*, New York: Simon & Schuster.

————. (1988) *The De-Militarized Society*, Montreal: Harvest House.

————. (2001) *After Capitalism: From Managerialism to Workplace Democracy*, New York: Alfred Knopf.

Moniz, D. and Eisler, P. (2004) 'U.S. Missed Need for Prison Personnel in War Plans,' *USA Today*, 24 June.

Morin, M. (2004) 'GI Gets 8-Year Sentence After Guilty Plea in Abuse Scandal,' *Los Angeles Times,* 22 October: A4.

Oshinsky, D. (1996) *'Worse Than Slavery': Parchman Farm and the Ordeal of Jim Crow Justice*, New York: The Free Press.

Paglen, T. and Thompson, A. C. (2006) *Torture Taxi: On the Trial of the CIA's Rendition Flights*, Hoboken, New Jersey: Melville House Publishing.

Patterson, O. (1982) *Slavery and Social Death: A Comparative Study*, Cambridge: Harvard University Press.

Pennsylvania Abolitionists. (2004) *Currently Employed SCI-Greene Prison Guard Supervised Torture of Prisoners in Iraq; PA Officials Covering up his PA Record*, 6 May 2004, viewed 21 November 2007, www.pa-abolitionists.org or www.thejerichomovement.com/5-6-04paudp.html

Pentagon. (2003) *Working Group Report on Detainee Interrogations in the Global War on Terrorism: Assessment of Legal, Historical, Policy, and Operational Considerations*, viewed 21 November 2007, http://antiwar.com/rep/military_0604.pdf

Pierce, P. (2004) 'Fayette Reservist Implicated in Scandal,' *Pittsburgh Tribune Review*, 5 May.

Pinar, W. (unpublished) 'Cultures of Torture.'

Priest, D. (2005) 'CIA Holds Terror Suspects in Secret Prisons: Debate Is Growing Within Agency About Legality and Morality of Overseas System Set Up After 9/11,' *The Washington Post,* 2 November: A01.

Puar, J. (2004) 'Abu Ghraib: Arguing Against Exceptionalism,' *Feminist Studies,* vol 30, no 2, pp.522–34.

Rasul, S. and Iqbal, A. (2005) 'Open Letter to President George W. Bush from Two Former Detainees' in R. Meerpool (ed) *America's Disappeared: Secret Imprisonment, Detainees, and the 'War on Terror,'* New York: Seven Stories Press, pp. 26–30.

Rhodes, L. (2004) *Total Confinement: Madness and Reason in the Maximum Security Prison,* Berkeley: University of California Press.

Rodríguez, D. (2006) *Forced Passages: Imprisoned Radical Intellectuals and the U.S. Prison Regime,* Minneapolis: University of Minnesota Press.

Ryder, D. (2003) 'Military and Civilian Corrections: The Professional Bond,' *Corrections Today,* December.

Samara, T. (2005) 'Policing Development: Crime, Security and Urban Renewal in Cape Town,' *Journal of Southern African Studie*s, 31, 1

Scarry, E. (1985) *The Body in Pain: The Making and Unmaking of the World,* New York: Oxford University Press.

Serrano, R. (2006) 'The Slow Rot at Supermax,' *Los Angeles Times,* 5 May: A1.

Shamsi, S. and Pearlstein, D. (2006) *Command's Responsibility: Detainee Deaths in U.S. Custody in Iraq and Afghanistan,* New York and Washington, DC: Human Rights First.

Singer, P. W. (2003) *Corporate Warriors: The Rise of the Privatized Military Industry,* Ithaca: Cornell University Press.

Smith, R. J. (2004) 'Abuse at US Prisons in Iraq Mirrored at Jails in Afghanistan,' *San Francisco Chronicle,* 3 December.

Solomon-Godeau, A. (unpublished) 'Torture at Abu Ghraib: In and Out of the Media'

U.S. Department of Justice. (2006) 'Prisoners in 2005,' *Bureau of Justice Statistics Bulletin,* Washington, DC: Office of Justice Programs.

Vera Institute of Justice. (2006), *Commission on Safety and Abuse in America's Prisons,* viewed 21 November 2007, www.prisoncommission.org/report.asp

Ward, D. and Werlich, T. (2003) 'Alcatraz and Marion: Evaluating super-maximum custody,' *Punishment and Society,* vol 5, no 1, pp.53–75.

Wilkin, P. (2002) 'Global Poverty and Orthodox Security,' *Third World Quarterly,* vol 23, no 4.

Williams, C. (2006) 'At Guantánamo,' *Los Angeles Times,* 7 October.

Williams, K. (2006) *American Methods: Torture and the Logic of Domination,* Boston: South End Press.

Zernike, K. (2005) 'Government Defies an Order to Release Iraq Abuse Photos,' *The New York Times,* 23 July.

10 A Reign of Penal Terror
United States Global Statecraft and the Technology of Punishment and Capture

Dylan Rodríguez

INTRODUCTION: THE GLOBAL CRAFTING OF CARCERAL VIOLENCE

An encompassing carceral violence has been central to the post-1970s national formation and global dominance of the United States. American hegemony in the current moment of militarised globalisation and post-Cold War 'empire' is inscribed by a specific production of power that enmeshes, alters and fundamentally forms United States economic and political global ascendancy. I reference this period-specific enactment of dominance—and its strategic rearrangements of relatively discrete technologies of power—as American 'globality.' This will foreground the vacillations and frequent structural-institutional overlap between *ad hoc* (allegedly temporary and reactive) and rigidly formalised (rigorously institutionalised, as well as juridically and culturally legitimated) techniques of domination across political geographies large and small. I contend that the particular production of United States global power in which we are all differently encircled, (dis)located and implicated at the current moment works and weaves through the institutionality, state violence and socially ordering/disrupting logic of the United States prison regime. The eminently visceral and persistently abstracted logic of bodily domination that crystallises in the regime of the American prison is *fundamental,* not ancillary, to United States state-mediated and state-sanctioned methods of legitimated 'local' violence at sites across the planetary horizon.

While massive state-produced violence is inseparable from the history of United States statecraft generally, the emergence of the prison as a labour-intensive, *political and cultural naturalisation* of a symbiosis between a) technologies of strategic bodily immobilization and b) intimately (though no less systemically) formed methodologies of coercion, manipulation and bodily violence (in excess of human rights conceptions of 'prison torture') is an authentically new *global* project. Within the enactment of hegemonic United States State projects that stretch across the world with increasing force, a logic of carceral violence has become inseparable from the conceptual and military apparatus of Global Americana at this historical conjuncture. The American prison regime plays a central and amplified role within the emergence of a militarised American global legitimacy (that is, a 'legitimacy' ordained by breathtaking military capacities and deployments). By way of example, a recent public relations visit by a delegation of United States elected officials to the maximum security units at the military prison in Guantánamo Bay, Cuba, signified the importance of the global United States prison apparatus to the fabrication of American globality as something *good for the world*. The visit was, in one sense, a ritualised performance of 'war on terror' cultural/knowledge production. What, literally and allegorically, does Guantánamo Bay *mean* within the global schema of contemporary United States dominance? Here, it is the prominence of the prison as a staged scene, forming an institutional base for the statecraft of Global Americana, that demands theoretical attention:

> As part of a major Pentagon public relations offensive, dozens of law-makers are being flown to the maximum-security units here for VIP tours conducted by generals who portray the cells as safe and even comfortable places for suspected terrorists to spend their days. One aim of the PR offensive is to head off calls from lawmakers of both parties for an independent commission . . . to look into the conditions and activities at the Guantánamo Bay prison. The administration is also trying to fend off proposed Senate GOP legislation to ensure humane treatment of prisoners and to restrict interrogation tactics. Republican and Democratic lawmakers say they are drawn to the prison out of curiosity and concern about the physical conditions and treatment of prisoners. House Government Reform Committee Chairman Thomas M. Davis III (R-Va.), who led a small delegation Monday, said close scrutiny is essential to improving the United States' image abroad and 'winning the hearts and minds of the modern Arab world.' (Allen 2005: A01, emphasis added)

In this chapter, I am concerned with the integral role of the United States prison regime in the material/cultural production of American globality, as well as with the prison's particular function as a *methodology of power and dominance* that specifically reproduces the perpetuity (that is, the presumptive endlessness) of the 'war on terror.' In the previous passage, the State's attempt to structure public discourse and debate does not revolve around the question of *whether* the prison should be a central component of perpetual global war-making, but rather around the fabrication of a 'moral high ground' that *preserves and enhances* the prison's mobilisation as a technology of righteous war. To 'win the hearts and minds of the Arab world' through a carceral *administrative strategy* (here, a vague notion of 'close scrutiny') enlightens a critical component of American globality's discursive and institutional architecture. Even utterances of transparent absurdity, within this arrangement of state-formed ideological labour and militarised power, illuminate the centrality of the prison regime to United States war-making and 'peace-keeping':

> The tours appear to be having the intended effect. Some lawmakers who have made the trip one or more times have praised the conditions there in interviews with their hometown television stations and newspapers. Rep. Jon Porter (Rep-Nevada), part of Monday's tour, said of the inmates he had seen from a distance: '*Many of them are happy to be there.*' (Allen 2005: A01; emphasis added]

It would be an egregious political and intellectual mistake to dismiss— hence under-theorise and politically minimise—such public relations campaigns and state-organised knowledge productions as simple reflections of the United States Government's endemic corruption, arrogance or stupidity. Rather, I am interested in meditating on the historical question that envelops the moment of this particular pronouncement of global power: What are the *conditions of possibility* for Porter's absurdly profound assertion, particularly in the face of massively accumulated evidence (including mounting survivors' testimonials) indicating that the structure of feeling coerced by the United States prison regime is, in fact, terror?

The remainder of this chapter examines how layered, complex technologies of imprisonment, across scales of individualising and mass-based techniques of bodily immobilisation, have come to form the premises of a global antisocial formation that is fundamental to the very intelligibility of 'America'—as an ideological and cultural gravity of identity and identification, global formation of material and spatial dominion/occupation, and, perhaps most importantly, as a *racially* constituted mobilisation of militarised policing and juridical force. 'The Prison' (as both a geographic and discursive production)[1] is conceptually and institutionally constitutive of contemporary 'empire,' the earthly social ordering that is simultaneously emblematised and mobilised by the United States in the current historical moment. This is to suggest, at the outset, that the arrangement of juridically coded bodily violence that is breathtakingly coordinated and institutionalised by the United States carceral regime generates a logic of (anti)social formation that fundamentally exceeds the 'national' geography within which it is nominally situated. By way of elaboration, I consider the historical and theoretical specificity of the emergent *global institutionality* of the United States prison, by which I mean the modality of the prison's material signification of American occupation and hegemony across localities, as well as its qualitative expansion as a working architecture of global relations of dominance. This suggests that the making and remaking, mapping and remapping of the United States prison as a specific arrangement of state-mediated domination and global dominion also situates the prison as a *constitutive* rather than ancillary or marginally complementary component of the current global order.

WHITE SUPREMACY AND THE UNITED
STATES PRISON REGIME

I have argued elsewhere for a conception of the United States prison regime that focuses on the processes, mediating structures and vernaculars that compose the United States state's self-articulation and 'rule' across variable scales of jurisdiction, cultural production and global hegemony (Rodríguez 2006). Here, I expand on the notion that the United States prison is best understood as a dynamic arrangement (regime) of intersecting and generally symbiotic trajectories of *violence* that radically exceed the physical and juridical parameters of 'The Prison' as a self-contained 'total institution,' criminological datum or social scientific problematic. To centre such a notion of the prison regime is to critically reframe common sense conceptions. It is to think of the prison as a popularly reified American juridical structure *and cultural production* that is inseparable from the mystified (White) national imagination of societal well-being (or 'law and order') in the nominal post-slavery era. In using the concept of reification, I mean to invoke the mystification of 'The Prison' in a manner that obscures the *material relations of power* and *normalised racist bodily violence* that render the carceral site as a central presence in the social and racial formation of the United States.

Reification, in this case, describes the set of political and conceptual labours that make prisons appear as a naturalised, inevitable, and indispensable feature of a functioning and coherent society. Marxist literary and cultural theorist Georg Lukács (1968: 83) elaborates the implications of reification as producing a condition in which a 'relation between people takes on the character of a thing and thus acquires a "phantom objectivity," an autonomy that seems so strictly rational and all-embracing as to conceal every trace of its fundamental nature: the relation between people.'

Following Lukács' critique, it is especially incumbent on current critical praxis to generate decisive and transformative disruptions of reified notions of 'The Prison' that instead attempt to address how the power relations crystallised in the intimate 'everyday' of the United States prison industrial complex[2]—from the sites of the prison yard, visiting room and warden's office to the household, highway and high school—are *mutually* implicated in the relations of global violence that dynamically compose United States hegemony at home and abroad. Here I am suggesting a particular elaboration of political geographer and abolitionist scholar-activist Ruth Wilson Gilmore's contention that:

> The expansion of prison constitutes a geographical solution to socio-economic problems, politically organized by the state which is itself in the process of radical restructuring. This view brings the complexities and contradictions of globalization home, by showing how already existing social, political and economic relations constitute the conditions

of possibility (but not inevitability) for ways to solve major problems. (Gilmore 1998/1999: 174) [3]

Since the formal abolition of racial plantation slavery and the 13th Amendment's juridical *recodification* of 'involuntary servitude' as a punishment reserved for people convicted of crimes, the United States prison apparatus has both negotiated and facilitated multiple transformations of the American social order. More specifically, the prison has formed a central institutional site through which the social formation has articulated broader relations of social power and hierarchy through the biopolitics of racialised immobilisation and bodily disintegration. One-time Black Liberation Army soldier and former United States political prisoner Ashanti Alston, whose continuing work with the Zapatistas in Chiapas, Mexico, has significantly framed his theorisation of the global significance of contemporary technologies of United States anti-Black and anti-Indigenous state violence, has recently argued:

> . . . people need to see the connection between this real sweet business deal between politicians, industries, and those agencies of repression. How can we keep these prisons full to serve the need of United States capitalism in today's times, in the present times? So our communities get devastated—the gentrification, the militarization of the police. It becomes clear why the prison industrial complex is necessary, and it becomes clear why you got to also focus it on people of color, especially people of African descent, and Native Americans as well, because those people on the bottom are always going to be your most dangerous classes if we should ever pull together and build the kind of revolutionary movement where we can throw off these shackles.

> . . . [T]his why people use the term neoliberalism. This is a shift . . . and what the shift means is that we also have to shift in terms of our thinking, in terms of how to change this. What does revolution mean now? Who do we focus on? What areas should we see as maybe more dangerous than others, and how do we organize people in these times? Our situation becomes not too much different from what we see happening in Chiapas, or in parts of Africa that are being pretty much raped by world corporate powers. There's these connections here and it's important that we see it—it's not simple as it may have been a hundred years ago. There's been some changes that we need to be more astute about.[4]

According to Alston, the emergence of the United States prison industrial complex exceeds the self-contained utilitarian mandates of any 'criminal justice' agenda. This carceral formation instead signifies a *global* (neoliberal) 'shift' in the larger White supremacist genealogy of American nation building. Sustained within the structural elaboration of this shift, however, is a logic of racial domination and bodily violence, a historical continuum of power that precipitates through what Alston references in shorthand as the state's 'agencies of repression.'

Following the trajectory of Alston's historical-theoretical narrative, I contend that Gilmore's conception of prison expansion should be understood in organic historical connection to the genealogies of two other 'expansionist' movements that have been both fundamental to and ongoing within the global American project: 'frontier' expansion (the conquest-driven pushing of United States White/nationalist settlements, colonies, and political hegemonies across and beyond the North American continent) and the expansion of White supremacist plantation slavery (as a geographic production of White supremacist socio-economic order, and primary United States White/nationalist idiom of power). The latter 'classical' United States expansionist projects were (and, in complex ways we will not address here, *are*) galvanised by a logic of genocide and persistently *culturally* produced as the necessary institutions of an incipient American civilisation (from Manifest Destiny onward).[5] Both the frontier and the slave plantation, moreover, are inseparable from the 20th century emergence of the United States as a global hegemon by virtue of *enacting* the conditions of possibility for nationhood as well as for the slippery American renditions of freedom, democracy and civic life (none of these conditions of national existence, in other words, are conceivable outside genocidal frontier conquest and genocidal racial slavery).

Finally, the expansions of the frontier and slave plantation encompassed a statecraft that constructed and dialogued with an authentic and usually explicit White (and Christian) *racial* consensus that effectively produced a progenocide, proslavery common sense—in fact, many of the most celebrated and canonised White American critics of Indigenous/Black genocide and slavery were articulating their arguments from within the sets of assumptions posited by this common-sense (essential Indian savagery, Black racial inferiority/subhumanity, etc.). It is in genealogical connection to this historical production of White supremacist common-sense—a racial/national consensus that styles and materially orchestrates such 'expansionisms'—that the formation of the United States prison regime can and must be analysed and critically intervened upon. Historian Reginald Horsman, in his classic exploration of the mid-19th century ideological articulation of American 'Anglo-Saxonism' and racial Manifest Destiny, writes:

> It became obvious in these years that the United States had now rejected the idea that most other peoples of the world could share in the free government, power, and prosperity of the United States. . . . Most peoples, they believed, lacked the innate abilities to take advantage of

free institutions. Some races were doomed to permanent inferiority, some to extinction . . . [I]f other peoples could not be instructed in the establishment of free republican states, what would happen to the population in the areas into which the American Anglo-Saxons were expanding? The Americans had two immediate racial models—the Indians and the blacks. Wherever the whites had moved in large numbers the Indians had disappeared . . . The blacks were not disappearing but were increasing in numbers. They were surviving, argued the advocates of slavery, because they had been totally subordinated to a superior race. Even many of those who opposed slavery believed that free blacks could not survive and prosper in close proximity to the white race. (Horsman 1981: 229–230)

This White supremacist common-sense, which permeates the discrete formulations of the United States as an *essentially racial* national project, as well as its various historical aspirations toward extraterritorial dominion and political-economic ascendancy, is inseparable from the ideological, discursive and 'on the ground' material structures of American globality—including and especially in its carceral forms. Hence, Gilmore's theorisation of late 20th century California (and, by extension, the United States) prison expansion marks a crucial moment within a larger historical continuum of genocidal, White supremacist expansionisms, while also describing a *disjunctive* moment (that is, both a quantitative and qualitative shift) within the longer material history of United States prisons.

INTEGRATED POWER: TOWARD A REARTICULATED GLOBAL 'LAW AND ORDER'

The prison regime forms the condition of possibility and *constitutive logic*[6] of the United States global formation in the broadest and most permeating sense. I am suggesting that the lived surfaces, institutional productions, coercive practices and global statecraft of carceral violence compose a crucial theoretical and pragmatic problem for opponents of United States global hegemony (that is, critics of American hegemonic globalisation and empire) as well as progressive-to-abolitionist critics of the putatively localised United States prison industrial complex. More polemically, I posit that conventional *symptomatic* treatments of 'violence in prison' as episodes of institutional excess, bungled protocol, unconstitutionality or illegality—vis-à-vis a critical focusing on specific imprisonment policies and/or particular case studies and patterns of state-organised and state-sanctioned brutality, torture and abuse—only scratch the surface of a more substantial and comprehensive conceptualisation of carceral violence.

The dynamic and symbiotic constitution of structures linking incarceration to technologies of bodily violence (of which *imprisonment* is the prototypic form) is, in our moment, an epoch-shaping production of global power relations. A new paradigm of state and state-sanctioned, mass-based and intimate coercion posits strategic, racially articulated human capture as the *premise* (rather than the utilitarian and self-contained 'means') of hegemonic power itself. Thus, American global statecraft has become unimaginable outside its prominent productions of incarcerating technologies as material paradigms of dominance, occupation and political ascendancy.

The recently published policy document, *Integrated Power: A National Security Strategy for the 21st Century*, provides an especially rich and significant articulation of the United States prison regime as the silent partner of emergent American globality. Co-authored by Lawrence Korb (former Assistant Secretary for Defense under the Reagan administration) and Robert Boorstin (a Clinton-era member of the National Security Council and one-time adviser to Secretary of State Warren Christopher), the June 2005 publication of *Integrated Power* inscribes an increasingly durable strain within a statecraft and public discourse that entangles the future trajectories of globalising United States state hegemony with the prison regime's organic technologies of domination.

Conceived by the Washington, DC-based think tank, the Center for American Progress (www.americanprogress.org), the Korb–Boorstin proposal departs from the implosive and openly corrupt praxis of global domination institutionalised by the Bush administration, and has been hailed as 'a ready-made foreign and security policy for the United States' that

> . . . sees the Department of Homeland Security and the State Department, the Commerce Department and the CIA, the Pentagon and the FBI, the Treasury and the US Trade Representative's office as parts of a single whole that need to be singing in harmony rather than trying to shout one another down as they vie for their share of the budget. (Walker 2005)

While there is a significant question as to whether the Korb–Boorstin strategy will substantively or immediately alter the current state formation (the document is suggested as a viable policy pathway for a revitalised Democratic Party), the proposal is groundbreaking in the content of its conceptualisation of a militarised (and, as I will discuss, carceral) United States globality, as well as for the institutional context in which it was produced.

While Korb and Boorstin's political biographies flout any common perception of a progressive politic, the Center for American Progress is nonetheless recognised (and self-represents) as a worthy 'left' counterpoint to such established right-wing think tanks as the Heritage Foundation and the American Enterprise Institute, and, at its inception in 2003, boasted an operating budget of $10 to $12 million per year, funded by such well-known liberal/progressive philanthropists as George Soros. The Center's founding President and CEO, John D. Podesta (Clinton's former Chief of Staff) has been credited with developing a comprehensive strategy that will 'update the liberal agenda while beating back the conservative tide,' while also establishing a *political-intellectual* apparatus that can 'discover, train and promote a new generation of liberal spokesmen [sic]' (Von Drehle 2003: A29).

Thus, while structures of global White supremacist violence enlivened by the contemporary hegemonic American 'right' seem to be generously available for critical engagement, I am concerned with the possibilities inherent to—if not already actualising within—a 'left'/ liberal/ progressive trajectory of United States globality that *presumes* the peculiar carceral regimes that are more commonly identified with post-civil rights and post-Cold War American conservatism. I am not suggesting that the political articulations of this incipient liberal 'left' establishment (of which the Center for American Progress is only an especially viable 'mainstream' representative) are either willing or capable of assimilating a critical engagement that will displace or abolish their reliance on durable renditions of racist United States state violence. To the contrary, I am meditating on the *premises of political articulability* shared across an institutionalised political spectrum that *rationalise, justify, debate and desire* the material procedures of United States globality. They may also overlap with other critical, progressive or otherwise oppositional discourses that address the problematics of globalisation, 'global civil society,' and 'Empire.' More specifically, there is a coalescence of moral imperative, social ordering, and legitimised juridico-military force that defines a peculiar *indispensability* to the constitutive logic of the United States prison regime as a *modality of social order* within and beyond the 'domestic' domains of its instantiation. The Korb–Boorstin publication, in this context, encompasses a genealogy of the United States state that is inseparable from the historically indelible technologies of White supremacy crystallised in the prison industrial complex.

Integrated Power attempts to dissolve the classical governmental distinction between the 'domestic' and 'international' fronts in its formulation of a 'national security' paradigm. While the document predictably valorises the alleged incontestability and essential righteousness of American globality, it also envisions a relative restructuring of United States state power such that its *policing capabilities* become horizontally integrated with the juridical, economic and ideological imperatives of United States global hegemony and 'international' world order. Addressing an anticipated audience of elected officials, policy makers, government liaisons and administrators and state officials, the text commences:

> One thing is clear: in the years since the end of the Cold War, the United States has firmly established its position as a power without peer. We are the dominant global military force, our economy drives many others, and our cultural influence is unsurpassed. Today we have the opportunity to increase the security and prosperity of the American people,

to increase our influence in critical regions and countries, and to help others achieve economic growth and build democratic institutions. The strategy presented here is designed to help the United States exercise the broad range of our instruments of power, [emphasis added] exploit the opportunities ahead, and defeat the enemies we confront. It concludes that the interests of the United States will be served best by following a strategy of integrated power, a new concept that reflects the challenges and promise of the 21st century. (Korb and Boorstin 2005: i)

The seamless vista of a global United States state dominion infers an expansiveness, perhaps a pre-emptive and extra-domestic movement, to the technology of 'national security.' Refraining from (and in places repudiating) the procedural and discursive protocols of declared (interstate) warfare, *Integrated Power* inscribes its conceptualisation of police power with a mobilisation of 'national security' *as global statecraft*. In other words, it is absolutely *not* 'national' in either its conceptualisation or envisioned deployment. The domain of the national within 'national security' crystallises *beyond the reach of the American 'domestic,'* and already encompasses a White nationalist locality of the American Homeland that is 'globalised' and, therefore, in need of nationally protective policing. The United States state reinvents itself, and actually renders itself intelligible, through an anticipated activation of *nonwar state violence* that is juridically—and culturally—coded as the necessary exercise of (White nationalist) self-defence. Thus, 'a national security strategy should provide solid and steady principles to guide our actions—to help us define where we want to go, to seize opportunities, and to stop those who would do us harm' (Korb and Boorstin 2005: iv).

There is a surface resonance here with Negri and Hardt's conceptualisation of Empire as the 'right of the police':

In order to take control of and dominate such a completely fluid situation, it is necessary to grant the intervening authority (1) the capacity to define, every time in an exceptional way, the demands of intervention, and (2) the capacity to set in motion the forces and instruments that in various ways can be applied to the diversity and the plurality of the arrangements in crisis. Here, therefore, is born, in the name of the exceptionality of the intervention, a form of right that is really a right of the police. The formation of a new right is inscribed in the deployment of prevention, repression, and rhetorical force aimed at the reconstruction of social equilibrium: all this is proper to the activity of the police. (Hardt and Negri 2000: 16–17)

Plumbing the depth of presumption upon which the labour of American globality instantiates as a *racist formation*, and more pointedly as a mobilisation of *White supremacist social formation*, compels a revision of Negri and Hardt's framing of Empire's juridicality.

Immobilisation and death, which I understand here as creative and dynamic compositions of United States state-building and extra-domestic dominion-making, compose the sturdy technologies of American national coherence and its irrevocable conflation of two things: biopolitical White racial/nationalist ascendancy and the lived and laboured *telos* of United States civilisation-making as the perpetual planetary obligation endemic to the moral, spiritual and cultural inscription of Manifest Destiny (and its descendant material cultural and state-building articulations) across different historical moments. Fundamental to our historical present, then, is a specific articulation of immobilisation and death in which the staid juridical rationality of an American global policing doggedly sustains its intelligibility and structural integrity while constantly collapsing into mind-boggling productions of period-specific carceral violence.

While collapsing juridical rationality into unprecedented carceral violence forms the raw material of a necessary discursive labour—how is the right of the United States-as-police to kill, detain, obliterate to be *voiced, juridically coded and culturally recoded?*—it is most often privileged as a *tacit condition of globality*. Hence, the political question of whether, how and upon whom such carceral technologies of state violence are exercised is most easily deferred or forfeited even within critical conceptualisations of globalisation and 'Empire.' The relative unspeakability of the prison's centrality to the logic of American globality, in this sense, is precisely evidence of the formative and fundamental power of the United States prison regime within the larger schema of American hegemony. Wedged within the broader, accelerating project of revising the political geography of 'national security' is a formulation of world order in which massively scaled, endlessly strategised technologies of human immobilisation address (while never fully resolving) the socio-political crises of globalisation. These technologies of capture, moreover, are less defined by the extra-domestic 'exportation' or extra-territorial institutional 'expansion' of the United States prison industrial complex (although both are clearly occurring) than they are by the *logic of social organisation* that the United States prison regime constitutes, mobilises and prototypes across various localities. *Integrated Power*, for example, invokes an expansive formation of carceral violence—again, a violence other than 'war' traditionally conceived—as an assumptive and tacit condition of globalisation's incipient progress.

> Making globalization work—increasing economic opportunities in developing countries and helping governments provide basic services—can also help reduce the potential pool of recruits for global terrorist networks, and reduce the chances that resource competition will lead to conflict . . . The creation of wealth in developing countries is an integral element of a 21st century national security strategy. So, too, is a

rational approach to the unprecedented mobility of populations. In almost every sphere, mobility presents huge opportunities and tremendous
risks. (Korb and Boorstin 2005: 10)

Herein appears the spectre of large-scale, institutionalised human capture—including and exceeding actual imprisonment—as a central and
'rational' modality, perpetual endpoint, and socially constitutive condition of neoliberalism. The crisis of 'unprecedented mobility of populations' requires unprecedented deliberation on the technologies of strategic
containment and immobilisation. Thus, while the Center for American
Progress situates itself as a staunch antagonist of the overlapping conservative and neoconservative blocs, and names its mission as the development of 'a long term vision of a progressive America,' it enshrines the
pillars of an aspiring liberal/ progressive consensus within the political
ontology of the post-1970s 'law and order' state, or what I have discussed
elsewhere as the late-20th century movement of White Reconstruction
in the aftermath of global movements against colonial domination and
United States apartheid.[7]

The American carceral apparatus is becoming a way of the world, and
is only increasing in its globally formative significance to the extent that
its complex circulations as a material institutionalisation of United States
globality and as an accessible, indispensable technology and matrix of
state-mediated power within the emergent global order *are generally unre-
markable, and almost always unremarked upon.* Thus, the Center's particular articulation of neoliberal progressivism signifies the larger, qualitative
transformation of the racialised 'law and order' United States *nation-build-
ing* project into an authentic, post-Cold War praxis of American globality
that posits punitive carcerality—the naturalised symbiosis of violence and
incarceration—as the presumptive bottom line of 'world-building,' that
is, the anchoring disciplinary and/or socially liquidating violence of any
impending civilisational order.

We are living the germinal moments of a United States state that reproduces through a racially overdetermined global formation of carceral death.
The hegemony of the United States as the effective institutional architect—
and already formed social architecture—of perpetual global crisis management thus rests on an articulation of state dominion in which the densely
layered technologies of the prison regime (human immobilisation, racist
criminalisation and programmatic bodily disintegration) form a sturdy,
available and *already legitimated* lexicon of power and dominance. *Integrated Power* suggestively indicates that a viable national security entails
an interventionist American statecraft that reforms and reorders extrado-
mestic localities through an extension of the material genealogy of 'law
and order' crisis management. While the rhetoric of policing and criminal
jurisprudence is perhaps only vaguely evident, the formatting of 'capable'

states and effectively 'governing' governments culls from the assumptive structural logics of the United States carceral formation.

> [T]oday it is no exaggeration to say that the weakest states pose as great an immediate danger to the American people and international stability as do potential conflicts among the great powers. Our strategy must be to manage these burgeoning crises—by acting to prevent where possible, and moving swiftly to respond when necessary. Our goal is a world in which a maximum number of states are capable (i.e. able to maintain secure borders, protect their citizens, and provide basic services), democratic, and committed to the free exchange of goods and ideas. In pursuit of this goal, the United States must invest in crisis prevention and respond to a broad range of challenges, including chronic poverty, weak states, situations of active crisis or conflict, post-crisis transitions, and the demands of reconstruction or rehabilitation . . .

> [T]he United States must remain focused on building capacity—the capacity of governments to govern; the capacity of citizens to participate in the decision-making that affects them; the capacity of regional institutions to foster trade and promote security; and the capacity of the international system to increase economic growth, protect regional stability, and strengthen the position of capable, democratic states. (Korb and Boorstin 2005: 48–49)

In its concluding pages, the document stakes an even clearer affinity to the United States prison regime's enabling vernacular of power:

> In conflict situations such as Iraq, we should take steps to ensure that the absence or collapse of law and order does not undermine the political transition. In post-conflict situations, we should place greater emphasis on the need to help countries develop law enforcement and judicial bodies with the capacity to provide law and order. (Korb and Boorstin 2005: 55)

Integrated Power eloquently illustrates how the 'organic intellectuals' of White civil society and its corresponding racist state galvanise a *global structure of self-identity* (signified through the rhetoric of 'national security') through technologies of violence that are depersonalised, diffused into the mind-boggling realm of the institutional and the bureaucratic. The political and cultural technology of 'law and order' is, in part, an expressive rhetoric of solidarity between the dependable White supremacist logic of global American statecraft and the telos of globalisation as couched in the terms of 'development.' Thus, a broadly engaged (re)theorisation of White supremacy remains a crucial facet of any potential struggle against the carceral form of White civil society's law and order globality.

THEORISING THE INTERSECTIONS OF
VIOLENCE AND INCARCERATION

The American prison regime forms an increasingly global way of life rather than a discrete institutional location outside the realm of the normative everyday of civil society ('global' or otherwise). This conception fundamentally displaces the historical mystification of the United States prison as a permanent 'elsewhere,' alienated and isolated from the social intercourse of the world outside the prison's institutional grounds. Rather, the unprecedented White supremacist formation of the prison industrial complex situates the technology of imprisonment—in our moment, a racially structured immobilisation more massive than history has ever before witnessed—within a larger historical genealogy of White supremacist hegemony and domestic/continental warfare. What happens, then, when the prison itself becomes a *central apparatus* of militarised neoliberal 'globalisation,' and thus explodes the assumption that the United States imprisonment regime is either a discretely 'domestic' apparatus or a relatively contained application of carceral violence? Within this historical context, the critical theorisation of 'violence' as a fundamental global social force, specifically organised and constantly re-engineered and innovated by the United States prison regime, becomes an urgent grassroots intellectual task that can perhaps produce new modalities of political praxis that disturb, fracture and transform a global United States (prison) hegemony. What would it mean to consider state-crafted, White supremacist modalities of imprisonment as the *perpetual end* rather than the self-contained means of American global domination and dominion?

The prison regime is the organic descendant of durable and gender-specific mobilisations of anti-Black geopolitical and socioeconomic containment—what Massey and Denton (1993) have called an authentic 'American Apartheid'—and programmatic state terror vis-à-vis domestic police ground wars (alternately named in state popular cultural productions as 'wars' on crime, drugs and terror), which can be conceptualised as apparatuses of civil elimination that approximate and rearticulate slavery's fundamental 'idiom of power': social death. Orlando Patterson's comparative archaeology of slavery's originating vernaculars of social order, natal alienation and property dominion (in which he visits upon the slave orders of Rome, Greece, China and medieval Europe as well as the racial enactments of slavery in the Americas) suggests 'two ways in which social death was represented and culturally "explained," depending on the dominant early mode of recruiting slaves.' Marking the schematic relation between 'intrusive' and 'extrusive' modalities, Patterson's conception of slaveholding societies' ideological ordering facilitates an excavation of the global present that recentres (racial) slavery as constitutive to the social genetics of Western civilisation in the post-conquest period.

In the intrusive mode of representing social death the slave was ritually incorporated as the permanent enemy on the inside—the 'domestic enemy,' as he was known in medieval Tuscany. He did not and could not belong because he was the product of a hostile, alien culture. He stood, on the one hand, as a living affront to the local gods, an intruder in the sacred space. . . . In sharp contrast with the intrusive conception of death was the extrusive representation. Here the dominant image of the slave was that of an insider who had fallen, one who ceased to belong and had been expelled from normal participation in the community because of a failure to meet certain minimal legal or socioeconomic norms of behaviour. The destitute were included in this group, for while they perhaps had committed no overt crime their failure to survive on their own was taken as a sign of innate incompetence and divine disfavor. (Patterson 1982: 39–41)

To critically theorise the structuring racial and White supremacist vernaculars of American national formation and contemporary globality suggests a particular elaboration of Patterson's schema: the historical formation of White supremacist state and state-sanctioned violence inscribes the centrality of (anti-Black) social death as the *fundamental historical idiom of power* defining the convergence and mutual constitution between 'racial' regimes and 'carceral' regimes.

By invoking Patterson's well-known theorisation of slavery's unique production of societal and interpersonal domination, I do not mean to posit a simplistic metaphorical or vulgar comparative depiction that vaguely metaphorises the historical and institutional symbiosis between the United States prison and slave plantation. Rather, I am invoking a conception of the prison regime as a particular 'formation of violence' (Feldman 1991), which in turn anchors the contemporary articulation of White supremacy as a global technology of coercion and hegemony. Feldman (ibid: 5) writes,

> The growing autonomy of violence as a self-legitimating sphere of social discourse and transaction points to the inability of any sphere of social practice to totalize society. Violence itself both reflects and accelerates the experience of society as an incomplete project, as something to be made.

The contemporary American carceral apparatus, as a material artifact and technological blueprinting of global dominance, derives its significance as a fathomable and culturally accessible production of power from the institutionalised collapsing of state violence into the multiple 'incomplete projects' of United States social formation in its local and global habitats. In this sense, the specificity and irreducibility of the United States prison regime as a formation of racial and White supremacist violence, and its centrality to the viability of the United States as both a national and global hegemony, is only partially signified by its institutional massiveness. What this condition requires is a working theorisation of the *constitutive logic of power and domination* that the United States prison regime simultaneously prototypes, institutionalises and mobilises in our global moment.

The United States prison regime's local points of origin have literally and figuratively housed the mobilisation of an epochal (and peculiar) White supremacist global logic. This contention should not be confused with the sometimes parochial (if not politically chauvinistic) proposition that American state and state-sanctioned regimes of bodily violence and human immobilisation are somehow self-contained 'domestic' productions that are exceptional to the United States, and that other 'global' sites simply 'import,' imitate or re-enact these institutionalisations of power.

In fact, I am suggesting the opposite: the United States prison regime exceeds as it enmeshes the ensemble of social relations that cohere United States civil society, and is fundamental to the geographic transformations, institutional vicissitudes and militarised/ economic mobilisations of 'globalisation' generally. To assert this, however, is to also argue that the constituting violence of the United States prison regime has remained somewhat undertheorised and objectified in the overlapping realms of public discourse, activist mobilisation, and (grassroots as well as professional) scholarly praxis. Thus, I am arguing that it is not possible to conceptualise and critically address the emergence and global proliferation of the (United States/ global) prison-industrial complex outside a fundamental understanding of what are literally its technical and technological premises: namely, its complex organisation and creative production of racial bodily violence. How is 'The Prison' a *modality* (and not just a reified product or outcome) of American statecraft in the current political moment, particularly as it crystallises multiple abstractions and (juridical) metaphors of state power and legitimated violence at a rather discrete (though still often metaphorised and abstracted) institutional site?

We must also ask what it would mean to theoretically centre a complex conception of carceral violence—at the dynamic and uneven intersections of neoliberal globalisation, White supremacist patriarchy, and what Ruth Wilson Gilmore (1993: 26) has called the essential racist violence of American nationalism's reactionary 'restorative tendencies'—as the *animating force* of United States globality in its various forms. By way of illustration, since the 1990s this animus has haunted and shaped the shifting *management imperatives* endemic to prison expansions, administrative reformations and incarceration strategies in different parts of the world, even as the 'American concept' of imprisonment is subtly renounced and loudly decried for its excesses of violence. In a 1997 report for the United Kingdom Home Office entitled *Monitoring and Evaluation of Wolds Remand Prison*, an ensemble of British criminologists summarised and explicated a strategy of incarceration that closely blueprints—and explicitly invokes—the institutional imperatives that have repeatedly surfaced in the United States prisoners' rights and prison reform movements since at least the 1970s:

> There was a strong consensus amongst the management team about the aims and objectives of Wolds. Their aim was to produce a regime offering a much higher degree of freedom and movement for prisoners than was found in public-sector prisons and to subject prisoners only to such restrictions as were an inevitable concomitant of their imprisonment. (Bottomley, James, Clare and Leibling 1997: 17)

While the incorporation of American prison reformist initiatives into the United Kingdom's penal system—in this case, through its first 'contracted out' or privately run prison opened in 1992—is an interesting and significant development in and of itself, I am more interested in the report's impulse to differentiate and qualify the British appropriation of United States imprisonment strategies:

> A key element in trying to achieve their aims and objectives, and a major innovation in terms of prison management and prisoner control, was the introduction of the philosophy of 'direct supervision' which was untested in Britain. Direct supervision is a style of prisoner management in operation in a number of American prisons, where it had been introduced because it was cheaper than more traditional approaches. It was based on the view that by treating prisoners more positively in the context of closer contact with prison officers, disruptive behaviour would be reduced. As a result, the cost of building prisons could be reduced since they would not be required to withstand such high levels of destructive behaviour and could therefore be built to lower specifications.

> Although the main principles of direct supervision were adopted at Wolds . . . the American concept was not adopted in its entirety and modifications were necessary because of legal, practical and cultural differences between the American and the British penal systems—e.g. differences in prison design; the authority vested in American prison officers to deploy sanctions such as long-term preemptive segregation against disruptive prisoners; differences in the rights of prisoners; and the potential threat of the use of firearms that exists in American prisons. In short, the more coercive context of American prisons, in which direct supervision was developed and implemented and on which its effectiveness partly depends, does not exist in the British penal system. (Bottomley, James, Clare and Leibling 1997: 18)

The anxious denial of a wholesale British reflection, importation or 'adoption' of carceral Americana is especially significant as an indicator of the largely inescapable globality of the United States prison regime as a modality of power and domination. The coercive logic, statecrafted racism and violent technologies of the American prison regime *reflexively* extract a global response, as if inscribing a conceptual problematic within which other carceral formations must negotiate institutional legitimacy and stake claims of effectiveness *relative to the American carceral paradigm*. Herein reflects the extra-domesticity and constitutive excess of the United States prison-industrial complex as an architecture and incipient social genetics of global power.

Currently imprisoned people as well as numerous survivors of state captivity have consistently reflected on the meaning of racial, gender and sexual violence when it is generated from a condition of state-formed legitimacy and institutional ascendancy. The 2004 CD *The We That Sets Us Free*, a cross-textual compilation of music, interviews and spoken word produced by the California-based prison abolitionist organisation *Justice Now* (a cofounder of which is a contributor to this anthology), includes multiple critiques of the misogynist White supremacist state that insist on a feminist redefinition of sexist and patriarchal violence *that analytically centres the routinised gender violence of the prison regime*. Simultaneously, the critical articulations of many voices on *The We That Sets Us Free* rearticulate and transform parochial definitions of the racist state, displacing the stubborn androcentrist politic that envisions the prototypical (or even universalised) body of the imprisoned to be that of the racially pathologised male. More than a simple supplementation of conventional antiracist discourse, the trajectory of this critique points towards a *qualitative* transformation of analytical method. By substantiating the specificity and complexity of carceral violence and closely illustrating the *multiplicity of institutionalised forms* this violence takes on once constituted by the differentiating and hierarchical axes of race, gender, sexuality, age and mental health, we begin to understand that the United States prison regime is a formation of state power that requires multiple and intersecting theorisations. In one of the CD's most lucid examinations of racist gender violence, Beverly Henry (2004; imprisoned at the Central California Women's Facility) contends:

> It's very important for people to recognize that prisons are a form of violence against women. In my seven years in prison, I've seen many, many women suffer from extreme medical neglect in here, and I've watched several women die. Sexual harassment and abuse of women is constant, and it is important for people to think about the fact that this is violence perpetrated by the employees of the state. Women who have mental health issues are warehoused here, instead of being helped in the community. So when people think about violence against women, I believe that they need to expand their definition to think about women who are survivors of violence at the hands of the state.

This critical theorisation focuses on a logic of carceral violence not reducible to a singular (or 'ideal type') articulation or modality of the White supremacist state, but rather is premised on the capacity of the state to dynamically, strategically and opportunistically reform and shift its techniques of bodily coercion—even as certain racially pathologised bodies remain the abiding 'control' group for policing and normalised state violence within a hegemonic White supremacist social formation. Following the conceptual implications of this meditation, this chapter offers a partial framework for conceiving the historical specificity of the United States prison regime as a flexible deployment of domestic and global warfare technologies that simultaneously disrupt, reorganise and coercively form the normative condition and parameters of civil society and the global 'social.' My intention has been to generate a theoretical trajectory and vision of praxis that will facilitate an end to the treatment of carceral violence as *symptomatic* of some 'other' corruption or flaw in the prison's institutionality, and instead *centre* this violence as the core historical logic of the global United States prison regime and, by extension, American 'globalisation(s)' writ large.

CONCLUSION: SOCIAL LIQUIDATION AND THE GLOBAL CRISES OF THE UNITED STATES PRISON REGIME

Examined schematically, and with the understanding that requisite analytical nuances must be applied to the following rendition, we can see that paradigmatic shifts in the late 19th and 20th and early 21st century American racial formation have been fundamentally mediated and generated by a prison regime that variously crystallises these transformations as crises. The first is Black bodily and social mobility, condensing the structuring contradiction between postemancipation Black civil and biological existence as an alleged entitlement and right, versus the circumscription of 'free' Black existence as a concession and privilege variously granted and contracted by the vicissitudes of a White supremacist state and social formation. Second is post-conquest, genocidal domestic colonial and protocolonial dominance over indigenous populations, wherein the overarching national structure of Indian incarceration organically bridges carceral 'reservations' with prisons. Third includes the political-economic displacements of Black and Brown migrant populations from underdeveloped geographies of the global South *and North*, including and especially the post-1965 and post-NAFTA migrations of political/ economic refugee and undocumented populations. Finally are the perpetualised, declared and undeclared global warfare and militarisation in which United States and United States-influenced prison regimes proliferate across zones of occupation as vehicles of active warmaking *and* militarised hegemony.

At a global scale, this regime is dialogically linked to a state of perpetual warfare, sustained 'on the ground' through multiple, simultaneous juridical, cultural and paramilitary policing technologies, and composing a relatively coherent apparatus (or 'regime') of strategically harnessed state violence. It is the technology of the 'prison fix' as a *logic of social liquidation* that composes the prison industrial complex in its most localised manifestations. To the extent that the statistical and sociological outcomes of this structure of mass imprisonment are significantly compatible with progressive and revised definitions of biological, cultural and/ or physical genocide,[8] I have offered reflections on how the regime of violence organised by the prison additionally articulates through overlapping strategies of immobilisation and bodily disintegration, as well as complex techniques of civil and social death.

The United States prison regime is a historically dynamic, though relatively coherent arrangement of state and state-proctored acts of violence that simultaneously contextualise, enable and actively articulate with the relations of dominance that compose the United States social formation in its most localised *and globalised* sites and moments of production, from the initiating moments of frontier warfare and racial chattel slavery to the present era of American globality. We must begin to comprehend the enormity of the implication, then, that to critically examine and radically intervene on the United States prison regime is, in this context, to suggest the fundamental disarticulation—perhaps unavoidably, the abolition—of 'America' itself.

NOTES

1. Ruth Wilson Gilmore (University of Southern California) has been the most notable and nuanced voice on the formation of the United States prison apparatus as a political geography that is, at the same time, enabled and materially constructed by a particular discursive structure that links the crises of racism and globalisation to state-ordained, mass-based punishment. While I most thoroughly absorbed her ideas on the conceptual-material relation between geography and discourse in the context of a Fall 1999 seminar in the Department of Geography at the University of California, Berkeley, her scholarly publications (noted following) have formed a readily accessible foundation from which to develop other ideas in this chapter.
2. While there are various conceptual and descriptive definitions of the prison industrial complex, I will distill my version here: The prison-industrial complex is a set of symbiotic institutional and historical relationships dynamically linking private business and government/ state (that is, 'public') apparatuses in projects of multiply scaled human immobilisation and imprisonment. These projects are, in turn, contextualised by variable forms of domestic warfare, declared and undeclared international wars, and the structures of global empire. The texts from which I have most substantively drawn in this formulation include Davis (1998); Davis (1995); Evans and Goldberg (1998); and Gilmore (1999–2000).
3. See also Gilmore (2007).
4. Interview with Ashanti Alston, April 17, 2006.
5. For valuable discussions of the historical continuum that United States White supremacy has inscribed through multiple genocidal and protogenocidal

state and state-organised practices, see Churchill (1997); Marable (1983); Robinson (1983); Smith (2005).
6. For a full discussion of the notion that contemporary (late-20th century) hegemonies are marked by multiple, moving, though still identifiable sites of power marked by specific 'constitutive logics' of social formation see Melucci (1994).
7. See Dylan Rodríguez (2006): 'Introduction: American Apocalypse.'
8. See Churchill's (1997) useful critique of the historical processes culminating in the rather narrow and conservative juridical inscriptions of genocide in the United Nations forum, as well as his 'proposed' redefinition of genocide jurisprudence and enforcement.

REFERENCES

Allen, M. (2005) 'Lawmaker Tours Become Part of Guantánamo Life; Pentagon Responds to Critics With a PR Push,' *The Washington Post*, 6 August.
Bottomley, A. K., James, A., Clare, E. and Leibling A. (1997) *Monitoring and Evaluation of Wolds Remand Prison: A Report for the Home Office Research and Statistics Directorate*, Centre for Criminology and Criminal Justice, University of Hull, and the Institute of Criminology, University of Cambridge.
Churchill, W. (1997) *A Little Matter of Genocide: Holocaust and Denial in the Americas, 1492 to the Present*, San Francisco: City Lights.
Davis, A. Y. (1998) 'Masked Racism: Reflections on the Prison Industrial Complex,' *Colorlines*, Fall, vol. 1, no. 2, pp.11–13.
Davis, M. (1995) 'Hell Factories in the Field: A Prison-Industrial Complex,' *The Nation*, February, vol. 260, no. 7, pp. 229–234.
Evans, L and Goldberg, E. (1998) *The Prison Industrial Complex and the Global Economy*, Berkeley: Agit Press.
Feldman, A. (1991) *Formations of Violence: The Narrative of the Body and Political Terror in Northern Ireland*, Chicago: University of Chicago Press.
Gilmore, R. W. (1993) 'Terror Austerity Race Gender Excess Theater,' in R. Gooding-Williams (ed) *Reading Rodney King, Reading Urban Uprising*, New York: Routledge, pp. 23–37.
———. (1998/1999) 'Globalisation and US Prison Growth: From Military Keynesianism to Post-Keynesian Militarism,' *Race & Class*, vol. 40, no. 2/3, pp.171–188.
———. (1999–2000) 'Behind the Power of 41 Bullets: An Interview With Ruth Wilson Gilmore,' *Colorlines*, vol. 2, no. 4, Winter.
———. (2007) *Golden Gulag: Prisons, Surplus, Crisis and Opposition in Globalizing California*, Berkeley: University of California Press.
Hardt, M. and Negri, A. (2000) *Empire*, Cambridge, MA: Harvard University Press.
Henry, B. (2004) 'The We That Sets Us Free: Building a World Without Prisons,' Audio Recording, Track 5, *Prisons Are Violence Against Women*, Oakland, CA: Justice Now.
Horsman, R. (1981) *Race and Manifest Destiny: The Origins of Racial Anglo-Saxonism*, Cambridge, MA: Harvard University Press.
Korb, L. J. and Boorstin, R. O. (2005) *Integrated Power: A National Security Strategy for the 21st Century*, Washington, DC: The Center for American Progress.
Lukács, G. (1968) *History and Class Consciousness*, Cambridge: MIT Press.

Marable, M. (1983) *How Capitalism Underdeveloped Black America*, Boston: South End Press.

Massey, D. S. and Denton, N. A. (1993) *American Apartheid: Segregation and the Making of the Underclass*, Cambridge, MA: Harvard University Press.

Melucci, A. (1994) 'A Strange Kind of Newness: What's 'New' in New Social Movements?' in E. Laraña, H. Johnston and J. R. Gusfield (eds) *New Social Movements: From Ideology to Identity*, Philadelphia: Temple University Press, pp. 101–130.

Patterson, O. (1982) *Slavery and Social Death: A Comparative Study*, Cambridge, MA: Harvard University Press.

Robinson, C. (1983) *Black Marxism: The Making of the Black Radical Tradition*, Chapel Hill: University of North Carolina Press.

Rodríguez, D. (2006) *Forced Passages: Imprisoned Radical Intellectuals and the U.S. Prison Regime*, Minneapolis: University of Minnesota Press.

Smith, A. (2005) *Conquest: Sexual Violence and American Indian Genocide*, Cambridge, MA: South End Press.

Von Drehle, D. (2003) 'Liberals Get a Think Tank of Their Own,' *The Washington Post*, 23 October, A29.

Walker, M. (2005) 'Walker's World: Democrats Thinking at Last,' *United Press International*, June 8 (accessed via Lexis-Nexis on 15 June 2006).

11 Indigenous Incarceration
The Violence of Colonial Law and Justice

Chris Cunneen

INTRODUCTION

This chapter explores the issue of violence in relation to Indigenous people. I begin by setting out a number of assumptions underpinning the argument, using a broad concept of violence which includes overt physical violence, as well as the use of cruel, inhuman and other forms of ill-treatment. Such an approach is consistent with human rights standards which, in the United Nations Convention against Torture, prohibit cruel, inhuman and degrading treatment. I have also discussed the failure to exercise a reasonable duty of care to persons in custody within the category of violence. The outcomes which arise when custodial authorities fail to adequately perform their responsibilities are often disastrous. Many Indigenous deaths in custody, and much mistreatment of Indigenous people, arise through a failure to exercise a required duty of care. I have termed the results of this failure 'the violence of neglect.'

This chapter is specifically focused on the violence of incarceration for Indigenous people in Australia. However, the over-representation of Indigenous people in criminal justice systems is an international phenomenon. The social, economic, health and educational status of Indigenous peoples are indicative of the most marginalised groups globally.[1] There is also a particular resonance between the experience of Indigenous people in Australia with those in other 'settler' countries of Canada, New Zealand and the United States. Similarities can be found in the experience of colonisation as well as the contemporary levels of mass imprisonment (see Cunneen 2006). In each country, Indigenous people are massively over-represented in local, state and federal prisons. In Australia, in 2005, the imprisonment rate per 100,000 of the non-Indigenous population was 125.3. For Indigenous people, the comparable rate was 2021.2 (Australian Bureau of Statistics [ABS] 2005:31).

A further assumption underpinning this chapter is the 'location' of violence I have taken to include both police and prison authorities. There is a specific reason for this broader consideration of violence. Many Indigenous people come into contact with the criminal justice system and are locked up in local police cells (or local jails to use American terminology). This is an issue for Indigenous people living in rural and remote areas where they are not transported to a major prison for their period of incarceration, particularly in relation to minor offences. In these cases, the person is held in custody until the matter is determined by a magistrate, which might take several weeks if it is in a remote area where the court only sits on a monthly schedule. To properly understand the 'violence of incarceration' as it applies to Indigenous people, we need to include police in their role as a custodial authority.

The final assumption underpinning the chapter is the importance of the history of colonial dispossession and control. The state claims monopoly over the legitimate use of violence against its own citizenry, largely through the application of the criminal law and its systems of punishment. Yet we can only understand this monopoly of violence in the context of Indigenous peoples when it is symbiotically linked to the historical process of colonisation. Colonisers claimed the moral and political right to impose specific systems of law and punishment over Indigenous peoples—systems which were alien to the colonised. In this sense, the original 'violence of incarceration' has its roots in dispossession from land and denial of sovereignty.

THE HISTORICAL CONTEXT

Much has been written concerning colonial violence against Indigenous people in Australia and elsewhere; it is not my purpose here to recount the role of the colonial state in perpetrating that violence, or in turning a blind eye to its occurrence. There is also enough literature to demonstrate the role of the criminal justice system as an agent of colonial policy and often involved in outright violence, or as an instrument of policies of containment, control and removal (Cunneen 2001; Human Rights and Equal Opportunity Commission 1991; Johnston 1991; NISATSIC 1997). With regard to the long-term impact of this violence, it has been noted that trauma is greater, more severe and longer lasting when it is caused by human agency, than by those who experience natural disasters. For Indigenous people, this trauma has been inter-generational and has its roots in the colonial experience (Atkinson 2002).

Violence was at the foundational core of the *civilising* processes embarked on by state authorities in their efforts to contain native resistance. The history of terror, torture, violence and ill-treatment is intimately bound up with the various stages of warfare across Australia, New Zealand and North America as Indigenous peoples were dispossessed from their land. As Taussig (1987) has argued, violence and terror were an essential part of maintaining colonial hegemony. The criminal justice system during the early colonial period was characterised both by its repressiveness and military character. In Australia, police actions in 'dispersing' Aboriginal people became an important part of colonial policy in ensuring the removal and control of the traditional landowners. 'Dispersal' became the euphemism for armed conflict, and some 20,000 Aboriginal people were killed during the 'settlement' of an 'unoccupied' land (Reynolds 1987:1).

During the late nineteenth and early twentieth century, a period of government 'protection' of Indigenous peoples was introduced. Protection legislation racially segregated Aboriginal people from Australia citizens and then proceeded to criminalise certain types of behaviour. For example, the criminalisation of Indigenous people for alcohol offences and their subsequent incarceration began with the introduction of the Western Australian protection legislation in 1905 (Haebich 1992: 110). Thus, a significant feature of protection legislation was the exercise of criminal sanctions over Indigenous people. Although legislation was couched in the language of protection, essentially the model for administration and maintenance of control utilised the institutions of the criminal justice system through extensive surveillance and penal sanctions built around the deprivation of liberty. In observing the racially defined and arbitrary nature of justice for Indigenous people, the Australian anthropologist Charles Rowley remarked in the early 1970s, that it was 'still true that in Queensland one can be incarcerated either for crime or for being an Aboriginal' (Rowley 1972:123). Indigenous writers like Atkinson (2002) have referred to these policies of containment and enforced dependency as the structural violence of colonisation.

The historical memory of massacres, containment on reserves, the forced removal of children and a discriminatory criminal justice system is very much alive in Indigenous histories. This history informs Indigenous understandings of the criminal justice system. It also means that there is a particular structural relationship between Indigenous peoples and criminal justice systems which is quite different from other groups. The legal system is one that is firmly entrenched in a colonial paradigm and built on assumptions and processes that removed Indigenous people from whatever legal protections may have existed for other groups.

CONTEMPORARY ACCOUNTS OF VIOLENCE

Perhaps the most extensive documentation regarding Indigenous complaints of violence against criminal justice agencies can be found in the report of the National Inquiry into Racist Violence (Human Rights and Equal Opportunity Commission 1991). The Inquiry was established to investigate the incidence of racist violence against all communities in Australia. What is particularly telling about the evidence from Indigenous people was their complaint that the main perpetrator of racist violence was the criminal justice system. By way of contrast, non-Indigenous racial and ethnic minority groups tended to see the perpetrators of racist violence as more diffuse, including individuals in the community and organised racist groups.

There were many allegations of physical violence by criminal justice officials including police and prison officers. In some cases, there were witnesses, and in a few cases formal complaints were made. In a small number of complaints, there was also successful civil litigation. It was clear from all the evidence presented to the Inquiry that the treatment of Indigenous people in the criminal justice system was an issue of national significance.

One study prepared for the National Inquiry into Racist Violence concerned Indigenous juveniles and their relations with police. It found that over eighty per cent of Aboriginal juveniles in detention centres in New South Wales, Queensland and Western Australia alleged that they had been assaulted by police on at least one occasion (Cunneen 1991). Aboriginal girls who were interviewed reported similar assaults to the males, as well as the incidence of sexist verbal abuse. Overall, the research found that there were widespread complaints in relation to violence across the three States, that the allegations were geographically widespread within each State and that there was an internal consistency in the types of complaints which were made across the nation. In addition, there was a strong tendency on the part of those interviewed to see the violence as something normal and to be expected. The violence was not seen as unusual, and in some cases the significance of the violence was downplayed by the victims. Violence by police officers was found to take a number of forms, including verbal abuse, physical assault, provocation and harassment. Less than ten per cent of Indigenous young people interviewed recollected making any form of complaint about the incidents of violence. In the majority of cases, there was simply seen to be 'no point' (Cunneen 1991).

More recently, the Australia Bureau of Statistics (ABS 1995; 2004) national Aboriginal and Torres Strait Islander surveys have provided disturbing data on the contact between Indigenous people and the criminal justice system. The 1994 survey found that approximately ten per cent of all persons aged thirteen years and over reported being 'hassled' by police during the twelve months prior to being interviewed. Some fourteen per cent of males and five per cent of females said they were hassled. The same survey estimated twenty-two per cent of males aged between fifteen and nineteen years reported being hassled. Approximately three per cent of persons aged thirteen years and over said they were physically assaulted by the police in the twelve months before the interview (ABS 1995:59). The later ABS survey conducted in 2002 did not require information on the nature of contact with police. However, sixteen per cent of Indigenous people aged fifteen or over reported being arrested at least once in the previous five years, and seven per cent reported being imprisoned during the same time frame (ABS 2004: 14).

STATE VIOLENCE AND MISCARRIAGES OF JUSTICE

Violence and intimidation against Indigenous people lead to significant miscarriages of justice, including lengthy periods of imprisonment. The case of Kelvin Condren provides an extreme illustration of this point. Condren was sentenced to life imprisonment in 1984 for the murder of Patricia Carlton. Both Condren and Carlton were Aboriginal people living in Mt Isa. The case caused considerable controversy and the conviction was finally set aside by the Queensland Court of Criminal Appeal in June 1990. Condren had, by this time, spent six years in prison.

Condren had always claimed that he was assaulted and 'verballed' by police over the murder he had supposedly confessed to committing. Specifically, Condren claimed that he had been subjected to assault and intimidation prior to making a police record of interview, that the record of interview was largely fabricated by police, and that the oral admissions which police claimed he had made prior to the record of interview were also fabricated. In addition, three Aboriginal witnesses also claimed that the statements they had made to police in the matter were false and had been obtained through intimidation, duress and assault (Criminal Justice Commission 1992).

In the first application to the Queensland Court of Criminal Appeal in 1987, evidence pointing to Condren's innocence had been rejected. The mode of reasoning in that rejection is illuminating. A linguistic expert with particular knowledge concerning Aboriginal English and the legal process, Dr Eades, had presented evidence to the court that the speech patterns in the police record of interview were inconsistent with the type of speech patterns used by Aboriginal people in Queensland. Eades' evidence was rejected by the court on a number of grounds including on the basis that Condren was only 'part-Aboriginal' and therefore not within the group described by Dr Eades (see Caruana, 1989). During the first appeal, the Court accepted the uncorroborated confession to police despite mounting evidence which cast doubt on its validity. The matter went back to the Queensland Court of Criminal Appeal for a second time in 1989, after intervention by the High Court of Australia and a commitment by the new Queensland Labour Attorney-General to review the case. Condren was released from gaol in 1990.[2] Condren's case points to another view or understanding of the violence of incarceration. The deprivation of liberty (itself an implicitly violent act) is an outcome from the actual violence exercised in earlier stages of the criminal justice process.

KILLED IN CUSTODY

Perhaps the more obvious way of thinking about the violence of incarceration relates to those cases where individuals are violently assaulted and killed. Deaths in custody have been a major issue for Indigenous people and were the subject of an extensive Royal Commission in the later part of the 1980s and early 1990s. The Royal Commission into Aboriginal Deaths in Custody (RCADIC) was established because there had been a number of deaths in police and prison custody, which caused serious alarm among Aboriginal communities across the country. These included in particular the deaths of John Pat in Western Australia (kicked to death by police after a pub brawl), and Eddie Murray in New South Wales (picked up by police for public drunkenness and died from hanging in a police cell) (see Cunneen 2006).

Situations where Indigenous people are killed by police and correctional authorities *whilst in custody* (as compared to being killed while being taken into or escaping from custody) are undoubtedly the most controversial of deaths. One of the most recent and notorious cases in Australia involved thirty-six-year-old Mulrunji (Cameron Doomadgee), who died in police custody on Palm Island in November 2004. Palm Island is a major Indigenous community near Townsville in Queensland. Mulrunji was arrested for drunk and disorderly behaviour. He was healthy man when arrested, was not known as a troublemaker, and had not been previously arrested on Palm Island. The postmortem examination revealed that Mulrunji suffered four broken ribs, a ruptured spleen and a liver that was almost cleaved in two. A riot occurred on the Island after the release of the autopsy results. During the riot, the police station and local courthouse were destroyed.

The community's anger over the death of Mulrunji was vindicated by the Coroner's report into the death, which was released in September 2006. Coroner Clements found that Mulrunji had punched Sergeant Hurley after being arrested and transported to the police station, and that Hurley had punched Mulrunji in response. Both men fell to the ground and Hurley lost his temper and hit Mulrunji several times after falling to the floor. 'I conclude that these actions of Senior Sergeant Hurley caused the fatal injuries' (Clements 2006:27). After being beaten, Mulrunji was dragged away and deposited in the police cells. According to the Coroner, 'there was no attempt whatsoever to check on Mulrunji's state of health after the fall and its sequelae. . . . No attempt at resuscitation was made by any police officer even when there was a degree of uncertainty about whether Mulrunji had died' (Clements 2006:27).

The Coroner found that the decision to arrest Mulrunji in the first instance for drunk and disorderly was an inappropriate use of police discretion and could easily have been addressed by means other than arrest. In other words, Mulrunji should never have been in police custody in the first place.

The Coroner was critical of the failure to check on the health of Mulrunji after the fall and the assault.

> Mulrunji cried out for help from the cell after being fatally injured, and no help came. The images from the cell video tape of Mulrunji, writhing in pain as he lay dying on the cell floor, were shocking and terribly distressing to family and anyone who sat through that portion of the evidence. The sounds from the cell surveillance tape are unlikely to

be forgotten by anyone who was in court and heard that tape played. There is clear evidence that this must have been able to be heard from the police station dayroom where the monitor was running. Indeed the timing of Senior Sergeant Hurley's visit to the cell suggests that the sounds were heard. But the response was completely inadequate and offered no proper review of Mulrunji's condition or call for medical attention. The inspections were cursory and dangerous even had Mulrunji been merely intoxicated. The so-called arousal technique of nudging Mulrunji with a foot is not appropriate. It cannot be sanctioned. (Clements 2006: 32)

The Coroner was highly critical of the investigation, which failed to meet the standards of thoroughness, competency or impartiality. One investigating officer was a friend of Sergeant Hurley—the police officer most likely to be under investigation—and both investigating officers visited Hurley's house for dinner after the investigation had begun.

Adding to the community's view of a cover-up over the killing was the fact that Mulrunji's sister had visited the police station bringing lunch for him. At this time, he was known by police to be dead. She was simply told to go away. The family was not informed of the death until four hours after it had occurred.

The death of Mulrunji is really a 'worst case' example of someone who should not have been in custody in the first place, who is then beaten by custodial authorities and simply left to die. At the time of writing, the matter had been referred to the Director of Public Prosecutions to make a decision on bringing criminal charges against the police responsible for the death.

THE VIOLENCE OF NEGLECT

Violence is often associated with the actions of individuals on others. However, it can also be seen in the *inaction* of authorities which have specific responsibilities and duties. At the most extreme, these inactions can result in death. The RCADIC found that there was a significant failure by custodial authorities to exercise a proper duty of care for Indigenous people held in custody. The Commission found that there was little understanding of the duty of care owed by custodial authorities and there were many system defects in relation to exercising care. There were many failures to exercise proper care. In some cases, the failure to offer proper care directly contributed to or caused the death in custody.

Royal Commissioner Wootten, in his report on New South Wales, Victoria and Tasmania noted that 'everyone of the (18) deaths was potentially avoidable and in a more enlightened and efficient system . . . might not have occurred. Many of those who died should not or need not have been in custody at all' (Wootten 1991a: 7). He found that 'negligence, lack of care, and/or breach of instructions on the part of custodial authorities was found to have played an important role in the circumstances leading to 13 of the 18 deaths investigated' (Wootten 1991a: 63).

In Queensland, the Royal Commission found that five of the twenty-seven deaths investigated 'were preventable in that they would not have occurred if the custodial authorities had adequately attended to their responsibilities' (Wyvill 1991: 27). At least two other deaths may have been preventable. In particular, 'a lack of understanding of the duty of care owed to a person in custody; a failure on the part of one or more individuals to perform their custodial duties; [and] entrenched habits of non-compliance' contributed to the deaths (Wyvill 1991: 27).

In Western Australia, the Royal Commission reports were equally damning of the indifference to the duty of care demonstrated by custodial authorities. For example, there were five Aboriginal deaths in custody in Kalgoorlie police lock-up during the 1980s. In the last four of these deaths, police ignored procedures relating to cell checks, which had been specifically introduced after the first Aboriginal death in custody in the lock-up (O'Dea 1991: 456–457).

The stories of this neglect and indifference to Indigenous people in custody seem barely comprehensible to those non-Indigenous people with little experience of the criminal justice system. Yet the treatment of Indigenous people revealed by the RCADIC represented the day-to-day experiences of people when they came into contact with non-Indigenous institutions. Two cases examined by the Royal Commission, one from NSW (Quayle) and one from Queensland (Kulla Kulla), illustrate the point, and show a similar pattern of institutional abuse.

In these cases, the neglect and indifference is exacerbated by both the criminal justice system and the health system and arise when Indigenous people have taken a sick relative to hospital for treatment. Charlie Kulla Kulla was admitted to Coen hospital by members of his family in a seriously ill condition. It was assumed by medical staff that he was drunk and there was no proper diagnosis of his condition—despite his complaints about pain. Although he was not troublesome in any way at the hospital, the police were called; they too assumed that he was drunk and proceeded to arrest him as he lay on a hospital trolley. He was taken and placed in the police watchhouse with eighteen other men and women. All but one of these people were incarcerated for public drunkenness. The local sergeant had decided that those arrested over the weekend would not be allowed bail. Charlie Kulla Kulla died in the watchhouse the following day from lobar pneumonia (Wyvill 1990). A similar series of events occurred with Mark Quayle. In this case, Commissioner Wootten found that the death of Quayle

 . . . resulted from shocking and callous disregard for his welfare on the part of a hospital sister, a doctor of the Royal Flying Doctor Service and two police officers. I find it impossible to believe that so many experienced people could have been so reckless in the care of a seriously ill person dependent on them, were it not for the dehumanised stereotype of Aboriginals so common in Australia and in the small towns of western NSW in particular. In that stereotype a police cell is a natural and proper place for an Aboriginal. (Wootten 1991b:2)

It might be reasonable to expect an improvement after the completion of the RCADIC and the subsequent release of its findings and recommendations. The most extensive examination of deaths in custody since the Royal Commission has been prepared by the Office of the Aboriginal and Torres Strait Islander Social Justice Commissioner (1996). It examined ninety-six Indigenous deaths in custody during the period 1989 to 1996 and used the findings of coronial inquests as a means of auditing the implementation of Royal Commission recommendations.

The report found that there were numerous breaches of Royal Commission recommendations, including the lack of proper assessment procedures; the lack protocols for dealing with intoxicated persons; insufficient training to distinguish intoxication from injuries; irregular cell observations; 'at risk' information about prisoners was not passed between medical and prison staff or police and custodial authorities; and in some cases there was a lack of awareness of the duty of care to detainees. Health services in prisons were also substantially below community standards (Office of the Aboriginal and Torres Strait Islander Social Justice Commissioner 1996: xv–xvii).

The response to minimising Indigenous deaths in custody has been very inconsistent. The RCADIC, reported in 1991, made 339 recommendations and showed clearly how deaths could be minimised. When the situation was reviewed in the mid-1990s by the Aboriginal and Torres Strait Islander Social Justice Commissioner, it was still found that major recommendations which could prevent deaths in custody were being ignored. And now a more recent review of Indigenous deaths in custody since 2000 continues to show that basic recommendations to prevent deaths have not been implemented (Cunneen 2006). To demonstrate these current problems, two relatively recent Indigenous deaths in prison are summarised below, that of Trent Lantry in New South Wales and Craig Allen in South Australia.

Trent Lantry took his own life whilst in prison in March 2000. He was nineteen years of age when he hanged himself by using a bed sheet fixed to an obvious hanging point: the vertical bar in front of a grill at the top of the door of the cell. The young man died on the same day he was released from an Acute Crisis Management Unit (ACMU). He had been previously admitted to the ACMU on a number of occasions. On this particular occasion he had been held there as a result of self-inflicted lacerations to his arm and swallowing razor blades. The Unit was described by the Department of Corrective Services as 'a safe and temporary environment for inmates assessed as being highly at-risk or suicidal or who have previous self-harm histories and are currently in crisis' (Smith 2005:10).

On the day of his release from the Crisis Unit, the young man was placed into a cell on his own with a bed supported by four moveable milk crates. There were various accessible hanging points in the cell. There was little monitoring or supervision by correctional staff, who had not been informed of his circumstances (Smith 2005:10). The mother of Trent Lantry, Mrs Veronica Appleton, brought a negligence action against the Department of Corrective Services, alleging breach of duty of care towards the deceased and breach of a duty of care towards herself. Mrs Appleton was not notified of her son's death by the Department of Corrective Services but through a telephone call from a friend who worked at a juvenile detention centre. She attended the prison to view her son's body. She was unaware that she would be taken to his cell and not warned about the condition of his body (Smith 2005:10).

Despite his young age, Trent Lantry had a long history of incarceration and previous suicide and self-harm attempts, including while detained in juvenile correctional facilities. At the time of his death, Trent had been in the adult correctional system for around six months and had been in the ACMU several times because of self-harm.

In relation to the negligence action regarding Trent Lantry, the court found that

> The defendant breached its duty of care in not taking further precautions to prevent impulsive self-harm by Trent after his discharge from the ACMU and in particular by placing him in a cell with easy and immediate access to a hanging point by movable milk crates. By placing Trent in a cell with movable milk crates supporting his bed, the defendant provided him with the opportunity to kill himself. I also find that not monitoring him or assessing him in some fashion and placing him in a cell alone amounted to breaches of its duty. (*Veronica Appleton v State of New South Wales*, Unreported, District Court of New South Wales, Quirk, J. 28 July 2005, 26)

The death of Trent Lantry, like many contemporary Indigenous deaths in custody, shows how little has changed in terms of improved procedures following the Royal Commission. In many respects, Lantry's death is a carbon copy of the circumstances of deaths investigated by the Royal Commission. As Smith notes:

> The circumstances of this case demonstrate fundamental deficiencies in custodial procedures. These include poor standard of cells, inadequate training of correctional staff and an unreliable system of communication for the exchange of relevant information between staff

members about inmates that are at high-risk of suicide or self-harm (Smith 2005:11) .

There was a range of recommendations from the Royal Commission precisely designed to remedy these deficiencies. These included forty-five recommendations specifically aimed at improving custodial health and safety (Johnston 1991: (5) 95–107).

Allan was twenty-nine years of age when he died as a result of hanging in Yatala prison in South Australia in October 2000. He had been convicted of assault against his partner Ms Bowden and was serving one month of a seven-month prison sentence (with the remainder suspended subject to a bond). He had been placed in cell 211, which was a management cell. The deceased made a noose from bed clothing, attached it to an upper rail of a double bunk and hanged himself. Mr Allan had a long involvement with the criminal justice system, his mother giving evidence that he had been in trouble with the police since he was eight years old and had been in and out of prison since becoming an adult. Craig Allen had a previous history of amphetamine use and alcohol abuse. He was receiving psychiatric help for depression and had been proscribed Prozac. Mr Allen also had previous suicide attempts, including one by hanging whilst in police custody ten years earlier.

On admission to Yatala prison, eight days before his death, Mr Allan was subject to various assessments. His Clinical Assessment Record and Health Assessment form, completed by nursing staff, noted his psychiatric assessments of personality disorder and depression, his Prozac daily dosage, his heavy alcohol consumption, his history of attempted hangings and his 'active emotional problems.' Under Special Medical Recommendations it was written, 'shared cell recommended.' Correctional staff completed a Prison Stress Screening form designed to assess prisoner risk, where, despite knowledge of the factors identified here, he was assessed as not at risk. The deceased continued on his Prozac medication and in addition was prescribed Valium to combat the affects of alcohol withdrawal.

Cell 211 was used to accommodate 'recalcitrant' prisoners for up to forty-eight hours, and the deceased was placed there the morning before he took his own life. Cell 211 is a solitary confinement cell with no television, minimal reading material and only one hour exercise per day (instead of the usual six through eight hours). Mr Allan was placed in cell 211 because, contrary to prison regulations, he was wearing two rings on his fingers. A married person was entitled to wear a wedding band only. Prison staff determined that because the deceased was not married he was not entitled to wear any rings. Mr Allan refused to remove the rings and was thus placed in the management cell. He was then threatened with removal to the maximum security G Division, which has a regime of potential long-term solitary confinement. Mr Allan agreed to remove the rings, which he did during the middle of the day. He was left in cell 211.

The Coroner noted that, 'the decision to place the deceased within cell 211 was made without regard to the material contained in the Health Assessment form and, in particular, the recommendation regarding shared cell accommodation. . . . The fact that the material set out [in the form] was not referred to before making the decision was taken . . . was a serious oversight' (State Coroner 2003).

The prison 'Local Operating Procedure No 26' required that prisoners be observed by correctional staff every two hours. The deceased was discovered in his cell at 7.30 am. Taking into account the medical examiners approximate time of death and other factors, the Coroner estimated that the deceased took his own life sometime between 1 am and 2.50 am. Officer observation patrols at 3 am, 5 am and 7 am failed to observe that the deceased had hanged himself from a rung on the top bunk.

The death of Mr Allan highlights the failure to ensure proper medical assessments are made available and for the assessments to inform decision making, the failure to remove hanging points (especially in cells where agitated prisoners are likely to be held in solitary confinement) and the failure to properly observe prisoners as required by prison regulations. In South Australia, the State and Deputy State Coroner have consistently recommended that 'safe cell' principles be implemented as a matter of priority in the State's prisons. However, the government's response to this has been that while safe cell design principles are incorporated in new cell accommodation, 'the refurbishment of existing cells to meet safe cell standards is beyond the current resources of the Department.' The government went on to respond to the Coroner as follows:

> The financial priorities of the Government are related to issues of health, education and police. The cost associated with upgrading all prison cells so they are consistent with 'safe cell' principles would be in excess of $40m. Expenditure of such proportions would reduce the ability of the Government to provide the wider community with better security, education and health related services. (State Coroner 2006)

It is hard to imagine a clearer statement from government that the lives of prisoners are unimportant.

Negligence and lack of attention to duty of care obligations are still endemic in custodial settings. This is despite the accepted legal view that authorities have a duty of care for those in their custody. Indeed, when an individual loses his or her liberty there is a heightened responsibility on the State to exercise a duty of care and prevent harm. For this reason, negligence on the part of authorities can be legitimately considered as part of the violence of incarceration. It is the violence inflicted by neglect. Yet we see basic failings: hanging points remain commonplace, medical assessments and other vital information are not communicated or do not impact on decision making, there is a lack of training in how to respond to vulnerable persons such as the mentally ill, and there is a failure to follow instructions or procedure.

RACISM, TRAUMA AND VIOLENCE

It is also important to consider the links between violence in the criminal justice system and the psychological impacts of racism. I am thinking here of the impacts of racist abuse, racist taunts and degrading treatment based on race. In the research on violence against Indigenous juveniles in custody referred to previously, some eighty-one per cent of the Indigenous young people interviewed said they had been subjected to racist abuse, while many also alleged that they had been threatened with hanging or had suggestions made about committing suicide (Cunneen 1991). The National Inquiry into Racist Violence also documented humiliating treatment. For example, a non-Aboriginal women who was arrested with Aboriginal people in Western Australia and gave evidence to the Inquiry stated that Aboriginal detainees were 'humiliated . . . laughed at, jeered at, enticed to say something wrong so that the punishment would be even greater, threatened with the padded cell, abused with the most insidious remarks . . . I have never [before] seen this kind of human abuse, this mental torture, never' (Human Rights Equal Opportunity Commission 1991:105–106). Degrading treatment while in custody was also recounted. For instance, it was alleged that in the Pilbara region of Western Australia, Aboriginal men had been forced, through lack of water, to drink from toilet bowls while they were held in police cells (ibid: 104–105).

This type of treatment reflects what has been referred to as the psycho-social domination that underpins racism and the denigration of Indigenous culture and Indigenous being. As Judy Atkinson writes, 'Aboriginal people would call this the greatest violence, the violence that brings the loss of spirit, the destruction of self, of the soul' (Atkinson 2002: 69). This is the racialized violence of incarceration. It may involve physical violence, racist behaviour or verbal abuse. However, it is aimed at destroying the sense of self-worth through an attack on the person's ethnic or racial background. An extreme incident of this type of racist psychological violence against Indigenous (both Aboriginal and Maori) prisoners was exhibited in the Victorian prison system in the later part of the 1980s. There was a persistent campaign of violence and intimidation against Maori and Aboriginal prisoners in Pentridge prison, which involved Ku Klux Klan-type activities.

Some of these activities were found to have occurred by internal prison investigations, including those involving KKK activities. However, prison activists also alleged that the investigations were inadequate and aimed at covering up the existence of violence and intimidation. The major allegations included 'cross-burning' by prison officers and prison officers appearing in cell doors at night wearing Ku Klux Klan hoods. There was also photographic evidence that showed prison officers wearing a hood, as well as standing beside a prisoner wearing the Ku Klux Klan hood. Seven prison officers were charged with internal disciplinary matters under the *Public Service Act*. The charges were determined by the Director of Prisons. Three prison officers were found guilty of disciplinary offences. One officer was charged with misconduct for 'the construction and burning of a wooden cross while on duty in 'H' Division in 1986 and during the let out procedure of [a] Maori prisoner'. A chief prison officer was charged with misconduct for taking a photograph of two prison officers with a prisoner wearing a KKK hood. Another chief prison officer was charged with misconduct for allowing himself to be photographed wearing a KKK hood. The officers were 'reprimanded' for their behaviour (Cunneen 1997: 145–147).

CONCLUSION

This chapter has considered the violence of incarceration in the specific context of Indigenous people. The focus has been on Australian Indigenous experiences; however, there are similarities internationally, particularly in the other 'settler' countries of New Zealand and North America. The first point in understanding the violence of incarceration for Indigenous people is to draw the link to the original violence of invasion, occupation and dispossession. Law was a foundational tool in this original violence, and the criminal justice system has continued to operate in a structural context which criminalises Indigenous people in a highly disproportionate manner. Criminalisation is an endemic problem in Indigenous communities. While it remains such an extensive problem, the Indigenous people will continue to bare the brunt of the violence of the system.

State violence through the criminal justice system and against Indigenous people has been widely documented. There is no doubt that violence or the threat of violence is an integral part of the way the criminal justice system operates. Indeed, incarceration is built on an act of violence—the deprivation of liberty, and the criminal justice system lays claim to moral and legal authority for the legitimate use of violence. The massive over-representation of Indigenous people in prison means that they are more susceptible to the use of routine violence. However, beyond the routine violence of incarceration, there is also racialised violence, which is specific to the experiences of Indigenous people in the criminal justice system. In more extreme cases, the prison may be home to organised racist groups who victimise Indigenous prisoners.

This chapter has identified the type of overt violence used against Indigenous people, where in cases like Condren it leads to gross miscarriages of justice. In Condren's case, the six years of incarceration was directly the result of earlier violence by police and unquestioning racial stereotypes used by the judiciary. In cases like Mulrunji, the violence is palpable—he was beaten to death by police whilst in their custody. However, the type of violence which is far more pervasive and probably more damaging in terms of loss of life is the violence of neglect and indifference. Despite the need for basic safeguards which have been identified time and time again over the last couple of decades, Indigenous people continue to die in custody in circumstances that could be easily avoided. They die in custody for very simple reasons: safe cells are not available, proper health facilities are not available, proper procedures are not followed.

The type of solutions which flow from this analysis are evident. They partly relate to changing the way the justice system operates—and there have been enough inquiries and recommendations to clearly indicate how some of the more overt failings of the system could be avoided. However, there is also the deeper need to fundamentally change the relationship of Indigenous people with the criminal justice system—and this is basically a question of decolonising that relationship. The decolonising of criminal justice will involve both the recognition of a rights-based agenda (primarily Indigenous self-determination rights and other political and legal rights) and a process of practically developing alternatives to the current modes of intervention. These alternatives in policing, sentencing and punishment processes are likely to be organic to the particular needs of communities. However, we see examples in a range of initiatives like women's night patrols, elders' groups and community justice groups.

NOTES

1. See generally, the United Nations *Permanent Forum on Indigenous Issues* for discussion on these issues. http://www.un.org/esa/socdev/unpfii/
2. See *Condren v The Queen* (1987) 28 A Crim R 261; *Condren v The Queen*, appeal, High Court of Australia, 16 November 1989, unreported.

REFERENCES

Atkinson, J. (2002) *Trauma Trails. Recreating Songlines*, North Melbourne: Spinifex.

Australian Bureau of Statistics (ABS). (1995) *National Aboriginal and Torres Strait Islander Survey 1994. Detailed Findings*. Catalogue No. 4190.0. Canberra: ABS.

———. (2004) *National Aboriginal and Torres Strait Islander Survey 2002*. Catalogue No. 4714.0. Canberra: ABS.

———. (2005) *Prisoners in Australia*. Catalogue No. 4517.0 Canberra: ABS.

Caruana, C. (1989) 'Trial by Endurance,' *Aboriginal Law Bulletin*, 2(41): 4–6.

Clements, C. (2006) *Inquest Into the Death of Mulrunji*, Office of the State Coroner. Brisbane. http://www.justice.qld.gov.au/courts/coroner/findings/mulrunji270906.doc

Criminal Justice Commission. (1992) *Report on the Investigation Into the Complaints of Kelvin Ronald Condren and Others*, Brisbane: Goprint.

Cunneen, C. (1991) *A Study of Aboriginal Juveniles and Police Violence*, Report Commissioned by the National Inquiry into Racist Violence, Sydney: Human Rights and Equal Opportunity Commission.

———. (1997) 'Hate and Hysteria: The Vilification of Aboriginal and Torres Strait Islander People' in C. Cunneen, D. Fraser and S. Tomsen (eds) *Faces of Hate*, Annandale: Federation Press, pp. 137–161.

———. (2001) *Conflict, Politics and Crime*, St Leonards: Allen and Unwin.

———. (2006) 'Aboriginal Deaths in Custody: A Continuing Systematic Abuse,' *Social Justice* vol 33, no 4.

Haebich, A. (1992) *For Their Own Good*, Nedlands: University of Western Australia Press.

Human Rights and Equal Opportunity Commission (HREOC). (1991) *Racist Violence*, Canberra Report of the National Inquiry into Racist Violence, AGPS.

Johnston, E. (1991) *National Report, 5 Vols*, Canberra: Royal Commission into Aboriginal Deaths in Custody, AGPS.

NISATSIC. (1997) *Bringing Them Home, Report of the National Inquiry Into the Separation of Aboriginal and Torres Strait Islander Children From Their Families*, Sydney: HREOC.

O'Dea, D. (1991) *Regional Report of Inquiry Into Individual Deaths in Custody in Western Australia, Vol.1*, Canberra: Royal Commission into Aboriginal Deaths in Custody, AGPS.

Office of the Aboriginal and Torres Strait Islander Social Justice Commissioner. (1996) *Indigenous Deaths in Custody 1989–1996* Sydney: Human Rights and Equal Opportunity Commission.

Reynolds, H. (1987) *Frontier. Aborigines, Settlers and Land*, Sydney: Allen and Unwin.

Rowley, C. (1972) *Outcastes in White Australia* Harmondsworth: Penguin.

Smith, C. (2005) 'Broken Beds and Broken Lives: Veronica Appleton v State of New South Wales' *Indigenous Law Bulletin*, vol 6, no 14, pp.10–11, October.

State Coroner, South Australia (2003) *Finding of Inquest Craig Mark Allan*. Inquest No. 17/2002 (2689/2000) http://www.courts.sa.gov.au/courts/coroner/ Accessed 5/7/06

———. (2006) *Finding of Inquest Troy Michael Glennie*. Inquest No. 17/2006 (0397/04 & 2943/04) http://www.courts.sa.gov.au/courts/coroner/ Accessed 10/11/06

Taussig, M. (1987) *Shamanism, Colonialism and the Wild Man. A Study in Terror and Healing*, Chicago: University of Chicago Press.

Wootten, H. (1991a) *Regional Report of Inquiry in New South Wales, Victoria and Tasmania*, Canberra: Royal Commission into Aboriginal Deaths in Custody, AGPS.

———. (1991b) *Report of Inquiry Into the Death of Mark Anthony Quayle*, Canberra: Royal Commission into Aboriginal Deaths in Custody, AGPS.

Wyvill, L. (1990) *Report of the Inquiry Into the Death of Charlie Kulla Kulla*, Canberra: Royal Commission into Aboriginal Deaths in Custody, AGPS.

12 The Violence of Refugee Incarceration

Jude McCulloch and Sharon Pickering

> *We came to a country we heard has human rights and freedom. We can't believe what's happening to us. . . . We haven't any human rights. We are just like animals. We do not have a normal life like a human. Our feeling is dead. Our thinking is dead. We are very sad about everything. We can't smile.*
>
> (Ibrahim Ishret, asylum seeker, Australia, quoted in Amnesty International 2005).

INTRODUCTION

Increasingly, the global north uses detention to repel, deter and contain asylum seekers from the global south. Forms of immigration detention operate in states including the United States, the United Kingdom, Sweden, Denmark, Finland, Ireland, France, Belgium, Spain, Portugal, Austria, Germany and the Netherlands. People detained include visa overstayers, those whose claims for refugee status under the Refugee Convention and associated domestic legislation are rejected, increasingly, those seeking asylum and awaiting determination of their claims. This chapter focuses on the detention by Australia of asylum seekers in on- and offshore locations. It describes the profound impact of this detention on the bodies and minds of refugees, and the systematic official denial of the harm and injustice integral to practices of prolonged mandatory detention of asylum seekers and refugees. As the majority of asylum seekers held in Australian detention centres are eventually determined to be refugees, the terms refugee and asylum seeker are used interchangeably throughout the chapter (Mares 2002: 50).

Exposing the violence of Australian refugee detention is a worthwhile task. Australia has the dubious honour of being a world leader in asylum-seeker incarceration (Carrington 2006: 179; Weber 2006: 26). It has been at the forefront of punitive responses to onshore asylum seekers through the use of mandatory, often lengthy and potentially indefinite detention; detention in remote, harsh and isolated locations; the redrawing of Australian borders specifically to thwart asylum claims and naval blockades aimed at repelling boats carrying asylum seekers (see, for example: Mares 2002; Marr and Wilkinson 2003: 289–290). There is a growing body of research in Australia and testimony from detainees which attests to the gross inhumanity and high costs in human pain and suffering of these policies. Exposing the damage that such policies have done, not only to asylum seekers but also to Australia's body politic, is important if other countries are to be dissuaded from following this lead.

Another reason for examining the violence of incarceration in immigration detention from an Australian perspective is that much of the work in this area has located the contemporary situation in the context of Europe or the United States. Australia's detention regime reflects many aspects of a global punitive trend directed against asylum seekers. In Australia, as elsewhere, the events of 11 September 2001 have intensified this trend. As Perera (2007: 7) points out, 'the bodies of asylum seekers' have become 'the interface between the war on terror and the war at home.'

While much of what has been written internationally is pertinent to detention in Australia, Australia nevertheless is geographically and historically distinct in ways that impact on the political dynamic and contemporary practices of detention. Australia is an island continent, with no shared borders, but which for a number of reasons, including a vast difficult-to-defend coastline, sparse population, particularly in the north, and race-based fears of migrating 'Asian hordes,' suffers from 'invasion anxiety' (Burke 2001; Mares 2002: 27–30). Australia's unique convict and colonial history are also significant factors in the genesis and contemporary context of asylum-seeker detention (Carrington 2006: 197–201; Wadiwel 2007: 158–159). Australia has a long and violent history of detaining and punishing convicts and Indigenous people in and on remote inland and island locations (Hughes 1987: 460–484; Wadiwel 2007). Broader lessons can be found in the story of asylum-seeker detention in Australia. This is a story not only about the violation of human rights and the suffering flowing from that, but also about the way the Government has manoeuvred to profit from that suffering and hide its human costs through systematic and sustained tactics of denial.

The global north has made much of its claim as a civilising influence internationally. These claims are substantially founded on a purported culture of respect for human rights and adherence to the rule of law. Such claims to the moral high ground are exaggerated and unsupportable particularly in the face of the long and brutal history of colonial power (see, for example, Eisenstein 2004; Saada 2003). White Australia was founded on the wholesale denial of Indigenous people's human rights and remains a neo- rather than post-colonial country. As Cunneen argues, the criminalisation of Indigenous people continues the colonial relationship, working to eclipse Indigenous people's standing as citizens with legitimate claims on the nation state (Cunneen 2001). Claims to moral superiority based on respect for human rights demand exposure of ongoing and systematic violation of these same rights by the claim makers. Despite its continuing colonial history, Australia promotes itself as a state that respects human rights and in this context its denial of refugee rights needs to be exposed.

A state's claim to uphold refugees' human rights, combined with a systemic failure to do so, are matters of paramount importance, sometimes even life and death. As one Australian asylum seeker puts it:

> I and my fellow detainees came in search of freedom after suffering extreme persecution in our home countries. What has shocked us most is that our human rights have been profoundly violated again, this time by a country that is supposed to respect the principals of human rights. If a western country can do this and get away with it, what hope do we have? (Silove et al. 2001: 1436)

The evolution of Australia's policies in relation to refugees, particularly mandatory detention, is not only a story about violation of rights and the tactics of power. It is also a story that makes clear the positive force of collective action against such practices and tactics. Six years ago, the conservative Howard government was re-elected largely on the basis of its punitive and uncompromising response to asylum seekers (Marr and Wilkinson 2003). Influential sections of the media, leading politicians and the federal police comprehensively vilified asylum seekers as dangerous, criminal, immoral, manipulative and most importantly 'not like us' (see: Marr and Wilkinson 2003; McCulloch 2004; Perera 2007; Pickering 2004; 2005: 22–25; 32–37; Poynting 2002; Poynting, et al. 2004: 153–178).

In the face of vilification and politically manipulated crisis, a myriad of lawyers, minor political parties, academics, non-government organisations, church groups, trade unions, journalists, individual refugee advocates, former detention centre employees and released detainees worked to counter the negative popular sentiment. They did this by cataloguing the Australian Government's failure to meet its human rights obligations under refugee conventions, documenting the human costs of government policy and challenging official disinformation (see: Australian Council of Heads of Schools of Social Work 2006).

Detainees, despite concerted official efforts to isolate and silence them, have gone to extraordinary lengths to draw attention to their plight, engaging in a whole range of individual and collective, organised, spontaneous, desperate and sometimes extremely creative acts. Ultimately, there was a major shift in popular opinion in Australia, and the Government was forced to mitigate some of the harshest aspects of its mandatory detention policy (Carrington 2006). This chapter aims to contribute to the task of bringing the Australian Government to account for its treatment of asylum seekers. It also aims to acknowledge and go some small way towards documenting the unconscionable pain and suffering inflicted on people whose only 'crime' is to be in need of safe harbour and protection after suffering persecution in their home country. It begins by considering the politicised nature of border politics and, in particular, the way that the human rights of asylum seekers have been sacrificed for political gain. The nature and conditions of mandatory detention of refugees in Australia and offshore are described and explored along with the profound impact of this detention on asylum seekers. Finally, the way the violence of incarceration is denied through tactics designed to deny, minimise and blame the victim is considered.

(IN)SECURITY POLITICS ON THE BORDER

The mandatory detention of onshore asylum seekers was introduced by the federal Labour Government in 1992 (Carrington 2006: 193). The treatment of asylum seekers, however, became an issue of political pre-eminence with the arrival in Australian waters of the Norwegian ship, the MV *Tampa* carrying 433 asylum seekers (McCulloch 2004). The *Tampa* was the harbinger to both an increasingly punitive political climate and an exacerbation in the use of a well-established and increasingly harsh detention regime backed by laws and policies designed to ensure that asylum seekers have little opportunity to engage Australia's refugee protection obligations. Summing up the sea change in Australian politics heralded by the *Tampa*, Marr and Wilkinson (2003: 93) conclude that '[n]ascent racism, ancient fears of invasion by immigration and talkback radio ranting about Asian crime' fused into a 'new and extraordinarily potent political force.'

On 26 August 2001, in the midst of a federal election campaign, the *Tampa*, responding to an Australian Government request, rescued the asylum seekers, mainly from Afghanistan and Iraq, from a sinking boat in the Indian Ocean, 140 kilometres from Australian territory. The Government did not allow the *Tampa* to disembark the asylum seekers at the closest Australian port, instead refusing it entry into Australian waters and closing the nearest port. Three days later, the ship, carrying nearly 400 more passengers than it was licensed for, was declared in distress by its captain. Many of the asylum seekers, including fifty-six children and a number of pregnant women, were sick, some seriously so with more than ten unconscious at any one time (Marr and Wilkinson 2003: 68; 187). In what was to become emblematic of the denial that characterised reports of refugees' suffering in detention, the Prime Minister publicly denied claims of medical problems on the ship, effectively implying that those making them were lying (Marr and Wilkinson 2003: 70). When the ship moved into Australian waters without permission, it was boarded by the military's Special Air Services who took control. On 31 August, proceedings were commenced in the Federal Court for a writ of *habeas corpus* against the Government for the detention of the asylum seekers aboard the ship. The

Government, typical of the semantics that came to frame its position on detainees, argued that they were not illegally held and were free to go anywhere other than Australia. The writ was successful on 11 September 2001 but later defeated on appeal. That the asylum seekers had nowhere to go and no means of getting there was literally ruled out of court in the charged atmosphere that accompanied the 2001 attacks on the United States (Marr and Wilkinson 2003: 142–157; 121–127) .

In the midst of the Government's carefully constructed, logically absurd, but politically successful construction of the *Tampa* and its human cargo as significant threats to Australia's sovereignty, media attention and public anxiety were stoked by the false allegation that asylum seekers on another vessel threw their children overboard (Mares 2002: 135–9). The Immigration Minister commented that 'I regard these as some of the most disturbing practices I've come across in public life.' Prime Minister Howard said 'I don't want in this country people, who are prepared, if those reports are true, to throw their own children overboard' (quoted in Marr and Wilkinson 2003: 188–9). The vilification of the asylum seekers and the fear generated by the Government about 'illegal boat people' were important elements in its re-election (Mares 2002: 121–141; Marr and Wilkinson 2003; McCulloch 2004; Perera 2007).

In the wake of the *Tampa*, legislation was enacted to create an extra-territorial frontier, excising territory from Australia's migration zone and establishing offshore detention centres on Manus Island, Papua New Guinea and the small island nation of Nauru. In a significant policy shift, the Australian Government sought to ensure that asylum seekers arriving by boat would be prevented from reaching the mainland so that they could be processed under different rules with fewer rights (Pickering 2005: 114–118). The 'Pacific solution,' as it is called, similar to Guantánamo Bay, has been described by a former Australian High Court judge as a 'legal no man's land' and by an academic lawyer as operating in a 'legal vacuum' (see: Weber 2006: 28). The 'Pacific solution' opened up extra-territorial space for the exercise of largely unchecked state power. According to David Manne, the coordinator of the Refugee and Immigration Legal Centre and representative for some of those detained on Pacific islands, the detainees are 'are fundamentally out of sight, out of mind, out of rights' (quoted in Gordon 2007: 8).

MANDATORY DETENTION

Australia's most controversial detention centres were established in deliberately remote and hostile physical environments, geographically isolated from large metropolitan population centres. Port Hedland detention centre, for example, is approximately 1,640 kilometres from Western Australia's capital Perth, described as the most isolated city in the world (Lonely Planet

2007). Metropolitan detention centres tend to contain only short-term detainees. Approximately half the detainee population is held in remote centres (Carrington 2006: 189). Detention centres at Port Hedland, Baxter, Woomera and the Curtin Immigration and Processing and Reception centre have been described as 'desert boot camps' (Carrington 2006: 189). Such is the isolation of the detention centres and the detainees within them that they have been said to exist in a space 'within not-Australia' (Cohn, quoted in Weber 2006: 26). There is also an immigration processing centre at Christmas Island, a tiny island more than 2,000 kilometres from Perth in the Indian Ocean. Detention on remote islands and in the desert adds another dimension of intensity to the isolation and inaccessibility of detainees that is deliberately enforced by government.

While Woomera and Curtin have been closed, Manus Island is no longer being used, and other camps are almost empty, in the recent past thousands of refugees, including hundreds of children, have been detained in desert and island detention, many for several years (Carrington 2006; Gordon 2007; Jackson 2007). On average, between 1997 and 2006, there were more than 6,000 asylum seekers held in detention each year (Senate Legal and Constitutional Legislation Committee 2006: 17).

Asylum seekers are detained for the time it takes to assess their claims, which may be several years. People found not to be refugees but unable to return safely to their homeland for various reasons have been incarcerated for many years. Adverse security assessment by the Australian Security Intelligence Organisation has meant continued incarceration even for those with successful refugee claims. As Amnesty International points out:

> Currently the Department of Immigration can detain anyone they consider to be a so called unlawful non-citizen forever. Australian courts do not have the opportunity to determine the need or appropriateness of that detention. The denial of such a fundamental right means that a person in Australia can be detained without end. (Dr Thom, Amnesty International Australia's Refugee Coordinator, quoted in Amnesty International Australia, 2005: para 5)

Mandatory detention was introduced to deter asylum seekers who were considered to be abusing Australia's humanitarian generosity (Pickering 2005: 82–122). The rationale of immigration detention is to deter refugees from travelling to Australia prior to determination of their claims and to encourage them to apply for refugee status offshore. In 2002, the Immigration Minister stated: 'Detention arrangements have been a very important mechanism for ensuring that people are available for processing and available for removal, and thereby a very important deterrent in preventing people from getting into boats' (quoted in Ozdowski 2003: para 26).

The policy has resulted in the differential treatment of asylum seekers based on whether they seek asylum offshore or when they arrive in Australia.

There is no doubt that such an approach goes against the spirit of Australia's international obligations under the Refugee Convention and other international instruments. These provide that refugees who flee when their lives or freedom are threatened should not be penalised for arriving in a country without authorisation (Pickering 2005: 83).

The mandatory detention of asylum seekers and the conditions of detention have created enormous controversy and division within Australia. There has been a substantial shift in government policy away from long-term detention in the face of mounting public pressure (Carrington 2006: 192). Inquiries and protests outside the detention centres have been matched in intensity and frequency by protests inside. These protests have taken the form of riots, lip sewing, organised hunger strikes and mass escapes (see, for example: Mares 2002). While the media has often tended to view these acts as inexplicable or evidence of bad character, including a ready willingness to resort to violence, many of the actions have clearly been designed as explicitly political protests against detention. Journalist and author Peter Mares (2002: 10), for example, describes a well-organised protest by Iraqi detainees at Curtin processing centre in 2000 that combined a mass hunger strike, lip sewing, speeches, chants for freedom and 'a large professionally drawn banner, which depicted the dictator Saddam Hussein expressing gratitude to DIMA [Department of Immigration and Multicultural Affairs] for its cooperation in locking up his critics.' The protests by detainees and the response by authorities, tear gas, water cannon and overwhelming force has meant that detention centres have at times become battle grounds (Carey 2007; Mares 2002: 49–50; Marr and Wilkinson 2003: 44).

THE VIOLENCE OF REFUGEE INCARCERATION

The violence of incarceration in immigration detention in Australia is well-documented. Despite government attempts to control information, dehumanise asylum seekers, and discredit critics, issues we return to later, increasing evidence of physical abuse and the abuse of detainees' basic human rights has emerged. There have been at least 25 inquiries into Australia's detention centres. These are usefully summarized in a chapter by Kerry Carrington (2006: 189–191). The physical abuse of detainees and denial of rights includes the use of brutality and gratuitous violence, the provision of limited and inadequate food, exposure to extremes of temperature, overcrowding, extreme isolation, including limited or no access to phones, limited or no mail, denial of access to legal assistance, transporting detainees without provision of adequate water, food, or breaks, limited and inadequate medical care, lack of education for children, inadequate psychiatric care and a range of other issues. The Department of Immigration Multicultural and Indigenous Affairs was the government department with the responsibility for refugee and asylum-seeker detention. Although not commenting directly on the conditions of detention, the findings of a 2005 Inquiry into the wrongful deportation of an Australian citizen are nevertheless instructive as to the culture of the department and its attitude towards its responsibilities. The report of the inquiry concluded that:

> It is difficult to form any conclusion other than that the culture of DIMIA was so motivated by imperatives associated with the removal of unlawful non-citizens that officers failed to take into account the basic human rights obligations that characterise a democratic society. For some DIMIA officers, removing suspected, unlawful non-citizens has become a dehumanised, mechanical process. The inquiry is particularly worried by the fact that some DIMIA officers it interviewed said they thought they would be criticised for pursuing welfare-related matters instead of focusing on the key performance indicators for removal. (Comrie 2005: 31)

While the myriad of harms committed against refugees in detention remains a major concern, the psychological violence endured by detainees is possibly the most comprehensively documented and arguably the most serious aspect of the violence of refugee incarceration. The ongoing psychological harm inflicted on detainees is not separate from physical harms and closely related to the conditions of detention, some of which are described earlier. There is now a strong body of research which collectively evidences the negative impact of immigration detention on the mental health of asylum seekers. Amnesty International reports that:

> The psychological impact of indefinite detention is irrefutable. Amnesty International continues to receive allegations of ill-treatment of detainees held in immigration detention centres. If substantiated, such treatment would breach international principles of humane treatment of persons in detention and the prohibition of cruel, inhuman or degrading treatment. This would be consistent with findings by other bodies of cruel, inhuman or degrading treatment or punishment regarding similar allegations. Reports of hunger strikes, suicide attempts, riots and protests within immigration detention centres are symptomatic of the complete disempowerment and desperation of human beings who are arbitrarily detained with no access to an effective remedy. (Amnesty International 2005)

There are high rates of post-traumatic stress disorder, depression, anxiety and panic attacks, attempted suicide and self-harm amongst detainees. One study documented the psychiatric status of ten families including fourteen adults and twenty children held in detention for more than two years. They argue that the rates of mental illness amongst the ten families surveyed appear unparalleled in contemporary medical literature. All adults and children met diagnostic criteria for at least one current psychiatric disorder with twenty-six disorders identified amongst the fourteen adults and fifty-two disorders amongst the twenty children. The adults displayed a threefold increase and children a tenfold increase in disorders subsequent to detention. All adults and the majority of children were regularly distressed by sudden and upsetting memories of detention and feelings of sadness and hopelessness. The majority of parents felt that they were no longer able to care for, support or control their children (Steel et al. 2004).

Other studies similarly have found very high levels of psychopathology in child and adult asylum seekers, attributable to traumatic experiences in detention and the impact of indefinite detention. Mares and Jurcidini (2004) found all detainee children in their study had at least one parent with a mental illness. All of the children aged six to seventeen years fulfilled criteria for post-traumatic stress disorder and major depression with suicidal thoughts. Eighty per cent of these had made significant attempts to self-harm. Of the eleven-months to six-year-old age group, eighty per cent were identified with developmental delay or emotional disturbance. Further, multiple obstacles to adequate service provision were identified and adequate intervention and care was not possible.

The contradictions between Government suicide prevention programmes in the community and the suicide producing circumstances of detention are stark. Dudley (2003: 102) concludes:

> The Australian government's policies supporting successful suicide prevention programs stand in contrast to its policy regarding indefinite mandatory detention of on-shore asylum seekers. Men's and women's rates of suicidal behaviours in Australian immigration detention centres, while imprecise, are calculated as 41 and 26 times the national average. . . . Self-harm in detention reflects a convergence of health, protection and human rights concerns, and is driven by the extremity of detention and the detention environment.

Concern has been raised that actions in detention, including hunger strikes, demonstrations, self-harm, suicide attempts and forcible removal procedures, adversely impact on children's sense of security and stability (Sultan and O'Sullivan 2001). Children in detention have also been exposed to the effects of tear gas (Gilsenan 2006).

The 2005 Joint Standing Committee on Migration, Report of Inspections of Baxter Immigration Detention found that the accounts by detainees indicate that the strain on detainees awaiting the results of appeals for prolonged periods is immense. The Committee argued that it believed that the length of detention has a close correlation with the development or exacerbation of depressive conditions in a number of cases. Moreover, it found psychiatric visits to be inadequate for the number of detainees on tranquilisers and antidepressants. The Palmer Report (2005) likewise highlighted the inadequate mental health care in Baxter, noting that the detainee population requires a much higher level of care than the general population.

Some research suggests that the levels of harm inflicted by the detention process outweigh experiences of persecution in countries of origin. The head of the Department of Psychological Medicine at the Adelaide Women's and Children's Hospital records that 'All the adults and most of the children I've seen have been extremely badly damaged—more damaged by their detention experience than by their experiences before arriving' (quoted in Grattan 2005a).

The impact of mandatory detention on children has been the focus of intense controversy. As a result of this, and the growing evidence of the negative impact of detention, children have been released from mandatory detention. However, in the recent past approximately 100 children were held in immigration detention at any one time (Carrington 2006: 193). A 2004 inquiry found that the average period for a child in detention was one year, eight months and eleven days (Human Rights and Equal Opportunity Commission 2004: Chapter 3).The highest number of children in detention was 842 in 2001 and the longest a child was in detention was five years, five months and twenty days before being assessed as a refugee (Amnesty International 2005).

An expert in Australian child welfare examined the conditions of detention and the evidence of its impact on children (Bessant 2002). She considered whether the circumstances under which children were held in detention centres constituted a basis for determining that they were at risk within the terms of domestic child protection legislation and whether, if the normal rule of law was applied, these children would be brought under the protection of that legislation. She found that they would be. In other words, if parents treated their children the way the Government treated children in detention, the State would intervene to change their living conditions or remove them.

The Human Rights and Equal Opportunity Commission (2002) documented the case of Shayan Badraie, an Iranian boy, who lodged a complaint against Department of Immigration Multicultural and Indigenous Affairs (DIMIA) over his detention and the harm he suffered as a result. He was held in detention for two years between the ages of five and seven. The Commission found his human rights were breached and that he had witnessed suicide attempts, self-harm and abuse. He developed post-traumatic stress disorder, refused to eat, drink or talk and was hospitalised on numerous occasions. Health professionals were constrained from acting in the child's best interests because of the policy of mandatory detention. The treatment he received in hospital would inevitably fail because he would always return to detention which caused the problems (Zwi et al. 2003). The Commission recommended that the Government should pay Shayan $70,000 compensation for the harm he had suffered and that he should receive a written apology. The

Government refused. Subsequently the Immigration Department was sued over his experiences in detention and he was paid a $400,000 settlement (*Sydney Morning Herald*, 3 March 2006).

The impact of the body of research about the seriously detrimental impacts of mandatory detention on practices of immigration detention was limited until recently. The turning point came with the revelation that Australians (as opposed to non-citizens) had wrongfully and unlawfully been detained. In one case, a permanent resident, Cornelia Rau, suffering from a severe mental illness, was held in immigration detention for nearly a year. She spent months at Baxter detention centre where she was kept for several periods in solitary confinement in high security management units. Other detainees expressed concern about her mental health to refugee advocacy groups who alerted journalists to her plight. Her family recognised her instantly from a newspaper article in January 2005 and secured her release to a psychiatric hospital (Palmer 2005).

Cornelia Rau's sister questioned the lack of human rights for detainees commenting that:

> While she [Cornelia] was an unnamed illegal immigrant the only treatment she got for mental illness was longer periods in lock-up as punishment for bad behaviour. And yet as soon as she was found to be an Australian resident she was whisked away to a teaching hospital, seen by psychiatrists and medicated. During which leg of her flight from Baxter to Adelaide did she suddenly gain the basic human right to medical treatment? How many cases will it take like Cornelia's until detainees get the rights they deserve or, more importantly taken out of conditions that themselves cause mental illness? (Rau 2005)

In the light of the Rau case and another high profile case, DIMIA now admits to other cases between July 2000 and April 2005 where citizens or lawful residents have been arrested and detained (Commonwealth Ombudsman 2006). In the face of growing scandal, the Government finally made substantial changes to the nature and circumstances of immigration detention. Children have been released from mandatory detention, detention has been restricted to twenty-eight days, except in exceptional circumstances and enhanced mental health services have been provided for detainees (Carrington 2006: 192). There is still, however, a group of offshore detainees on Nauru who face spending years on the tiny island (Gordon 2007). In addition, the excising of Australian territory from the migration zone combined with offshore detention means that any future asylum seekers who arrive by boat are likely to be held offshore (Forbes 2007).

While the release from detention of children and many others—some after having spent years languishing—and major shifts in policy are welcome, they are long overdue in light of the evidence of human rights abuses in detention and evidence of the harmful impact of lengthy and indefinite detention on asylum seekers. Tactics of denial were characteristic of the Government's approach to (dis)information about asylum seekers and the circumstances and condition of their detention.

DENIAL

Violence is a physical and emotional act upon the recipient. When the state is the perpetrator of such violence, it also amounts to an attack on the body politic which turns away or even embraces as necessary and normal the harm committed. The violence of incarceration depends substantially on discourses that mitigate its practice in the public imagination. In *States of Denial* (2001) Stanley Cohen explores the way that systematic human rights abuses and widespread suffering are denied. The Australian Government has sought to deny the violence of its refugee detention policy by hiding it, minimising it, and blaming the victim.

At the most basic level, the Government has sought to hide the violence of incarceration by hiding detainees and detention centres. The remote location of the desert and island centres created real practical barriers to seeing. The Government exacerbated the geographical isolation of detention by limiting detainees' opportunities to communicate with the outside world (Mares 2002: 12; 44–5; Marr and Wilkinson 2003: 135–136). A Media, Entertainment and Arts Alliance report (2006:18) on press freedoms in Australia notes the great lengths (often legislative) that the Government has gone to in making it all but impossible to report in any detail on the conditions of incarceration. When parliamentarians have sought direct physical access to immigration detention centres, they too have been actively prevented by Ministers and the Department of Immigration (Grattan 2005b).

Offshore detention has enhanced the Government's ability to hide detainees and the conditions of detention. Many advocates and lawyers who have wanted to travel to Nauru to assist asylum seekers have been denied visas. The Migration Amendment Bill (Senate Report) 2006 records that the Human Rights and Equal Opportunity Commission, a body charged with some official oversight of immigration detention, was challenged by the Department when seeking to visit Nauru and was unable to go in the face of an uncooperative and unsupportive Department.

At another level, the Government hides the violence of incarceration by diminishing the humanity of refugees. There is a substantial body of literature that points to discursive strategies used by the Government to represent asylum seekers as dangerous 'others' (see, for example: Pickering 2004; Poynting 2002). We refer to only two examples here. During the *Tampa* incident, discussed earlier, the Government specifically directed that no 'personalising or humanising images' were to be taken of those on board (Marr and Wilkinson 2003: 135–36). In another instance, the Minister for Immigration refused to acknowledge the humanity of a young boy in detention, referring to him repeatedly as 'it' rather than using his name. In response to a media story about the boy's precarious mental health, the Minister stated: 'I understand *it* receives food and liquids'; 'We are working at getting the child into an environment in which *its* condition can be managed'; '*It's* a step child' (ABC 2001).

Hiding the violence of immigration detention has included attacking and discrediting critics of mandatory detention. Steel et al. (2004: 527) note:

> The key public health dilemma to emerge from this and other such research is that the Australian Federal Government has, and continues to be, unresponsive to findings regarding detention practices, choosing instead to attempt to challenge the validity of the research and the integrity of the researchers involved.

Privatisation of immigration detention centres has also worked to hide human rights abuses and provide a means for government to avoid scrutiny and accountability (Palmer 2005).

MINIMISING

The Government has sought to minimise the violence of refugee detention by downplaying its seriousness and renaming coercive practices to make them appear harmless. When questioned about solitary confinement in immigration detention, the Immigration Ministers used the term 'separation detention' and argued it was not a form of punishment but a practice of 'monitoring those for their own safety' (Crock et al. 2006). Responding to reports of the deteriorating mental health of detainees, the Immigration Minister maintained that 'I'm not sure that everybody would regard depression as a mental illness' (quoted in Lawrence 2003). In one instance, the then Minister for Immigration responded to media questions surrounding suicide threats made by fifteen unaccompanied minors in detention by stating: 'Look, I take all of these issues seriously. I don't want to see some *mishap* occur' (ABC 2002 emphasis added). The equation of mass suicide of teenage children with a 'mishap' is even more shocking, given that the Minister was the legal guardian of any unaccompanied minors.

The Government has also tried to soften the image of detention centres visually. In 2005, Villawood detention centre was surrounded by cyclone fencing and razor wire. Sensitive to criticisms, and in an effort to make detention centres *look* less like prisons, the Minister cut down the razor wire before the assembled media. It was soon replaced with less visually confronting but equally effective electric fencing (Crock et al. 2006). It has even been suggested that those asylum seekers held on Nauru are not actually detained. Department officials in the Migration Amendment Bill (Senate Report) stated:

> People who are on Nauru are not in detention. They are residing on Nauru under conditions established under special visa arrangements with the Nauru government. Anyone lawfully in Nauru is free to leave. If they wish to return to their country of residence they can. (2006: 53)

BLAMING THE VICTIM

The 'blame the victim' approach is replete in discourses around asylum seekers, who have been blamed for jumping (non-existent) queues, paying people smugglers, being terrorists, abusing their children by throwing them overboard, being manipulative and ungrateful. One manifestation of this approach has been to argue that suicide attempts and self-harm are simply strategies for gaining attention rather than signs of desperation. In a 2003 interview, for example, the Immigration Minister argued that self-harm and suicide were not symptoms of mental illness but attempts to gain refugee status:

> ... there were perceptions in the centres themselves that, by action of self-harm, people had achieved outcomes. . . . And it led to a belief amongst a proportion of the Afghan population that the only way in which they were going to obtain visas was to be involved in the same sort of conduct. (ABC 2003)

In the civil action involving Shayan Badraie, already discussed, the Government contested the case, arguing that it was Shayan's family who made him sick as part of a scheme to escape detention. The Government's contention that Shayan, not then eight years old, could be persuaded to not eat or drink for days on end as part of a ploy to access visas for his family was quickly dismissed by expert witnesses as not possible for a young boy. Psychiatrists gave evidence that his parents were caring and sensitive people doing everything they could for a very sick child. The Government continued its defence regardless, not making an acceptable offer of settlement until the thirteenth week of a trial, placing enormous further stress on the family (Carey 2007).

Prime Minister John Howard expressed a similarly hard attitude towards the suffering of refugee children in detention. In an interview after the change of policy in relation to the mandatory detention of children in 2005, a journalist put it to the Prime Minister:

> You've had alarm bells going off all over the place over years. You've had serious psychiatric warnings, quite serious ones, from whole groups of psychiatrists, particularly about children, you've had the

Human Rights Commission, you've had other groups saying—and having made the admission that the changes are—not just overdue but long overdue, which suggests a long period, have you stopped to ask yourself how many of these children now face life as seriously damaged human beings, not to mention their parents? (ABC 2005)

Howard replied:

[P]erhaps their parents should have stopped to ask themselves whether they should have tried to come to this country in an unauthorised way in the first place. (ABC 2005)

CONCLUSION

Australia stakes it claim to being an advanced democratic state substantially on its respect for human rights. The treatment of asylum seekers undermines these claims. Australia's policy of refugee detention has been at the forefront of increasingly harsh and punitive responses to refugees internationally. Australia instituted a programme of mandatory, prolonged and even indefinite detention unprecedented amongst countries in the global north. Additionally, in an effort to thwart the asylum claims of those arriving by boat, it excised significant swaths of Australian territory from its migration zone and removed asylum seekers off shore to Pacific islands creating a virtual rights-free zone.

The precursors of contemporary detention centres are to be found in Australia's systems of reserves, missions and punishment islands used to segregate, exile and punish Indigenous people and, in the case of the latter, convicts (Carrington 2006: 199–200; see Hughes 1987; Morris 2002; Wadiwel 2007 on the use of punishment islands). As Wadiwel (2007: 159) points out in his reflection on the historical antecedents of refugee incarceration:

[T]he Australian camp archipelago of the late 1800s and early 1900s does not sit at a distance from the contemporary camp, nor can it be said that it functions through a different logic; on the contrary the modern camp relies on the colonial camp as its evolutionary point of origin.

The denials of the basic human rights of asylum-seeker detainees, their isolation and the prolonged nature of their incarceration have had a devastating impact on their psychological health. Children in detention have felt these impacts particularly acutely. While the harsh treatment of asylum seekers was originally popular with the public, information about the profound suffering of refugees in detention has led to a change in popular sentiment so that the government has had to alter some aspects of its punitive policy.

The Government was only able to gain and maintain strong public support for its policies through a systematic programme designed to hide and minimise the suffering inflicted by its policy and ultimately to blame the victims for their own suffering. The vilification of asylum seekers through various strategies, for example, suggesting that those fleeing from repressive regimes are masters of manipulation, terrorists and child abusers, is typical of the way states seek to hide their crimes of violence (Green and Ward 2004). When faced with the unwelcome attention accompanying the triple suicide of detainees held indefinitely at Guantánamo Bay, Rear Admiral Harris stated that the men did not kill themselves out of despair but rather:

> They are smart. They are creative, they are committed. They have no regard for life, either ours or their own. I believe this was not an act of desperation, but an act of asymmetrical warfare waged against us. (*BBC News*, 11 June 2006)

In the same 'blame the victim mode,' military psychiatrists at Guantánamo Bay had previously reclassified suicide attempts as 'manipulative self-injurious behaviour' (Amnesty International Australia 2006).

The violence and incarceration of asylum seekers by the Australian Government illustrates the increasing tendency of states to withdraw guarantees of legal protection and entitlements from individuals and abandon especially non-citizens to the intensifying coercive powers of the national security state. In October 2001, the Australian Prime Minister and the Minister for Immigration expressed outrage and moral revulsion in the face of (false) allegations that asylum seekers had thrown their children overboard. This claim was used by the Government to bolster popular support for its punitive stand against asylum seekers and assisted it to electoral victory. The purported concern for the welfare of refugee children is significant in the light of the Government's treatment of these same children in detention. The bogus claim of child abuse against asylum seekers is valid and credible when directed to the Australian Government's treatment of asylum-seeker children in detention. Such a conclusion provides evidence for Australian anthropologist Michael Taussig's (1987: 9) astute observation that '[t]he military and the New Right, like the conquerors of old, discover the evil they have imputed to these aliens, and mimic the savagery they have imputed.'

REFERENCES

ABC. (2001) 7.30 Report: 'Ruddock Replies to Community Concerns' 14 August. http://www.abc.net.au/7.30/content/2001/s346319.htm

————. (2002) Lateline: 'Labour Rethinks Detention Stance' 28 January http://www.abc.net.au/lateline/stories/s468643.htm

————. (2003) 7.30 Report: 'Woomera Problems Historical: Ruddock' 20 May http://www.abc.net.au/7.30/content/2003/s859558.htm

————. (2005) 7.30 Report: 'PM Admits Immigration Changes Long Overdue' 20 June http://abc.net.au/7.30/content/2005/s1396449

Amnesty International. (2005) 'The Impact of Indefinite Detention: The Case to Change Australia's Mandatory Detention Regime' http://safecom.org.au/amnesty-report2005.htm

Amnesty International Australia media release. (2005) 'Immigration Detention: Safeguards Must Be in Place' 20 June http://action.amnesty.org.au/index.php/news/comments/immigration_detention_safeguards_must_be_in_place/

Amnesty International Australia. (2006) USA: Independent Investigation Must Be Held Into Deaths of Three Guantánamo Detainees http//www.amnesty.org.au/news_features/news/hrs/usa_independent_investigation_

Australian Council of Heads of Schools of Social Work. (2006) 'We Have Boundless Plains to Share: The First Report of the People's Inquiry Into Detention' http://www.safecom.org.au/peoples-inquiry.htm

Bessant, J. (2002) 'Normal Rules of Law, Child Protection Legislation and Australia's Detention of Child Asylum Seekers,' *Alternative Law Journal* vol. 27, no 4, August, pp.165–170.

Burke, A. (2001) *In Fear of Security: Australia's Invasion Anxiety*, Sydney: Pluto Press.

Carey, C. (2007) 'Woomera: Victims of the War Zone,' 25 February, *The Age.*

Carrington, K.(2006) 'Law and Order on the Border in the Neo-Colonial Antipodes' in S. Pickering and L. Weber (eds) *Borders, Mobility and the Technologies of Control*, Dordrecht, the Netherlands: Springer, pp. 179–206.

Cohen, S. (2001) *States of Denial: Knowing About Atrocities and Suffering*, Cambridge: Polity.

Commonwealth Ombudsman. (2006) Ombudsman Releases Three Reports on Immigration Detention 6 December www.comb.gov.au/commonwealth/publish.nsf/Content/mediarelease_2006_15

Comrie, N. (2005) 'Inquiry Into the Circumstances of the Vivian Alvarez Matter' http://www.ombudsman.gov.au/commonwealth/publish.nsf/attachmentsbytitle/reports_2005_03_dimia.pdf/$file/alvarez_report03.pdf

Crock, M., Saul, B and Dastyari, A. (2006) *Future Seekers II Refugees and Irregular Migration in Australia*, Sydney: The Federation Press.

Cunneen, C. (2001) *Conflict Politics and Crime: Aboriginal Communities and the Police*, Crows Nest, NSW: Allen and Unwin.

Dudley, M. (2003) 'Contradictory Australian National Policies on Self-Harm and Suicide: The Case of Asylum Seekers in Mandatory Detention,' *Australian Psychiatry* vol 11, pp.102–108.

Eisenstein, Z. (2004) *Against Empire: Feminism, Racism and the West*, Melbourne: Spinifex Press.

Forbes, M. (2007) 'Asylum Seekers to Be Sent Back to Sri Lanka' 24 February, *The Age.*

Gilsenan, R. (2006) 'In Denial Over a Living Hell,' 7 March, *The Australian.*

Gordon, M. (2007) 'Asylum Seekers Fear Return to Malaysia' 17 February, *The Age.*

Grattan, M. (2005a) 'A Mickey Mouse Inquiry,' 9 February, *The Age.*

————. (2005b) 'MP's Bid to Meet Detainees Foiled' 18 February, *The Age.*

Green, P. and Ward, T. (2004) *State Crime: Governments, Violence and Corruption*, London: Pluto Press.

Hughes, R. (1987) *The Fatal Shore*, London: Pan Books.

Human Rights and Equal Opportunity Commission. (2002) Report of an Inquiry Into a Complaint by Mr Mohammed Badraie on Behalf of his Son Shayan Regarding Acts or Practices of the Commonwealth of Australia (the Department of Immigration, Multicultural and Indigenous Affairs) HREOC Report No. 25 http://www.hreoc.gov.au/human_rights/human_rights_reports/hrc_25.html

———. (2004) 'A Last Resort? The Report of the National Inquiry Into Children in Immigration Detention' http://www.hreoc.gov.au/human_right/children_deten-tion_report/summaryguide/summary.pdf

Jackson, A. (2007) 'Baxter Near Empty and costing $30 Million a Year to Maintain' 10 February, *The Age*.

Lawrence, C. (2003) 'Institutionalised Sadism' 2 June, *Sydney Morning Herald*.

Lonely Planet. (2007) World Guide. http://www.lonelyplanet.com/worldguide/des-tinations/pacific/australia/perth/

Mares, P. (2002) *Borderline: Australia's Response to Refugees and Asylum Seekers in the Wake of the Tampa*, Sydney: UNSW Press.

Mares, S., and Jureidini, J. (2004) 'Psychiatric Assessment of Children and Families in Immigration Detention—Clinical, Administrative and Ethical Issues,' *Australian and New Zealand Journal of Public Health* 28 No. 6, pp. 520–526.

Marr, D. and Wilkinson, M. (2003) *Dark Victory*, Crows Nest, New South Wales: Allen and Unwin.

McCulloch, J. (2004) 'National (In)security Politics in Australia: Fear and the Federal Election,' *Alternative Law Journal*, vol 29, pp.87–91.

Media, Entertainment and Arts Alliance. (2006) '*Turning Up the Heat: The Decline of Press Freedom in Australia 2001–2005*' http://www.alliance.org.au/sections/media/press-freedom-turning-up-the-heat.html

Morris, N. (2002) *Maconochie's Gentlemen: The Story of Norfolk Island and the Roots of Modern Prison Reform*, Oxford: Oxford University Press.

Ozdowski, S. (2003) 'Long-Term Immigration Detention and Mental Health' 27–29 October at http://www.hreoc.gov.au/speeches/human_rights/health_diversity.html

Palmer, M. (2005) 'Inquiry Into the Circumstances of the Immigration Detention of Cornelia Rau Report' http://www.minister.immi.gov.au/media_releases/media05/palmer-report.pdf

Perera, S. (2007) 'Introduction: Acting Sovereign' in S. Perera (ed) *Our Patch: Enacting Sovereignty Post-2001*, Curtin University, Perth: Network Books, pp.1–22.

Pickering, S. (2004) 'The Production of Sovereignty and the Rise of Transversal Policing: People-smuggling and Federal Policing' *The Australian and New Zealand Journal of Criminology*, vol 37, pp.362–379.

———. (2005) *Refugees and State Crime*, Annandale, New South Wales: The Federation Press.

Poynting, S. (2002) 'Bin Laden in the Suburbs: Attacks on Arab and Muslim Australians Before and After 11 September,' *Current Issues in Criminal Justice*, vol 14, no 1, pp.43–64.

Poynting, S., Noble, G., Tabar, P. and Collins, J. (2004) *Bin Laden in the Suburbs: Criminalising the Arab Other*, Sydney: Sydney Institute of Criminology

Rau, C. (2005) 'My Sister Lost her Mind and Australia Lost Its Heart,' 7 February, *The Age*.

Saada, E. (2003) 'The History Lessons: Power and Rule in Imperial Formations,' *Items and Issues*, Social Science Research Council, vol 4, no 4, Fall/Winter.

Senate Legal and Constitutional Legislation Committee. (June 2006) 'Provisions of the Migration Amendment (Designated Unauthorised Arrivals) Bill 2006, http://www.aph.gov.au/senate/committee/legcon_ctte/migration_unauthor-ised_arrivals/report/report.pdf

Silove, D., Steel, Z., Mollica,R. and Sultan, A. (2001) 'Detention of Asylum Seek-ers: Assault on Health, Human Rights and Social Development,' *The Lancet*, vol 357, pp.1436–1437.

Steel, Z., Momartin, S., Bateman, C., Hafshejani, A., Silove, D., Everson, N., Salehi, J.K., Roy, K., Dudley, M., Newman, L., Blick, B. and Mares, P. (2004) 'Psychiatric Status of Asylum Seeker Families Held For a Protracted Period in a Remote Detention Centre in Australia,' *Australian and New Zealand Journal of Public Health* 28 No. 6: 527–36.

Sultan, A. and O'Sullivan, K. (2001) 'Psychological Disturbances in Asylum Seek-ers Held in Long Term Detention: A Participant-Observer Account,' *Medical Journal of Australia*, vol 175, pp.593–596.

Taussig, M. (1987) *Shamanism, Colonialism, and the Wild Man: A Study of Ter-ror and Healing* Chicago: The University of Chicago Press

Wadiwel, D. (2007) '"A Particularly Governmental Form of Warfare": Palm Island and Australian Sovereignty' in S. Perera (ed.) *Our Patch: Enacting Sovereignty Post-2001*, Curtin University Perth: Network Books, pp.149–166.

Weber, L. (2006) 'The Shifting Frontiers of Migration Control' in S. Pickering and L. Weber (eds) *Borders, Mobility and Technologies of Control*, Dordrecht, The Netherlands: Springer, pp. 21–44.

Zwi, K., Herzberg, B., Dossetor, D. and Field, J. (2003) 'A Child in Detention: Dilemmas Faced by Health Professionals,' *Medical Journal of Australia* vol 179, pp.319–322.

13 Preventing Torture and Casual Cruelty in Prisons Through Independent Monitoring

Diana Medlicott

INTRODUCTION

In this chapter, I consider the effectiveness of preventing torture and inhumane treatment in prisons and other places of detention through independent monitoring, a requirement for those states that are signatories to the Optional Protocol to the United Nations Convention against Torture and Other Cruel, Inhuman or Degrading Treatment or Punishment (OPCAT). I make special reference to the United Kingdom because it has a well-established system of monitoring, involving independent experts and lay people. I show that, despite the longevity and embedding of this system of independent monitoring, it has not prevented inhumane treatment and routine casual cruelty in the prisons of England and Wales. I consider the reasons for this.

INTERNATIONAL BACKGROUND TO THE PROBLEM OF TORTURE

Since the 1970s, the problem of preventing torture in places of detention has attracted growing attention from international bodies. Data from a range of bodies, including Amnesty International and the United States State Department, have shown that torture and ill treatment remain a routine and systematic part of detention worldwide, with incidences reported in 165 countries. In ninety-seven per cent of cases, it occurred in state custody police detention or prison (Rytter, Jefferson and Worm 2005). Two strands of international response can be detected. First, an intention to break the self-perpetuating cycle of general acceptance and awareness of impunity within states by the firm prosecution of perpetrators. This philosophy is encapsulated in the United Nations Convention Against Torture (UNCAT). As Malcolm Evans (1999:23) points out, there are serious difficulties in preventing torture in this way:

> Prevention requires the active engagement of the State. Since most violations of human rights come about as a consequence of State action,

prevention requires an intrusion into the laws and legal system of the State itself. Moreover, since many violations are the result of direct acts by State agents—such as police, armed forces . . . it requires penetration into the very heart of the State's system of power and control. In essence, the prevention of human rights abuses requires persuading a State to change fundamental aspects of its relationship with its citizens. This is a very threatening undertaking and is more likely to be successful if there is a relationship of trust between those concerned. Unfortunately, much of the international protection of human rights is based on allegations of breach and results in condemnation. It is confrontational in nature and thus renders the task of prevention even more difficult.

The second strand of international action concerns the establishment of relations of trust with the relevant authorities so that torture, and the climate that encourages and legitimises torture, can be prevented from happening. Independent visits can be an important, if not central, means through which this change in climate is achieved, and this chapter outlines some existing mechanisms of independent visits, before considering the case of England and Wales in more detail.

INDEPENDENT VISITS TO PLACES OF DETENTION

Several bodies at the international and regional levels are mandated to make official visits to places of detention in a range of contexts. The United Nations Committee Against Torture and the Human Rights Committee are authorised at the international level under international human rights law to systematically visit places of detention. During armed conflict or occupation, the International Committee of the Red Cross is authorised under international humanitarian law to visit any place where protected persons are detained. At the regional level, the European Committee for the Prevention of Torture under the Council of Europe has conducted regular visits to places of detention since 1989.

Although there is a range of existing mechanisms that may be effective within their particular mandate, only some conduct visits on a routine basis and in a nonconfrontational environment. Neither do they link up at national and international levels (Rytter, Jefferson and Worm 2005: 5). A desire for a systematic and overarching approach that would strengthen the protection of the incarcerated led to the adoption, by an overwhelming majority at the United Nations General Assembly in 2002, of the Optional Protocol to the United Nations Convention Against Torture and Other Cruel, Inhuman or Degrading Treatment or Punishment (OPCAT). OPCAT advocates a universal system of independent regular visits to all places of detention by a range of mechanisms prescribed to link up their preventive initiatives at international and national levels, so that international standards will be effectively implemented even at the local level. In particular, it is intended that the new instrument will provide the power to intervene to prevent torture from occurring, rather than as a reaction after the event. Additionally, it will not adopt the practice of public condemnation of states found to be in breach of the Protocol, but will work with them through a confidential process of dialogue and cooperation. In these ways, it is intended that the gaps in the existing systems will be bridged.

This instrument formally came into force on the 22 June 2006, when, following the simultaneous ratification by Bolivia and Honduras, the instrument reached the twenty ratifications necessary for it to come into effect. OPCAT will have both a national and international capability. The national capability will revolve around the composition, in each State Party, of what Article 3 of the OPCAT terms 'national preventive mechanisms.' These will consist of 'one or several visiting bodies' that are 'set up, designated or maintained at the domestic level' (IIHR and APT 2004). Their brief is to prevent 'torture and other cruel, inhuman or degrading treatment or punishment' (IIHR and APT 2004). Internationally there will be a Sub-Committee of ten members elected by states that are party to the Protocol, and this Sub-Committee will visit all places of detention in those states and make recommendations. In addition, the Sub-Committee will assist and advise states in establishing and maintaining direct contact with the national preventive mechanisms. It is thus a two-tier system for prevention, and has been described by Manfred Nowak, the United Nations Special Rapporteur on Torture, as the most important development for the effective prevention of torture at the universal level (APT 2006).

Although national preventive mechanisms (NPMs) must fulfil certain criteria in terms of independence, capabilities, professional knowledge and the representativeness of their composition with regard to gender, ethnicity and minority interests, states are free to choose whatever type of mechanism is considered fit for the purpose. Where there are established mechanisms in place that meet the criteria, these can be designated as NPMs and must be maintained accordingly. Several states already have national mechanisms that monitor conditions of those held in places of detention. There are, for example, Ombudsman institutions in Denmark, Poland, Colombia and Russia; Parliamentary Commissions in Switzerland; Human Rights Commissions in India, Nepal, Uganda, Senegal, South Africa, Austria (IIDH and APT 2004). Other states lack mechanisms, and some are looking to the example of the United Kingdom, where there are several domestic visiting mechanisms. There is a perception that England and Wales have valuable and effective mechanisms that could be readily followed. But how effective have the domestic visiting mechanisms been in the England and Wales in the prevention of torture and inhuman or degrading treatment?

In answering this question, we must address the appropriateness of comparing jurisdictions with very different starting bases. There is a difference of degree between England and Wales and states such as Kenya, where independent evidence shows that state-sponsored torture is routinely practiced in places of detention (Wafula and Kalebi 2004). Each state that ratifies OPCAT starts at a different base of culture and practice, and effectiveness of monitoring mechanisms should be measured by the progress of each state from that base. The inclination of states to adopt the domestic visiting mechanisms of England and Wales suggests they consider them to have been effective. But they can only be said to have been effective if they have, over time, improved standards of humanity and justice and reduced the occurrence of instances of inhumane and degrading treatment. Following an exploration of the domestic visiting mechanisms in England and Wales, I will return to this issue of effectiveness.

There is a range of domestic visiting mechanisms for places of detention in England and Wales, but it is the triumvirate of the Ombudsman, HM Prisons Inspectorate and Independent Monitoring Boards that have caught the attention of other states looking to ratify the OPCAT. The Ombudsman was set up in 1994 as a resource for individual prisoners to make official complaints when all other means of complaint within prisons have been exhausted. The Ombudsman is also tasked with carrying out independent investigations following a death in custody. (S)he has a mission 'to provide prisoners and those under community supervision with an accessible, independent and effective means to resolve their complaints, and to contribute to a just and humane penal system' (Prisons and Probation Ombudsman for England and Wales 2005). The Ombudsman service is also dedicated to helping the Prison Service improve its handling of complaints, helping them to support their staff effectively and achieve a positive working environment. Wherever possible, the Ombudsman avoids a bureaucratic, paper-based approach and uses local, more restorative methods that are in accord with the conciliatory intent of OPCAT. Thus, less than one in twenty complaints leads to a formal report. Most are resolved through informal recommendations, except where the Prison Service declines to do so.

During the years 2003 through 2004, the Ombudsman received a total of 3,527 complaints about the Prison Service. Forty-six per cent of these met the criteria for eligibility. The most common reason for the ineligibility of complaints was that the internal complaints system had not been fully exhausted. Complaints covered many issues, including adjudications, assaults, security, food, general conditions, regime activities, medical care, property, race, segregation and transfers (Prisons and Probation Ombudsman for England and Wales 2005). It is clearly important to have an accessible, independent and effective means of resolving prisoners' complaints. That said, I do not propose to dwell on this function. It does not have systematised monitoring visits as part of its remit, and it is essentially a service which responds to individuals after perceived deficits in treatment. However, it is reasonable to assume that it has some effect in preventing torture and inhumane treatment, in that it contributes to an awareness of prisoners' rights in relation to the general conditions of imprisonment, and to the prevention of a torture-prone culture. Nevertheless, it is worth noting that young prisoners have consistently been under-represented in the Prison Ombudsman's caseload, despite there being more disquiet over alleged cruel, inhumane or degrading treatment of young prisoners than of any other section of the prison population, an issue that this chapter revisits later.

Her Majesty's Prisons Inspectorate has a statutory responsibility to inspect all prisons and immigration removal centres, using five inspection teams consisting of paid specialists of high calibre, each team specialising in the inspection of a particular type of establishment (HMCIP Reports 2006). There are four types of inspection, full and announced, short and unannounced, full unannounced and annual juvenile. In between, there are education inspections, carried out jointly with the Office for Standards in Education (OFSTED) and one-day monitoring visits. Inspection reports are published within fifteen weeks of the inspection, and the establishment is then expected to produce an action plan based on the recommendations of the report, within two months of its being published (HMCIP Reports 2006). It was the case that the Minister responsible had to produce a written response to every Inspection report, with an account of actions that would be taken. These could then be reviewed and updated. This practice, an important dimension of accountability, has been discontinued (Ramsbotham 2003: 247).

The Inspectorate has evolved its own methodology and criteria for inspection, grounded in the standards of international human rights. It has developed the concept of a 'healthy prison' using four tests from the World Health Organisation. The tests ask if prisoners 'are held in safety, treated with respect for their human rights, offered purposeful activity and prepared for re-settlement into the community.'[1] The Inspectorate has criteria which are based on best practice and published in 2001 as an annex to its Annual Report (HM Inspectorate of Prisons 2001) as *Expectations*. Since then, *Expectations* has been shared with other countries attempting to safeguard conditions in prison. Ninety-seven of these criteria are evidenced against international human rights standards, but they have not been developed without a struggle. Sir David Ramsbotham, previously Chief Inspector, describes how the then Home Secretary tried to delay and prevent the publication of *Expectations* (Ramsbotham 2003: 229).

Independent monitoring at the local level by volunteer and unpaid members of the public has a long history in prisons and has recently been extended to include immigration removal centres. Independent Monitoring Boards (IMBs, formerly Boards of Visitors) have a statutory basis in law through the Prison Act 1952, Prison Rule 1964, the Young Offender Institution Rules 1988, the Immigration and Asylum Act 1999, and Detention Centre Rules 2001. Members are appointed for three years by the Home Secretary, but they are independent of the Home Office. Boards are independent of the Prison Service. Board members are required to report to the Secretary of State any matter that they consider expedient (Independent Monitoring Boards 2006).

Unlike the Prisons Inspectorate, where an intense inspection period may last for one week, board members attend prisons on a daily basis. Each member is expected to conduct a regular rota duty and produce a report of their rota visit, which is a regular and contemporaneous overview of the day-to-day life of the establishment. They must: take applications from individual prisoners who wish to see them privately; monitor the use of segregation; be present at and monitor the resolution of serious incidents. Board members try to resolve problems on an ongoing basis with the appropriate staff members. Unresolved problems are taken up with the Governor, the Area Manager and, in the last resort, the Secretary of State. They meet as a Board monthly with the Governor in attendance. Each Board must submit an Annual Report to the Secretary of State covering the previous twelve-month period. The work of IMBs, including their annual reports, is published in accord with Section 19 (1) of the Freedom of Information Act 2000 and the IMB Secretariat is responsible for operating a scheme of publication.

There are approximately 1,800 lay members working in 137 prison establishments and nine immigration removal centres throughout England and Wales. Members come from all sectors of society, and vary in ethnicity, religion and age. This voluntary work by lay members of the public is recognised as a public duty and under the Employment Act 1996, and employers must allow employees reasonable time off work to carry out duties. Despite this, there is a problem in achieving diversity, particularly in relation to ethnicity, social class and age, and, as is the case with much voluntary work, there is an over-representation of retirees.

In 2001, a review of the work of the Boards found that prisoners were often confused about the role of Board members and their supposed independence. Prisoners were often uncertain as to whether or not Board members were part of the prison management team (Lloyd 2001). This is a serious finding because it neutralises the very independence under which Boards are mandated to operate. However, this failure to demonstrate independence adequately to prisoners within each institution is not surprising, since requests for access to Board members are processed and controlled by prison staff. A frequent complaint mentioned in many Annual Reports of Boards is that prisoners' requests to meet with Board members are not passed on. A striking example is recorded in the Annual Report of Feltham Young Offenders Institution in 1999, the year in which Zahid Mubarek was placed in a shared cell with a known violent racist who murdered him (Annual Reports of Independent Monitoring Boards 2006).

The 2001 Review also reported that Board members considered they were ignored. They suffered from a lack of leadership and often felt unsupported by the National Advisory Council and the Secretariat. Most seriously, their core purpose was not sufficiently clarified. A relaunch in 2003 attempted greater effectiveness, announcing better training and support for members, and clearer lines of communication with Governors, Area Managers and the Home Secretary.

It is clear that the three mechanisms I have described are immensely valuable in their potential to protect human rights in closed institutions. The Ombudsman responds effectively to those complaints which have exhausted every other avenue. HM Prisons Inspectorate is robustly independent, and a model that other countries look to emulate. It is a national system, and the statutory obligation to report directly to the Home Secretary gives it a powerful lever. The Inspectorate, however, currently faces a serious intention by Government to weaken its powers. The current plan is to merge it with other Inspectorates into a single criminal justice inspectorate responsible for the whole system of policing, ensuring defendants attend court and managing those convicted. The Government has suggested that the Inspectorate should work to government criteria, rather than independent criteria devised by the Inspectorate.

Thus the existence, the long-cherished values and direct focus of the Inspectorate, admired internationally for its robust independence, are under political attack. Unless the Inspectorate can work to independent criteria and give independent advice, it cannot propel this public service toward increasing performance. Nor can the Inspectorate mesh with international preventive mechanisms unless it retains its independence from the Prison Service and from Government. At the time of writing, this threat has been staved off by a defeat of the relevant legislative instrument in the House of Lords and the Government has backed down in the face of overwhelming distrust of its proposal. It is worth noting that a harsh and punitive system of imprisonment flourished in the 19th century precisely in parallel with the removal of powers from prison inspectors and the curtailment of the powers of local justice watchdogs. Thus attacks by the State on the principle of independent inspection are not new.

It is at the local level, in each establishment, that the principle of monitoring has potential value. I use the word 'potential' advisedly, because it is clear that, in the past, local Boards have not had clear goals, sufficient training or adequate visibility. There has been a lack of accountability and they have not demonstrated their independence. Where they have, it has sometimes been in an iconoclastic way, ignoring the advice of the National Advisory Council or the Secretariat. Some boards have been colonised by the prison management in their institution, and have identified their role as co-managing, rather than stepping back and monitoring prison management. Boards tread a very fine line inside a prison. It is easy to become unduly complicit with the senior management team, in which case they may fail prisoners through a lack of objectivity. Alternatively, they may become unnecessarily adversarial in their relations with the senior management team, and jeopardise the chances of encouraging good practice in the resolution of day-to-day problems.

It is not yet clear how recent minor changes in Independent Monitoring Boards might result over time in establishing a more robust and independent means of lay monitoring. Boards have the capacity to provide local, day-to-day monitoring of each institution in ways the Inspectorate cannot. Each, therefore, has the capacity to complement the work of the other. Between them, with some much needed joined-up communication, both mechanisms have the capacity to provide direct connections between the public, the prisons, government ministers and Parliament. IMBs have the potential to prevent abuses of power, and it is understandable that other states, such as Japan, are considering the implementation of a type of IMB (Stern 2004). Perhaps, however, the failures are most instructive, particularly recent instances where the United Kingdom has been found to have violated the European Convention on Human Rights. Three of these cases resulted in death because of inadequacies in care and treatment. In each of the following cases, it is important to note that Board members were visiting the prisons daily, monitoring and recording all significant issues regarding inhuman or degrading treatment.

FAILURES IN PREVENTING INHUMANE TREATMENT

The first European Court of Human Rights' finding against United Kingdom prison conditions, because of a violation of Article 3, concerned a paranoid schizophrenic, whose time in prison consisted of being shuffled between the healthcare unit and the segregation unit. In the healthcare unit, he attacked staff. Finally in the segregation unit, he killed himself (Owers 2004). Other mentally ill patients are restrained by whatever means is available, such as a young man of eighteen restrained in a body belt for three days, because without it he tore strips off his anti-tear clothing and attempted to hang himself. Given a television, he broke the glass and tried to eat it. Inspectors have seen young women vomiting and having fits in their cells because of lack of supervised detoxification. Board members, untrained and ill-equipped to deal with serious mental illness, have to deal on a daily basis with prisoners exhibiting extreme signs of suffering, such as a distressed young man of eighteen who flooded or trashed every clean cell he was put into, who inserted into his arm razor blades, excrement, paper clips, broken glass or any object at hand. When his arm was stitched at the local hospital, he tore out the stitches and began the process all over again (personal observation).

These cases are deeply distressing to staff, who are recruited as prison officers and find themselves spending their working lives engaged in fire-fighting and crisis management of the mentally ill. The distortion between their expectations and their experiences can produce an overwhelming sense of powerlessness that contributes, in turn, to high levels of long-term sickness through stress, suicide and early retirement. In 2003, the Inspectorate inspected a prison where, each month, seventy-five new suicide-at-risk forms had been opened on prisoners, 129 self-harm incidents were recorded and every bed in the prison hospital and cells in the segregation unit was occupied by mentally ill prisoners. Of the girls under twenty-one, fourteen were on suicide watch and three seventeen–year-olds were self-harming every day (Owers 2004).

Children in prison are particularly vulnerable. Precisely because of their physical and psychological vulnerability, forms of treatment may not be inhumane when applied to adults, but applied to children they may amount to cruel and degrading treatment. Children are deserving of the highest standards of care and protection, not just because of their age, but because in their short lives they have almost without exception been deprived of care and protection by those closest to them. Children in the juvenile wings of prisons in England and Wales, either on remand or sentenced, are the most damaged and disfigured images of society. Their lives are a record of poverty, neglect, drug and alcohol misuse, mental illness, physical ill health, self-harm and loneliness. They have had little education, frequently they have been sexually and physically abused, and often they have been homeless prior to coming into prison or in the care of the state (Goldson 2002).

Despite the glaring vulnerability of children in prison, however, systemic failures to prevent cruel, inhuman and degrading treatment are clearly evidenced in successive Inspectorate and Boards' reports. There is a consistent failure to tackle the issue strategically. These are children who have been discarded as if they were garbage (Lyon, Dennison and Wilson 2000). Even when juvenile crime has been falling, and the Government has voiced its commitment to abolish imprisonment for children, the numbers in custody have continued to rise (Goldson 2002). This has led to a lottery, in which good conditions prevail at certain institutions, whereas in others horrors are repeatedly identified by successive Chief Inspectors, often to no avail because of political inertia.

In April 2004, Gareth Myatt died while being restrained by officers in Rainsbrook Secure Training Centre. He was fifteen years old and weighed seven stone, or forty-five kilos. This provoked an official Inquiry by Lord Carlile of Berriew, QC, to investigate the use of mechanical and physical restraint, solitary confinement and forcible strip searching of children in prisons, secure training centres and local authority secure children's homes. The Inquiry report was published on 17 February 2006, and subsequent exchanges in Parliament showed Lord Carlile's dedication to exposing abuses whilst at the same time identifying and commending good practice where it occurred (Carlile 2006). The report refrained from confrontation with the Government and sought to establish a situation of trust, a position identified at the outset of this chapter as consistent with the aims of OPCAT.

In the light of the United Nations Convention on the Rights of the Child, how can forcible strip searching, the use of physical or mechanical restraint and solitary confinement be used with impunity on children in prison? Why cannot the local IMB prevent such things? A partial answer is that these practices are embedded in the system. It is a system arguably stronger than the monitoring apparatus, and behind the system stands an indifferent State. Until recently, the Children Act 1989 did not apply to the prison system, and prisons therefore had immunity from the primary instrument of child welfare legislation. Of all parts of the Prison Service, it was the treatment of young prisoners that gave HM Chief Inspector of Prisons the most concern during his tenure from 1995 to 2001 (Ramsbotham 2003).

Despite concerns raised over a number of years by national systems of monitoring and inspection, by 2000 a culture of violence was reported as embedded in the worst prisons, where the Director General of the Prison Service agreed that prison officers could abuse inmates with impunity, and colleagues were too frightened to report abuse by fellow officers (*The Observer*, 3 February 2000). Amnesty International (2002: 5–6) declared that the conditions of imprisonment in several young offender institutions amounted to 'cruel, inhuman and degrading treatment; (they) are in violation of international human rights law; and are not consistent with internationally recognised standards for the treatment of children and young people in detention.'

The report named several institutions where violence was endemic. In each, the Chief Inspector of Prisons already had drawn attention to the alleged violence in his reports, pointing out that if the Children Act 1989 had applied to young offenders' institutions at the time, emergency protection orders could have been applied for, in order to remove some of the children at risk. Additionally, in their annual reports Boards had drawn attention to serious shortcomings. Yet, in some cases, this was not enough to prevent those shortcomings from continuing.

In 2000, persistent campaigning by the Howard League for Penal Reform, a non-governmental organisation, led to allegedly prevalent abuses at Portland YOI for fourteen years finally surfacing in the public domain. Evidence was published of abuse, assaults and neglect (Amnesty International 2002). Portland was well-known for its authoritarian regime. Mistreatment and brutality had previously been reported by the Chief Inspector in his reports in 1993, 1997 and 2000. Concerns had been expressed by the then Board of Visitors in annual reports. Crucially, however, it was a voluntary sector organisation that played a vital role in campaigning, disclosure, dissemination and independent legal scrutiny that should have resulted in prosecution. The Howard League took evidence from a random sample of ten children between fifteen and seventeen years old who had been in Portland in 1999. This testimony was important. It established that there were no avenues for complaint. Whatever the children wrote had to be shown first to a prison officer who would prevent it from reaching the Governor or a member of the Board of Visitors.

The most recent HMCIP report for Portland refers to residual staff attitudes of authoritarianism, to unacceptable physical conditions on four wings, to insufficient activity and insufficient proactive staff involvement.

Forty-two per cent of prisoners reported feeling unsafe, and there was racial tension (*Independent Monitor* 2005). More recently, a regime of inhumane treatment, involving savage beatings, death threats and sexual assault extending over nine years, was uncovered at Wormwood Scrubs prison, London. Despite a police investigation that began in 1998, and allegations widely reported in the press, the Government refused a public inquiry. The Prison Service conducted its own inquiry and its reports remained confidential. The author of one report, Peter Quinn, is reported (*The Guardian* 20 November 2006) to have turned whistleblower because of the continuing risk of assault on prisoners. Once embedded in an institution, the culture of inhumane treatment is hard to shift. It is to this context of entrenched culture that I now turn.

CONTEXT AND CULTURE

To understand the enormity of the task for IMBs, an appreciation is needed of the highly difficult and complex context in which they operate. Prisons in England and Wales hold large numbers of people suffering chronic and acute mental illness. Some statistics put this as high as eighty per cent of the prison population. Prison is a cheap solution for those who have already been excluded from society and for those damaged by addiction to alcohol, drugs or violence. In England and Wales a place in a local male prison costs £30,000 a year, while a bed in a regional secure NHS facility costs £136,000. A place in a women's prison costs £36,000 a year, while a bed in regional secure hospital costs £163,000. The difference in cost reflects the numbers of skilled and specialist staff available. A shortage of beds in mental health facilities means that prison has become the dumping ground for thousands of sick people.

Torture sanctioned by the state and carried out on a regular basis is not the glaring and well-documented problem in prisons in England and Wales that it is in other states. What is overt and clearly sanctioned by the State are problems of overcrowding, failures of political will and a lack of strategic thinking. These are the defining features of a system which cause it to be vulnerable to abuse and which allows a culture of casual cruelty to flourish with impunity. It is overcrowding that has led to a six-fold increase in violent assaults against other prisoners and prison staff since 1997, so that the figure for such assaults in 2005 was 20,000 (*Justice and Crime News* 2006).

Overcrowding is not a problem that has developed suddenly. It has been identified as a danger for many years. There are more people in prison in England and Wales per capita than in any other Western European state. When the Council of Europe's Committee for the Prevention of Torture or Degrading Treatment or Punishment (CPT) visited prisons in England and Wales in 1997 and in 2001, it criticised the Prison Service's use of the notion of 'safe' overcrowding, and the number of prisoners held two to a cell in cell space of less than 8.5 square metres. Overcrowding, however, has been accepted as part of the system, in that the spaces available are actually calculated on the capacity being twenty-four per cent overcrowded (Owers 2004). New prison accommodation is being brought into use which still does not meet CPT's standards. This is a flagrant disregard on the part of Government for internationally agreed standards in human rights. It produces inhumane conditions for those incarcerated and those who manage them. Overcrowding means two prisoners routinely sharing cells built for one, with an unscreened lavatory in the cell. Overcrowding means they may spend twenty-three hours a day locked up. Overcrowding means some prisoners being held on a berthed ship with no access to training or activity, to natural air or light except for one hour a day. Overcrowding means prisoners being moved around the system, never allowed time at a prison to settle and address their offending behaviour.

The entrenched nature of overcrowding in the system has contributed to other problems that involve inhumane treatment and conditions. Suicides, self-harm and mental illness have been accepted as 'normal' aspects of a system strained almost to breaking point. Self-inflicted death in custody happens at the approximate rate of two per week, and those who kill themselves are among the most vulnerable members of society. They are frequently new to prison and not even sentenced. They are often suffering from mental illness and many are forced into rapid and involuntary withdrawal from drugs. Qualitative research with suicidal prisoners has shown that lives can be 'saved' by the humanity of individual officers, but often this is not enough to overcome the desperation produced by inhumane conditions, a culture of routine neglect, insensitive routines and callous treatment (Medlicott 2001).

The conditions within prison also affect staff. Many members of staff begin their service with high ideals, only to meet persistent failures in management, strategy and support for staff. It is not surprising that many lapse into defensive postures of indifference toward the prisoners in their care. Indifference, combined with poor conditions, produces degrading and abusive treatment for prisoners. The former Chief Inspector of Prisons pointed out that when, during an inspection visit, officers were asked to discuss with him a particular item of their good practice, they asked to meet him privately to avoid pressure and derisory comment from colleagues who despised their efforts. This illustrates how hard it is for officers to hold to ideals of good practice (Ramsbotham 2003).

THE INTRACTABILITY OF CULTURE

The cases of Portland and Wormwood Scrubs illustrate the intractability of culture in an individual institution. Unless the state, or its agent, takes the lead in challenging such powerful and embedded cultures, they present an insuperable problem to independent monitoring mechanisms. Quite apart from the individual culture in each prison, the nature of prison means that it is a place where casual cruelty flourishes, cruelty that takes as its natural target those most vulnerable, cruelty that is such a commonplace there is no attempt to hide it from visiting researchers (Medlicott 2005). Prison officer culture in overcrowded prisons is predicated on the principle of *less eligibility*: the belief that prisoners have a status as inferior beings is deeply engrained in the psyche and belief systems of prison officers (Medlicott 2005: 78). Even doctors practice the casual cruelty that this belief system produces in an unself-conscious way (Sim 2003). This cruelty flourishes all the more readily if the system is underfunded, overcrowded and ineffectively monitored. Clearly, if monitoring is absent or ineffective, the ubiquity of casual cruelty can develop into something much worse—an entrenched culture of violence and torture such as happened in Portland and Wormwood Scrubs.

The role of the IMB is to monitor the management of prisons and the conditions produced by such management. In so doing, Boards grapple not only with intractable prison culture on the wings and landings, but also with intransigent cultures at the level of management. The former Chief Inspector of Prisons has written graphically about those responsible for preventing the good management of prisons:

> (The enemy) was not prisons, prisoners or the staff who worked in or with them. It was not Parliament. It was not the public or the media. . . . The enemy was exactly the same group—although made up of different individuals—that had ignored, or resisted, all the efforts of so many distinguished and knowledgeable people over the years to improve the conduct of imprisonment. . . . The enemy of successful imprisonment was a triumvirate: ministers, Home Office officials, and the hierarchy of the Prison Service. (Ramsbotham 2003: 86)

He indicts this trio for their lack of strategy, their obsession with managerialism, their slavish attention to targets, performance indicators and compliance with regulations unrelated to quality of service. In addition, there are ongoing failures in management structure, accountability and responsibility. There may well be deficits in resources, but without a strategy, there can be no progress made in directing resources to where they are most needed—eliminating the waste caused by current managerial practices and estimating how much money is needed to put things right.

It is into these wider and deeply embedded contexts of strategic failure that Chairs of IMBs are drawn, when they identify weaknesses and bring them to the attention of the Governor and senior staff. And when they go further, and join others in calling for a public inquiry, as happened in the infamous and long-running problems of alleged abuses at

Wormwood Scrubs, it is not a vote of confidence in Boards when such calls are ignored (Lockhart-Mummery 2005). These failures show the enormity of the task facing domestic visiting mechanisms such as IMBs. Past cases have provided evidence that many prisoners are too frightened to complain. In their perception, lodging a complaint can lead to further abuse and intimidation. This is particularly the case with young and other vulnerable prisoners. In some young offender institutions, there is a widespread belief by young prisoners that prison staff can act as they wish, and there is no way to curb them (Amnesty International 2002). Clearly IMBs have a job to do in getting their independence across to prisoners and in transcending the entrenched culture of some prisons. They can only do this if they are sufficiently empowered by the State in terms of aims and objectives, status, training and accountability.

THE FUTURE

The OPCAT advocates *systems* of regular inspection by independent international and national bodies. Any fully functioning system must be multi-layered, and bring in the existing layers of monitoring and inspection which currently work to prevent torture and other cruel, inhuman or degrading treatment or punishment. Non-governmental organisations play an energetic and vital preventive role in the United Kingdom, and they will be involved, along with the Prisons Inspectorate and the IMBs, in the implementation of OPCAT. The quality of domestic visiting mechanisms designated as national preventive mechanisms under the OPCAT is crucial. It is understandable that states that are party to OPCAT are scrutinising the domestic mechanisms of the United Kingdom. At the local level, IMBs are potentially of great value, and countries with embedded traditions of voluntary service in civil society are rightly interested in this aspect of United Kingdom monitoring. The principle of independent lay monitoring is a principle worth defending, even if, in practice, lay monitoring currently has some obvious weaknesses. It is clearly healthy to have volunteer members of the general public visiting prisons on a daily basis to monitor the treatment of prisoners.

Despite the 2003 relaunch and subsequent improvements, there remains room for improving the status, visibility, robustness and legitimacy of IMBs. There are still no guidelines or objective criteria for members to work towards. Given that these are lay members of the public, not fully trained, it is clear that relying on individual judgement and discretion is not satisfactory. As I have indicated, there is a tendency for Board members within an establishment to lean toward the staff agenda and forget the primacy of their responsibilities toward prisoners. This is hardly surprising when they rely on the Governor and his/ her staff for their accommodation, administrative and secretarial support within the prison. Much more could be done to make IMBs independent, in terms of resources, culture and practice. It is vital that members are empowered by sufficient appropriate training so that they have the confidence to raise issues effectively, appropriately and to the right people, when it is necessary.

The performance of IMBs could be considerably improved by adopting objective criteria for monitoring, visiting, inspecting and reporting. These criteria should not be shaped by the very systems of detention themselves. The Prisons Inspectorate has achieved the development of objective criteria in *Expectations*, benchmarked against international human rights standards. If the IMBs, the Prisons Inspectorate, and the national/international OPCAT mechanisms each adopted the same criteria, there would be a fully functional multi-layered system, in which the different agencies could communicate concerns in a meaningful way, through operating with the same criteria and goals. With such cohesion, they would be better placed not only to establish relations of trust with government but also to bring consistent, reasoned and irresistible pressure on government. Without this synthesis, there is a danger of fragmentation. Governments are easily able to fend off criticism when it comes from a plethora of bodies working to different criteria and with disparate goals. For instance, it is disappointing that despite the remit of various visiting mechanisms in the United Kingdom, they have not managed to combine and produce an effective evidenced case against the use of prison to contain seriously ill and addicted people.

But it is the international layers of OPCAT that are potential and exciting levers for change in the United Kingdom and other participating states. Establishing and designating NPMs with powers of independent scrutiny and reporting at the *national* level are of primary importance, but it is the ways in which these are disseminated to the Sub-Committee, and how the Sub-Committee follows up and responds, that will prove crucial in illuminating and preventing human rights abuses. The extent to which the Sub-Committee is proactive, and not just responsive, will also prove vital. The quality of coordinating arrangements, and how they will produce formal, regular and recorded encounters between mutually reinforcing national and international mechanisms, remains to be seen.

There are, I suggest, lessons here for states considering setting up monitoring mechanisms. The layers of inspection and monitoring in the United Kingdom are clearly a useful starting point for protecting prisoners' human rights against widespread or systematic torture, and, for those states with no monitoring mechanisms, their historical longevity and embeddedness in our system might appear enviable. But it is worth reflecting how, in a prosperous economy such as the United Kingdom, a better resourced and more joined-up approach could have had greater effectiveness, not just in identifying actual abuses and cultures of violence, but in pressing for more strategic overall management of all places of detention, and more appropriate attention to the inhumane conditions in which many prisoners, particularly children, the suicidal and the mentally ill, have to live.

What is clear is that the apparently powerful triumvirate of Ombudsman, Inspectorate and IMBs, with their plethora of visiting mechanisms, have not managed to change the culture of casual cruelty in prisons in England and Wales, because they have been thwarted by serious failures of political will, an engrained political refusal to tackle the problems of overcrowding and an apparently intractable culture of casual cruelty. This chapter began by emphasising the enormity of the task of preventing torture and inhumane treatment in prisons, because prevention requires 'the active engagement of the state' and 'penetration into the very heart of the State's system of power and control' (Evans 1999 cited in Rytter, Jefferson and Worm 2005: 4). States looking to the United Kingdom's domestic visiting mechanisms as effective ways of implementing the national aspects of OPCAT would do well to take note that, despite the obvious virtues of the Ombudsman, the Inspectorate and the IMBs, the United Kingdom has not yet managed to achieve the active engagement of the State to a sufficient degree. This weakness stems from the same inherent vulnerabilities that beset such mechanisms in all other OPCAT participating states, and that concerns their relationship with the state itself. Nevertheless, this does not mean we should relinquish domestic mechanisms. As an intrinsic part of active citizenship there is an obligation to maintain them, to apply pressure in order to make them more powerful and to use them to continue challenging the inadequacies of the state's system of power and control. The international preventive mechanism of the OPCAT will be a crucial element not only in the prevention of torture, but also in strengthening the impact of domestic mechanisms, and sharing with them the huge responsibility of making real and sustainable impacts on the legal systems and power structures of state parties.

REFERENCES

Amnesty International. (2002) *United Kingdom: Failing Children and Young People in Detention: Concerns Regarding Young Offenders Institutions,* http://www.amnesty.org/resources.

Annual Reports of Independent Monitoring Boards. (2006) HMYOI Portland 1999/2000; 2000/2001; HMYOI Feltham 1999/2000, http://www.imb.gov.uk

APT. (2006) *APT Special Coverage for the Entry into Force, October 9th 2006,* http://www.apt.ch/indexlb.shtml

Carlile, Lord. (2006) *The Carlile Inquiry,* London: Howard League for Penal Reform.

Goldson, B. (2002) *Vulnerable Inside: Children in Secure and Penal Settings,* London: The Children's Society.

HM Inspectorate of Prisons. (2001) *Annual Report to Parliament December 1999–December 2000,* 17 July. www.hmprisonservice.gov.uk

HMCIP Reports. (2006) www.hmprisonservice.gov.uk

Independent Monitoring Boards. (2006) http://www.homeoffice.gov.uk/justice/prisons/imb/index.html

IIHR and APT. (2004) *Optional Protocol to the United Nations Convention Against Torture and Other Cruel, Inhuman or Degrading Treatment or Punishment, a Manual for Prevention*, Inter-American Institute of Human Rights and Association for the Prevention of Torture.

Justice and Crime News. (2006), http://www.libdems.org.uk/justice/prisons

Lloyd, Sir Peter. (2001) *Review of the Boards of Visitors: A Report of the Working Group*, London: Home Office.

Lockhart-Mummery, L. (2005) 'One Year On,' *Independent Monitor*, February.

Lyon, J., Dennison, C. and Wilson, A. (2000) *'Tell them so they listen': Messages from Young People in Custody,* London: Home Office.

Medlicott, D. (2001) *Surviving the Prison Place: Narratives of Suicidal Prisoners,* Aldershot: Ashgate pp. 75–85.

———. (2005) 'The Unbearable Brutality of Being: Casual Cruelty in Prison and What This Tells Us About Who We Really Are,' in M. Breen (ed) *Minding Evil: Explorations of Human Iniquity*, Amsterdam: Rodopi.

Owers, A. (2004) 'Rights Behind Bars, The Conditions and Treatment of Those in Detention,' *Prison Service Journal* vol 158, pp.63–71

Prisons and Probation Ombudsman for England and Wales. (2005) *Annual Report 2003–2004*. http://www.ppo.gov.uk

Ramsbotham, D. (2003) *Prisongate: The Shocking State of Britain's Prisons and the Need for Visionary Change*, London: Simon & Schuster, The Free Press.

Rytter, T., Jefferson A.M. and Worm, L. (2005) *Preventing Torture in Places of Detention Through Systems of Regular Visits: Concept Paper,* Copenhagen: Rehabilitation and Research Centre for Torture Victims.

Sim, J. (2003) 'Whose Side Are We Not On? Researching Medical Power in Prisons,' in S. Tombs and D. Whyte (eds) *Unmasking the Crimes of the Powerful*, New York: Peter Lang, pp. 239–260.

Stern, V. (2004) 'IMBs—A Prison Monitoring Model for the Rest of the World?' *Independent Monitor,* October.

Wafula, E. and Kalebi, A. (2004) *Rolling Back Torture: IMLU Annual Report* Nairobi: Independent Medico-Legal Unit. 1.

Contributors

Bree Carlton PhD is Lecturer in Criminology in the School of Social and Political Inquiry at Monash University. Her research interests include histories of punishment, high-security and supermax prisons and the impact of criminal justice institutions and state practices on individuals and communities. Her first book, *Imprisoning Resistance: Life and Death in an Australian Supermax* was published in 2007.

Chris Cunneen PhD is Global Chair in Criminology at the University of New South Wales, Sydney, Australia. He has worked with a number of Australian Royal Commissions and Inquiries and Aboriginal organisations. His research interests are: Indigenous People and the Law, Juvenile Justice, Restorative Justice, Policing, Prison Issues, Hate Crime. He has published widely and his books include: *Juvenile Justice, Youth and Crime in Australia* (Oxford University Press, 2002); *Indigenous People and the Law in Australia* (Butterworths, 1995); *Faces of Hate* (Federation Press, 1997); *Conflict, Politics and Crime* (Allen and Unwin, 2001).

Amanda George is a lawyer and Lecturer in Law at the Institute of Koorie Education, Deakin University. She is a prison activist and founding member of Flat Out, an accommodation service for women leaving prison. Amanda undertook a Churchill Fellowship looking at Prisoner Committees in Women's Prisons in Canada, South Africa and California and has written on the privatization of women's prisons in Victoria.

Barry Goldson PhD is Professor of Criminology and Social Policy at the University of Liverpool. His most recent books include: *In The Care of the State: Child Deaths in Penal Custody in England and Wales* (2005); *Youth Crime and Justice* (2006); *Comparative Youth Justice* (2006) and the *Dictionary of Youth Justice* (2008). He is currently co-editing three volumes of international 'major works' on youth crime and juvenile justice for the Sage Library of Criminology. He is also the founding editor of *Youth Justice: An International Journal*. He provided expert evidence to the United Nations Secretary General's study on violence against children, and he was a member of an independent inquiry into the use of physical restraint, solitary confinement and strip searching of children in prisons and other penal institutions in England and Wales. He is a non-executive Director/Trustee of the Howard League for Penal Reform, and he has long-standing relations with a range of other national and international non-governmental, human rights and progressive penal reform organisations.

Avery F. Gordon PhD is Professor of Sociology and Law and Society at the University of California, Santa Barbara, and Visiting Faculty at the Centre for Research Architecture, Goldsmiths College, University of London. She is the author of *Keeping Good Time: Reflections on Knowledge, Power and People*; *Ghostly Matters: Haunting and the Sociological Imagination*; and the co-editor of *Mapping Multiculturalism* and *Body Politics*, among other works. She is co-host of the weekly radio programme *No Alibis* on KCSB 91.9 FM Santa Barbara. She is currently writing about captivity, war and utopia.

Jude McCulloch PhD is Associate Professor and Head of Criminology in the School of Social and Political Inquiry at Monash University, Melbourne, Australia. Her research interrogates institutionalised state violence. She has published extensively in academic journals, magazines and the media on topics such as deaths in custody, police violence, police shootings and paramilitary policing. Her recent work focuses on state crime in the 'war on terror'. She is author of *Blue Army: Paramilitary Policing in Australia* (Melbourne University Press, 2001) and co-editor of the special issues of *Social Justice* on deaths in custody and detention (2006) and transnational crime (2008).

Laurence McKeown PhD is Research Coordinator with Coiste na nIarchimí, the umbrella organisation for former Irish republican prisoners. He was imprisoned in Long Kesh/Maze Prison in the North of Ireland from 1976–1992. During that time he took part in the protests for the return of political status and spent seventy days on hunger strike in 1981, during which ten other prisoners died. On release, he completed a doctoral study at Queen's University, Belfast. He has also written and co-written several plays and a feature film, *H3*, based on the 1981 hunger strike. He is co-author of *Nor Meekly Serve My Time: The H-Block Struggle 1976–1981* (Beyond the Pale, 1994, revd 2006) and author of *Out of Time: Irish Republican Prisoners, Long Kesh 1972–2000* (Beyond the Pale, 2001).

Diana Medlicott PhD is Professor and an independent scholar writing about and working in the areas of restorative justice and torture prevention. Her forthcoming book, *How to Design and Deliver Engaging Modules*

(McGraw-Hill, Spring 2009), takes restorative ideas into higher education delivery. She is the author of *Surviving the Prison Place: Narratives of Suicidal Prisoners* (Ashgate 2001).

Linda Moore PhD is Lecturer in Criminology in the School of Policy Studies at the University of Ulster. Formerly she was a senior research and investigations officer at the Northern Ireland Human Rights Commission. Her most recent research has focused on the imprisonment of children and young people, the detention of refugees and asylum seekers and the imprisonment of women. Her recent co-authored publications include: *In Our Care: Promoting the Rights of Children in Custody* (NIHRC, 2002); *The Hurt Inside: The Imprisonment of Women and Girls in Northern Ireland* (NIHRC, 2005); *Children's Rights in Northern Ireland* (NICCY, 2005); *Still in Our Care: Protecting Children's Rights in Custody* (NIHRC, 2006); *The Prison Within* (NIHRC, 2007)

Sharon Pickering PhD is Associate Professor, Criminology, in the School of Social and Political Inquiry at Monash University, Melbourne, Australia. Her research interests include policing, human rights, criminalisation and state crime. She has published on refugees, borders and justice; policing, terrorism and security; human rights and state crime; and gender persecution. Her books are: *Women, Policing and Resistance in Northern Ireland* (Beyond the Pale, 2002); *Critical Chatter: Women and Human Rights in South East Asia* (Carolina Academic Press, 2003); *Refugees and State Crime* (Federation Press, 2005) and *Borders, Mobility and Technologies of Control* (ed. Springer, 2006).

Dylan Rodríguez PhD is Associate Professor in the Department of Ethnic Studies, University of California at Riverside. He received his PhD and his MA degrees in Ethnic Studies from the University of California, Berkeley, and is an interdisciplinary scholar-activist whose research interests include critical race studies and cultural studies, focusing on intersections of race, state violence and community/identity formation. He has worked with *Critical Resistance* on prison abolition and INCITE! a progressive antiviolence movement led by radical women of colour and the Critical Filipino and Filipina Studies Collective. He has published widely, is on the editorial board of *Social Justice* and is author of *Forced Passages: Imprisoned Radical Intellectuals and the U.S. Prison Regime* (University of Minnesota Press, 2006).

Phil Scraton PhD is Professor of Criminology in the Institute of Criminology and Criminal Justice, School of Law, Queen's University, Belfast. His research includes: the regulation and criminalisation of children and young people; controversial deaths and the state; the rights of the bereaved and survivors in the aftermath of disasters; violence and incarceration; the politics of truth and official inquiry; critical analysis and its application. His most recent publications include: *'Childhood' in 'Crisis'?* (ed. Routledge, 1997); *Hillsborough: The Truth* (Mainstream, 2000); *Beyond September 11* (ed. Pluto, 2002); *The Hurt Inside: The Imprisonment of Women and Girls in Northern Ireland* (co-author, NIHRC, 2005); *Children's Rights in Northern Ireland 2004* (co-author, NICCY, 2005); *The Prison Within* (co-author, NIHRC, 2007); *Power, Conflict and Criminalisation* (Routledge, 2007) and a special issue of *Social Justice* (co-editor 2006) on deaths in custody and detention. He is founder of INQUEST: United Campaigns for Justice.

Cassandra Shaylor is an attorney and activist and co-founder and co-director of *Justice Now*, a prison organization and training centre focused on people in women's prisons in the United States. She is a PhD candidate in the History of Consciousness Department at the University of California at Santa Cruz; her thesis is derived on this legal and activist work. Her research and publications focus on women in prison, prison abolition and the intersections of race and sexuality in the prison-industrial complex. In 2006, she was awarded a Soros Justice Fellowship to research practical, viable alternatives to prison that contribute to safer, more democratic societies.

Index

racial stereotypes, racism, white supremacy

racial stereotypes, 154; of African and Indigenous Americans, 192; of Indigenous Australians, 223. *See also* colonisation, race inequality, racism

racism, 151, 154; as 'racialized sadism' in US prisons, 172, 178; integral to US prison regime, 190–191, 198, 204; in US prisons, 178; towards asylum seekers in Australia, 228; towards Indigenous Australians, 221–222. See also colonisation, race inequality, racial stereotypes, racism, white supremacy

Rau, Cornelia, 235

Red Cross, 245

refugees, detention of. *See* asylum seekers

Richardson, Paula, suicide in custody, 116–117, 122

Rookes vs Barnard, 1964 case of, 32

Royal Commission into Aboriginal Deaths in Custody (RCADIC), 213–217

Royal Ulster Constabulary (RUC), 28, 29, 30, 31, 35–368n

S

Sands, Bobby, 20, 21, 181–1823n

San Quentin State Penitentiary, USA, 62, 63

Schwarzenegger, Governor Arnold, 147, 149, 158

segregation, 40, 48; in prisons in England and Wales, 252, monitoring of, 247; in Scottish prisons, 65, 69, 71, 72; in US prisons, 81, 82, 174, 176, 203; of children prisoners, 95, 99; of Indigenous Australians, 211; of women prisoners at Mourne House Women's Unit, Maghaberry, Northern Ireland, 137, 142. *See also* isolation, solitary confinement

self-harm: of asylum seekers in Australian detention centres, 232–233, 238; of Australian women prisoners, 115; of incarcerated children, 95; of prisoners in the UK, 252, 255;

of women prisoners, 125; prisoner, at Jika Jika High Security Unit, Australia, 49; prisoner, at Peterhead Prison, Scotland, 79; prisoner, in Northern Ireland, 134

sensory deprivation: as normal practice in US prisons, 174; psychological studies of effects of, 41–42, 44. *See also* behaviour modification; violence, physical; violence, psychological; torture

sexism, 151, 153. *See also* gender, sexist stereotyping

sexist stereotyping, of prisoners, 152–155. *See also* gender, sexism

sexual assault: as normal practice in US prisons, 172; increased incidence for women prisoners prior to incarceration, 113; of transgender prisoners, 153; strip search as equivalent to, 3, 8, 108, 122, 127–130

Sherbaghan: abuses and torture at, 165; number of prisoners held at, 168

slavery, in the US: 178, 200; abolition of, 191

social death, 179–180, 200, 206

solitary confinement: as normal practice in US prisons, 174; at Peterhead Prison, Scotland, 65, 67, 68, 69, 74; of asylum seekers in Australian detention centres, 237; of child prisoners, 94, 95, 99, 252; of Indigenous Australian prisoners, 219

State Correctional Institute at Greene (SCI-Greene), 170

Stewart, Terry, 171

Storey, Bobby, 23, 24, 25, 26, 27, 28, 30

strip searching: as equivalent to sexual assault, 3, 8, 108, 122, 127–130; at Mourne House Women's Unit, Maghaberry, Northern Ireland, 127–130, 131, 142; campaigns against, 110, 118, 119, 120–121; contraband seized from, 118–119; of child prisoners, 94–95, 252; of transgender prisoners, 153; of women prisoners, 107–122; psychological impact of, 112–117, 119–120, 122, 128–130

suicide, asylum seekers, 232–233, 238